Business Law and Organizations for Paralegals

Business Law and Organizations for Paralegals

THIRD EDITION

Emily Lynch Morissette

CAROLINA ACADEMIC PRESS
Durham, North Carolina

Library of Congress Cataloging-in-Publication Data

Names: Morissette, Emily Lynch, author.
Title: Business law and organizations for paralegals / by Emily Lynch
Morissette.
Description: Third edition. | Durham, North Carolina : Carolina Academic
Press, 2021. | Includes index.
Identifiers: LCCN 2021017741 (print) | LCCN 2021017742 (ebook) | ISBN
9781531020583 (paperback) | ISBN 9781531020590 (ebook)
Subjects: LCSH: Corporation law--United States. | Business enterprises--Law
and legislation--United States. | Legal assistants--United
States--Handbooks, manuals, etc.
Classification: LCC KF1414.85 .M67 2021 (print) | LCC KF1414.85 (ebook) |
DDC 346.73/066--dc23
LC record available at https://lccn.loc.gov/2021017741
LC ebook record available at https://lccn.loc.gov/2021017742

Carolina Academic Press
700 Kent Street
Durham, North Carolina 27701
Telephone (919) 489-7486
www.cap-press.com

To my daughter, Isabelle.
I write this book now to make college more affordable for students, and
hope that you will be able to go college affordably
when you're eighteen.

Contents

SECTION III • NON-CORPORATE BUSINESS ENTITIES

SECTION IV • THE CORPORATION

SECTION V • THE BUSINESS ENTITY AS A LITIGANT

Table of Cases

Section I

Agency and Employment

Chapter 1

Agency

Chapter Outline

Chapter Objectives

- Learn what a principal-agency relationship is.
- Determine how to form a principal-agent relationship.
- Explain the differences between the types of authority an agent may possess.
- Be able to identify the duties of agents and principals.
- Understand the liability of principals and agents to third parties.
- Discuss how to terminate an agency relationship.

1.1 Introduction to Agency

Agency is one of the building blocks of corporate law and so is discussed first. It is a key building block to corporate law because most business organizations are run by agents. A sole proprietor can hire employees, who would be agents of the sole proprietor. The general partners in a partnership are agents of one another and of the partnership. Officers and directors of a corporation are agents to the corporation.

In agency, one person acts for another. The person acting is the agent and the person being acted for is the principal. Both of the parties, the principal and the agent, have to consent to and have the capacity to consent to the principal agent relationship, though this consent does not have to be written or even verbal! An agent is a person who has either an implied or express, verbal or a written agreement to perform tasks on behalf of the principal, in regards to third parties. The agent is someone who does work for the principal, whether paid or not. The agent gets his authority to act from his principal. The agent performs specified or general tasks. General agents are authorized to transact all the types of business of the principal. Special agents are only authorized to do certain acts. Any acts done outside of those certain acts, by a special agent, would be unauthorized. As a general rule, a principal can authorize an agent to do any acts he would be able to do himself.

An agent is usually subject to some control by the principal. Since agents perform tasks for the principal, the principal can, at times, be held liable for the agent's actions. In essence, when an agent acts, it as if the principal acted. So long as the agent's actions appear to be authorized by the principal, then the principal probably will be held responsible for that agent's actions. There are three main ways in which actions can be or appear to be authorized by the principal:

- actual authority,
- apparent authority, and
- ratified authority.

These three ways will be discussed later in the chapter. Estoppel is a way a principal-agency relationship can be found by a court and will be discussed last.

The principal-agent relationship is broader than that of an employer-employee relationship; the employer-employee relationship does fall under the principal-agent relationship. The principal-agent relationship is broader because an agent does not have to be paid, whereas an employee typically does have to be paid. The Restatement (Third) of Agency defines agency as a relationship "that arises when one person (a "principal") manifests assent to another person (an "agent") that the agent shall act on the principal's behalf and subject to the principal's control, and the agent manifests assent or otherwise consents so to act." § 1.01.

In recent years, there has been a lot of discussion about whether an unpaid intern has to be classified as a paid employee or not. This issue, as indicated in the below request for appeal, will be heard in late 2015. According to the case prior to appeal, there are six factors in determining whether someone can be an unpaid:

- whether the intern gets educational-like training,
- the internship being for the benefit of the intern,
- the intern does not cause employees to be fired,
- the employer does not get immediate advantage from the intern,
- the intern is not entitled to a job at the end of the internship, and
- both the employer and intern understand that the intern will not be paid.

Glatt v. Fox Searchlight Pictures, Inc.
811 F.3d 528 (2016)

Plaintiffs, who were hired as unpaid interns, claim compensation as employees under the Fair Labor Standards Act and New York Labor Law. Plaintiffs Eric Glatt and Alexander Footman moved for partial summary judgment on their employment status. Plaintiff Eden Antalik moved to certify a class of all New York interns working at certain of defendants' divisions between 2005 and 2010 and to conditionally certify a nationwide collective of all interns working at those same divisions between 2008 and 2010. The district court (William H. Pauley III, *J.*) granted Glatt and Footman's motion for partial summary judgment, certified Antalik's New York class, and conditionally certified Antalik's nationwide collective. On defendants' interlocutory appeal, we VACATE the district court's order granting partial summary judgment to Glatt and Footman, VACATE its order certifying Antalik's New York class, VACATE its order conditionally certifying Antalik's nationwide collective, and REMAND for further proceedings.

BACKGROUND

Plaintiffs worked as unpaid interns either on the Fox Searchlight-distributed film *Black Swan* or at the Fox corporate offices in New York City. They contend that the defendants, Fox Searchlight and Fox Entertainment Group, violated the Fair Labor Standards Act (FLSA), 29 U.S.C. §§ 206–07, and New York Labor (NYLL), N.Y. Labor Law § 652, by failing to pay them as employees during their internships as required by the FLSA's and NYLL's minimum wage and overtime provisions. The following background facts are undisputed except where noted.

Eric Glatt

Eric Glatt graduated with a degree in multimedia instructional design from New York University. Glatt was enrolled in a non-matriculated (non-degree) graduate program at NYU's School of Education when he started working on *Black Swan*. His graduate program did not offer him credit for his internship.

From December 2, 2009, through the end of February 2010, Glatt interned in *Black Swan's* accounting department under the supervision of Production Accountant Theodore Au. He worked from approximately 9:00 a.m. to 7:00 p.m. five days a week.

As an accounting intern, Glatt's responsibilities included copying, scanning, and filing documents; tracking purchase orders; transporting paperwork and items to and from the *Black Swan* set; maintaining employee personnel files; and answering questions about the accounting department.

Glatt interned a second time in *Black Swan's* post-production department from March 2010 to August 2010, under the supervision of Post Production Supervisor Jeff Robinson. Glatt worked two days a week from approximately 11:00 a.m. until 6:00 or 7:00 p.m. His post-production responsibilities included drafting cover letters for mailings; organizing filing cabinets; filing paperwork; making photocopies; keeping the takeout menus up-to-date and organized; bringing documents to the payroll company; and running errands, one of which required him to purchase a non-allergenic pillow for Director Darren Aronofsky.

Alexander Footman

Alexander Footman graduated from Wesleyan University with a degree in film studies. He was not enrolled in a degree program at the time of his *Black Swan* internship. From September 29, 2009, through late February or early March 2010, Footman interned in the production department under the supervision of Production Office Coordinator Lindsay Feldman and Assistant Production Office Coordinator Jodi Arneson. Footman worked approximately ten-hour days. At first, Footman worked five days a week, but, beginning in November 2009, he worked only three days a week. After this schedule change, *Black Swan* replaced Footman with another unpaid intern in the production department.

Footman's responsibilities included picking up and setting up office furniture; arranging lodging for cast and crew; taking out the trash; taking lunch orders; answering phone calls; watermarking scripts; drafting daily call sheets; photocopying; making coffee; making deliveries to and from the film production set, rental houses, and the payroll office; accepting deliveries; admitting guests to the office; compiling lists of local vendors; breaking down, removing, and selling office furniture and supplies at the end of production; internet research; sending invitations to the wrap party; and other similar tasks and errands, including bringing tea to Aronofsky and dropping off a DVD of *Black Swan* footage at Aronofsky's apartment.

Eden Antalik

Eden Antalik worked as an unpaid publicity intern in Fox Searchlight's corporate office in New York from the beginning of May 2009 until the second week of August 2009. During her internship, Antalik was enrolled in a degree program at Duquesne University that required her to have an internship in order to graduate. Antalik was supposed to receive credit for her internship at Fox Searchlight, but, for reasons that are unclear from the record, she never actually received the credit.

Antalik began work each morning around 8:00 a.m. by assembling a brief, referred to as "the breaks," summarizing mentions of various Fox Searchlight films in the media. She also made travel arrangements, organized catering, shipped documents, and set up rooms for press events.

Prior Proceedings

On October 19, 2012, plaintiffs filed their first amended class complaint seeking unpaid minimum wages and overtime for themselves and all others similarly situated. Thereafter, Glatt and Footman abandoned their class claims and proceeded as individuals. After discovery, Glatt and Footman moved for partial summary judgment, contending that they were employees under the FLSA and NYLL. The defendants cross-moved for summary judgment claiming that Glatt and Footman were not employees under either statute. At about the same time, Antalik moved to certify a class of New York State interns working at certain Fox divisions and a nationwide FLSA collective of interns working at those same divisions.

On June 11, 2013, the district court concluded that Glatt and Footman had been improperly classified as unpaid interns rather than employees and granted their partial motion for summary judgment. The district court also granted Antalik's motions to certify the class of New York interns and to conditionally certify the nationwide FLSA collective.

On September 17, 2013, the district court, acting on defendants' motion, certified its order for immediate appeal under 28 U.S.C. § 1292(b). On November 26, 2013, we granted defendants' petition for leave to file an interlocutory appeal from the district court's orders. For the reasons that follow, we vacate the district court's orders and remand.

DISCUSSION

At its core, this interlocutory appeal raises the broad question of under what circumstances an unpaid intern must be deemed an "employee" under the FLSA and therefore compensated for his work. That broad question underlies our answers to the three specific questions on appeal. First, did the district court apply the correct standard in evaluating whether Glatt and Footman were employees, and, if so, did it reach the correct result. Second, did the district court err by certifying Antalik's class of New York interns. Third, did the district court err by conditionally certifying Antalik's nationwide collective.

I. Glatt's and Footman's Employment Status

We review the district court's order granting partial summary judgment to Glatt and Footman de novo. *See Velez v. Sanchez*, 693 F.3d 308, 313–14 (2d Cir. 2012). Summary judgment is appropriate only if, drawing all reasonable inferences in favor of the nonmoving party, there is no genuine issue of material fact and the moving party is entitled to judgment as a matter of law. *Id.* at 314.

With certain exceptions not relevant here, the FLSA requires employers to pay all employees a specified minimum wage, and overtime of time and one-half for hours worked in excess of forty hours per week. 29 U.S.C. §§ 206–07. NYLL requires the same, except that it specifies a higher wage rate than the federal minimum. *See* N.Y. Labor Law § 652. An employee cannot waive his right to the minimum wage and overtime pay because waiver "would nullify the purposes of the [FLSA] and thwart the legislative policies it was designed to effectuate." *Barrenline v. Arkansas-Best Freight Sys., Inc.*, 450 U.S. 728, 740, 101 S. Ct. 1437, 67 L. Ed. 2d 641 (1981)....

The strictures of both the FLSA and NYLL apply only to employees. The FLSA unhelpfully defines "employee" as an "individual employed by an employer." 29 U.S.C. § 203(e)(1). "Employ" is defined as "to suffer or permit to work." *Id.* § 203(g). New York likewise defines "employee" as "any individual employed, suffered or permitted to work by an employer." 12 N.Y.C.R.R. § 142-2.14(a). Because the statutes define "employee" in nearly identical terms, we construe the NYLL definition as the same in substance as the definition in the FLSA. *See Zheng v. Liberty Apparel Co.*, 355 F.3d 61, 78 (2d Cir. 2003).

The Supreme Court has yet to address the difference between unpaid interns and paid employees under the FLSA. In 1947, however, the Court recognized that unpaid railroad brakemen trainees should not be treated as employees, and thus that they were beyond the reach of the FLSA's minimum wage provision. *See Walling v. Portland Terminal Co.*, 330 U.S. 148, 67 S. Ct. 639, 91 L. Ed. 809 (1947). The Court adduced several facts. First, the brakemen trainees at issue did not displace any regular employees, and their work did not expedite the employer's business. *Id.* at 149–50. Second, the brakemen-trainees did not expect to receive any compensation and would not necessarily be hired upon successful completion of the course. *See id.* at 150. Third, the training course was similar to one offered by a vocational school. *Id.* at 152. Finally, the employer received no immediate advantage from the work done by the trainees. *Id.* at 153.

In 1967, the Department of Labor ("DOL") issued informal guidance on trainees as part of its Field Operations Handbook. The guidance enumerated six criteria and stated that the trainee is not an employee only if all of the criteria were met. *See* DOL, Wage & Hour Div., Field Operations Handbook, Ch. 10, ¶ 10b11 (Oct. 20, 1993), *available at* http://www.dol.gov/whd/FOH/FOH_Ch10.pdf. In 2010, the DOL published similar guidance for unpaid interns working in the for-profit private sector. This Intern Fact Sheet provides that an employment relationship does not exist if all of the following factors apply:

1. The internship, even though it includes actual operation of the facilities of the employer, is similar to training which would be given in an educational environment;

2. The internship experience is for the benefit of the intern;

3. The intern does not displace regular employees, but works under close supervision of existing staff;

4. The employer that provides the training derives no immediate advantage from the activities of the intern; and on occasion its operations may actually be impeded;

5. The intern is not necessarily entitled to a job at the conclusion of the internship; and

6. The employer and the intern understand that the intern is not entitled to wages for the time spent in the internship.

DOL, Wage & Hour Div., Fact Sheet #71, Internship Programs Under The Fair Labor Standards Act (April 2010), *available at* http://www.dol.gov/whd/regs/compliance/whdfs71.pdf.

The district court evaluated Glatt's and Footman's employment using a version of the DOL's six-factor test. However, the district court, unlike the DOL, did not explicitly require that all six factors be present to establish that the intern is not an employee and instead balanced the factors. The district court found that the first four factors weighed in favor of finding that Glatt and Footman were employees and the last two factors favored finding them to be trainees. As a result, the district court concluded that Glatt and Footman had been improperly classified as unpaid interns and granted their motion for partial summary judgment.

The specific issue we face — when is an unpaid intern entitled to compensation as an employee under the FLSA? — is a matter of first impression in this Circuit. When properly designed, unpaid internship programs can greatly benefit interns. For this reason, internships are widely supported by educators and by employers looking to hire well-trained recent graduates. However, employers can also exploit unpaid interns by using their free labor without providing them with an appreciable benefit in education or experience. Recognizing this concern, all parties agree that there are circumstances in which someone who is labeled an unpaid intern is actually an employee entitled to compensation under the FLSA. All parties also agree that there are circumstances in which unpaid interns are not employees under the FLSA. They do not agree on what those circumstances are or what standard we should use to identify them.

The plaintiffs urge us to adopt a test whereby interns will be considered employees whenever the employer receives an immediate advantage from the interns' work. Plaintiffs argue that focusing on any immediate advantage that accrues to the employer is appropriate because, in their view, the Supreme Court in *Portland Terminal* rested its holding on the finding that the brakemen trainees provided no immediate advantage to the employer.

The defendants urge us to adopt a more nuanced primary beneficiary test. Under this standard, an employment relationship is not created when the tangible and intangible benefits provided to the intern are greater than the intern's contribution to the employer's operation. They argue that the primary beneficiary test best reflects the economic realities of the relationship between intern and employer. They further contend that a primary beneficiary test that considers the totality of the circumstances is in accordance with how we decide whether individuals are employees in other circumstances.

DOL, appearing as amicus curiae in support of the plaintiffs, defends the six factors enumerated in its Intern Fact Sheet and its requirement that every factor be present before the employer can escape its obligation to pay the worker. DOL argues (1) that its views on employee status are entitled to deference because it is the agency charged with administering the FLSA and (2) that we should use the six factors because they come directly from *Portland Terminal.*

We decline DOL's invitation to defer to the test laid out in the Intern Fact Sheet. As DOL makes clear in its brief, its six-part test is essentially a distillation of the facts discussed in *Portland Terminal.* DOL Br. at 11–12, 21. Unlike an agency's interpretation of ambiguous statutory terms or its own regulations, "an agency has no special competence or role in interpreting a judicial decision." *State of N.Y. v. Shalala*, 119 F.3d 175, 180 (2d Cir. 1997). And as DOL concedes, DOL Br. at 21, this interpretation is entitled, at most, to *Skidmore* deference to the extent we find it persuasive. *See Skidmore v. Swift & Co.*, 323 U.S. 134, 140, 65 S. Ct. 161, 89 L. Ed. 124 (1944) (the weight given to the Administrator's judgment depends on "all those factors which give it power to persuade"). Because the DOL test attempts to fit *Portland Terminal's* particular facts to all workplaces, and because the test is too rigid for our precedent to withstand, *see, e.g., Velez*, 693 F.3d at 326, we do not find it persuasive, and we will not defer to it.

Instead, we agree with defendants that the proper question is whether the intern or the employer is the primary beneficiary of the relationship. The primary beneficiary test has three salient features. First, it focuses on what the intern receives in exchange for his work. *See Portland Terminal*, 330 U.S. at 152 (focusing on the trainee's interests). Second, it also accords courts the flexibility to examine the economic reality as it exists between the intern and the employer. *See Barfield v. N.Y.C. Health & Hosps. Corp.*, 537 F.3d 132, 141–42 (2d Cir. 2008) (employment for FLSA purposes is "a flexible concept to be determined on a case-by-case basis by review of the totality of the circumstances"). Third, it acknowledges that the intern-employer relationship should not be analyzed in the same manner as the standard employer-employee relationship because the intern enters into the relationship with the expectation of receiving educational or vocational benefits that are not necessarily expected with all forms of employment (though such benefits may be a product of experience on the job).

Although the flexibility of the primary beneficiary test is primarily a virtue, this virtue is not unalloyed. The defendants' conception of the primary beneficiary test requires courts to weigh a diverse set of benefits to the intern against an equally diverse set of benefits received by the employer without specifying the relevance of particular facts. *Cf. Brown v. N.Y.C. Dep't of Educ.*, 755 F.3d 154, 163 (2d Cir. 2014) ("While our ultimate determination [of employment status] is based on the totality of circumstances, our discussion necessarily focuses on discrete facts relevant to particular statutory and regulatory criteria." (internal citation omitted)).

In somewhat analogous contexts, we have articulated a set of nonexhaustive factors to aid courts in determining whether a worker is an employee for purposes of the FLSA. *See, e.g., Velez*, 693 F.3d at 330 (domestic workers); *Brock v. Superior Care, Inc.*, 840 F.2d 1054, 1058–59 (2d Cir. 1988) (independent contractors). In the context of unpaid internships, we think a non-exhaustive set of considerations should include:

1. The extent to which the intern and the employer clearly understand that there is no expectation of compensation. Any promise of compensation, express or implied, suggests that the intern is an employee — and vice versa.

2. The extent to which the internship provides training that would be similar to that which would be given in an educational environment, including the clinical and other hands-on training provided by educational institutions.

3. The extent to which the internship is tied to the intern's formal education program by integrated coursework or the receipt of academic credit.

4. The extent to which the internship accommodates the intern's academic commitments by corresponding to the academic calendar.

5. The extent to which the internship's duration is limited to the period in which the internship provides the intern with beneficial learning.

6. The extent to which the intern's work complements, rather than displaces, the work of paid employees while providing significant educational benefits to the intern.

7. The extent to which the intern and the employer understand that the internship is conducted without entitlement to a paid job at the conclusion of the internship.

Applying these considerations requires weighing and balancing all of the circumstances. No one factor is dispositive and every factor need not point in the same direction for the court to conclude that the intern is not an employee entitled to the minimum wage. In addition, the factors we specify are non-exhaustive — courts may consider relevant evidence beyond the specified factors in appropriate cases. And because the touchstone of this analysis is the "economic reality" of the relationship, *Barfield*, 537 F.3d at 141, a court may elect in certain cases, including cases that can proceed as collective actions, to consider evidence about an internship program as a whole rather than the experience of a specific intern.

This flexible approach is faithful to *Portland Terminal*. Nothing in the Supreme Court's decision suggests that any particular fact was essential to its conclusion or that the facts on which it relied would have the same relevance in every workplace. *See Portland Terminal*, 330 U.S. at 150–53; *see also Solis v. Laurelbrook Sanitarium & Sch., Inc.*, 642 F.3d 518, 526 n.2 (6th Cir. 2011) ("While the Court's recitation of the facts [in *Portland Terminal*] included those that resemble the Secretary's six factors, the Court gave no indication that such facts must be present in future cases to foreclose an employment relationship." (internal citation omitted)).

The approach we adopt also reflects a central feature of the modern internship — the relationship between the internship and the intern's formal education — and is confined to internships and does not apply to training programs in other contexts. The purpose of a bona-fide internship is to integrate classroom learning with practical skill development in a real-world setting, and, unlike the brakemen at issue in *Portland Terminal*, all of the plaintiffs were enrolled in or had recently completed a formal course of post-secondary education. By focusing on the educational aspects of the internship, our approach better reflects the role of internships in today's economy than the DOL factors, which were derived from a 68-year old Supreme Court decision that dealt with a single training course offered to prospective railroad brakemen.

In sum, we agree with the defendants that the proper question is whether the intern or the employer is the primary beneficiary of the relationship, and we propose the above list of non-exhaustive factors to aid courts in answering that question. The district court limited its review to the six factors in DOL's Intern Fact Sheet. Therefore, we vacate the district court's order granting partial summary judgment to Glatt and Footman and remand for further proceedings. On remand, the district court may, in its discretion, permit the parties to submit additional evidence relevant to the plaintiffs' employment status, such as evidence on Glatt's and Footman's formal education. Of course, we express no opinion with respect to the outcome of any renewed motions for summary judgment the parties might make based on the primary beneficiary test we have set forth....

CONCLUSION

For the foregoing reasons, the district court's orders are VACATED and the case REMANDED for further proceedings consistent with this opinion.

An example of a typically free principal-agent relationship is that created by a durable power of attorney for healthcare. This document simply lets one person make medical decisions on behalf of another, when that person is incapable of making those decisions himself. It is a written principal-agency agreement. Often, no money is exchanged to be an agent for healthcare. A son-in-law, who has a power-of-attorney for an aging mother-in-law, does not act as the mother-in-law's power-of-attorney for money. However, he is still an agent because he is acting on his mother-in-law's behalf. Other examples of agents include realtors, attorneys, partners, directors, and often salespeople.

A durable power of attorney for health care is different from a general power of attorney. A general power of attorney allows an attorney in fact to act for a principal on all issues, not just those of healthcare. An attorney-in-fact does not have to be an attorney at all. An attorney in fact can be someone who has authority, though a power of attorney, to act on behalf of another. In essence, an attorney-in-fact is an agent.

The following document is an example durable power of attorney for health care, from the state of Rhode Island.

Rhode Island Statutory Form:
Durable Power of Attorney for Health Care
WARNING TO PERSON EXECUTING THIS DOCUMENT

This is an important legal document which is authorized by the general laws of Rhode Island. Before executing this document, you should know these important facts:

You must be at least eighteen (18) years of age and a resident of the state for this document to be legally valid and binding.

This document gives the person you designate as your agent (the attorney in fact) the power to make health care decisions for you. Your agent must act consistently with your desires as stated in this document or otherwise made known.

Except as you otherwise specify in this document, this document gives your agent the power to consent to your doctor not giving treatment or stopping treatment necessary to keep you alive.

Notwithstanding this document, you have the right to make medical and other health care decisions for yourself so long as you can give informed consent with respect to the particular decision. In addition, no treatment may be given to you over your objection at the time, and health care necessary to keep you alive may not be stopped or withheld if you object at the time.

This document gives your agent authority to consent, to refuse to consent, or to withdraw consent to any care, treatment, service, or procedure to maintain, diagnose, or treat a physical or mental condition. This power is subject to any statement of your desires and any limitation that you include in this document. You may state in this document any types of treatment that you do not desire. In addition, a court can take away the power of your agent to make health care decisions for you if your agent:

(1) Authorizes anything that is illegal,

(2) Acts contrary to your known desires, or

(3) Where your desires are not known, does anything that is clearly contrary to your best interests.

Unless you specify a specific period, this power will exist until you revoke it. Your agent's power and authority ceases upon your death except to inform your family or next of kin of your desire, if any, to be an organ and tissue owner.

You have the right to revoke the authority of your agent by notifying your agent or your treating doctor, hospital, or other health care provider orally or in writing of the revocation.

Your agent has the right to examine your medical records and to consent to their disclosure unless you limit this right in this document.

This document revokes any prior durable power of attorney for health care.

You should carefully read and follow the witnessing procedure described at the end of this form. This document will not be valid unless you comply with the witnessing procedure.

If there is anything in this document that you do not understand, you should ask a lawyer to explain it to you.

Your agent may need this document immediately in case of an emergency that requires a decision concerning your health care. Either keep this document where it is immediately available to your agent and alternate agents or give each of them an executed copy of this document. You may also want to give your doctor an executed copy of this document.

(1) DESIGNATION OF HEALTH CARE AGENT. I, (insert your name and address) do hereby designate and appoint:

(Insert name, address, and telephone number of one individual only as your agent to make health care decisions for you. None of the following may be designated as your agent: (1) your treating health care provider, (2) a nonrelative employee of your treating health care provider, (3) an operator of a community care facility, or (4) a nonrelative employee of an operator of a community care facility.) as my attorney in fact (agent) to make health care decisions for me as authorized in this document. For the purposes of this document, "health care decision" means consent, refusal of consent, or withdrawal of consent to any care, treatment, service, or procedure to maintain, diagnose, or treat an individual's physical or mental condition.

(2) CREATION OF DURABLE POWER OF ATTORNEY FOR HEALTH CARE. By this document I intend to create a durable power of attorney for health care.

(3) GENERAL STATEMENT OF AUTHORITY GRANTED. Subject to any limitations in this document, I hereby grant to my agent full power and authority to make health care decisions for me to the same extent that I could make such decisions for myself if I had the capacity to do so. In exercising this authority, my agent shall make health care decisions that are consistent with my desires as stated in this document or otherwise made known to my agent, including, but not limited to, my desires concerning obtaining or refusing or withdrawing life-prolonging care, treatment, services, and procedures and informing my family or next of kin of my desire, if any, to be an organ or tissue donor.

(If you want to limit the authority of your agent to make health care decisions for you, you can state the limitations in paragraph (4) ("Statement of Desires, Special Provisions, and Limitations") below. You can indicate your desires by including a statement of your desires in the same paragraph.)

(4) STATEMENT OF DESIRES, SPECIAL PROVISIONS, AND LIMITATIONS. (Your agent must make health care decisions that are consistent with your known desires. You can, but are not required to, state your desires in the space provided below. You should consider whether you want to include a statement of your desires concerning life-prolonging care, treatment, services, and procedures. You can also include a statement of your desires concerning other matters relating to your health care. You can also make your desires known to your agent by discussing your desires with your agent or by some other means. If there are any types of treatment that you do not want to be used, you should state them in the space below. If you want to limit in any other way the authority given your agent by this document, you should state the limits in the space below. If you do not state any limits, your agent will have broad powers to make health care decisions for you, except to the extent that there are limits provided by law.)

In exercising the authority under this durable power of attorney for health care, my agent shall act consistently with my desires as stated below and is subject to the special provisions and limitations stated below:

(a) Statement of desires concerning life-prolonging care, treatment, services, and procedures:

(b) Additional statement of desires, special provisions, and limitations regarding health care decisions:

(c) Statement of desire regarding organ and tissue donation:

Initial if applicable:

[ ] In the event of my death, I request that my agent inform my family/next of kin of my desire to be an organ and tissue donor, if possible.

(You may attach additional pages if you need more space to complete your statement. If you attach additional pages, you must date and sign EACH of the additional pages at the same time you date and sign this document.)

(5) INSPECTION AND DISCLOSURE OF INFORMATION RELATING TO MY PHYSICAL OR MENTAL HEALTH. Subject to any limitations in this document, my agent has the power and authority to do all of the following:

(a) Request, review, and receive any information, verbal or written, regarding my physical or mental health, including, but not limited to, medical and hospital records.

(b) Execute on my behalf any releases or other documents that may be required in order to obtain this information.

(c) Consent to the disclosure of this information.

(If you want to limit the authority of your agent to receive and disclose information relating to your health, you must state the limitations in paragraph (4) ("Statement of desires, special provisions, and limitations") above.)

(6) SIGNING DOCUMENTS, WAIVERS, AND RELEASES. Where necessary to implement the health care decisions that my agent is authorized by this document to make, my agent has the power and authority to execute on my behalf all of the following:

(a) Documents titled or purporting to be a "Refusal to Permit Treatment" and "Leaving Hospital Against Medical Advice."

(b) Any necessary waiver or release from liability required by a hospital or physician.

(7) DURATION. (Unless you specify a shorter period in the space below, this power of attorney will exist until it is revoked.)

This durable power of attorney for health care expires on

(Fill in this space ONLY if you want the authority of your agent to end on a specific date.)

(8) DESIGNATION OF ALTERNATE AGENTS.

(You are not required to designate any alternate agents but you may do so. Any alternate agent you designate will be able to make the same health care decisions as the agent you designated in paragraph (1), above, in the event that agent is unable or ineligible to act as your agent. If the agent you designated is your spouse, he or she becomes ineligible to act as your agent if your marriage is dissolved.)

If the person designated as my agent in paragraph (1) is not available or becomes ineligible to act as my agent to make a health care decision for me or loses the mental capacity to make health care decisions for me, or if I revoke that person's appointment or authority to act as my agent to make health care decisions for me, then I designate and appoint the following persons to serve as my agent to make health care decisions for me as authorized in this document, such persons to serve in the order listed below:

(A) First Alternate Agent:

(Insert name, address, and telephone number of first alternate agent.)

(B) Second Alternate Agent:

(Insert name, address, and telephone number of second alternate agent.)

(9) PRIOR DESIGNATIONS REVOKED. I revoke any prior durable power of attorney for health care.

DATE AND SIGNATURE OF PRINCIPAL

(YOU MUST DATE AND SIGN THIS POWER OF ATTORNEY)

I sign my name to this Statutory Form Durable Power of Attorney for Health Care on _____ (Date) at _____ (City), _____ (State) _____ (You sign here)

(THIS POWER OF ATTORNEY WILL NOT BE VALID UNLESS IT IS SIGNED BY TWO (2) QUALIFIED WITNESSES WHO ARE PRESENT WHEN YOU SIGN OR ACKNOWLEDGE YOUR SIGNATURE. IF YOU HAVE ATTACHED ANY ADDITIONAL PAGES TO THIS FORM, YOU MUST DATE AND SIGN EACH OF THE ADDITIONAL PAGES AT THE SAME TIME YOU DATE AND SIGN THIS POWER OF ATTORNEY.)

STATEMENT OF WITNESSES

(This document must be witnessed by two (2) qualified adult witnesses. None of the following may be used as a witness:

(1) A person you designate as your agent or alternate agent,

(2) A health care provider,

(3) An employee of a health care provider,

(4) The operator of a community care facility,

(5) An employee of an operator of a community care facility.

At least one of the witnesses must make the additional declaration set out following the place where the witnesses sign.)

I declare under penalty of perjury that the person who signed or acknowledged this document is personally known to me to be the principal, that the principal signed or acknowledged this durable power of attorney in my presence, that the principal appears to be of sound mind and under no duress, fraud, or undue influence, that I am not the person appointed as attorney in fact by this document, and that I am not a health care provider, an employee of a health care provider, the operator of a community care facility, nor an employee of an operator of a community care facility.

Signature: _____ Residence Address: _____

Print Name: _____ Date: _____

Signature: _____ Residence Address: _____

Print Name: _____ Date: _____

(AT LEAST ONE OF THE ABOVE WITNESSES MUST ALSO SIGN THE FOLLOWING DECLARATION.)

I further declare under penalty of perjury that I am not related to the principal by blood, marriage, or adoption, and, to the best of my knowledge, I am not entitled to any part of the estate of the principal upon the death of the principal under a will now existing or by operation of law.

Signature: _____ Signature: _____

Print Name: _____ Print Name: _____

Petition for Appointment of Conservator

Form is Also Available at: https://courts.michigan.gov/Administration/SCAO/Forms/courtforms/pc639.pdf

1.2 Formation of a Principal-Agent Relationship

Before looking at how the principal-agent relationship is formed, whether a person can be in an agency relationship needs to be determined. The principal must have the capacity to appoint an agent to act on her behalf, or in other words. A mentally insane or underage person usually cannot appoint an agent. The court has the authority to appoint an agent on behalf of those people.

Please either look at the form "Petition for Appointment of Conservator" or go to the form through the weblink below.

"a. The individual is an adult unable to manage his/her property and business affairs effectively because of:

- mental illness
- chronic use of drugs
- detention by a foreign power
- mental deficiency
- chronic intoxication
- disappearance
- physical illness or

- disability confinement

and

either the adult has property that will be wasted or dissipated unless proper management is provided,

or

the adult or his/her dependents are in need of money for support, care, and welfare, and protection is necessary to obtain or provide money.

b. The adult petitioner is mentally competent but because of age or physical infirmity is unable to manage his/her property and affairs effectively, and recognizing the disability, requests appointment of a conservator.

c. The individual is a minor who owns money or property that requires management or protection that cannot otherwise be provided. has or may have business affairs that may be jeopardized or prevented by minority. needs money for support and education, and protection is necessary or desirable to obtain or provide money.

d. I am the guardian of the ward and it is in the ward's best interests to sell or otherwise dispose of the ward's real property or interest in real property."

https://courts.michigan.gov/Administration/SCAO/Forms/courtforms/pc639.pdf

Please note that some of the times a court may be able to appoint a conservator (or agent) are when the principal has a mental illness, physical illness or disability, chronic abuse of drugs, and/or chronic abuse of alcohol.

However, an agent does not have to have capacity to act as an agent; an agent could be mentally insane or a minor! There is a caveat about the agent being mentally insane or a minor: the agent must be able to understand the act(s) that they need to execute for the principal.

Another important observation to make is that an agency for something illegal is not a valid agency relationship. Hence, an agency relationship established to buy and sell illicit drugs would not be a valid agency relationship. The news has made a big deal out of murder for hire contracts. It is ironic that someone wanting to murder another would be concerned about a contract. If this were true though, the contract would be invalid as would the principal-agent relationship, as murder is not a legal act. Take a look at the Murder for Hire Act at https://www.justice.gov/archives/jm/criminal-resource-manual-1107-murder-hire-offense. What is the travel requirement?

How the principal-agent relationship can be formed is through:

- Actual Authority (this can be either express or implied),
- Apparent Authority,
- Ratified Authority, or
- Estoppel.

Each of these ways in which to form a principal-agent relationship will be discussed in more detail below.

1.3 An Agent's Authority

a. Actual Authority

Actual authority occurs when a principal purposefully gives the agent certain power. To have a principal-agent relationship, both parties must have the capacity to consent and both parties must consent to it. The agreement can be implied or express. Express would be the principal and agent saying or writing words down to the effect that they have a principal-agent relationship. While most agency agreements can be oral (though it is better to have written agency agreement), some agency relationships are required by law to be written, such as a contract to sell land. Another example of agency by a written agreement is a written agreement by a seller of a house to be represented by one real estate agent. Implied authority would be acts or conduct from which a principal-agency agreement could be inferred.

b. Apparent Authority

Apparent authority is similar in nature to agency by estoppel (discussed in section d below). The emphasis is placed upon what a third party reasonably believed about the alleged agent's status and not what the principal and agent themselves believed. This is usually the case when someone is standing behind the cash register in a store. It seems apparent that they have authority to act on behalf of the principal; otherwise, why would they be standing behind the cash register?

If Abdi goes to a dog grooming shop and sees someone in an apron, holding an electric shaver, he is reasonable in believing that the person wearing the apron is acting on behalf of the owners of the dog grooming shop. The fact that someone might have walked in off the street, put on the employee apron and grabbed an electronic shaver does not matter (the owner of the shop should prevent people from doing this), and Abdi has a reasonable belief. The owner of the shop made it look like someone who walked in off the street had authority by not preventing that person from grabbing an employee apron and electric shaver.

Apparent agency is caused by the principal making it look like there is an agency relationship. The action is the principal's usually and not the agent's. The law holds it is fair to find a principal-agency relationship because it was reasonable for a third party to believe there was one. There are three major factors to apparent authority. They include the conduct of the principal, which implies that a person is acting as his agent. Next, to have apparent authority, a third party must rely on that implication. Finally, the third party has to have acted to her detriment in relying on that implication. Thus, it is not as simple as it initially sounds to prove apparent authority.

c. Ratified Authority

Ratified authority happens after the fact. Hence, the person did not originally have the authority to act on behalf of the principal, but they did anyway. After the action, the principal might come by and say, "Good job on buying that office equipment." This would be ratified authority, if the agent did not have the authority to by the equipment prior to buying it. The principal only has the power to ratify the entire transaction of the agent, and not just part of the transaction.

Ratified authority has several different elements to it:

- The agent has to have acted on behalf of the principal, who then ratifies the act,

- The principal has to know all of the material facts in the act,

- The act must be ratified in its entirety,

- The principal has to have had authority to authorize the act when it happened and when it was ratified, and

- The ratification must happen before the third party voids the act.

d. Estoppel

There is yet another way that a principal-agent relationship can be found. Sometimes, it is simply unfair if a principal-agency arrangement is not found, so a court will find one. This usually occurs when it is reasonable for a third party to believe that someone is an agent on another person's behalf. That third person is normally considered innocent in the transaction. In this way, estoppel is similar to apparent authority. Estoppel is a public policy argument, which changes what the law would otherwise hold, based upon a "fairness" argument and can involve the actions of the agent as well. This element is different from apparent authority.

Using the same example from above of the dog grooming salon owner who did not secure employee aprons or electric shavers, what if the dog grooming salon owner had secured the employee aprons? What if the agent went into the employee break room to get an employee apron, and then picked up an electric shaver that was not secured an anyway? The owner did not secure the electric shaver. The agent went into an employee break room. Both acted to make a third party think that the person off the street was an employee of the dog grooming salon.

An estoppel argument also has the added arguments about the size and bargaining position of the parties. If the dog grooming salon is a bigger salon, like a national chain, it is much more likely a court will find the national chain helped create a principal-agent relationship expectation. If the dog grooming salon is a smaller salon, like a mom and pop operation, it is much less likely a court will find the smaller salon helped create a principal-agent relationship expectation.

For example, Jill, a legal intern, goes with a law firm associate attorney, Mark, on an office supply run. Jill is an unpaid intern, for the summer. However, while on the office supply run, the associate, Mark, mentions to the manager of the store that Jill is a great "asset to the firm." The manager of the store now has a reasonable belief that Jill works for the law firm. If Jill orders supplies for the law firm, the law firm will need to pay for those supplies. While Jill might know that she does not typically have authority to buy expensive equipment for the law office, the manager of the store does not know that. The office supply store might argue apparent authority.

Later, the intern went back to the office supply store by herself. She tells the office supply store she has been asked to get more supplies on credit, when she has not. She does buy more office supplies on credit. Now the law firm does not want to pay, stating she did not have authority to purchase the supplies. The office supply store could argue estoppel in addition to apparent authority, as the agent's actions also contributed to the office supply store believing she had authority and it would not be fair to hold otherwise.

Typically, the fairness part of estoppel has to do with the size and the bargaining power of the parties. If the equipment seller is small versus large, it is much more likely that a court would find in favor of the equipment seller, rather than a large law firm that allowed a legal intern to look like a representative of the company. If the parties were the same size, there would not be a strong estoppel argument.

Agency by estoppel is very similar to agency through apparent authority. However, there is usually an unfairness argument added to the agency by estoppel, often based upon size. In addition, another difference between the two is that with apparent authority, the issue is often the principal's actions, whereas with estoppel, it often has to do more with the agent's actions.

1.4 Duties Agents and Principals Owe Each Other

a. Agent's Duties

In general, a principal-agency relationship is one in which the agent has a fiduciary duty to the principal. A fiduciary relationship is one in which one person has a legal and/or ethical obligation to another and that other person should be able to trust the fiduciary. In addition to the other duties of an agent discussed below, an agent is also supposed to act in good faith and with due care. The fiduciary relationship and good faith requirement go hand in hand. The fiduciary relationship requires the agent to act responsibly or in good faith, in regards to the principal's money and interests. Thus, an agent embezzling his principal's assets would be in violation of the fiduciary duty. The duty of care, also known as the duty of due care, requires the agent to use that amount of care a reasonably prudent agent would use under similar circumstances.

1. Performance

It seems very basic, but the agent is supposed to perform his tasks for the principal. Usually these tasks should be completed as soon as possible, unless the principal has specified another time frame. Essentially this equates to what is known as due diligence — actually performing the tasks and doing so in a timely manner. These tasks should be performed in a conscientious manner, taking care to do the tasks properly.

In the law, this is frequently referred to as the duty of due care and due care is also required specifically to performance. The duty of due care is the duty to not act with negligence, which equates again to acting as a reasonably prudent agent would under similar circumstances. What is considered acting with due care also, in part, relies on what society expects is reasonable.

Thus, the agent is expected to perform the duties covered in the contract, whether or not this was a written or oral contract. If a paid agent did not perform, then the agent would be in breach, though it can be harder to prove a breach of an oral contract than a written contract. If an unpaid agent acts negligently, then while he may not be in breach of contract, he may still be liable under tort law.

2. Notification

An agent is supposed to notify the principal about material matters relating to the tasks the agent is supposed to perform for the principal. In fact, the principal is assumed to have imputed knowledge, which is having the same knowledge that the agent has about the agency. Material matters are important matters, such as the facts necessary to make a decision. Material matters include information that can affect the principal's rights or actions.

For example, an attorney is an agent of the client, who is the principal. If the attorney receives a reasonable settlement offer, the attorney is required to convey that settlement offer to the client. Depending upon the state, an attorney may not be required to convey an unreasonable settlement offer, such as one-tenth of the value of the case, to the client. Different states have different rules on conveyance of settlement offers by attorneys, but in general, an agent would not be required to convey a completely unreasonable settlement offer.

3. Loyalty

Duty of loyalty is also known as the duty not to compete with the principal or to help others compete against the principal. The agent could compete with the principal by taking business advantages meant for the principal and using them for himself. The duty of loyalty, owed by an agent to his principal, is to act solely in the interest in the principal. The agent should not be skimming any money off the top and pocketing it before giving the remainder to the principal. This is self-dealing. The agent might have to put the needs of the principal above his own.

In addition, the duty of loyalty is the duty not to have a conflict of interest. In general, an agent violates this duty if he tries to work for more than one principal with similar interests. This is known as dual agency. It is only allowed if all parties agree to it.

4. Accounting

If the agent has to expend money in performing the tasks for the principal, he should keep detailed records of the expenditures. For example, if the agent has to drive to perform his task, he may be able to claim mileage. An internet readout of the number of miles travelled would help to substantiate his claim. If the agent had to pay for parking, the parking stubs would help substantiate his claim. Accounting can be very simple as below:

Expenditure for:	Amount paid to:	Amount:	Paid from which account:	Date:

In addition, anything of value given to the agent by a third party during the relationship typically belongs to the principal. Thus, the agent is required to take good care of those items of value and make sure that all are passed over to the principal.

b. Principal's Duties

1. Compensation

Although this sounds very basic, the principal is required to pay the agent, so long as it is not a free agency (such as a durable power of attorney for healthcare) or a valid unpaid internship. However, it is best to negotiate the payment prior to doing the work. If no payment is negotiated previously, then legally the payment should be whatever is normal and customary in the industry. If that cannot be determined, then "reasonable" payment is due. Proving what is reasonable payment is difficult, so it is better to discuss the terms of payment prior to the start of work.

2. Reimbursement

The principal is required to reimburse the agent for the amounts of money the agent had to spend to perform the tasks for the principal. The expenses must have been authorized by the principal, within the scope contemplated by the agency, and the expenses must be necessary for the agent to perform her duties. If this is the case, then essentially, the expenses paid for by the agent are considered the principal's expenses, for which he must reimburse the agent. To be reimbursed, the agent should provide an accounting of his expenses. The agent should not expect payment without an accounting.

3. Indemnification

In addition, if the agent acts negligently (for example, causing an accident) then typically the employer is required to indemnify, or hold harmless, the employee for a lawsuit against the agent. If the behavior were intentional, the principal would not be required to pay. If the behavior was reckless and willful, the principal may be required to pay, depending on how pro-corporation or pro-plaintiff the state is and how severe the behavior of the agent was. Reckless and willful behavior is behavior that is substantially likely to cause an injury. Drunk driving is often used as an example of reckless and willful behavior. The driver probably did not intend to cause an injury, but by driving while drunk, it is substantially certain that the driver will cause an injury Most people do not realize how little alcohol it takes to drive impaired, although they are aware alcohol can impair driving ability [look at the Figure on Blood Alcohol Content at https://www.dmv.ca.gov/portal/dmv/detail/pubs/hdbk/actions_aps_court It shows that the only safe driving limit is a .00 blood alcohol limit (shown in green). It shows that driving skills are impaired between .02 and .07 blood alcohol content (shown in yellow). It shows that people are legally intoxicated (at least in the state of California) with a blood alcohol content of .08 or higher (shown in red)]. If the principal did nothing to encourage the agent to drink and drive, then typically the principal would not be liable for the agent's behavior while.

4. Cooperation

The principal is expected to cooperate with the agent so that the agent can do his job. The principal should help the agent in performing the tasks, at least in terms of providing a company credit card for large expenditures or a place to work, if needed.

1.5 Liability of Principal and Agent to Third Parties

Vicarious liability is when one person (here the principal) can be held liable for another person's (here the agent's) negligence. In other words, the principal is liable for an injury that was caused by his agent. This does not mean that the agent is not held liable for his own actions, unless and until the principal decides to indemnify him. Thus, vicarious liability is closely tied to indemnification, which was discussed earlier as one of the principal's duties to the agent.

For the principal to be found vicariously liable for the acts of his agent, the agent must be acting within the course and scope of employment when he committed the act. Another requirement for the principal to be found vicariously liable for the acts of his agent is that the relationship must be a principal-agency one (often, an employment principal-agency relationship) and not an independent contractor one (which will be discussed more later in the text at section 2.2).

In the following case, the company that hired the weed control company is attempting to avoid the liability of herbicide spraying. The court held that the hirer could not avoid liability under the concept of respondeat superior, also known as vicarious liability. A more complete definition of respondeat superior is when an employee is responsible for torts he committed during the course and scope of his employment, then the employer is also responsible.

Warner v. Southwest Desert Images
218 Ariz. 121, 180 P.3d 986 (2008)

… Southwest Desert Images, LLC (SDI) was hired by Warner's employer, Aegis Communications (Aegis), to perform landscaping and weed control. On September

29, 2003, SDI employee Hoggatt began spraying an herbicide on weeds on the property around Aegis's building. The parties dispute whether other SDI employees had been present and engaged in spraying. After approximately an hour and a half of spraying, Hoggatt was informed that people inside Aegis's building were complaining. The herbicide spray had entered the building through its air conditioning system and had circulated throughout the building. After being informed of the situation, Hoggatt stopped spraying. Emergency services arrived as the building was being evacuated. Employees in the building complained of respiratory problems and itching and burning eyes.

Prior to and during the evacuation, Warner began having difficulty breathing, was coughing violently, and felt burning in her eyes, nose, and throat. As she exited building, Warner began to feel faint and felt "extreme chest pain" and heart palpitations. Warner had had heart attacks in January 1998 and April 2003, and had undergone heart surgery in May 2003. Warner apparently had been instructed to carry nitroglycerine and take it if she felt angina, or heart pain, so she took some after she left the Aegis building. She was then transported by ambulance to the hospital, where she was treated and released after about four hours. She returned to Aegis and drove home.

Warner testified she continued to have angina and palpitations that night. She visited her doctor two days later. He concluded she had suffered a heart attack the day of the evacuation. Warner continued to have a "scratchy throat and watery eyes" for about ten days after the incident, continued to suffer from chest pain, balance problems, short-term memory loss and other neurological problems, nausea, muscle aches, and fatigue, and has not worked since the incident. Warner had heart surgery that October, and again in January 2004. She suffered another heart attack shortly after the latter surgery, which was followed by emergency surgery and further surgery in September 2004. Warner had a pacemaker implanted in June 2005.

Warner sued SDI for negligence in September 2004, later amending her complaint to include as defendants Hoggatt, Wilson, and Sierra Pest, Wilson's employer. She alleged SDI was a "branch office" of Sierra Pest and operated under Wilson's qualifying party license, and thus that Wilson and Sierra Pest were liable for Hoggatt's negligent herbicide spraying and "for the [negligent] supervision and training of ... Hoggatt." SDI admitted it operated under Wilson's qualifying party license.

The jury found SDI to be completely responsible for the injuries Warner suffered by inhaling the herbicide.... This appeal followed....

"... [T]he evidence [wa]s undisputed that Mr. Hoggatt [had] acted within the scope of his employment for [SDI]," and, thus, that SDI was "clearly liable in this situation for whatever damages the jury does find in this matter...." ("According to the doctrine of *respondeat superior*, 'an employer is vicariously liable ... for the behavior of an employee who was acting within the course and scope of his employment.... '")

"It is well-established law that an agent will not be excused from responsibility for tortious conduct [merely] because he is acting for his principal...." ("An agent is subject to liability to a third party harmed by the agent's tortious conduct. Unless an applicable statute provides otherwise, an actor remains subject to liability although the actor acts ... within the scope of employment....")

First, in order for an employer to be liable for punitive damages, the alleged basis for punitive damages must spring from either (1) the employer's independent actions for which it is liable, or (2) the actions of its employee for which it is liable under the doctrine of respondeat superior.... Thus, for SDI's own actions, such as possibly having used unlicensed applicators, to form the basis for a punitive damages award, SDI must be independently liable for negligence....

Furthermore, even if Warner had alleged SDI was independently liable, mere usage of unlicensed herbicide applicators cannot, as a matter of law, justify an award of punitive damages. Warner argues the use of unlicensed applicators can, without more, show the "conscious disregard" necessary to justify a punitive damages instruction.... To support her assertion, Warner relies on several cases from other jurisdictions in which the defendant's use of unlicensed employees or entrustment of vehicles to unlicensed drivers, who later commit a tort, justifies an award of punitive damages against the defendant....

We agree with Warner that the likely purpose of the licenses in those cases was, like here, public safety. In those cases, however, it was illegal for an unlicensed person to perform the underlying activity.... Despite Warner's assumption that the use of unlicensed herbicide applicators would be illegal, A.R.S. § 32-2312(F) allows companies to use unlicensed applicators so long as they "work under the direct supervision of a licensed applicator at all times." "Direct supervision" merely requires that the unlicensed applicators work "under the instruction, control and responsibility of a licensed applicator who is available if needed for consultation or assistance even though the licensed applicator is not physically present at the time and place the [herb]icide is used...." Warner presented no evidence suggesting Hoggatt, SDI's licensed applicator, was unavailable, nor that any unlicensed workers SDI may have used were otherwise not under Hoggatt's "instruction, control and responsibility." Without more, the legal use of unlicensed herbicide applicators is not the type of "outrageous, oppressive or intolerable" conduct that would support an award of punitive damages....

1.6 Termination of Agency

There are four ways in which the parties can arrange to properly terminate a principal agency relationship. These ways will not cause a breach of contract. They are: mutual agreement, lapse of a specified amount of time, the achievement of the purpose of the agency, or when a certain event occurs. If both parties agree, then it will terminate the relationship, but it will not be a breach of the relationship. The agency may be for an indefinite amount of time, or it may have a limited amount of time placed upon it. If the agency is for a stated period, then the agency will terminate at the end of that period. If the agency is just for as long as is necessary for the agent to complete a task, then once that task is completed, then the agency will terminate. A certain event occurring may or may not be tied to the tasks required in the principal-agency relationship. For example, the relationship might be contracted to last as long as a prior agent, out on maternity leave, does not return to work.

The relationship can be terminated by the actions of either party. Neither party is legally forced to stay in the relationship if either one no longer wants to be in the relationship. However, if terminating puts one side in breach, then legally, that party may have to pay damages for terminating to the other. To not be in breach for ending the relationship early, both parties would have to mutually agree to end the principal-agency relationship early.

How one party terminates is usually by notice. Once the principal is notified, then the principal has a duty to notify specific third parties about the termination of the agency. If the principal does not, and there looks like there is apparent authority, then principal would be liable to the third parties who relied on that appearance. The principal is generally responsible for notifying those persons who dealt with or knew of the agency relationship; the principal would not be responsible for telling persons who did not know of the principal-agency relationship.

If one of the parties, either the principal or the agent, dies or otherwise becomes incapacitated (for example, by death, insanity, bankruptcy, and/or war), then the relationship will terminate by operation of law. Remember, from earlier in the chapter, if an agent is insane, he can still be an agent, so long as he is able to understand what he is agreeing to do. In general, if it becomes impossible to perform the tasks of the agency for the principal, then the relationship will terminate.

Chapter Summary

In agency, one person acts for another. The person acting is the agent and the person being acted for is the principal. The agent acts on behalf of the principal toward third parties. Both parties have to agree to the principal-agent relationship for the agent to have actual authority. While a written contract for the principal-agency relationship is better, it is not required to form an agency relationship. There could be an oral contract for a principal-agency relationship. Principal-agency relationships made by oral or written words are known as express agency agreements. Some principal-agent relationships are financially compensated and some are not, such as a durable power of attorney for health care.

Sometimes, principal-agency agreements can be created by the actions, rather than the written or oral words of the parties. This would be known as an implied agency, because the relationship is inferred from the actions. There is also apparent authority, when the principal makes it look or sound like there is an agency relationship, even when there is not. Agency can occur after the fact as well; a person may do something on behalf of another and if it is approved by the principal after the fact, then agency by ratification has occurred. Finally, there can be agency by estoppel. The principal will be estopped, or stopped, from denying the relationship. While very similar to apparent authority, estoppel focuses more on the actions of the agent than the principal. Agency by estoppel is also based on a fairness argument; it can occur when the principal is large, and better equipped to bear the loss, than the third party, who is small.

In general, the agent has a fiduciary duty to act in good faith and with due care towards the principal. In addition, the agent has several duties to the principal, which include performing reasonably, notifying the principal of material information, and loyalty (the duty not to compete). The agent should also account for all the items of value that are bought and sold on behalf of the principal.

In return, the principal has several duties to the agent. Primarily, the principal is responsible for paying the agent, also known as compensation. If there is not an agreement as to the amount to be paid, the amount to be paid should be what is normal and customary in the industry. The principal has a duty to reimburse the agent for the expenses the agent makes in performing his duties. The principal should indemnify the agent for certain acts committed within the course and scope of the relationship. Whether the principal does have to indemnify the agent depends upon the employee's actions. Typically, an employer would not be reasonable for an employee's intentional bad acts, but would be responsible for an employee's negligent bad acts. Finally, the principal needs to cooperate with the agent so that the agent can perform his job.

The parties can decide to terminate the principal-agency relationship through the following ways, none of which causes a breach of contract: mutual agreement, lapse of a specified amount of time, the achievement of the purpose of the agency, or when a certain event occurs. If the parties terminate in any of these four ways, then notice should be given by the principal to the third parties who knew of the principal-agency relationship. If however, only one party wants to terminate the relationship, this is normally considered a breach of contract; the other party may be entitled to damages. Principal-agency relationships can also be terminated by operation of law or certain events. Examples of termination by operation of law include death, mental insanity, bankruptcy, impossibility, and war.

Key Terms

Actual authority	Apparent authority
Agency	Duty
Agency by estoppel	Duty of care
Agency by ratification	Duty of due care
Agency law	Duty of loyalty
Agent	Duty to compensate
Apparent agency	Duty to cooperate

Duty to indemnify
Duty to notify
Duty to perform
Duty to reimburse
Employer-employee relationship
Estoppel
Express agency
Fiduciary relationship
Implied authority

Indemnification
Independent contractor
Limited personal liability
Principal
Principal-agent relationship
Ratify
Respondeat superior
Termination
Vicarious liability

Review Questions

1. What are the parties called in an agency relationship?

2. Explain what an agent is.

3. What is the main goal of an agency relationship?

4. Explain the concept of apparent authority and how it differs from agency by estoppel.

5. Is it a good idea to create a principal-agency agreement without a written contract? Can an oral agreement be used for all types of principal-agency relationships?

6. Is financial remuneration necessary to create a principal-agency relationship?

7. What duties does an agent owe to her principal?

8. Does a principal owe an agent a duty to indemnify that agent?

9. In the *Warner v. Southwestern Desert Images* case in this chapter, did the court allow punitive damages? Why or why not?

10. How can a principal-agency relationship be terminated?

11. Identify a time in which you have acted as an agent for another.

Web Links

For more information on agency law, go to Hieros Gamos explanation and accompanying articles at http://www.hg.org/agency-law.html. Hieros Gamos is a large legal resources website.

Go to your state's secretary of state's website and determine how to designate an agent for service of process.

Exercises

1. Jackie is a manager of a pet hotel for the owner, Ian. Jackie has been told by Ian to charge thirty-five dollars a day for dogs, and twenty-five dollars a day for cats.

Unbeknownst to Ian, when customers are paying in cash, Jackie has raised the rates to forty-five dollars a day for dogs, and thirty-five dollars a day for cats. She has been pocketing the difference. What duties, if any, has Jackie violated in regards to her principal, Ian?

2. Using the facts from the last question, Ian has warned Jackie that all pets staying at the pet hotel must be vaccinated for kennel cough prior to boarding at the facility. However, Jackie has not required pet owners to produce the record of vaccination, so that she can board as many animals as possible. What duties, if any, has Jackie now violated in regards to her principal, Ian?

3. A rental unit is being sold. The seller warrants that there are no plumbing problems. However, after the buyer buys the property, major plumbing problems become known. In a lawsuit against the seller, if the buyer can prove the seller's property manager knew of the plumbing problems prior to the sale, how will the court rule?

4. Pretend that your spouse is leaving the country for an eight-month deployment. Find and revise a power of attorney for your spouse to sign prior their departure, which will give you the right to sign on their behalf, while they are gone. Note that this document is different from a durable power of attorney for healthcare.

5. Research the status of the *Glatt v. Fox Searchlight Pictures, Inc.* case.

6. Start preparing timesheets for the work you do in this class, so you can get used to preparing timesheets in a law firm.

Time should be keep in increments of 6 minutes. This means that the hour is divided into 10 segments. Most attorney-client fee agreements (which also cover paralegals, state that if we work 8 minutes, for example, we round UP to the nearest increment, which would be a .2). Once we get to over an hour, we put time in the following format: 1.2 for an hour and twelve minutes.

0–6 minutes = .1

7–12 minutes = .2

13–18 minutes = .3

19–24 minutes = .4

25–30 minutes = .5

31–36 minutes = 6

37–42 minutes = .7

43–48 minutes = .8

49–54 minutes = .9

55–60 minutes = 1.0

You also need to learn how to phrase your time so that your supervising attorney will approve it. Instead of writing: "Read Chapter 1," write "Review and Analyze Chapter 1." Review and Analyze is what you should write whenever you read something in law.

When you write something for a homework assignment, you should call it "Draft," so for example, you "Draft Removal Pleading." If you edit your pleading, then you could separately bill for that as: "Finalized Removal Pleading."

For timekeeper, you put down two initials. Thus, Arabella Jimenez would be aj (lowercase for paralegals).

The date should always be the date you performed the task.

Typical format:

Date	Assignment	Description	Timekeeper	Time

Chapter 2

Employment

Chapter Outline

Chapter Objectives

- Discuss how an employer-employee relationship is formed.

- Determine which federal laws govern hours and wages, and give the rules on both.

- List some of the protections provided to private pensions under the Employee Retirement Income Security Act (ERISA).

- Review the Family and Medical Leave Act (FMLA) protections for employees.

- Describe employment-at-will.

- Overview employment agreements.

- Illustrate how workers' compensation works.

- Emphasize the difference between employees and independent contractors.

- Cover the Occupational Safety and Health Act (OSHA) regarding the requirement that employers provide safe working conditions.

- Provide some information on immigration laws in connection with employment.

2.1 Introduction to Employment

Chapter 2 covers a myriad of employment issues. Note, however, that some employment issues, such as unemployment insurance and social security have been left to Chapter 3, as those issues are common to almost any business entity. In addition, employment discrimination is discussed in Chapter 16, as it also falls under the category of the business entity as a defendant. What this chapter does cover is:

- how the employer-employee relationship is formed,

- the duties an employer owes (some of those duties overlap with principal duties),

- the Fair Labor Standards Act (FLSA),

- pension plans,

- the Family and Medical Leave Act (for those employees who need to take time to care for an infant or sick family member),

- employment-at-will versus employment agreements,

- workers' compensation,

- how independent contractors differ from employees,

- the Occupational Safety and Health Act (OSHA), and

- some of the immigration laws that apply to employment.

**Graphic of Principal-Agency Relationship in Relation to
Employer-Employee Relationship**

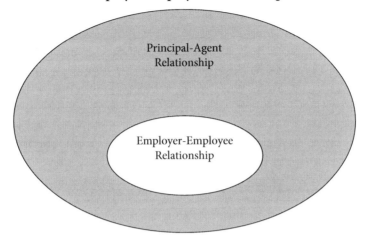

2.2 Formation of an Employer-Employee Relationship

There are several different classifications of workers an employer can hire. There are full-time and part-time employees, independent contractors, and interns. These distinctions are also important when determining the duties of employers, especially to third parties. The formation of an employer-employee relationship is somewhat similar to the formation of a principal-agency relationship, though with employment, the employer will almost certainly be in control of the employer's work performance and must pay the employee.

With a full-time employee and part-time employees, the employer needs to pay payroll taxes. With an independent contractor, the employer does not. However, it might cost more per hour to hire an independent contractor than an employee. Independent contractors will be discussed later in this chapter, but basically, the employer does not control how an independent contractor performs his job, the employer just controls the end result. Though a fine distinction, it is an important one that merits more discussion in Section 2.10. If the employer misclassifies someone as an independent contractor, then the employer may have to pay fines and back taxes for Social Security, Medicare, income taxes, and unemployment taxes. Interns are typically unpaid, and the employer will not need to pay payroll taxes. However, as discussed in Chapter 1, the rules about interns are currently in flux.

2.3 Duties of Employers

The duties of principals discussed in the last chapter also apply to employers. Remember, employers are a subset of principals. The duties the principal owed to the agent in Chapter 1, that the employer owes to the employee are compensation, reimbursement, indemnification, and cooperation. Thus, here indemnification and vicarious liability are discussed in relation to employment. When an employee is responsible for torts he committed during the course and scope of his employment, then the employer is often also responsible. A tort is a wrong done by one person to another that results in jury to a person or her property. With a tort, money is often paid in order to try to compensate the injured party.

The principle of holding an employer responsible for the actions of the employee is known as respondeat superior. Usually, the type of tort involved in respondeat superior cases is negligence. The reasoning behind respondeat superior is that employees are not working for themselves, but for the employer and for the employer's benefit. In other words, the employee would not have been doing the work which caused the harm had he not been working for the employer, so the employer should be vicariously liable. Another big reason for the principle of respondeat superior is: who typically has more money? Does the employer or the employee often have more money? The employer usually has more money. If a third-party plaintiff can hold the employer responsible for the acts of his employee, then the plaintiff will be more likely to win a monetary award than if he were only able to sue the employee. While this may seem inequitable to the employer, employers are able to obtain insurance for their business more easily than an employee is able to insure his work. Thus, the employer will often be required to indemnify his employee.

There are also several additional duties imposed upon employers by employment law. Duties and laws covered in this chapter are minimum wage, overtime, pensions, the Family and Medical Leave Act, workers' compensation, the Occupational Health and Safety Act, and immigration.

2.4 Fair Labor Standards Act

When discussing the exempt and non-exempt status of employees, the reference is whether they are exempt or not from the Fair Labor Standards Act (FLSA). In general, the Fair Labor Standards Act regulates workers' wages as well as child labor. It applies more to private employees than to public ones. The FLSA covers those employers who operate in interstate commerce (commerce in between states), make goods for interstate commerce, or are in certain businesses. Typically, exempt employees do not have to be paid overtime, but non-exempt employees do.

There are several criteria for determining whether someone is exempt or non-exempt. Exempt employees have to get at least four hundred and fifty-five dollars a week (that is twenty-three thousand, six hundred and sixty dollars a year). Just because someone is salaried, does not make them automatically exempt; the worker must still be earning more than minimum wage. In general, professional and administrative jobs are exempt.

In more detail, the FLSA overtime rules do not apply to executives, administrative employees, learned professionals, highly compensated employees, computer employees, and outside sales representatives. These exemptions are as named by the FLSA. The executive exemption covers executives in management, who can hire employees, manage two or more employees, and are paid a salary. The administrative employee exemption covers either employees who are paid a salary or a fee, who do office work rather than manual work, and who have some discretion and judgment that they can exercise in performing their tasks. The learned professional exemption again covers employees paid either a salary or a fee, have an intellectual job, and who had to go through years of specialized academic training. The highly compensated employee exemption applies to employees making over one hundred thousand dollars, and who do some sort of executive, administrative, or professional job. The computer employee exemption also applies to those employees paid a salary or a fee, who work in computer systems, programming, or engineering as a designer, analyst, or tester of computer systems. The outside sales representative exemption is for salespeople who are usually not at the employer's place of work, are out making sales, and are paid by the customer.

These are exempt employees, not covered by the FLSA. Therefore, a law firm, for instance, could potentially pay for a forty-hour workweek but expect some of their employees to work much more than a forty-hour workweek under the Fair Labor Standards Act.

Workers that are covered by the Fair Labor Standards Act should receive time-and-a-half for hours worked over forty hours in one week. Therefore, non-exempt employees are covered by the FLSA and must get at least minimum wage, along with time-and-a-half pay for overtime when they work more than forty hours a week.

One of the goals of the FLSA is to prevent extreme child labor. Generally, the minimum working age is sixteen, unless the child is working on a farm. A minor cannot work in hazardous work environments. Occasionally, a fourteen- or fifteen-year-old may have limited work, i.e., three hours per school day, after school, with more hours allowed on weekends. A fourteen-year-old would also be allowed to deliver newspapers and have limited rights to work in entertainment.

a. Minimum Wage

At the time of writing this second edition, the federal minimum wage was still $7.25 per hour and applied to non-exempt workers. Servers are slightly different. Federal law allows the employer to include tips when calculating the minimum wage, but the employer must still pay $2.13 per hour. If, with tips, the server does not make minimum wage, then the employer must pay the difference. Students and apprentices may be paid less than the federal minimum wage.

While the federal government has a certain federal minimum wage, states are free to set a minimum wage that is higher than the federal minimum. These higher wages are called living wage laws. Since the first edition of this textbook, several states have enacted living wage laws and now the majority of states have living wage laws. The amount above minimum wage between the states that do have living wage laws varies. States with higher than the federal minimum wage are:

- Alaska,
- Arkansas,
- Arizona,
- California,
- Colorado,
- Connecticut,
- Delaware,
- Florida,
- Hawaii,
- Illinois,
- Maine,
- Maryland,
- Massachusetts,
- Michigan,
- Minnesota,
- Missouri,
- Montana,
- Nebraska,
- Nevada,
- New Jersey,
- New Mexico,
- Nevada,
- New York,
- Ohio,
- Oregon,
- Rhode Island,
- South Dakota,
- Vermont,
- Washington, and
- West Virginia.

Go to the following webpage: https://www.dol.gov/agencies/whd/minimum-wage/state There is a clickable map of the United States. Select the state that you are currently living in. Determine what the minimum wage in your state is.

b. Overtime

The overtime rate is one-and-a-half times the regular rate of pay for every hour over forty hours of work in a week. This applies only for non-exempt employees. Thus, if a non-exempt employee eats at work, while doing work, that must be paid. Typically, short work breaks are paid as well. An individual state may require additional breaks.

2.5 Employee Benefit Plans

An employer might provide for retirement plans separate from Federal Social Security, which can allow an employee to better prepare for retirement. Defined benefit plans are retirement plans where there is a specific monetary amount the employee would get per month in retirement. This would be the same no matter what the stock market did. However, many businesses no longer use a defined benefit plan because it is expensive. Nowadays, the retirement plans are more likely what is called a defined contribution plan. This is a type of qualified plan, discussed more below. These types of plans do not promise a certain amount when an employee retires, but do require a set amount that the employer will contribute each year prior to retirement. Perhaps the most common type of these plans that you may recognize is a 401k plan.

With a 401k plan, the employee might contribute and then be matched up to a certain amount by the employer. For example, if an employee puts in eight percent of his annual paycheck, an employer might match that up to fifty percent, so that the employer would be putting four percent of the employee's annual salary into the 401k as well. Combined, twelve percent of the employee's annual salary would be going into a 401k.

Typically, an employer, depending upon the employer, is not required to give a benefit plan, but may receive a tax incentive to do so. A plan could be qualified or nonqualified. The big difference between these two is that a qualified plan typically gives the employer a tax benefit, whereas a nonqualified plan does not. As nonqualified plans are not as popular a qualified, nonqualified plans will not be discussed any further here.

a. Qualified Plans

What a qualified plan does is give a tax deduction to the employer for providing certain employee benefits. In a qualified plan, typically the employee does not pay taxes on the money he invests in the qualified plan until he withdraws the money.

With a qualified plan, the goal is to set up retirement income to the employee. The employee is supposed to take only the money out once he is retired, but there are some exceptions, such as becoming disabled, which would allow the money to be withdrawn earlier than retirement.

The Employee Retirement Income Security Act (ERISA) is supposed to protect employees in these plans. Employers do not have to set up a plan, but once the employer does, it must follow ERISA. ERISA particularly helps retired employees should their employer go bankrupt.

2.6 Family and Medical Leave Act (FMLA)

The Family Medical Leave Act was instituted in 1993. Eligible employees, working for covered employers, may receive up to twelve weeks of unpaid leave during a twelve-month period. In addition to the leave, the employer must continue the health care coverage and make sure that the employee will be able to come back to the same or a substantially similar position when they return. An event such as one of the following would have to occur for an employee to eligible, when working for a covered employer:

- the birth of a new child of the employee (this applies to moms as well as dads);
- adopting or fostering of a new child (this also applies to moms as well as dads);

- care of a very sick family member;
- or the employee's own serious health problem, which prevents her or him from being able to work.

Note however, that if the employee leaves for the birth, fostering, or adoption of a child, the employee should not take the leave intermittently unless the employer agrees to it.

One of the questions then becomes, who are qualifying family members in terms of whom the employee might be taking care of? These include wives or husbands, children under eighteen, or parents of the employee. The next question might then be, who is a covered employer? A covered employer is one that employs fifty or greater employees each business day for the last twenty weeks, or twenty weeks the prior year. Another question might be who is an eligible employee? An eligible employee is one that has worked with a covered employer for at least twelve months, and during that time has worked a minimum of one thousand, two hundred and fifty hours.

There are exceptions to the FMLA, which includes key employees, employees who have worked at the company for less than a year, and/or employees who have worked twenty-five hours or less a week in the past year. A key employee is an employee in the top ten-percent pay bracket at the company. The employer can forgo giving a key employee his job back if doing so is necessary to prevent a large and serious economic injury to the employer's business.

The following case looks at the application of the Family and Medical Leave Act to men.

Nevada Department of Human Resources v. Hibbs
538 U.S. 721 (2003)

The Family and Medical Leave Act of 1993 (FMLA or Act) entitles eligible employees to take up to 12 work weeks of unpaid leave annually for any of several reasons, including the onset of a "serious health condition" in an employee's spouse, child, or parent.... The Act creates a private right of action to seek both equitable relief and money damages "against any employer (including a public agency) in any Federal or State court of competent jurisdiction ..." should that employer "interfere with, restrain, or deny the exercise of" FMLA rights.... We hold that employees of the State of Nevada may recover money damages in the event of the State's failure to comply with the family-care provision of the Act.

Petitioners include the Nevada Department of Human Resources (Department) and two of its officers. Respondent William Hibbs (hereinafter respondent) worked for the Department's Welfare Division. In April and May 1997, he sought leave under the FMLA to care for his ailing wife, who was recovering from a car accident and neck surgery. The Department granted his request for the full 12 weeks of FMLA leave and authorized him to use the leave intermittently as needed between May and December 1997. Respondent did so until August 5, 1997, after which he did not return to work. In October 1997, the Department informed respondent that he had exhausted his FMLA leave, that no further leave would be granted, and that he must report to work by November 12, 1997. Respondent failed to do so and was terminated....

The FMLA aims to protect the right to be free from gender-based discrimination in the workplace. We have held that statutory classifications that distinguish between males and females are subject to heightened scrutiny.... For a gender-based classification to withstand such scrutiny, it must "serv[e] important governmental objectives," and "the discriminatory means employed [must be] substantially related to the achievement of those objectives...." The State's justification for such a classification "must not rely on overbroad generalizations about the different talents, capacities, or preferences of males and females...." We now inquire whether Congress had evidence of a pattern of constitutional violations on the part of the States in this area.

The history of the many state laws limiting women's employment opportunities is chronicled in — and, until relatively recently, was sanctioned by — this Court's own opinions. For example, in *Bradwell v. State* ... and *Goesaert v. Cleary* ... the Court upheld state laws prohibiting women from practicing law and tending bar, respectively. State laws frequently subjected women to distinctive restrictions, terms, conditions, and benefits for those jobs they could take. In *Muller v. Oregon* ... for example, this Court approved a state law limiting the hours that women could work for wages, and observed that 19 States had such laws at the time. Such laws were based on the related beliefs that (1) a woman is, and should remain, "the center of home and family life ..." and (2) "a proper discharge of [a woman's] maternal functions — having in view not merely her own health, but the well-being of the race — justif[ies] legislation to protect her from the greed as well as the passion of man...." Until our decision in *Reed v. Reed*..., "it remained the prevailing doctrine that government, both federal and state, could withhold from women opportunities accorded men so long as any 'basis in reason'" — such as the above beliefs — "could be conceived for the discrimination...."

Congress responded to this history of discrimination by abrogating States' sovereign immunity in Title VII of the Civil Rights Act of 1964 ... and we sustained this abrogation in *Fitzpatrick*. But state gender discrimination did not cease. "[I]t can hardly be doubted that ... women still face pervasive, although at times more subtle, discrimination ... in the job market...." According to evidence that was before Congress when it enacted the FMLA, States continue to rely on invalid gender stereotypes in the employment context, specifically in the administration of leave benefits. Reliance on such stereotypes cannot justify the States' gender discrimination in this area.... The long and extensive history of sex discrimination prompted us to hold that measures that differentiate on the basis of gender warrant heightened scrutiny; here, as in *Fitzpatrick,* the persistence of such unconstitutional discrimination by the States justifies Congress' passage of prophylactic § 5 legislation.

As the FMLA's legislative record reflects, a 1990 Bureau of Labor Statistics (BLS) survey stated that 37 percent of surveyed private-sector employees were covered by maternity leave policies, while only 18 percent were covered by paternity leave policies.... The corresponding numbers from a similar BLS survey the previous year were 33 percent and 16 percent, respectively.... While these data show an increase in the percentage of employees eligible for such leave, they also show a widening of the gender gap during the same period. Thus, stereotype-based beliefs about the allocation of family duties remained firmly rooted, and employers' reliance on them in establishing discriminatory leave policies remained widespread.

Congress also heard testimony that "[p]arental leave for fathers ... is rare. Even ... [w]here child-care leave policies do exist, men, *both in the public and private sectors,* receive notoriously discriminatory treatment in their requests for such leave...." Many States offered women extended "maternity" leave that far exceeded the typical 4- to 8-week period of physical disability due to pregnancy and childbirth, but very few States granted men a parallel benefit: Fifteen States provided women up to one year of extended maternity leave, while only four provided men with the same.... This and other differential leave policies were not attributable to any differential physical needs of men and women, but rather to the pervasive sex-role stereotype that caring for family members is women's work.

Here, however, Congress directed its attention to state gender discrimination, which triggers a heightened level of scrutiny.... Because the standard for demonstrating the constitutionality of a gender-based classification is more difficult to meet than our rational-basis test — it must "serv[e] important governmental objectives" and be "substantially related to the achievement of those objectives ..." — it was easier for Congress to show a pattern of state constitutional violations. Congress was similarly successful in *South Carolina v. Katzenbach*, where we upheld the Voting Rights Act of 1965: Because racial classifications are presumptively invalid, most of the States' acts of race discrimination violated the Fourteenth Amendment.

The impact of the discrimination targeted by the FMLA is significant. Congress determined:

> "Historically, denial or curtailment of women's employment opportunities has been traceable directly to the pervasive presumption that women are mothers first, and workers second. This prevailing ideology about women's roles has in turn justified discrimination against women when they are mothers or mothers-to-be...."

Stereotypes about women's domestic roles are reinforced by parallel stereotypes presuming a lack of domestic responsibilities for men. Because employers continued to regard the family as the woman's domain, they often denied men similar accommodations or discouraged them from taking leave. These mutually reinforcing stereotypes created a self-fulfilling cycle of discrimination that forced women to continue to assume the role of primary family caregiver, and fostered employers' stereotypical views about women's commitment to work and their value as employees. Those perceptions, in turn, Congress reasoned, lead to subtle discrimination that may be difficult to detect on a case-by-case basis.

We believe that Congress' chosen remedy, the family-care leave provision of the FMLA, is "congruent and proportional to the targeted violation," *Garrett*.... Congress had already tried unsuccessfully to address this problem through Title VII and the amendment of Title VII by the Pregnancy Discrimination Act....

By creating an across-the-board, routine employment benefit for all eligible employees, Congress sought to ensure that family-care leave would no longer be stigmatized as an inordinate drain on the workplace caused by female employees, and that employers could not evade leave obligations simply by hiring men. By setting a minimum standard of family leave for *all* eligible employees, irrespective of gender, the FMLA attacks the formerly state-sanctioned stereotype that only women are responsible for family caregiving, thereby reducing employers' incentives to engage in discrimination by basing hiring and promotion decisions on stereotypes.

2.7 Employment-at-Will

Unless there is a contract for a certain amount of time, then in general an employer can fire an employee without cause, whenever the employer choses. This is known as employment-at-will. There are exceptions to this general rule, such as the employer cannot fire employees for participating in union events.[1] In addition, members of unions or public sector employees may have to be fired for "just" cause. The largest exception to employment-at-will is wrongful discharge. Wrongful discharge is the concept that an employer should not be allowed to fire a worker for a reason against basic rights. Three basic rights that fall under wrongful discharge include an employee should not be forced to agree to violate the law, an employee should be allowed to use his legal rights, and an employee should be allowed to perform a legal duty. Not being forced to agree to violate the law is straightforward, and just like it sounds. An example of using one's legal rights is if an employee files a legitimate workers' compensation claim, then his employer should not fire him for doing so. Finally, employers should not be allowed to fire an employee for performing a legal duty, such as jury duty.

The *Wendeln* case illustrates a new public policy exception to the employment-at-will rule. Typically, an employee cannot be fired for reporting the employer's alleged violations of law. For example, in *Wendeln*, an employee who worked at a nursing home should not be fired for making a report of patient abuse.

Wendeln v. Beatrice Manor
271 Neb. 373, 712 N.W.2d 226 (2006)

NATURE OF CASE

The primary issue presented in this appeal is whether we should recognize a public policy-based cause of action for retaliatory discharge when an employer discharges an employee for making a report to the Nebraska Department of Health and Human Services (DHHS) as mandated by the Adult Protective Services Act (APSA)....

---

1. This is upheld under the National Labor Relations Act and the Wagner Act.

FACTUAL BACKGROUND

Rebecca Wendeln, a certified nursing assistant, began working at The Beatrice Manor, Inc. (Beatrice Manor), in May 2000 as a staffing coordinator. A particular patient at Beatrice Manor was wheelchair-bound, and it was Wendeln's understanding that any time the patient was lifted or transferred, such transfer needed to be done by two persons and with a gait belt (an ambulatory aid used to transfer or mobilize patients). In December 2001, a "very upset" medical aide approached Wendeln, describing that approximately 2 weeks prior, this patient had been improperly moved and had fallen and bruised herself. The aide reported that she had offered to assist another aide in the transfer of the patient, but that the other aide had refused to let her help. The next thing the aide observed was the patient on the floor with no gait belt in sight. The aide told Wendeln that she had informed the administrator and the acting director of nursing about the incident, but that the aide did not believe that it had been properly reported to DHHS or was otherwise being taken care of.

That same day, a licensed practical nurse at Beatrice Manor also approached Wendeln about the incident, expressing concern that nothing was being done about it. The nurse did not witness the incident, but was a relative of the patient. In response to these reports, Wendeln approached another aide who was working the day of the incident to confirm that it had actually occurred. That aide had been called to help the patient off of the floor and told Wendeln that pain medication had been given to the patient as a result of the fall.

Wendeln then called DHHS to make sure that it had been reported. When DHHS indicated that no incident had been reported, Wendeln made a report.

A few days after her report to DHHS, Wendeln was called into her supervisor's office. Wendeln said that her supervisor was very angry with her after having learned that Wendeln had made a report with DHHS without having first spoken to her. Wendeln testified that her supervisor was "very aggressive" and made her feel scared and intimidated. Wendeln, who was 21 years old at the time, asked for some time off work because she "didn't know how [she] was going to face [her supervisor] after the way she had aggressively approached [her]." Her supervisor granted her the time off. Wendeln testified that during this time, she felt very nervous and upset. She explained that she had never before been "attacked" in such a manner by either a peer or a supervisor.

Upon Wendeln's return to work on her next scheduled workday, Wendeln found that the locks to her office had been changed. Eventually, her supervisor appeared and told Wendeln to follow her to her office. There, Wendeln was asked to resign, and when she refused, she was told she was fired. Her official termination date was January 2, 2002....

ASSIGNMENTS OF ERROR

Beatrice Manor argues, summarized and restated, that the trial court erred in (1) failing to find that the applicable statute of limitations was the 300-day period set forth in §48-1118(2), rather than the general 4-year limitation period found in Neb.

Rev. Stat. § 25-207 ...; (2) failing to find as a matter of law that Wendeln's public policy retaliatory discharge claim sounded in contract....

STANDARD OF REVIEW

Which statute of limitations applies is a question of law that an appellate court must decide independently of the conclusion reached by the trial court....

A jury verdict will not be disturbed on appeal as excessive unless it is so clearly against the weight and reasonableness of the evidence and so disproportionate as to indicate that it was the result of passion, prejudice, mistake, or some means not apparent in the record, or that the jury disregarded the evidence or rules of law....

A motion for new trial is to be granted only when error prejudicial to the rights of the unsuccessful party has occurred....

ANALYSIS

STATUTE OF LIMITATIONS

We first address Beatrice Manor's assertion that Wendeln's claim is barred by the applicable statute of limitations, which it asserts is the 300-day period stated in the NFEPA. The trial court determined that Wendeln's action was governed by the general 4-year statute of limitations set forth by § 25-207.

In determining which statute of limitations applies to any given cause of action, we bear in mind that a special statute of limitations controls and takes precedence over a general statute of limitations because the special statute is a specific expression of legislative will concerning a particular subject.... Moreover, the essential nature of a proceeding may not be changed, thereby lengthening the statute of limitations, merely by denominating it as something other than what it actually is.... To determine the nature of an action, a court must examine and construe a complaint's essential and factual allegations by which the plaintiff requests relief, rather than the legal terminology utilized in the complaint or the form of a pleading.... However, just because there may be some overlap between relevant facts, it does not change the conclusion that various causes of action are stated based on separate and distinct factual occurrences....

Wendeln asserts that her amended complaint states only a cause of action for retaliatory discharge in violation of public policy, which constitutes a cause of action separate and distinct from a claim based on the NFEPA. Indeed, Wendeln argues that in her case, a careful examination of the essential allegations of her complaint would reveal that she does not state a cause of action under the NFEPA at all.

Instead, Wendeln asserts that she was discharged in retaliation for reporting a negligent act which was not unlawful. Specifically, she asserts that she was discharged in retaliation for filing a complaint as required by the APSA. Section 28-384 makes it a Class III misdemeanor for any person to willfully fail to make any report required by the APSA. Section 28-372(1) provides in part:

> When any physician, psychologist, physician assistant, nurse, nursing assistant, other medical, developmental disability, or mental health professional,

law enforcement personnel, caregiver or employee of a caregiver, operator
or employee of a sheltered workshop, owner, operator, or employee of any
facility licensed by the Department of Health and Human Services Regulation
and Licensure, or human services professional or paraprofessional not including a member of the clergy has reasonable cause to believe that a vulnerable adult has been subjected to abuse or observes such adult being
subjected to conditions or circumstances which reasonably would result in
abuse, he or she shall report the incident or cause a report to be made to the
appropriate law enforcement agency or to the department.

"Abuse" is defined in § 28-351 as "any knowing, intentional, or negligent act or omission on the part of a caregiver, a vulnerable adult, or any other person which results
in physical injury, unreasonable confinement, cruel punishment, sexual abuse, exploitation, or denial of essential services to a vulnerable adult." "Physical injury" is
defined in § 28-363 as "damage to bodily tissue caused by nontherapeutic conduct,
including, but not limited to, fractures, bruises, lacerations, internal injuries, or dis-
locations, and shall include, but not be limited to, physical pain, illness, or impairment
of physical function."

We agree with the trial court's determination that the essential nature of Wendeln's
stated cause of action does not lie in the NFEPA, but, rather, lies in the public policy
mandate that she alleges is expressed by the APSA. Without making any determination
as to the hypothetical complaint which simultaneously states a cause of action under
both the civil rights provisions of the NFEPA and under a public policy exception allowing a retaliatory discharge action for an at-will employee, it is clear in this case that
not only does the denomination of Wendeln's cause of action accurately reflect its true
nature, but that the facts alleged simply do not state a cause of action for a claim under
the NFEPA. Wendeln did not allege that she was discharged for opposing any unlawful
employment practice, participating in a proceeding under the NFEPA, or opposing
or refusing to carry out an unlawful act. Rather, she claimed that her employment was
terminated because she did what the law affirmatively required her to do …

Yet despite a line of cases allowing limited retaliatory discharge claims for discharge
in contravention of a clear mandate of public policy, this court has never clearly expressed exactly what statute of limitations period is applicable to these claims.… An
examination of authority from other jurisdictions reveals that generally, when a
wrongful discharge claim is based on public policy, and not on an implied or actual
employment contract, such claim sounds in tort.

We agree that a public policy-based retaliatory discharge claim is based in tort.
Accordingly, such a claim is governed by the general 4-year statute of limitations period found in § 25-207. Wendeln's claim is not barred by the applicable statute of
limitations.

PUBLIC POLICY EXCEPTION

The public policy upon which Wendeln relies for her retaliatory discharge claim
has not yet been recognized by this court. Beatrice Manor asserts that unlike other

retaliatory discharge cases decided by this court, "[t]here is no clear legislative enactment declaring an important public policy with such clarity as to provide a basis for [Wendeln's] civil action for wrongful discharge...."

The clear rule in Nebraska is that unless constitutionally, statutorily, or contractually prohibited, an employer, without incurring liability, may terminate an at-will employee at any time with or without reason.... We recognize, however, a public policy exception to the at-will employment doctrine.... Under the public policy exception, we will allow an employee to claim damages for wrongful discharge when the motivation for the firing contravenes public policy ... In *Ambroz v. Cornhusker Square Ltd*..., we explained, however, that it was important that abusive discharge claims of employees at will be limited to "manageable and clear standards." Thus, "[t]he right of an employer to terminate employees at will should be restricted only by exceptions created by statute or to those instances where a very clear mandate of public policy has been violated...."

In *Jackson v. Morris Communications Corp*..., we held that an employee could state a cause of action for retaliatory discharge based upon the allegation that the employee was terminated from her employment because she filed a workers' compensation claim. In so doing, we recognized that Nebraska law neither specifically prohibited an employer from discharging an employee for filing a workers' compensation claim, nor specifically made it a crime for an employer to do so. Nevertheless, we concluded that "the general purpose and unique nature of the Nebraska Workers' Compensation Act itself provides a mandate for public policy...." We explained that the Nebraska Workers' Compensation Act was meant to create substantive rights for employees and that such beneficent purpose would be undermined by failing to adopt a rule which allows a retaliatory discharge claim for employees discharged for filing a workers' compensation claim. This is because were we not to recognize such a public policy exception to the employment-at-will doctrine, the substantive rights granted by the Nebraska Workers' Compensation Act could simply be circumvented by the employer's threatening to discharge the employee if he or she exercised those rights.

We ... find that the purpose of the APSA would be circumvented if employees mandated by the APSA to report suspected patient abuse could be threatened with discharge for making such a report. The Legislature articulates public policy when it declares certain conduct to be in violation of the criminal law.... The APSA makes a clear public policy statement by utilizing the threat of criminal sanction to ensure the implementation of the reporting provisions set forth to protect the vulnerable adults with which the APSA is concerned. Thus, we determine that a public policy exception to the employment-at-will doctrine applies to allow a cause of action for retaliatory discharge when an employee is fired for making a report of abuse as mandated by the APSA....

Employment-at-will does not just apply to employers. In general, employees can also terminate at will, meaning employees can terminate at any time or for whatever reason.

2.8 Employment Agreements

The majority of employees do not have an employment agreement and can be fired at the will of the employer (also known as at-will employment, discussed above). Employment agreements are more commonly used when an employee might be around the company's proprietary information, to keep the employee from taking that information to another company. Proprietary information is nonpublic information that is considered the property of an employer. Employees are not supposed to misuse proprietary information. Proprietary information would include a company's secret recipe.

Nowadays, some courts are finding implied contracts even where there is not a formal, signed employment contract. For example, an employment handbook is a contract though not necessarily an employment contract, and if it states that the employee should not be fired without three warnings, than usually, court will find that this creates an implied contract not to fire the employee before three warnings.

a. Drafting

An employment agreement is a contract. Thus, it must satisfy the law of contracts, which includes having an offer, an acceptance, and some consideration (usually money exchanged). In general, employment agreements will have many of the same basic clauses. For instance, both the parties need to be identified in the contract; here, that would be the employer and the employee. There will be terms to the contract, which may vary from contract to contract. Most employment agreements will specify where the employment is to be performed. It may go into detail about the amount of hours the employee is expected to do and whether the employee is allowed to work a second job.

Since many employment contracts are about maintaining proprietary information, the contract will probably discuss whether the employee can share the secret recipe, sales information, intellectual property information, etc.

The employment agreement should discuss all types of compensation, benefits, vacations, holidays, and sick days. It should also include the period of time the agreement is good for. The law of the state that will be used to interpret the contract should be included. Finally, although there are still more clauses that could be added, the parties should date and sign the agreement.

A very basic example of a sample employment agreement follows. The clauses mentioned above, if missing, could be added as applicable to this contract.

Sample Employment Agreement

This Employment Agreement ("Agreement") is entered into as of _____, 2012, between _____ ("Company") and _____ ("Employee").

The parties feel it is in their mutual best interests to hire the Employee full-time as an employee of the Company.

Therefore, the parties agree as follows:

1.0 Employment. The company hires the Employee, and the Employee accepts employment with the Company.

2.0 Duties. The Employee is hired as manager. The Employee shall be assigned to a specific location, _____. The Employee may be needed to serve at other locations, as directed by the Company. The Employee is subject to the supervision and direction of his superiors in the Company, insofar as his duties.

3.0 Compensation. Employee shall get a weekly base salary of $_____, to be paid in accord with the regular payroll practices of the Company. In addition, the Employee shall be eligible for reimbursement of expenses incurred on behalf of the Company, in accordance with the Employment Manual.

4.0 Service. The Employee will give his full-time to this job and exclusively work for the Company during his business time.

5.0 Termination. Either party may terminate the Employee's employment by providing two-week written notice to the other party. If the Company is terminating the employment and the termination is not for cause, then the Employee shall be entitled to severance equal to two weeks' salary and any such compensation due but not yet paid to the Employee.

6.0 Entire Agreement; Modification; Waiver. This Agreement is the entire agreement between the parties regarding the employment and it supersedes all prior agreements or understanding between the parties. No modification of this Agreement is binding unless executed in writing by both parties. No waiver of this Agreement is binding unless executed in writing by the party making the waiver.

7.0 Notices. All notices required under this Agreement shall be in writing and sent first class mail, postage prepaid, to the last registered address on record with the company.

8.0 Arbitration. Any controversies arising out of this Agreement are to be settled by the American Arbitration Association, and such ruling shall be binding.

9.0 Governing Law. This Agreement shall be interpreted by the laws of the State of _____. If part of this Agreement is invalid, the remaining terms and conditions shall remain in full force and effect.

The parties execute and deliver this Agreement as of the day and year first written above.

_____   _____

"Employee"   "Company"

2.9 Workers' Compensation

Each year, there are thousands and thousands of on-the-job injuries, usually taking place at one of the types of business entities that will be covered in this textbook.

Workers' compensation allows the injured employee to receive compensation without having to prove that the employer was negligent in causing the injury. Therefore, workers' compensation is known as a no-fault system.

In workers' compensation, injured workers typically receive a set amount of money, which is less than they would normally receive in civil court. Employers pay for these claims through workers' compensation insurance, or if they are self-insured, straight out of their own pockets. An employer might be self-insured due to the great risks of the job, so that an insurance company does not want to insure the employer, or because the insurance premiums are too high for the employer to pay. To be self-insured, the employer has to show it is capable of paying workers' compensation claims out of its own pocket. Workers' compensation insurance premiums are high, and this is a very real expense to an employer. Workers' compensation insurance is provided through either private insurance companies or a state insurance fund, if the employer is not self-insured. A state insurance fund can potentially be a cheaper way in which for employers to insure themselves, rather than buying private insurance.

a. Injuries Covered by Workers' Compensation

1. The Injury Occurred within the Employment Relationship

If an injury occurred within the employment relationship, then the employee should file in workers' compensation court (which is actually an administrative hearing board with relaxed rules of evidence) and not necessarily in civil court. However, there are exceptions to this general rule, which include the employer hiring someone to perform an illegal activity or violating the Occupational Safety and Health Act (OSHA). If either of these or other exceptions apply, then the employee could sue in civil court. Sometimes, the employee might still elect to file in workers' compensation, as this is usually quicker than civil court. The trade-off of having a quicker hearing is that the injured worker typically receives less money in workers' compensation. The concept of an injury occurring within the employment relationship will be discussed in further detail in the section on course and scope of employment.

2. There Was a Contract

In order for an employee to be covered by workers' compensation, the employee must have a contract with the employer to work for the employer. The contract does not have to be written, it could be oral or implied by the conduct of the parties.

3. The Employer Controlled How the Work Was Accomplished

Presumptions are principles generally held to be true until rebutted. One presumption is that a worker is an employee. To prove that someone is not an employee, the court would look at whether the alleged employer had the right to control the way in which the alleged employee did his job. If the alleged employee were actually an independent contractor (someone able to control the way in which the job for another is done), then the independent contractor would not be covered under workers' compensation. There are approximately another thirteen factors in determining whether someone is an employee or an independent contractor, but the most important factor is who has the right to control the way in which the alleged employee performs his job.

b. Compensable Injuries

In order for workers' compensation to apply there must be a compensable injury, i.e. one that can be compensated for by the employer. Typically, this would be some sort of monetary compensation.

c. Proximate Cause

While workers' compensation does not have the same requirements as a negligence cause of action, a workers' compensation case must still show that the injury was proximately caused by the employment. Proximate cause means there has to be a connection between the work and the injury. This is only fair if the employer is being required to pay for the injury, that the injury have been sufficiently closely related to the work.

d. Course and Scope of Employment

For an employer to be found liable under workers' compensation, the employee must have been acting within the course and scope of his employment. Course and scope of employment is the behavior expected of an employee as part of her job duties. To determine whether the employee was acting in the course and scope of his employment, and therefore covered under workers' compensation, the workers' compensation administrative hearing board may ask:

- whether the conduct was authorized by the employer,
- whether the behavior was normal in performing the job,
- whether the employee's behavior was at least foreseeable to the employer, and
- whether the employee's behavior happened during normal business hours.

For example, if you are a paralegal for a law office, and you are asked to file something in person, rather than electronically, an injury on the way to the courthouse could be within the course and scope of employment. Even though you are not technically in the law office when the injury occurs, you are doing an authorized task that is related to your job, during normal business hours. In addition, as you were asked to do the filing in person, the behavior was foreseeable to the employer.

e. Exclusions to Workers' Compensation

There are exclusions to workers' compensation, meaning that under some circumstances, even if the employee was working during the injury, the employer will not have to pay for the injury. Illegal activity and OSHA violations were discussed earlier as exceptions wherein the employer may have to pay, but in civil court. If the employer intentionally causes the injury to the worker, than that behavior will be an exception to the exclusive remedy of workers' compensation as well, as the worker will be able to sue the employer civilly. Even if the worker does claim under workers' compensation, the worker is not prohibited from suing a third party who was responsible for causing the injury while the worker was on the job.

Now, we are discussing exceptions wherein the employer might not have to pay at all, either in workers' compensation or in civil court. A common exclusion an employer might not have to pay for at all is injuries caused by an employee's intoxication.

A major exception to the course and scope of employment rule is the "going and coming" rule. The going and coming rule holds that an employer is not vicariously liable for accidents that happen to an employee while the employee is either going to work or coming home from work. The rationale for the going and coming rule is the employer should not have to pay for these accidents because the employee has to go and come from his home to whatever job he would work at. This rule holds true even if the employer pays for the employee's car or other transportation costs!

The second major exception to the course and scope of employment is the "frolic and detour" exception. With a frolic and detour, the employee's conduct is so far from a rational business purpose that the employer should not be liable for these actions of the employee. It boils down to the employee doing something to benefit himself rather than his employer during business hours. An example of frolic and detour would be going to a strip club while on the job. For most jobs, there is no benefit to the employer of an employee going to a strip club while working! Examples can also include something as innocuous as the employee running a personal errand while on the clock, depending upon how much the employee frolics and detours. For example, if an employee was asked to pick up his employer's dry cleaning and picked up his own at the same time, he would probably still be covered under workers' compensation if he had an injury. However, if an employee was asked to pick up lunch for an employer, and then went across town to pick up his own dry cleaning, he probably would not be covered under workers' compensation for an injury that occurred while picking up his own dry cleaning, as he detoured substantially from his errand for his employer.

f. Exclusive Remedy

In general, if the worker is injured on the job, the employer will provide medical treatment and other types of compensation, such a temporary disability payments (this are often similar to unemployment payments in terms of the amount of money paid). Typically, workers' compensation is no fault — meaning the employee will not have to prove that the employer caused the injury. The employer will not be able to raise negligence defenses. However, to receive this benefit of not having to prove fault for the injury, then the employee is normally only allowed to pursue a workers' compensation claim and not a civil lawsuit. Workers may not like this, because normally, the workers' compensation remedy is less than a civil lawsuit's compensation. However, as discussed before, the payments from workers' compensation usually start much more quickly than seeking an award in civil court, so there is still a benefit from workers' compensation.

2.10 Differences between Employees and Independent Contractors

Independent contractors are people who are hired by another person to perform a specific task(s). Note, however, that the independent contractor is not retained to represent another in a representative capacity. The Restatement (Second) of Agency states an independent contractor is "a person who contracts with another to do something for him who is not controlled by the other nor subject to the others right to control with respect to his physical conduct in the performance of the undertaking."[2] The Restatement (Third) of Agency did away with the term independent contractor, as it was felt the term was confusing. However, the new terms of "nonemployee agents" and "nonagents" arguably are not much clearer, so this text will stick with the term "independent contractor."

The number one way in which to differentiate between an independent contractor and an employee is whether the alleged employer has the authority to control the way in which the job is done. With an independent contractor, the alleged employer does not have control over the manner in which the independent contractor accomplishes the job. With an employee, the employer does have control over the manner in which the independent contractor accomplishes the job.

There are several other factors used in determining whether a person is acting as an independent contractor or as an employee. If the person has her own business, which is separate from the principal's, then it is much more likely that the person is an independent contractor. An independent contractor might then have her own office and own employees. If the job(s) being performed are usually performed by employees, it is more likely the person is an employee. If the person provides her own tools and workspace for the job, it is more likely she is an independent contractor. The length of the employment also has bearing on whether someone is considered an independent contractor or an employee. The longer the length of the employment (i.e., years versus days or weeks), the more likely it is the person is an employee. If the person submits a bill for payment of her services, it is more likely the person is an independent contractor. In addition, what the parties understand their relationship to be is also a factor in determining independent contractor versus employee status.

---

2. Section 2.

The reason why this distinction is so important is that employers are typically held liable for the negligent acts of their employees, but not for the same acts of their independent contractors. This was discussed previously under duties of employers, specifically the concept of respondeat superior. Therefore, if an alleged employer can validly assert a person is an independent contractor, the alleged employer would not have to pay a lawsuit for the negligent acts of the independent contractor. The reasoning behind this is that an independent contractor acts independently from the principal. The independent contractor is her own boss and as such, should be responsible for her own actions. The independent contractor may also have his own liability insurance. In addition, this status as independent contractor can affect someone's ability to obtain workers' compensation.

There are two exceptions to this general rule: inherently dangerous activities and if the hirer was negligent in selecting the independent contractor. In those two cases, the employer could still be held responsible for paying for the independent contractor's negligent behavior. Otherwise, the principal would be able to avoid liability for doing very dangerous activities, such as using bombs, by giving that job to an independent contractor. If the principal is negligent in the hiring, then he can be held liable if the independent contractor injuries someone while performing tasks for him.

Paralegals can be independent contractors, especially if they work for several different attorneys, at different law firms. An independent contractor paralegal would be able to set their own hours and determine the order in which to complete assignments. If you decide to become an independent contractor, you will still need to perform work under a supervising attorney. You may want to consider having your own liability insurance as well. Some states are now offering limited licenses to people as legal document assistants or law technicians. The rules about each of these vary by state and need to be researched separately. Other examples of people who often work as independent contracts are doctors, stockbrokers, tax advisors, and realtors.

Please review the 1099 form from the Internal Revenue Service below. You can see that this is intended to account for things that might not normally be accounted for, such as rent, royalty, other income, fishing boat proceeds, medical and healthcare payments, payments to attorneys, etc.

The form is a red and white form for Miscellaneous Income. It requires a payor to provide its address, its taxpayer identification number, the payee's taxpayer identification number, the payee's name, the payee's address, rents/royalties/other income, taxes withheld, and medical and healthcare payments.

2.11 Health and Safety in the Workplace

There are a variety of state and federal statutes that protect employees. Federally, the major statute for protecting employees' health and safety is the Occupational

Internal Revenue Service Form 1099 for an Independent Contractor

9595	☐ VOID	☐ CORRECTED		
PAYER'S name, street address, city or town, state or province, country, ZIP or foreign postal code, and telephone no.		**1** Rents $	OMB No. 1545-0115 20**20** Form **1099-MISC**	**Miscellaneous Income**
		2 Royalties $		
		3 Other income $	**4** Federal income tax withheld $	**Copy A** For
PAYER'S TIN	RECIPIENT'S TIN	**5** Fishing boat proceeds $	**6** Medical and health care payments $	**Internal Revenue Service Center** File with Form 1096.
RECIPIENT'S name		**7** Payer made direct sales of $5,000 or more of consumer products to a buyer (recipient) for resale ☐	**8** Substitute payments in lieu of dividends or interest $	For Privacy Act and Paperwork Reduction Act Notice, see the
Street address (including apt. no.)		**9** Crop insurance proceeds $	**10** Gross proceeds paid to an attorney $	**2020 General Instructions for**
City or town, state or province, country, and ZIP or foreign postal code		**11**	**12** Section 409A deferrals $	**Certain Information Returns.**
Account number (see instructions)	FATCA filing requirement ☐	2nd TIN not. ☐	**13** Excess golden parachute payments $	**14** Nonqualified deferred compensation $
		15 State tax withheld $ $	**16** State/Payer's state no.	**17** State income $ $

Form **1099-MISC**   Cat. No. 14425J   www.irs.gov/Form1099MISC   Department of the Treasury - Internal Revenue Service

Do Not Cut or Separate Forms on This Page — Do Not Cut or Separate Forms on This Page

Safety and Health Act[3] (also known as OSHA). Under OSHA, employers have to meet certain health and safety standards. For example, hospital personnel working around blood must be given gloves that are impermeable to blood. This is an example of a specific duty standard. These standards look at safety requirements for specific equipment, hazardous chemicals, machinery, procedures, etc. OSHA also imposes a general duty upon employers to provide a workplace environment that is not likely to cause death or serious injury. This is in addition to the specific duties.

OSHA is enforced by the Occupational Safety and Health Administration (part of the Department of Labor), the National Institute for Occupational Safety and Health (part of the Department of Health and Human Services), and the Occupational Safety and Health Review Commission, which handles appeals.

If a place of work is covered by OSHA, then an OSHA compliance officer can inspect that place of work. In addition, employees can make allegations of OSHA violations against the employer. It is wrongful retaliation or discharge to fire an employee for doing so. If OSHA finds a violation, it issues a written citation. The employer needs to fix or lessen the cause of the written citation. If the employer contests the citation, it is taken to the Occupational Safety and Health Review Commission. Further, that decision can be appealed to the Federal Circuit Court of Appeals.

The last paragraph begs the question, which places of work are covered by OSHA? Almost all private employers are covered by OSHA. As far as government employers,

---

3. 29 U.S.C. §§ 553, 651–678.

whether at a local, state, or federal level, those employers are usually exempt. In addition, if there is another federal safety statute in place, that will exempt a business from being covered by OSHA.

If an employer employs more than eleven people, that employer is typically responsible for keeping records of occupational illnesses and injuries. The employer must produce the record when requested and when the injury or illness occurs. The more dire the incident, the more quickly the employer needs to report it to the Department of Labor. At the same time, OSHA lacks some teeth, as it is hard to prosecute employers criminally under this act. An employer can still be prosecuted criminally under state laws though.

2.12 Immigration Laws Related to Employment

Employers are not allowed to hire illegal immigrants.[4] Employers are required by law to look at documents to determine whether a potential employee can properly work in this country.

In general, to be hired, a prospective worker from another country must have an offer of full-time, permanent, in the United States work, from an employer who is permanently located here. The prospective worker should have the correct education and work experience for the job.

There are five employment preference categories:

- EB-1 Priority workers,
- EB-2 Workers with advanced degrees/exceptional abilities,
- EB-3 Professionals/skilled workers/unskilled workers,
- EB-4 Religious workers, and
- EB-5 Individual investors willing to invest.

A detailed discussion of each of these categories is outside the scope of this book, and these categories are broadly conveyed here.

There are different rules for temporary workers. The major categories of temporary workers are broadly outlined below:

- H1-B is for professionals in specialty occupations,
- H1-C is for some nurses,
- H2-A is for agricultural workers,
- H2-B is for nonagricultural workers, and

---

4. Immigration Reform and Control Act of 1986 (IRCA); Immigration Act of 1990.

- H-3 is for trainees.
- H-4 accompanying visa is granted to spouses and children.

The H-1B Foreign Guest Worker Visa is the most utilized temporary work visa. This visa is for nonimmigrants that are skilled in certain specialty occupations, such as engineering, math, computer science, physical science, or medicine. These areas are considered more professional than those required by an H-2B visa, which also is normally for a shorter time.

The employer must sponsor the foreign guest worker in order for this type of worker to secure the H-1B visa. It is hard to get this type of visa, as there is usually a set limit that can be authorized in any given year. A foreign guest worker is legally allowed to bring his immediate family into the United States; however, his family is not eligible to work in the U.S.

The length of the H-1B visa is three years, and it can be renewed once. If the employer desires the foreign guest worker to stay longer, the employer should help the guest worker apply for a green card and citizenship. An H-2B visa is usually for the length of time the employer needs the worker, which is generally a shorter time period than three years.

Chapter Summary

The duties employers owe to their employees are very similar to those owed by a principal to an agent. The duties include compensation, reimbursement, indemnification, and cooperation.

The Fair Labor Standards Act (FLSA) regulates minimum wage and overtime pay for a variety of private employers, but typically not public employers. If an employee is eligible for overtime pay, the employee should be paid one-and-a-half times the regular pay rate for hours worked more than forty in a week. The FLSA also attempts to prohibit or restrict child labor.

Many employers do take advantage of the tax deduction they receive for offering qualified plans to their employees. The employee who partakes will not normally pay taxes on these plans until the money is distributed. For private pensions, the Employee Retirement Income Security Act applies.

The Family and Medical Leave act allows employees up to twelve weeks of unpaid leave, every twelve months. This leave is for the birth or adoption of a child, caring for a sick family member (who must be closely related), and/or undergoing one's own medical treatment.

Under the common law, workers could be fired at will for any reason. Nowadays, if an employee is fired for a reason counter to the employee's basic rights, the employer may be liable for wrongful discharge. Basic rights the employee typically cannot be fired for include refusing to break the law, using a legal right (i.e., workers' compensation), or performing a legal duty (i.e., jury duty). Employment agreements are not as common as at-will employment, but are still used. These agreements are a contract between the employer and the employee. An employee handbook can be used to impose requirements upon an employer to uphold said handbook.

Almost all employers have to pay for workers' compensation insurance premiums or be self-insured for workers' compensation. Workers' compensation is an expensive part of doing business. If the employee makes a workers' compensation claim, he normally cannot also make a claim in civil court as well. Therefore, if a worker makes a workers' compensation claim, this is normally his exclusive remedy. With an independent contractor, the employer is not normally responsible for the actions of the independent contractor. Exceptions to this general rule are for inherently dangerous activities and for negligence in selecting the independent contractor. This status as an independent contractor can also affect a person's ability to collect workers' compensation.

Under OSHA, employers are supposed to provide a safer environment for their employees. There are specific duty standards under OSHA, which set standards for a certain type of machine or industry. In addition, there is also the general duty standard on employers to provide safe and healthy work environments for their employees.

Employers are not allowed to employ illegal immigrants. One way an employer can legally hire a foreign worker is through an H-1B Foreign Guest Worker Visa. This allows an employer to hire a foreign national who has skills in a certain occupation.

Key Terms

Course and scope of employment
Employee
Employment-at-will
Employee Retirement Income Security Act (ERISA)
Exclusive remedy
Exempt employee
Fair Labor Standards Act (FLSA)
Family and Medical Leave Act (FMLA)
Frolic and detour
General duty
Going-and-coming rule
Immigration Reform and Control Act of 1986 (IRCA)
Independent contractor
Inherently dangerous activity
Insurance
In the course and scope of employment

Living wage law
Minimum wage
Non-exempt employee
Non-qualified plans
Occupational Safety and Health Act (OSHA)
Occupational Safety and Health Administration (OSHA)
Overtime pay
Pension
Presumption
Proprietary information
Proximate cause
Qualified plans
Retaliatory discharge
Self-insurance
Specific duty standard
Tipping laws
Tort

Vesting

Vicarious liability

Workers' compensation

Review Questions

1. How is the principal-agency relationship similar to the employer-employee relationship?

2. What is one of the reasons behind the doctrine of respondeat superior?

3. Give an example of when an employer will be vicariously liable for an employee.

4. Which law sets the federal minimum wage and weekly working hours?

5. What is the maximum working week before overtime?

6. What are some reasons for an eligible employee to legally take family or medical leave?

7. In the *Nevada Department of Human Resources v. Hibbs* case, what scrutiny are gender based classifications given?

8. Provide a definition for employment at-will.

9. What is the holding of *Wendeln v. Beatrice Manor*?

10. Give some examples of how employees are different from independent contractors.

11. What are examples of proprietary information?

12. What are some of the exclusions to workers' compensation?

13. Who enforces OSHA?

14. Explain the difference between an H-1B visa and an H-2B visa.

Web Links

The Department of Labor's website is http://www.dol.gov.

Review ERISA at: http://www.dol.gov/dol/topic/health-plans/erisa.htm.

We will be using the California Secretary of State's website for business entities in the State of California quite a bit in this book. Please go to the forms website (located at: https://www.sos.ca.gov/business-programs/business-entities/forms/) and familiarize yourself with this website.

Exercises

1. The client is an employer. The employer hires a sales clerk for his new jean clothing company. He trains the sales clerk prior to the store opening. For the training,

he pays the sales clerk minimum wage. Once the store opens though, the employer pays the sales clerk ten dollars an hour. Is this legally allowed?

2. The client is a restaurant owner. He pays his wait staff $3.65 an hour. The employee makes another $3.75 in tips per hour. Is this allowed by the law?

3. The client is the partner in a law firm. His associate works eighty hours a week. The partner does not pay the associate overtime. Is this allowed under the law?

4. A man is interviewing for a job. During the job interview, the man mentions that his wife is pregnant. The employer decides not to hire the man because he believes the man will ask for time off under the Family and Medical Leave Act. Is this discriminatory behavior?

5. Look up the current minimum wage in your state.

Section II

Business Documents

Chapter 3

Documents Common to Almost Any Business Entity

Chapter Outline

Chapter Objectives

- Distinguish the difference between the factors in selecting a type of business entity and the types of paperwork common to all types of business entities.

- Explain why the paralegal must verify that the client has an appropriate professional license to undertake the business he is creating.

- Cover, in some depth, the four major types of intellectual property law, including patents, trademarks, copyrights, and trade secrets.

- Briefly discuss the America Invents Act.

- Make the point that, if applicable, a copyright can be much cheaper for a client than a patent.

- Provide details on when a fictitious business name must be filed on behalf of the client.

- Differentiate between the types of businesses that need a sales tax permit and those that do not.

- Mention the requirement that many local governments require businesses to have a business license, which is different from the professional license.

- Bring up workers' compensation insurance in this chapter as a necessary requirement for a business, and reference Chapter 2, wherein it was discussed in more detail.

- Explain how unemployment insurance works and who pays into it.

- Discuss the different components of Social Security.

- Delineate the requirement that businesses have an employer identification number if they have employees.

3.1 Introduction to Documents Common to Almost Any Business Entity

The documents common to almost any business entity are different from the factors the attorney and paralegal must consider when encouraging a client, who wants to start a business, to select a specific business entity. Those factors include the ease of creating the business entity and how long will the business last if it changes ownership (also known as continuity). Some clients want to leave their businesses to their children or to sell it upon retirement. Another consideration is how much the business entity will cost to form as well as to capitalize. Still other factors include how much control the client wants to have over the management of the business, how much limited liability the client has under that type of business entity, and how the business entity is taxed. These factors will be discussed in more detail in the chapters on each specific business entity.

In this chapter, paperwork that is generally common to all types of business entities is discussed. However, depending upon the client's situation, he may or may not need all eight types of paperwork. The paralegal should ask the client several questions during the initial client interview to determine which of the eight types of paperwork the client will need.

First, the legal professional should find out from the client the name of the business and a general description of the business. If the name is not the client's last name, a fictitious business name statement will be needed. The general description tips the paralegal off as to whether the client needs to maintain a professional license for that type of business. A general description is also important, because due to the paperwork discussed below, there are different types of paperwork that must be filled out when the client is selling goods. If the client is selling goods, a sales tax permit will need to be applied for, usually prior to starting sales. The client should also be queried as to where the business will be located, because this can affect the business license fees, which are imposed by local governments.

The client should be questioned whether he plans to hire employees. There are four types of paperwork discussed below that apply to employees. These four types of paperwork are:

- workers' compensation insurance,
- unemployment insurance,
- Social Security, and
- an employer identification number.

3.2 Professional Licensing

Paralegals and attorneys are not ethically allowed to help the client break the law. Therefore, before the client opens up a business, the lawyer and/or paralegal should verify the client has an appropriate professional license in that area of commerce. It is often easier to remember that professionals such as doctors and certified public accountants have professional licenses than it is to remember many cosmetologists and construction workers must have professional licenses as well. Which professions are licensed depends upon the state. The paralegal should review state law first to see if a professional license is needed and then verify the client has such a license.

3.3 Registration of Intellectual Property

Intellectual property law is made up several types of law: patents, trademarks, copyrights, and trade secrets. Intellectual property is harder to quantify than real property, as it is sometimes intangible and the thoughts or creativity of someone. Usually, to be protected, the intellectual property needs to be manifested in some way, such as writing it down, to help prove that someone came up with that concept first. You may know someone who says "I thought up that idea first," but if they cannot prove that they did so first, then their intellectual property is unlikely to be protected by the law. Intellectual property is sometimes the most expensive asset a company has. However, at the same time, it can be easiest to steal this type of property. Intellectual property can be so many things, such as a book, song, new drug, new software, a recipe, etc. Three of these four types of intellectual property law do not require registration with the United States Patent and Trademark Office ("USPTO"). Only patents actually require registration with the USPTO. Trademarks and copyrights also can be registered (though copyrights would be registered with the United States Copyright Office instead of USPTO), and this benefits the holder of the trademark or copyright. Trade secrets cannot be registered, but rather need to be closely guarded by a company so that they will not become common knowledge.

Intellectual property is actually provided for in the United States Constitution. Article 1, Section 8 states that Congress has the power "[t]o promote the Progress of Science and Useful Arts, by securing for limited Times to Authors and Inventors the exclusive Right to their respective Writings and Discoveries." Thus, Congress never meant to allow inventors indefinite protection to their inventions, as the act indicates the protection should be for "limited Times."

As indicated, intellectual property is creative ideas that lead to a new invention, novel, song, etc. It can be bought or sold, similar to real or personal property. The point of protecting intellectual property is that it encourages people to write a book or create an invention. Why else would people work so hard to create something new if it would not be of benefit to themselves? At the same time, the government does not want to encourage monopolies. The government wants to encourage a competitive market for the public. Thus, there are time limits on patents, trademarks, and copyrights so that those inventions and ideas can be used freely by society. Trade secrets, on the other hand, could be protected for as long as the holder is able to keep the secret from becoming public knowledge.

a. Patents

A patent gives its holder a monopoly for a limited period. It allows only that person, the patent holder, to make, copy, use, and market the invention. Federal law completely governs patents.[1] Thus, a patent can only be granted by the United States Patent and Trademark Office.

Depending upon the type of patent, the invention may be protected for fourteen or twenty years. There are three types of patents: plant, design, and utility. Design patents are protected for fourteen years from the date of issuance, and other patents (plant and utility) are protected for twenty years from the date of issuance. In order to obtain this exclusive use, the patent holder has to disclose information about his invention once his patent is up. While the inventor has the exclusive use of his invention, he can keep others from using a substantially similar product by suing for damages against anyone who uses or makes the product without his permission. However, once the patent period is up, anyone can use the patent.

There are certain requirements that apply to all types of patents. These are that the invention needs to be novel and nonobvious. The third requirement varies on the type of patent. If it is a utility patent, the third requirement is that the item be useful; if it is a plant patent, the third requirement is that the plant be distinctive; and if it is a design patent, the third requirement is that it be ornamental.

Novel means that the invention not already be in use or known of in the United States and that it has not been discussed in a publication anywhere in the world. Nonobvious is just as it sounds; the invention cannot be obvious to a person with

---

1. 35 U.S.C. §§ 100 et seq.

ordinary skills in that area. Finally, the patent has to be useful, distinctive, or ornamental, but does not have to be valuable in terms of cost.

A plant patent allows someone who invents a new type of plant, and who can reproduce the plant asexually, to obtain a patent on the plant. By asexually, the patent office means reproducing the plant through some other means other than just planting the seeds of the plant. A specific example of a plant patent is a hybrid rose. Easy-to-peel citrus is another example of a plant patent.

A design patent is all about how the product looks. A design patent does not change the function of the product. A specific example of a design patent is a shoe-shaped couch. While a couch is a useful item, it becomes an ornamental one when shaped like a shoe. Shaped as a shoe, the couch might have little-to-no actual sitting space. There is a lot of overlap between design patents and copyrights. It will be easier and cheaper usually to get a copyright, than a patent, and copyrights last longer.

A utility patent is what most people are referring to when they just use the word "patent." This is because most patents are utility ones. A utility patent improves or invents a product in the following areas:

- Mechanical,
- Electrical,
- Chemical,
- Process,
- Machine, or
- Composition of matter.

Some specific examples of utility patents include a computer, Velcro, and prescription drugs. As indicated above, utility patents should be useful. The usefulness requirement just means it must be something that helps humans in some way. This is a very broad definition.

However, some items are completely excluded from patent protection of any type. This includes things that are laws of nature (i.e. the law of gravity), printed materials, atomic weapons, and useless business methods.

One of the most important aspects of patent law is to do a good patent search prior to applying for one. The patent search generally starts with a search of the USPTO's records, but can become much more detailed than that. There are so many places that one could look for references to patents. If the invention has been in a printed publication in the world, then it is not eligible for a patent.

When the application process is actually started, it is called patent prosecution. Note that litigation has not started even though the process is called prosecution. In general, the application will include what is known as a specification, which goes over a description, instructions on how to make the invention, and the subject matter. The application should include drawings and an oath by the inventor that he is the original inventor (the requirements that the inventor must sign the patent application are changing to allow the assignee to be able to sign). The specification has to be very detailed so that others will be able to make the invention after the patent has expired. The specification is often the most costly part of the patent process.

The USPTO will respond, after which, the inventor has six months to answer any questions raised by the USPTO. Once issues have been properly addressed, then the inventor may get an issuance of the patent once the fees are paid. When you see the "patent pending" indication on a good, it means that the inventor is currently in the process of patent prosecution. Once the patent is issued, you will often see a patent number.

Patents are treated like personal property, so they can be sold, licensed, or inherited. Personal property is property that can be moved and is not attached to land. Issues arise when others improperly treat the patent like their own, or infringe. Infringement occurs when an unauthorized individual makes, uses, and/or sells the patented item. There are several types of defenses to infringement, including that it is not infringement, the patent is not valid, the patent is misused, etc. If there is not a legally valid defense however, the infringer may be enjoined from infringing and/or have to pay damages, including punitive damages and attorneys' fees. Damages could include royalties and/or lost profits.

1. The America Invents Act

The America Invents Act (AIA) was signed on September 16, 2011. The United States had a first-to-invent system protecting the first inventor. This made it difficult to reconcile with other countries, which have a first-inventor-to-file rule. Thus, the America Invents Act changed the first-to-invent laws to more in keeping with the first-to-file laws, as of March 16, 2013. The issue is now when was the patent application filed?

b. Trademarks

Generally, a trademark is a word, phrase, or even a logo, which is utilized by a manufacturer to distinguish his product. For example, when AT&T is mentioned, a person thinks slightly different things than when Sprint in mentioned. The trademark has to be distinctive and it has to be used in commerce. In fact, the trademark must be distinctive enough so that it will help buyers tell the difference between products.

There are many different purposes behind trademarks. As illustrated above, in the AT&T example versus Sprint, trademarks are supposed to distinguish products from multiple providers. Trademarks indicate from whom the goods came. They also make it easier for a purchaser to search for the specific product he wants. A trademark is a valuable marketing tool. Companies spend billions annually to make sure that certain characteristics are associated with their products. Trademarks promote consistency. If you are on vacation, and you are tired and just want to get a quick bite to eat, you know that the food at a McDonald's in France is going to taste substantially similar to a McDonald's in the United States. A trademark can thus be an assurance of quality. Trademarks also prevent other companies from 'free riding' off their more famous counterparts.

There are four major types of trademarks: trademarks, service marks, collective marks, and certification marks. The Lanham Act (discussed more *infra*) states that a mark includes any of these four marks. Examples of trademarks though would be Maker's Mark Bourbon and Kellogg's Raisin Bran.

A service mark is something, whether a name, a phrase, or logo, used to identify and distinguish services. Examples of service marks are Ernst & Young, Ruby Tuesday, or United Parcel Service (UPS). Ernst & Young provides accounting services, Ruby Tuesday provides food services, and UPS provides shipping services. Sometimes, a business can be both a trademark and a service mark, such as Dunkin' Donuts. Dunkin' Donuts has retail stores wherein it serves customers with its food (service mark), but it also sells pre-packaged coffee at many grocery stores as well (trademark).

A collective mark is a mark used by an organization to show membership in the organization. The National Association of Legal Assistants is a collective mark.

A certification mark is a word, symbol, or logo used on either goods or services to certify the quality or locale of the product or services. Perhaps the most famous certification mark is the Good Housekeeping Seal of Approval. Per the Good House-keeping website, the certification mark provides a limited warranty:

> If any product that bears our limited warranty Seal proves to be defective within two years from the date it was first sold to a consumer by an authorized retailer, we, Good Housekeeping, will refund the purchase price or $2,000, whichever is less or, at Good Housekeeping's sole discretion, repair or replace the product.[2]

There is still another type of mark, known as a house mark. General Mills would be an example of a house mark, which is used to indicate a wide variety of products, all produced by the same manufacturer. Some of the products under the snacking section of General Mills include: Annie's Cascadian Farm, Fiber One, LaraBar, Yoki, Bugles, Chex, Food Should Taste Good, Gardetto's, and Nature Valley.[3]

The common law in the United States holds that someone obtains the right to a trademark by adopting and using the mark, and not from registration. While registration is not required, the trademark user would have to show when it first used the trademark, because the first person to use a mark owns the rights to the mark. Most other countries require registration of the trademark in order to have any rights to the trademark. In the United States, the use has to be public and typically in interstate commerce. This requirement could be met by using the trademark on the World Wide Web.

---

2. https://www.goodhousekeeping.com/institute/about-the-institute/a22148/about-good-house keeping-seal/. Accessed January 3, 2021.

3. https://www.generalmills.com/en/Brands/Snacks. Accessed January 3, 2021.

The Lanham Act is the primary act that affects trademarks in the United States. It establishes two registers for trademarks, including the principal register and the supplemental register. The principal register is for the majority of trademarks. The supplemental register is for those trademarks that were not eligible for the principal register, due to using military insignia or something scandalous. Disparaging trademarks are not supposed to be trademarked at all.

Although registration is not necessary, there are still several benefits to registration. Some of the many benefits offered by registering on the principal register include that:

- the trademark is good for ten years, at which point it is renewable;
- the public, nationwide, is notified of the use of the trademark;
- it is easier to get registration of the trademark in other countries; and
- the trademark holder can prevent the importation of goods which infringe on his trademark.

Note that a trademark can be used indefinitely, as long as it is registered every ten years.

Registering allows the trademark holder to bring an infringement action. The holder of the trademark can now use the registered designation by the trademark symbol. Registration also gives the holder some rights to the internet name. Another important benefit to registration is that it puts others that would like to use the same trademark on notice that the mark is already being used. For registration, the trademark owner can apply as much as six months before he even plans to use the trademark.

Each state has its own laws about trademarks. If a trademark is only used in one state, then the Lanham Act will not apply. The downside to state registration is that the trademark is only good in that state.

There are five major strengths of marks, which are based upon the distinctiveness and the use of the mark. Please note that these strengths are different from the types of marks there are. The first is the generic category. This strength of mark is not offered trademark protection because it is not distinctive enough to warrant trademark protection. It is often the common name of a product or even a characteristic of the product. For example, calling your product the "best" typically would not be registerable under trademark law. Sometimes though, products become generic under a process known as genericide. Genericide occurs when a product's name is used so often as to become generic. Kleenex is one of the most recognized examples of genericide. Kleenex tries to combat genericide by stating it is Kleenex brand tissues rather than just saying "Kleenex" in its advertising. In general, companies do not want to lose trademark protection because the name of their product is so commonly used.

The second strength of mark is a descriptive one. Descriptive terms are not normally trademarketable because they just describe the good or service. If however, the descriptive term garners secondary meaning, it may be trademarketable. Secondary meaning is assumed once the term has been used continuously and exclusively for at least five years. A good example of a descriptive term that was allowed to be trade-marked is "Mr. Clean." The secondary meaning of Mr. Clean makes many consumers think about the bald-headed man named Mr. Clean. Note that generic and descriptive marks are the weakest strengths of trademarks and servicemarks.

The third strength of mark is a suggestive mark. This strength of mark is distinctive because it required some imagination to come to a conclusion about the nature of the goods. Windex would be a good example of a suggestive mark, as the first part of the work "Win" makes many people think of windows and Windex does clean windows.

The fourth strength of mark is an arbitrary mark. This is a commonly known word, but it is arbitrarily applied to the particular product. A prime example of an arbitrary mark would be Apple for computers. Apples do not, in general, have a lot to do with computers, so the use of Apple for computers is arbitrary.

The fifth and final strength of mark is a fanciful mark. These are provided trade-mark protection because they are distinctive. In fact, the word was entirely made up and not already in use in a dictionary. Hulu is an example of a fanciful mark. The strongest types of trademarks are suggestive, arbitrary, and fanciful, with fanciful being the strongest of all.

More than words can be used as trademarks. A combination of letters, not making up a word, could be trademarked, such as CBS. Symbols can be trademarked, such as lululemon's symbol for their company, which looks like woman's hair against a red circle background. If a shape is distinctive rather than functional, it can also be trademarked. Coca-Cola's traditional coke bottle shape is trademarked. Sounds can even be trademarked, such as Woody Woodpecker's laugh.

Liability for trademark infringement can be, in part, based upon the company failing to do a proper trademark search prior to registering. In general, a company wants to seek a trademark in an area where there are not a lot of other similar trademarks. This will make the company's trademark stronger. Monster is a trademark that has a lot of competition. There is Monster Energy, Monster Job Search, and Monster Cable. They are each allowed to have a trademark as they are in different areas, but each trademark would be stronger if there were not so much competition with that name. A search can be performed on Lexis, Westlaw, and the USPTO's website. This is a preliminary search, performed to make sure there are no exact matches for the specific trademark. The USPTO's search engine, called the Trademark Electronic Search System (TESS) is available via the USPTO's website. More comprehensive searches, including those of telephone books and magazines, can be performed by a company specializing in trademark searches. If a person is found to have committed trademark infringement, then they may be enjoined, forced to pay actual damages and punitive damages three times the actual damages, have the items which misused the trademark destroyed, and may have to pay costs and attorney fees.

One of the more famous examples of suing repeatedly for trademark infringement is Monster Cable. Monster Cable is a trademark because although it is a common word, it is unusual when applied to a cable. This is similar to Apple Computers. However, Monster Cable has sued many other companies using Monster to apply to their products (in part, because Monster Cable states that it produces more than just cables). Most of the time, the infringement lawsuits are settled out-of-court. However, other times, the newer companies using the word monster give up their trademark and then license (or pay for) the trademark from Monster Cable. Specifically, in the Monster.com case (this is the job search website), the job search website paid Monster Cable's legal fees and agreed to put a link to Monster cable on Monster.com. That link was located at the bottom of Monster.com's website.

The USPTO requires a user of a trademark make an affidavit after they have had the trademark for five years, in order to prove that the trademark is still in use. This is called a Section 8 Affidavit. The USPTO just wants to make sure that the trademark is being used, because if it is not, it could potentially go to another customer. Madewell is one such example. Madewell is run by the J Crew Corporation. The Madewell Trademark was originally a family trademark. That family stopped using it and J Crew eventually used the name. A trademark itself can be renewed in ten-year intervals, and this process should be started in year nine of using the trademark.

The trademark symbol should be on a product in some way, maybe by use of a label, and on advertisements. The mark should be the same each time it is used. In addition to the trademark symbol, the owner of the trademark should be identified.

In the following case, *Menashe v. V. Secret Catalogue*, the two companies had a disagreement as to which company used the trademark first and was thus entitled to it. Pay attention to how the court classifies the trademark "sexy little things" as a suggestive trademark.

Menashe v. V. Secret Catalogue, Inc.

409 F. Supp.2d 412 (2006)

... I. BACKGROUND

On January 11, 2005, Ronit Menashe ("Menashe") and Audrey Quock ("Quock") (together "Plaintiffs"), filed this declaratory judgment action for non-infringement of the trademark "SEXY LITTLE THINGS" (the "Mark") under the Lanham Act, 15 U.S.C. § 1051 *et seq.*, and at common law against Defendants V Secret Catalogue, Inc., Victoria's Secret Stores, Inc., Intimate Beauty Corporation, and Victoria's Secret Direct, LLC (collectively "Victoria's Secret"). Plaintiffs also sought a declaratory judgment of non-cybersquatting under the Anticybersquatting Consumer Protection Act ("ACPA"), 15 U.S.C. § 1125(d), a judgment of tortious/fraudulent misrepresentation, punitive damages, and reasonable attorney's fees....

II. FINDINGS OF FACT

A. *Plaintiffs' Adoption of the Mark*

On or about June 1, 2004, Menashe, a publicist, and Quock, a fashion model and actress, embarked on a joint business venture to produce and launch a line of women's underwear.... Sometime in July 2004, they decided to name their line "SEXY LITTLE

THINGS...." Also in July 2004, Quock purchased 400 sample pieces of plain stock underwear from a manufacturer in China and in late July or early August 2004, heat pressed her designs consisting of words and logos onto the stock underwear.... She also heat pressed the Mark onto the back of the underwear where a label would normally be attached....

In late July or early August 2004, Menashe and Quock came up with the phrase "SEXY LITTLE THING, SEXY LITTLE THINGS," a variation of their chosen name that they believed yielded many creative possibilities for design and advertising.... On August 31, 2004, Quock registered the domain name www.sexylittlethings.com in preparation for building a website to sell the underwear line over the Internet.... Subsequently, on September 13, 2004, after searching the website of the United States Patent and Trademark Office ("USPTO") and finding that the Mark was available, Menashe and Quock filed an intent-to-use ("ITU") application with the USPTO for "SEXY LITTLE THING, SEXY LITTLE THINGS" for lingerie.... About ten days later, Quock hired a website designer to create the www.sexylittlethings.com site.

By early September 2004, Quock initiated negotiations with her manufacturer in China to silkscreen print her designs on bulk shipments of underwear.... In October 2004, she sent the manufacturer eight designs to make prototype prints, and started negotiations for an order of 6,000 pieces of underwear.... The manufacturer sent Quock the eight prototypes on November 13, 2004.... By then, she had also sent the manufacturer diagrams for the production of labels carrying the mark "SEXY LITTLE THINGS...."

Meanwhile, Plaintiffs had also set about publicizing their line. Sometime in September or October 2004, Quock did an interview with www.ediets.com, and an article that mentioned the name of Plaintiffs' line and the www.sexylittlethings.com website appeared online at the ediets.com website in the week of November 19, 2004.... On August 19, 2004, Quock did a photo shoot for Stuff Magazine in which she modeled a pair of "SEXY LITTLE THINGS" underwear.... The photographs were published in Stuff Magazine in March of 2005 with an accompanying article that featured Quock's venture into women's lingerie, but did not mention the name of the line.... In late September or early October 2004, Quock did an interview with Beyond Fitness magazine in which she promoted her underwear line, but was unaware whether the article was ever published.... In mid-November, she flew to Milan for a photo shoot featuring "SEXY LITTLE THINGS" underwear.... The photographs were never published....

On October 14, 2004, Quock e-mailed Menashe an outline of a business plan for the underwear line and indicated that they were ready to seek buyers.... Sometime in November 2004, Quock contacted a friend who was a buyer for Fred Segal stores about selling the underwear line in boutiques in Los Angeles, California.... As noted below, this effort too was never consummated.

On November 16, 2004, Menashe received a letter from Victoria's Secret's outside counsel informing her that Victoria's Secret had been using "SEXY LITTLE THINGS" as a trademark for lingerie since prior to the filing date of Plaintiffs' ITU application.... The letter warned that "SEXY LITTLE THING, SEXY LITTLE THINGS," the subject of Plaintiffs' ITU application, was confusingly similar to Victoria's Secret's mark and, if used, would constitute trademark infringement.... Further, the letter demanded that Plaintiffs cease and desist all plans to use "SEXY LITTLE THING, SEXY LITTLE THINGS," abandon their ITU application, and transfer the domain name www.sexylittlethings.com to Victoria's Secret.... Finally, the letter requested a response by November 19, 2004....

Victoria's Secret's letter caused Plaintiffs to halt production of their underwear project, instruct Stuff Magazine not to mention the name of their underwear line, discontinue other publicity efforts, stop development of their website, and cease their attempts to find retail outlets for their product.... Plaintiffs also ordered two trademark investigations into Victoria's Secret's claims to the Mark.... They were informed that no one had used the Mark prior to the filing of their ITU application.... One investigation reported that Victoria's Secret's Resort 2005 catalogue, which had been sent with the cease and desist letter as proof of Victoria's Secret's use of the Mark, was not mailed out until December 28, 2004.... At trial—while it stretches credulity—Menashe testified that since the time she received the cease and desist letter, she has not been in a Victoria's Secret store or looked at a Victoria's Secret catalogue to see whether Victoria's Secret was selling merchandise under the name "SEXY LITTLE THINGS...." Quock testified that she did not visit a Victoria's Secret store nor look at a Victoria's Secret catalogue until some time after receipt of the cease and desist letter, when she walked into a Victoria's Secret store and saw a display for "SEXY LITTLE THINGS...."

B. *Victoria's Secret's Adoption and Use of the Mark*

As early as Fall 2002, Victoria's Secret began to develop the concept and marketing for a panty collection.... Victoria's Secret's decision to expand its panty business stemmed from a desire to capitalize on a major fashion trend that appeared to herald "decorated bottoms"—seen in the popularity of low rise pants and the vogue among young women for wearing lingerie style items as outerwear.... Sometime between March 30 and June 1, 2004, Victoria's Secret's marketing department settled on the name "SEXY LITTLE THINGS" for its panty collection.... The collection, characterized as "fun, flirty, and playfully sexy," was designed to appeal to women in their twenties and early thirties, and was comprised of over eighty items that included panties, camisoles, and other underwear.... Some of these items were already being sold in Victoria Secret stores as general merchandise prior to the introduction of the "SEXY LITTLE THINGS" collection (the "Collection"), but the majority of the items were placed in stores for the first time when the Collection was rolled out in July 2004....

On or around July 28, 2004, the Collection was scheduled to make its first appearance in five Victoria's Secret stores in Ohio, Michigan, and California.... On that date, the mark "SEXY LITTLE THINGS" was displayed with the Collection in four of the five stores in the form of hangtags, store signage, permanent fixtures, or in window exposures.... For example, in one of the Ohio stores, denominated Easton # 1300, the Mark appeared as a large illuminated sign on a "focal wall," a specially constructed vertical unit of nine compartments, each compartment containing a plastic "buttock" on which a pair of panties was displayed.... In that store, the Mark also appeared prominently on hangtags attached to hangers that displayed panties, on labels adhered to pull-out compartments of something called a "panty bar" — a horizontal case that displayed merchandise in each compartment — and with window displays of the same merchandise.... Further, on July 28, 2004, the testimony recites that the "selling environments" for "SEXY LITTLE THINGS" merchandise, comprising the various described displays, opened to consumers in the Ohio roll-out stores....

The roll-out at the Briarwood, Michigan store was delayed owing to technical difficulties related to signage.... Maria Thurston, a co-manager of the Briarwood store from October 2001 until November 27, 2004, testified that while construction for a "panty boutique" was completed on July 28, 2004, no "SEXY LITTLE THINGS" signs appeared in the store until the second week of September 2004.... Ms. Thurston also testified that through September 2004, she never received brand guides from corporate headquarters with instructions for displaying "SEXY LITTLE THINGS" merchandise in the store....

The "SEXY LITTLE THINGS" collection was rolled out to more Victoria's Secret stores in September and October 2004, and by October 19, 2004, the Collection was available to consumers in all nine hundred and twenty-three Victoria's Secret retail lingerie stores nationwide.... In each of the stores, there was some form of focal wall or table signage that displayed the "SEXY LITTLE THINGS" mark together with garments from the Collection.... No labels displaying the Mark were sewn on the merchandise, however, until June 2005.... Moreover, when the Collection was rolled out, store receipts did not indicate that the consumer had bought a "SEXY LITTLE THINGS" item....

The Collection was also available to consumers through catalogues and online. The Collection, according to the uncontradicted testimony and exhibits, first appeared in the Major Fall 2 edition of the Victoria's Secret catalogue that was mailed out to approximately 2.9 million consumers nationwide between September 4, 2004 and September 9, 2004.... Because Victoria's Secret Direct simultaneously makes most of its catalogues available online through its website, the Major Fall 2 catalogue became available online on or about September 9, 2004.... Beginning with the Major Fall 2 edition, the Collection has appeared in approximately twenty-two editions of the Victoria's Secret catalogue....

Typically, the catalogues contained several pages dedicated to the display of "SEXY LITTLE THINGS" merchandise.... The Mark was prominently displayed on these pages together with "SEXY LITTLE THINGS" items. Occasionally, together with "SEXY LITTLE THINGS" merchandise, these pages also displayed a few items from Victoria's Secret's other trademarked collections, subbrands such as Angels by Victoria, Body by Victoria, and Very Sexy, so as to suggest to the consumer various looks that could be created using pieces from different collections.... When this happened, the catalogue copy stated the name of the collection to which the item belonged.... In addition, a few items advertised as part of the "SEXY LITTLE THINGS" collection were advertised in other editions of the catalogue as part of another trademarked collection or simply as general merchandise not belonging to any particular collection....

In the period July 31, 2004 through November 19, 2005, Victoria's Secret sold over thirteen million units of "SEXY LITTLE THINGS" merchandise for total sales of $119,052,756.... The "SEXY LITTLE THINGS" brand accounted for approximately 4% of Victoria Secret Stores' total company sales for fiscal year 2005....

On November 11, 2004, Victoria's Secret applied to register "SEXY LITTLE THINGS" for lingerie on the USPTO's Principal Register based on first use in commerce dating from July 28, 2004.... At about this time, Victoria's Secret learnt of Plaintiffs' ITU application for "SEXY LITTLE THING, SEXY LITTLE THINGS" and of their registration of the domain name www.sexylittlethings.com.... On November 15, 2004..., Victoria's Secret's outside counsel sent Plaintiffs a cease and desist letter....

III. CONCLUSIONS OF LAW

... B. *Non-Infringement Under Lanham Act & Common Law*

Plaintiffs claim that Victoria's Secret has no right of priority in the Mark because "SEXY LITTLE THINGS" for lingerie is a descriptive term that had not attained secondary meaning by the time Plaintiffs filed their ITU application. Consequently, Plaintiffs assert that they have priority based on their constructive use rights that date back to the filing of their ITU application on September 13, 2004. Victoria's Secret counters that the Mark is suggestive and thus qualifies for trademark protection without proof of secondary meaning. Therefore, Victoria's Secret has priority by virtue of its bona fide use of the Mark in commerce beginning July 28, 2004.

15 U.S.C. Section 1125(a) governs the infringement of non-registered marks such as the one at issue. In determining infringement under this statute, the court first ascertains whether the mark is protectable.... Then, the court assesses whether there is a likelihood of consumer confusion.... Where, as here, the marks and goods are nearly identical, however, the focus in the second step shifts from likelihood of confusion to "basic rules of trademark priority" to "determine use and ownership of the mark...."

1. Protectability of the Mark

To merit trademark protection, a mark "must be capable of distinguishing the products it marks from those of others...." As set forth by Judge Friendly in the landmark case of Abercrombie & Fitch Co. v. Hunting World, Inc., the four categories of terms to be considered in determining the protectability of a mark, listed in order of the degree of protection accorded, are (i) generic, (ii) descriptive, (iii) suggestive, and (iv) arbitrary or fanciful.... A descriptive term "forthwith conveys an immediate idea of the ingredients, qualities or characteristics of the goods...." In contrast, a suggestive term "requires imagination, thought and perception to reach a conclusion as to the nature of the goods...." Suggestive marks are automatically protected because they are inherently distinctive, i.e. "[t]heir intrinsic nature serves to identify a particular source of a product...." Descriptive marks are not inherently distinctive and may only be protected on a showing of secondary meaning, i.e. that the purchasing public associates the mark with a particular source....

Classification of a mark is a question of fact.... The fact-finder must decide, based on the evidence, whether prospective purchasers would perceive the mark to be suggestive or merely descriptive.... A composite mark—one comprising more than one term—must be assessed as a whole and not by its parts.... A leading trademark authority has proposed the following three-part test to distinguish suggestive from descriptive marks: (i) whether the purchaser must use some imagination to connect the mark to some characteristic of the product; (ii) whether competitors have used the term descriptively or rather as a trademark; and (iii) whether the proposed use would deprive competitors of a way to describe their goods....

Applying this three-part test, I find "SEXY LITTLE THINGS" to be suggestive. First, while the term describes the erotically stimulating quality of the trademarked lingerie, it also calls to mind the phrase "sexy little thing" popularly used to refer to attractive lithe young women. Hence, the Mark prompts the purchaser to mentally associate the lingerie with its targeted twenty to thirty year-old consumers. Courts have classified marks that both describe the product and evoke other associations as inherently distinctive.... The second factor is not at issue here as neither party has submitted evidence of competitors' usage of the term. Considering the third factor, however, it is hard to believe that Victoria's Secret's use of the Mark will deprive competitors of ways to describe their lingerie products. Indeed, Victoria's Secret's own descriptions of its lingerie in its catalogues and website illustrate that there are numerous ways to describe provocative underwear.

2. Priority

Plaintiffs' alternative contention is that even though the Mark may be suggestive, Victoria's Secret has used it in a descriptive manner, i.e. that Victoria's Secret used the words "sexy little things" to describe its lingerie rather than to identify itself as the source of the goods. Although not crystal clear, the thrust of Plaintiffs' argument appears to be that Victoria's Secret never sold a distinct collection of lingerie under the "SEXY LITTLE THINGS" mark, and hence the term could not have been used as a trademark, but only as a description of various items of underwear drawn from Victoria's Secret's several subbrands or from the retailer's general merchandise. Consequently, Victoria's Secret is not entitled to priority in the Mark.

The Second Circuit has held that "the right to exclusive use of a trademark derives from its appropriation and subsequent use in the marketplace...." A single use suffices to prove priority if the proponent demonstrates that his subsequent use was "deliberate and continuous...." The later filing of an ITU application by another party does not defeat these use-based rights.... The use must, however, be bona fide "use in commerce" as defined in 15 U.S.C. Section 1127. Under this statute, the mark must be "placed in any manner on the goods or their containers or the displays associated therewith or on tags or labels affixed thereto...." Prominent use of a mark in a catalog with a picture and description of the product constitutes a display associated with goods and not mere advertising because of the "point of sale" nature of the display.... The same principle can reasonably be extended to "point of sale" website displays. Whether or not a term has been used as a trademark must be determined from the perspective of the prospective purchaser....

At trial, Plaintiffs highlighted the delay in the roll-out of the Collection to the Briarwood, Michigan store. They painstakingly pointed to evidence that a few items sold as "SEXY LITTLE THINGS" had previously been sold under one of Victoria's Secret's other trademarks, or as part of a store's general merchandise. Plaintiffs also made much of the fact that in Victoria's Secret's catalogues and on its website, a few items from other trademarked collections were included in pages displaying "SEXY LITTLE THINGS" lingerie. Finally, Plaintiffs argued that the late introduction of sewn-in garment labels bearing the Mark and the delay in indicating on receipts that an item was from the "SEXY LITTLE THINGS" collection proved that there was no "SEXY LITTLE THINGS" collection prior to the filing of their ITU application.

Plaintiffs' determination to ignore the model for the underwear fails to overcome the overwhelming evidence that Victoria's Secret used "SEXY LITTLE THINGS" as a trademark in commerce beginning on July 28, 2004. Commencing on that date, the prominent use of the Mark in four stores on focal wall and table signage, on hangtags, and in window and floor displays in close association with the lingerie satisfies the "use in commerce" requirement of 15 U.S.C. Section 1127. Similarly, Victoria's Secret's prominent use of the Mark in its catalogues beginning on September 4, 2004, and on its website beginning on or about September 9, 2004, together with pictures and descriptions of the goods meets the Lands' End test, as both mediums were "point of sale" displays. Moreover, Victoria's Secret produced abundant testimony that, dating from July 28, 2004, it continuously used the Mark in association with lingerie sold through its retail stores, catalogues, and online. That Victoria's Secret sold a few garments as part of more than one collection, or that it occasionally included garments from other collections in the catalogue spreads showing "SEXY LITTLE THINGS" lingerie do not detract from such trademark use. Prospective purchasers of underwear, whose perception is determinative on the question of trademark use here, are unlikely to undertake the type of microscopic scrutiny Plaintiffs engaged in to unearth these details for purposes of this litigation. I find that because Victoria's Secret made bona fide trademark use of "SEXY LITTLE THINGS" in commerce before Plaintiffs filed their ITU application, and has continued to use that Mark in commerce, Victoria Secret has acquired priority in the Mark. Consequently, Plaintiffs are not entitled to a declaratory judgment of non-infringement under the Lanham Act or at common law....

c. Copyrights

Copyrights protect computer programs, movies, pictures, music, some types of architecture, and literature. The copyright is for a certain tangible or fixed expression of a concept. The work must be original, though it does not have to be a new idea and it must be made independently by the author of the work. Thus, this book, even though it did not start the idea of business law, can be and is copyrighted because it is the author's tangible expression of the concept of business law. There should be at least some minimum spark of creativity in the making of a copyrightable work. Something like a list of ingredients would not be copyrightable, as this is not really a creative work.

A copyright is automatic once the work is in a tangible form. Under the Copyright Act of 1976, publication is not even necessary to obtain this protection. This protection allows creators the sole rights to reproduce their work and make money from doing so. However, if a person wishes to enforce the copyright infringement in a court of law, she must have registered the work with the Copyright Office of the Library of Congress. Copyrights are protected by federal law.[4] To prove a copyright violation in a court of law, the plaintiff has to show that the defendant copied the work or that the defendant was able to access the original and the defendant's work is very similar to the plaintiff's work.

Another major benefit to copyright registration is that the holder can record the registration with the U.S. Customs and Border Protection. This allows the Customs and Border Protection to confiscate unauthorized copies of the copyrighted work. The application fee for a copyright is thirty-five or more dollars, and the process takes only about three months. Thus, if an item can be copyrighted, this is often much cheaper and faster than a patent.

Copyrights last until seventy years after the death of the last living author of the work.[5] If the work was created by a corporation, then the copyright would last ninety-five years from publication or one hundred and twenty years from the creation of the idea. The public can use, free of charge, the copyrighted material, once the copyright has expired. Prior to the expiration of the copyright, there is a limited right of the public to use copyrighted material under the Fair Use Doctrine. Usually, this use is for critiquing the work or research. Another exception to copyright is that work prepared by a United States government agency is typically not protected and can be used by the public.

More specifically, the rights provided under copyright law include reproduction, adaptation, distribution, performance, and display. Each right can be transferred separately. Thus, a copyright holder can sometimes make more money by selling rights separately rather than altogether. The holder could give one buyer the right to perform the work but another buyer the right to distribute the work.

The right to reproduce means the copyright holder gets to keep others from reproducing his work. This is true even if the copier does not make any money from copying the work. Hence, technically, a person who copies music without making money for doing so could be infringing.

---

4. 17 U.S.C. §§ 101 et seq.
5. Sony Bono Copyright Term Extension Act.

Another right allowed a copyright holder is the right to prepare an adaptation. An example of this is a book, such as *Lord of the Rings*, being made into a movie. The movie is a new work and would get a new copyright. The book would keep the original copyright.

A copyright holder has the right to display his work publicly except for sound recordings and works of architecture. This right is exclusive. This then begs the question, what exactly is public? Public does not include displaying the work to a large number of family and friends. The public is people the copyright holder does not know. The holder has to display at a place where a substantial number of people will be that the holder does not know.

Once works have been distributed, however, these rights generally terminate to some extent. Under the first sale doctrine, the buyer of a specific copy of copyrighted material is free to lend and/or resell the item without liability for infringement because they are now the owner of that copy. This makes sense as the owner of downloaded music paid for it and should be able to use, lend, and/or resell it. There are exceptions though to the First Sale Doctrine. It typically will not apply to rental of computer programs, in large part because Microsoft protested such use. If a computer program was completely incapable of being copied, then and only then, could it be rented.

Some things, however, are excluded entirely from being copyright violations. If materials are validly being used in educational activities, such as the teacher using the material, it may not constitute infringement. Sometimes charities can also use copyrighted materials if they are fundraising, without having to pay royalties and without infringing. Finally, another exception to copyright infringement is a religious workshop. A church could decide to perform a passion play, for instance, and this may not be considered infringement.

When a work is made "for hire," then the copyright holder is the hirer. The author would not then have the copyright; the hirer would. There are two types of works for hire. The first type is a work drafted by an employee in the course and scope of her employment. The second type is when a person is commissioned. Whenever a work is created in the course and scope of employment, there is a presumption that the work is owned by the employer. Sometimes though, issues arise when someone is an independent contractor.

When transferring a copyright, the transfer needs to be in writing and needs to be signed by the owner of the copyright. The exception is nonexclusive agreements, which do not have to be in writing. While it is hard sometimes to visualize, copyrights can be transferred by bankruptcy, divorce, wills, or even intestate by people who did not leave wills. Essentially, copyrights are treated like property. The best course is to record the written transfer with the copyright office, to avoid legal disputes later on.

Damages for copyright infringement can include actual damages. In the alternative, the copyright holder could seek statutory damages. Statutory damages are between five hundred dollars and twenty thousand dollars, unless the infringement was done purposefully. If the infringement was done purposefully, the holder may be able to get up to one hundred thousand dollars in statutory damages. Costs and attorneys' fees can be sought for copyright infringement.

d. Trade Secrets

A trade secret is simply information, which if known by a competitor, would give the competitor an advantage. The "secret sauce" is a perfect example of a trade secret. Trade secrets can and do include patterns, devices, and processes. Further categories of trade secrets include customer lists, research, prices, manufacturing techniques, and information on how the company markets to its clients. Trade secrets can be protected under state law and through contracts. To be protectable, the secret must have some commercial value, not be easily known, and safeguards must be in place to prevent it being disclosed.

For the requirement that there be commercial value, there does not have to be massive amounts of commercial value. The value must come from the information not being known by the public.

With a trade secret, the business has taken steps to keep the secret. These steps must be reasonable. Examples of reasonable steps include somehow locking up formulas, research, plans, blueprints, etc. The business will even have to take reasonable steps to keep trade secrets from some of its employees. Many employers will make their employees sign contracts stating that they will not disclose trade secrets to people outside the company.

The owner of the trade secret has the sole right to it, and can decide to sell it to someone else. To protect trade secrets, a company may request an injunction. The injunction could prevent someone who learned the trade secret from using it himself or telling someone else about the trade secret. The owner of a trade secret can also request damages from those who wrongfully take the trade secret. Specifically, the Uniform Trade Secrets Act allows the trade secret owner to seek punitive damages that are twice the sum of the actual damages, if the trade secret was wrongfully taken. The owner may also be able to get costs and attorney fees.

A major benefit to a trade secret is that there are no time limits on how long it can last. As long as the trade secret is not disclosed to other people, it can last longer than a patent (fourteen to twenty years) or a copyright (seventy to one hundred and twenty years).

3.4 Fictitious Business Name Statement

a. When Is One Necessary?

When the client is not using their last name in a business name, then typically the client will need to file a fictitious business name statement so that plaintiffs suing the business can determine who owns the business. When the client does not use his last name in his business, then name of the company is a fictitious name. When a business entity chooses a fictitious business name it will often need to publish a notice of that fictitious business name in a widely distributed newspaper in the same area as the business. When suing a business with a fictitious business name, the company would be sued in the following format: Eduardo Gonzalez, doing business as (dba) Candle-makers 'R Us.

If there is only one last name in a company's name, then the client does not need to file a fictitious business name statement, as it will be easy to find the owner and sue him. However, if there is a last name and it implies that others are involved, such as the name Dion & Associates, then the owners of the company would still need to file a fictitious business name statement, as it is not clear who the associates are.

3.5 Sales Tax

Many states impose sales tax on goods. Goods are anything that can be moved. The paralegal needs to research the laws in the state the client is located in to determine how to apply for a sales tax permit for the client.

3.6 Business License

Local government will often make businesses file for a business license. This is not the same as a professional license and may be required of all businesses. The paralegal needs to research local law for the area the client is located in to determine how to apply for a business permit for the client.

3.7 Workers' Compensation Insurance

Every state requires workers' compensation to a differing degree. By this, it is meant that some states cover more workers than others and some states offer more benefits than others do. Workers that might be excluded are workers such as house-keepers and gardeners in a residential setting, agricultural workers, or temporary employees.

Workers' compensation insurance covers an injured employee when he is injured on the job. This could include medical expenses, rehabilitation for a new job, and/or lost wages. If the employer cannot pay the workers' compensation insurance premiums, then usually the employer will have to self-insure such injuries or use state sponsored insurance. In addition, if the employer's work is in a highly dangerous area of work, the employer may not be able to find an insurance company willing to insure it, and may have to be self-insured for that reason. Workers' compensation is discussed in detail in Chapter 2.

In general though, workers' compensation laws act to provide a procedure for workers to be compensated for injuries on the job. The worker files with the appropriate state agency, and then the business entity looks at the claim to see if it is legitimate, and if so, how much should be paid.

3.8 Unemployment Insurance

Unemployment compensation was set up by Congress in 1935. The Federal Unemployment Tax Act and state laws govern unemployment. Employers must pay taxes into federal and state unemployment. Although it is commonly perceived that employees do pay into this system, in fact, employees do not pay unemployment taxes. Employees usually pay into state disability.

Although different states have different regulations about unemployment, in general there are a couple of rules. To receive unemployment, employees should be looking for work. In addition, if an employee was fired for exceedingly bad conduct or quit voluntarily without cause, the employee typically will not be paid by unemployment insurance.

3.9 Social Security

In the same year as unemployment compensation was created, Congress also set up Social Security. Social Security benefits are mainly for the retired or disabled. It can also provide death benefits. Part of Social Security is a medical benefit as well. Since Social Security covers old age retirement, survivors, and disability insurance, you may hear it referred to as OASDI. Social security is administered by the Social Security Administration (SSA).

Employer and employees both pay into Social Security. The federal government makes employers deduct from their employee's paychecks taxes both Social Security and Medicare. Together, Social Security and Medicare are known as FICA (Federal Insurance Contributions Act). The employer must withhold these amounts and then send them to the appropriate place. In general, the employer and employee each pay 6.2 percent of the employee's gross income for Social Security. This comes to a combined 12.4 percent. For Medicare, the employee and employer each pay 1.45 percent of the employee's gross income. Thus, the amount paid into Social Security is based upon the employee's annual wages. If a person is self-employed, she is also supposed to pay into social security. The penalties are steep for not paying into Social Security, and include criminal prosecution.

One of the controversial issues about Social Security is that the money taken from employees goes towards paying current claims, rather than going into a bank account-like system for the employee paying into it. This has caused worry that by the time an employee actually retires, there will not be enough money left in the system to pay his own Social Security.

Medicare is a health-insurance program and is run by the SSA. In general, it applies to people over the age of sixty-five. It is divided into two parts, one that covers hospital expenses, and one that covers non-hospital expenses.

3.10 Federal Employer Identification Number (FEIN)

The Federal Employer Identification Number (FEIN) is used by the Internal Revenue Service. It identifies the business. It is similar to a social security number for a person. Employers must have a FEIN. The FEIN will be nine digits, and look something like this: 97-48592.

The sole proprietor has to get a tax identification number even if he only has one employee. If the sole proprietor has more than one sole proprietorship, usually only one FEIN is needed for all those businesses. If the sole proprietorship converts to a new business entity, then it will usually need a new FEIN.

Chapter Summary

There are many types of paperwork the paralegal must be aware of when effectively helping the client to set up any type of new business. The first is a professional license. Many professions have to have a license in order to practice that profession legally. The paralegal needs to verify the client has that license before helping the client to set up his new business in that area.

The federal government can grant patents. A patent lets an investor keep other people from using or selling the invention for fourteen or twenty years. The three types of patents are utility patents (the most common), design patents, and plant patents. In general, for an invention to be patented, it must be useful, novel, and nonobvious.

Before a patent is applied for, a search should be conducted to try to ensure the invention can be patented. The patent application requires an in-depth description of the invention.

Patents are treated like personal property that can be bought and sold. Problems arise when patented products are made, bought/sold, or used, without permission. An inventor can sue for patent infringement in federal court. There are defenses to patent infringement that the alleged infringer can bring up, such as the patent is not a valid one. If the inventor wins the litigation, the inventor can enjoin the infringer and get damages.

Trademarks help consumers identify different seller's products, as well as associate certain characteristics with different brands. There are four types of marks, including trademarks, service marks, certification marks, and collective marks.

Trademarks are for goods; service marks are for services, certification marks are like the Good Housekeeping Seal of Approval, and collective marks are marks used by an association.

To gain the rights to a trademark, one has to use it. Registration with the United States Patent and Trademark Office can give additional rights.

One of the biggest issues in trademark law is whether something is trademarketable. Generic and descriptive words typically cannot be, or at least a descriptive term has to gain a secondary meaning to be trademarketable. It is much easier to prove categories of marks such as suggestive, arbitrary, and fanciful should be trademarked.

Paralegals are expected in this area of law to search for trademark use before the trademark the client wants to use is registered. If a search is not made, then a court will often rule in favor of the other person using the trademark.

The USPTO office wants to make sure that trademarks are continually in use. Therefore, between five and six years after registration, and in the ninth year as well, the trademark owner has to sign an affidavit stating that it is continuing to use the trademark. This is known as a Section 8 Affidavit. Otherwise, trademarks are renewable every ten years.

Copyright law is federal law. Registering a copyright helps protect the author from others using or copying his work. The work does not have to be published to be copyrighted; it just has to be in a fixed form. To be something copyrightable, the work must be original and created by the author. Copyrightable items include literary works, musical works, dramatic works, pictures, sculptures, and architecture. Items that are excluded from copyright include purely useful items, such as a to-do list and the telephone directory.

Holders of registered copyrights have exclusive rights, which include copying the work, deriving the work (i.e., from a book into a movie), distributing the work, performing the work, and displaying the work. If someone else other than the copyright holder does so, whether for money or not, he has violated copyright laws unless he obtained permission ahead of time from the copyright holder. There are exemptions to copyright benefits, and these include for educational purposes, for religious purposes, etc.

The first sale doctrine states that once a copyrighted work has been sold by or on behalf of the copyright holder, that holder is not entitled to any further financial benefit from that item.

If an author creates a work for hire, then the author no longer has rights to the copyright; the hirer would.

Trade secrets are basically information of value that a business does not want disclosed outside of the business. A trade secret can include customer lists, research, and prices. If that information were found out by a competitor, it would economically benefit the competitor. The nice thing about trade secrets, is if they are properly guarded, they can last indefinitely. Most employers with trade secrets will make their employees sign a confidentiality agreement. If someone does use the trade secret, the holder of it may seek an injunction or damages.

If the client is not using his last name in his business name, he will need to file what is known as a fictitious business name (FBN). An FBN allows the public to look up who owns the company and properly sue the owner, as well as the company.

If the client sells goods, he will need to obtain a sales tax permit. Depending upon local government, the client may also need to obtain a business license.

Employers will need to obtain workers' compensation insurance, which covers workers injured on the job. If the employer cannot get insurance, he will have to self-insure. Employers also have to pay into unemployment insurance and social security for their employees. Finally, the Internal Revenue Service requires that employers seek an Employer Identification Number (EIN) to use on all important paperwork, and particularly on taxes.

Key Terms

Adaptation

Arbitrary mark

Attribution

Certification mark

Collective mark

Collective work

Copy

Copyright

Derivative work

Design patent

Distribution

Doing business as (dba)

Domain name

Dramatic work

Employer identification number (EIN)

Fair use

Fanciful mark

Federal Employer Identification Number (FEIN)

Fictitious business name (FBN)

First sale doctrine

Fixed

Generic

Genericide

Generic term

House mark

Independent contractor

Infringement

Injunction

Intellectual property

Literary work

Mark

Musical work

Nonobviousness

Novelty

Patent

Patent prosecution

Plant patent

Principal register

Public domain

Reproduction

Secondary meaning

Service mark

Sound recording

Specification

Suggestive mark

Trademark

Trademark Electronic Search System (TESS)

Trade secret

United States Patent and Trademark Office

Usefulness

Utility patent

Workers' compensation insurance

Works for hire

Review Questions

1. What is the difference between a professional license and a business license?

2. Why is intellectual property protected legally?

3. Delineate the process for requesting a patent.

4. What length of time do each of the different patents last for?

5. What are the four major types of marks that make up trademarks?

6. Why did the court rule in favor of Victoria's Secret in *Menashe v. V. Secret Catalogue, Inc.*?

7. Can you copyright lists?

8. What are the rights provided under copyright law?

9. How can trade secrets be preserved?

10. How can the holder of a trade secret enforce his right to the trade secret?

11. When might a trade secret be more beneficial than a patent?

12. If a client names their business Sampson and Associates, does the client need to file a fictitious business name statement? Why or why not?

13. When is a sales tax permit required?

14. What are the four types of paperwork that apply to a business that hires employees?

15. Who pays into unemployment insurance? Who pays into Social Security?

16. What is an employer identification number similar to?

Web Links

http://www.icann.org is the website for the organization that helps with domain name registrations.

http://tess2uspto.gov/tmdb/tmep is the website to go to for the Trademark Manual of Examining Procedure.

The website for the United States Patent and Trademark Office can be found at: http://www.uspto.gov.

The copyright office can be found online at: http://www.copyright.gov.

The United Customs and Border Protection plays an important role in intellectual property because they can confiscate pirated goods. http:/// http://www.cbp.gov/trade.

The paralegal will often have to help the client obtain a FEIN. The form is Form SS-4, Application for Employer Identification Number, located at www.IRS.gov. The state the client employer is in may also require an identification number.

Exercises

1. Is the American Association for Justice, aka American Association of Trial Lawyers, a trademark, service mark, collective mark, or certification mark?

2. Is Princess Cruises a trademark, service mark, collective mark or certification mark?

3. Is an individual likely to get a trademark for Circle Cookies?

4. If a client wants to use Circle Cookies as a trademark, what words would you need to search?

5. Georgette writes a song in 2011. How long will the copyright protection for the song last?

6. Several different photographers take pictures of Yosemite. Can any or all of them seek a copyright for their photographs?

7. You buy a DVD of your favorite television series. After you watch it, you resell the DVD on eBay. May you legally do so? Why or why not?

8. Is a highlighter a utility, design, or plant patent?

9. Bettie files a patent application on November 4, 2009. The patent is issued May 5, 2011. The patent is a utility one. When will the patent expire?

10. Research the status of the appeal by the Washington Redskins of the cancellation of their trademark in that name.

Chapter 4

Contracts

Chapter Outline

Chapter Objectives

- Define what a contract is, and give definitions of several types of contracts.
- List sources of contract law.
- Provide the basic requirements for forming a contract, including offer, acceptance, and consideration.
- Outline the requirements of an offer.
- Discuss acceptable consideration.
- Comprehend the requirements of a legally binding contract.
- Describe how voidable contracts are different from void contracts.
- Introduce negotiation concepts.
- Discuss common business contracts.
- Overview Article 2 and 2A of the Uniform Commercial Code.
- Raise issues brought on by e-contracts and e-signatures.
- Mention the Uniform Electronic Transactions Act (UETA).

4.1 Introduction to Contracts

A contract is an agreement, which can be legally enforced. There must be at least two people involved in the contract, known as the parties. These parties must agree to do something or not to do something. Contract is often abbreviated "k" in law.

There is a difference between express versus implied contracts. Express contracts occur when both sides to the contract state or write out all the terms of the contract. Implied contracts are contracts formed by the conduct of both sides to the contract. A person going to see a tax advisor for tax advice is implying a contract, though he does not sign a written contract. While in everyday life, a contract does not have to be written down, legal professionals should encourage clients to write down their agreements.

Express Contract

Did the defendant make a promise?

↓

Yes.

↓

Is there a contract?

↓

Yes.

↓

Therefore, there is an express contract, as the parties wanted to
contract, and they agreed upon the terms.

Valid contracts are ones that are enforceable by law. A valid contract has met all the requirements needed for a contract, i.e., offer, acceptance, and consideration, which are discussed in section 4.3. For there to be a valid contract, the parties generally have to have the capacity to contract. This means that the parties usually must not be minors. A minor is a person under the age of eighteen. There is an exception if the minor is making a contract for one of the necessities of life; if the minor is, then this type of contract will normally be valid. The necessities of life include health care, housing, clothes, and food. Sometimes, in some states, it can also include education. If the minor makes a contract for a necessity of life, then the minor only has to pay a reasonable price, and not the price that was contractually agreed upon.

The parties must have the mental capacity to consent too. A judge usually makes the determination whether someone is mentally competent or not. In general, intoxicated people are held not to have the ability at the time they are intoxicated to be bound by a contract. However, if someone purposefully got intoxicated to try to avoid being competent to contract, then that person will probably still be found to have had the sufficient mental capacity to contract.

A voidable contract is a contract that allows one party, by law to terminate the agreement. When the party does so, then that party will not suffer any liability for withdrawing. This is because, even if the contract is valid, it can be gotten out of by one of the parties. An example of something that could make a contract voidable is if one of the parties to the contract failed to disclose a material fact. The other party, once he learned of the material fact, could decide to void the contract based not having known that fact when he agreed to the contract. In the alternative, that party could ratify the contract, which would make it valid.

There are several other reasons a contract can be voidable. When one or more of the parties uses fraud or misrepresentation in a contract, then the contract is typically voidable. Fraud occurs when a party makes, intentionally, an incorrect statement of important information and the other side reasonably relies on that information to his detriment. This is slightly different from failing to disclose. Misrepresentation is very similar. Misrepresentation is making a statement that is incorrect with the intent to mislead the other party.

There are still other reasons a contract can be voidable. If someone coerces another to make a contract through force, also known as duress, then that contract is voidable by the person who was placed under duress. If one party is in a special relationship to the other, and they use this relationship unfairly to force the other party to make a contract, this is known as undue influence. Contracts gained through undue influence are also voidable.

With a void contract, neither party to the contract can legally enforce the contract because the contract was illegal. A void contract is different from a voidable contract. A voidable contract is not necessarily illegal; it is just that one of the parties was in an unfair bargaining position. A void contract is illegal, and it does not matter if the parties to try ratify it, it is still illegal. Gambling contracts, unless they are allowed by the particular state, are often illegal. Another example of a void contract is if a friend takes out an insurance policy on another friend; only family members are usually allowed to take out an insurance policy on a person. A contract to murder someone would be a void contract.

However, sometimes, even when there is not a valid contract, the law will allow a plaintiff to recover (this is usually not the case with void contracts). Promissory estoppel is one such way in which the plaintiff can recover. There are many different elements to promissory estoppel. A plaintiff must prove that she:

- has been injured,
- does not have a valid contract,
- can show a promise,
- reasonably relied on that promise, and
- that there is an injustice as a result of that.[1]

A promise is a statement that this will or will not happen in the future. The person making the promise is known as the promisor and the person who has the promise made to them is known as the promisee.

---

1. *See Norton v. Hoyt*, 278 F. Supp. 2d 214.

Another remedy for an invalid contract is quasi-contract. A quasi-contract is also called an implied-in-law contract. With a quasi-contract, the plaintiff has to show the defendant received a benefit, the plaintiff reasonably expected to be paid, and the defendant was unjustly enriched by not paying.[2] Usually, with quasi-contract there will not be a contract, because if there was a contract, there are other remedies for breach of contract. The point of quasi-contract is to keep one party from being unjustly enriched. Damages for quasi-contract are known as "quantum meruit." The plaintiff will receive as much as she is out under the concept of "quantum meruit."

4.2 Contract Law Sources

There are three main sources of contract law: the common law, the Uniform Commercial Code ("UCC"), and the Restatement of Contracts. The common law is different from the UCC and encompasses case law. In general, the UCC covers the sales of goods and promotes commerce. Goods are anything that could be moved by the strongest mythical person in the universe, Hercules. Therefore, for example, even though a recreational vehicle could not be moved by a normal human being, Hercules could move it, so it is considered a good. However, Hercules could not move an attached home because it is attached to the land. Thus, a house would not be considered a good.

The UCC can modify general contract law, for example, which says that terms to a contract should not be left indefinite. Under the UCC, a contract for a good can have an indefinite term if there is intent and there is a "reasonably certain basis for giving an appropriate remedy."[3] Examples of terms the parties might want to leave indefinite are price, output, delivery, and warranties.

The Restatement of Contracts originally was put together by the American Law Institute in the 1930s. It has gone through revisions since that time. It is used as a reference on contract law, especially when the common law and the UCC are silent on an issue.

4.3 Requirements to Find a Contract

In a contract, there must be an offer, acceptance of that offer, and consideration. Legality and capacity can be considered additional requirements. Offer, acceptance, and consideration are the minimum requirements of any contract. An offer and an acceptance together constitute an agreement.

---

2. *See Novak v. Credit Bureau Collection Service*, 877 N.E. 2d 1253.
3. UCC Section 2-204(3).

With an offer, there has to be intent to make an offer that is binding, with some definite terms, and a communication of that offer to the other party. The intention must be a serious one. It must at least look serious to an objective, reasonable, outside party. If it looks like the offer was a joke to a reasonable person, who is not involved, then the offer was not serious.

Several things do not count as an offer. An invite to bargain is not an offer. A price estimate or quote is not an offer. Ads are also not typically considered offers. Putting an item up for auction is not an offer. These things are normally considered a request for an offer to be made. If an offer is terminated before acceptance, then a contract has not been formed. An offer can be terminated by the offeror revoking it, by the offeree rejecting or counteroffering it, by a time limit expiring, or by law. An offeror is the party who makes the offer. The offeree is the party to the offer is being made.

For example, let us pretend you are looking to buy a motorcycle on-line. You see an ad for a motorcycle for one thousand dollars. When you click on the ad, it describes the motorcycle, indicates that the motorcycle is actually ten thousand dollars, and indicates that if you are interested, you should call or text. This is an invitation to make an offer. When you call or text, that can be the actual offer. To be a valid offer, you would probably need to offer ten thousand, if it were clear that the one thousand dollars was a typo.

With revocation, the offeror is taking back the offer before it has been accepted. However, some offers are irrevocable, so this would not work. When the offeree does not accept the offer, it is known as a rejection. If an offeree counteroffers, that does not make a contract. A counteroffer is treated like a rejection of the original offer. If one of the parties dies or becomes mentally incapacitated, then the offer is terminated by law. If the item the contract is about is destroyed by a third party, the offer is terminated by law as well.

There must be some sort of affirmative action taken by the offeree in order for the offeree to have accepted the offer. An acceptance, generally, is a voluntary act or words, which show agreement with the offer. The acceptance in a contract, under the mirror image concept, has to be for the same terms as the offer. The mirror image concept is that the acceptance must match the offer exactly. If it does not, then it is not an acceptance. It is a counteroffer. Remember, however, that the UCC can change general contract law, at least in regards to the sale of goods. Therefore, for goods, the acceptance might not have to be to the exact same terms as the offer, as long as there was intent to contract.

What type of acceptance the offeree should make is based upon whether the contract is a unilateral contract or a bilateral contract. In a unilateral contract, the offeree accepts by performing. There is only one promise in a unilateral contract. An example would be "I promise to do this; you do that." This is also referred to as a promise for performance or an act.

In a bilateral contract, the offeree generally accepts by making a promise. Thus, there are mutual promises in a bilateral contract, otherwise referred to as a promise for a promise. An example would be: "I promise to do this; you promise to do that." Performance does not need to take place immediately for there to be a binding contract.

Consideration is a bargaining that causes the parties to exchange something of value between them. Each side has an obligation to the other. A court typically does not look into the value of the consideration, but it does require that both sides have given consideration. However, at the same time, it cannot be completely insignificant consideration. The consideration must be for present or future consideration, not past consideration. This is why contracts will often say some nominal amount of money in them, such as $1, to try to make sure that they are legally binding. A court probably would not uphold a house selling for a dollar ... that is more of a gift.

Some of the remedies for breach of contract include compensatory damages or specific performance. Compensatory damages are supposed to compensate the plaintiff for the loss she suffered as a result of the breach of contract. Attorney's fees are usually not included as part of the compensatory damages, however. Sometimes the contract itself will allow for attorney's fees if the contract is breached. Specific performance occurs when the plaintiff gets a court order stating that the defendant must go ahead and perform the contract as was agreed. In the alternative, the plaintiff might also be able to cancel the contract.

4.4 Negotiation

Negotiation is the process wherein one party tries to convince the other party to do a specific thing. To be a better negotiator, it is important to recognize what type of negotiator you are and what type of negotiator the other person is. The three major types of negotiators are competitive, cooperative, and principled.

The type of negotiator who usually does the best in negotiations is a principled, otherwise known as a problem-solver, negotiator. A principled negotiator attempts to focus on the interests involved and not on the positions and wants each party to gain. The principled negotiator also tries to look at all the options.

A cooperative negotiator is not as beneficial a negotiation partner to have as originally sounds. A cooperative negotiator will listen a lot, agree a lot, but may not have viable solutions to the problem.

One of the more common negotiators you will deal with in the law is the competitive bargainer, who sees the situation as a win-lose. Do not sink to the competitive bargainer's level and tell him that his side is wrong. Try not to see their side as evil and your side as innocent. If you propose a small concession, known as gift-giving, during the negotiation and it is not reciprocated, you know that you are probably dealing with a competitive bargainer.

One of the foremost negotiation strategies is to, before you start negotiating, determine your best alternative to the negotiated agreement. If you and the other party do not reach an agreement, what is the best alternative? In addition, you will want to figure out the worst alternative to not reaching a negotiated agreement. If there is no agreement, which party will lose the most? Figuring out these two positions will help you evaluate who is in the better bargaining seat going into the negotiation.

Another common negotiation strategy is to avoid being the first one to state your position, unless necessary. This is because oftentimes, by being the first one to state your position, you have already lost. If you are asked during a job interview how much you would like to make, and you reply with a number that is less than what the employer was expecting to pay you, you have lost.

Another easy and effective thing to do in a negotiation is to listen. Frequently, by listening, the other party may be more willing to make concessions or you may be able to figure out how best to reach a settlement. People are reluctant to settle until they feel like they have been heard.

A final point, which can be helpful in negotiation, is to remember what the relationship is between you and the other party. If this is a relationship that you need to continue, you might want to be less confrontational.

4.5 Written Contracts

Certain contracts are required, by the Statute of Frauds, to be in writing. The Statutes of Frauds could thus actually be renamed, more accurately, the Statute to Help Prevent Frauds. This is to help make sure that these types of contracts have written evidence to be enforceable and thus help to prevent fraud. These types of contracts are usually considered more important. These contracts include:

- contracts for land,
- any contract that will not be completed within one year,
- contracts to take over another's debt,
- marital agreements (especially prenuptial agreements),
- contracts for stocks and bonds, and
- sales of goods worth over five hundred dollars.

4.6 Performance

Once there is a valid contract, then the duty of performance comes into play. Complete performance occurs when a party to the contract has satisfied every duty that was required of them under the contract. Substantial performance occurs when one party to the contract has not made complete performance, but the party has tried to perform much more than just minimally. With substantial performance, the substantially complying party will still be paid, just less any damages to the other party. A material breach occurs when the performance is unacceptable. The party that materially breached loses the right to sue the other party and often must pay the other party damages.

4.7 Common Business Contracts

a. Sales

Sales contracts are governed by Article 2 of the Uniform Commercial Code. If the UCC does not touch on an issue regarding sales contracts, then the common law will apply. The types of sales governed by the UCC are sales of goods (typically over five hundred dollars), but not sales of real property, services, or investments. If the parties do not want to be governed by the UCC, then wherever possible, their sales agreement should make other provisions.

A sale occurs when the title of a good goes from the seller of the good to the buyer for consideration. Remember from earlier discussions, that a good is any moveable property.

There are several differences between general contract law and sales law under the UCC. With sales, the original contract does not need to contain all the terms of the contract. However, the quantity sought of a good must be in the contract. In addition, in a sales contract, additional terms placed in the acceptance do not constitute rejection, unless acceptance is required by the buyer.

b. Equipment Purchase/Leasing

Leasing of goods is covered by Article 2A of the UCC. Article 2A is very similar to Article 2, except that 2A is discussing leases, rather than sales. A lessor sells the right to the use of his goods, by using a lease. A lessee buys the right to use the goods.

c. Office Leasing

Office leases must also be in writing, per the Statute of Frauds, if they are for more than one year. Terms of the lease should at least have:

- the name of the lessor and lessee,
- a description of the office being leased,
- the length of the lease, and
- the rent.

Additional terms, known as covenants might include:

- a security deposit,
- whom will take care of repairs, and
- how to end the lease.

d. Real Estate

The common law applies to sales of real estate. Earlier, under the section on written contracts, it stated that the Statute of Frauds requires real estate contracts to be in writing to be valid. At least, the writing must include:

- the names of the buyer and seller,
- a detailed description of the property be transferred,
- the price, and
- the buyer's and seller's signatures.

Almost all types of real estate transactions are required to be in writing. This includes mortgages. They should also be recorded at the county assessor's office or the appropriate entity in your jurisdiction.

4.8 E-Contracts

The law is currently trying to keep up with the special problems presented in contract law by having electronic contracts. In general, if the electronic contract is about a good, a court will try to apply common law or the UCC. However, new laws have also been adopted. In addition to buying goods online, many people also license products online, such as spyware.

It is especially important that when buying something on-line there be an on-line contract address to:

- contact regarding what should be done with a defective product,
- how goods should be paid for,
- refunds,
- liability, and
- privacy of the buyer's information.

Often, a consumer goes ahead and accepts an on-line agreement by just clicking a box to a long set of contract terms within a box with a scroll bar. Many times, consumers do not bother to scroll through the entire contract and read it. The failure of a consumer to object to these contract terms will probably be an acceptance. Courts have held that a binding legal contract can be and is made by the consumer acting to accept these agreements, such as checking a box. The law does not state that a person must read the contract for it to be legally binding. The following case, *Feldman v. Google, Inc.*, illustrates these concepts.

Feldman v. Google, Inc.

513 F.Supp.2d 229 (2007)

... The ultimate issues raised by the motions and determined by the court are whether a forum selection clause in an internet "clickwrap" agreement is enforceable under the facts of the case and, if so, whether transfer of this case to the Northern District of California is warranted. The court finds in the affirmative as to both, issues....

Defendant's motion seeks to enforce the forum selection clause in an online "click-wrap" agreement, which provides for venue in Santa Clara County, California, which is within the San Jose Division. In his original complaint, Plaintiff based his claims on a theory of express contract. In his Amended Complaint, however, Plaintiff offers a wholly new legal theory. He argues that no express contract existed because the agreement was not valid. Withdrawing his express contract allegations, Plaintiff advanced the theory of implied contract because he argues he did not have notice of and did not assent to the terms of the agreement and therefore there was no "meeting of the minds." Plaintiff also argues that, even if the agreement were controlling, it is a contract of adhesion and unconscionable, and that the forum selection clause is unenforceable....

II. Factual Background

A. General Background

On or about January 2003, Plaintiff, a lawyer with his own law firm, Lawrence E. Feldman & Associates, purchased advertising from Defendant Google, Inc.'s "Ad-Words" Program, to attract potential clients who may have been harmed by drugs under scrutiny by the U.S. Food and Drug Administration.

In the AdWords program, whenever an internet user searched on the internet search engine, Google.com, for keywords or "Adwords" purchased by Plaintiff, such as "Vioxx," "Bextra," and "Celebrex," Plaintiff's ad would appear. If the searcher clicked on Plaintiff's ad, Defendant would charge Plaintiff for each click made on the ad.

This procedure is known as "pay per click" advertising. The price per keyword is determined by a bidding process, wherein the highest bidder for a keyword would have its ad placed at the top of the list of results from a Google.com search by an internet user.

Plaintiff claims that he was the victim of "click fraud." Click fraud occurs when entities or persons, such as competitors or pranksters, without any interest in Plaintiff's services, click repeatedly on Plaintiff's ad, the result of which drives up his advertising cost and discourages him from advertising. Click fraud also may be referred to as "improper clicks" or, to coin a phrase, "trick clicks." Plaintiff alleges that twenty to thirty percent of all clicks for which he was charged were fraudulent. He claims that Google required him to pay for all clicks on his ads, including those which were fraudulent.

Plaintiff does not contend that Google actually knew that there were fraudulent clicks, but alleges that click fraud can be tracked and prevented by computer programs, which can count the number of clicks originating from a single source and whether a sale results, and can be tracked by mechanisms on websites. Plaintiff alleges, therefore, that Google had the capacity to determine which clicks were fraudulent, but did nothing to prevent the click fraud, and did not adequately warn him about click fraud or investigate his complaints about click fraud. Plaintiff alleges that Google informed him that it did not keep records on an advertiser's account and click history for more than the most recent three months, and that Google disclaimed liability for clicks older than sixty days....

Plaintiff alleges Google charged him over $100,000 for AdWords from about January 2003 to December 31, 2005....

B. The Online Agreement and Forum Selection Clause

... It is undisputed that advertisers, including Plaintiff, were required to enter into an AdWords contract before placing any ads or incurring any charges.... To open an AdWords account, an advertiser had to have gone through a series of steps in an online sign-up process.... To activate the AdWords account, the advertiser had to have visited his account page, where he was shown the AdWords contract....

Toward the top of the page displaying the AdWords contract, a notice in bold print appeared and stated, "Carefully read the following terms and conditions. If you agree with these terms, indicate your assent below...." The terms and conditions were offered in a window, with a scroll bar that allowed the advertiser to scroll down and read the entire contract. The contract itself included the pre-amble and seven paragraphs, in twelve-point font. The contract's pre-amble, the first paragraph, and part of the second paragraph were clearly visible before scrolling down to read the rest of the contract. The preamble, visible at first impression, stated that consent to the terms listed in the Agreement constituted a binding agreement with Google. A link to a printer-friendly version of the contract was offered at the top of the contract window for the advertiser who would rather read the contract printed on paper or view it on a full-screen instead of scrolling down the window....

At the bottom of the webpage, viewable without scrolling down, was a box and the words, "Yes, I agree to the above terms and conditions:...." The advertiser had to have clicked on this box in order to proceed to the next step.... If the advertiser did not click on "Yes, I agree ..." and instead tried to click the "Continue" button at the bottom of the webpage, the advertiser would have been returned to the same page and could not advance to the next step. If the advertiser did not agree to the AdWords contract, he could not activate his account, place any ads, or incur any charges. Plaintiff had an account activated. He placed ads and charges were incurred....

IV. Discussion

... B. The Online AdWords Agreement is a Valid Express Contract.

1. The Clickwrap Agreement is Enforceable.

Plaintiff contends that the, online Ad-Words Agreement was not a valid, express contract, and that the law of implied contract applies. In support of this contention, Plaintiff argues that he, did not have notice of and did not assent to the terms of the Agreement. Implying that the contract lacked definite essential terms, but failing to brief the issue, Plaintiff argues that the contract did not include fixed price terms for services. He further argues that the AdWords Agreement presented does not set out a date when Plaintiff may have entered into the contract. As to the latter argument, the unrebutted Hsu Declaration states that the AdWords Agreement and online process presented went into effect at the time that Plaintiff activated his AdWords account.... Plaintiff has not presented any evidence to the contrary, nor does he allege that any agreement he made was different from the one presented through the Hsu Declaration. Thus, there is undisputed evidence that the AdWords Agreement presented is the same that Plaintiff activated with Defendant.

"Contracts are 'express' when the parties state their terms and 'implied' when the parties do not state their terms. The distinction is based not on the contracts' legal effect but on the way the parties manifest their mutual assent." "... There cannot be an implied-in-fact contract if there is an express contract that covers the same subject matter...."

The type of contract at issue here is commonly referred to as a "clickwrap" agreement. A clickwrap agreement appears on an internet webpage and requires that a user consent to any terms or conditions by clicking on a dialog box on the screen in order to proceed with the internet transaction.... Even though they are electronic, clickwrap agreements are considered to be writings because they are printable and storable....

To determine whether a clickwrap agreement is enforceable, courts presented with the issue apply traditional principles of contract law and focus on whether the plaintiffs had reasonable notice of and manifested assent to the clickwrap agreement.... Absent a showing of fraud, failure to read an enforceable clickwrap agreement, as with any binding contract, will not excuse compliance with its terms....

a. There was Reasonable Notice of and Mutual Assent to the Ad-Words Agreement.

Plaintiff claims he did not have notice or knowledge of the forum selection clause, and therefore that there was no "meeting of the minds" required for contract formation. In support of this argument, Plaintiff cites *Specht v. Netscape Comms. Corp.,* in which the Second Circuit held that internet users did not have reasonable notice of the terms in an online agreement and therefore did not assent to the agreement under the facts of that case....

The facts in *Specht,* however, are easily distinguishable from this case. There, the internet users were urged to click on a button to download free software.... There was no visible indication that clicking on the button meant that the user agreed to the terms and conditions of a proposed contract that contained an arbitration clause.... The only reference to terms was located in text visible if the users scrolled down to the next screen, which was "submerged...." Even if a user did scroll down, the terms were not immediately displayed.... Users would have had to click onto a hyperlink, which would take the user to a separate webpage entitled "License & Support Agreements...." Only on that webpage was a user informed that the user must agree to the license terms before downloading a product.... The user would have to choose from a list of license agreements and again click on yet another hyperlink in order to see the terms and conditions for the downloading of that particular software....

The Second Circuit concluded on those facts that there was not sufficient or reasonably conspicuous notice of the terms and that the plaintiffs could not have manifested assent to the terms under these conditions … The Second Circuit was careful to differentiate the method just described from clickwrap agreements which do provide sufficient notice.… Notably, the issue of notice and assent was not at issue with respect to a second agreement addressed in *Specht*.… In that clickwrap agreement, when users proceeded to initiate installation of a program, "they were automatically shown a scrollable text of that program's license agreement and were not permitted to complete the installation until they had clicked on a 'Yes' button to indicate that they had accepted all the license terms. If a user attempted to install [the program] without clicking 'Yes,' the installation would be aborted."

Through a similar process, the AdWords Agreement gave reasonable notice of its terms. In order to activate an AdWords account, the user had to visit a webpage which displayed the Agreement in a scrollable text box. Unlike the impermissible agreement in *Specht*, the user did not have to scroll down to a submerged screen or click on a series of hyperlinks to view the Agreement. Instead, text of the AdWords Agreement was immediately visible to the user, as was a prominent admonition in boldface to read the terms and conditions carefully, and with instruction to indicate assent if the user agreed to the terms.

That the user would have to scroll through the text box of the Agreement to read it in its entirety does not defeat notice because there was sufficient notice of the Agreement itself and clicking "Yes" constituted assent to all of the terms. The preamble, which was immediately visible, also made clear that assent to the terms was binding. The Agreement was presented in readable 12-point font. It was only seven paragraphs long — not so long so as to render scrolling down to view all of the terms inconvenient or impossible. A printer-friendly, full-screen version was made readily available. The user had ample time to review the document.

Unlike the impermissible agreement in *Specht*, the user here had to take affirmative action and click the "Yes, I agree to the above terms and conditions" button in order to proceed to the next step. Clicking "Continue" without clicking the "Yes" button would have returned the user to the same webpage. If the user did not agree to all of the terms, he could not have activated his account, placed ads, or incurred charges.…

A reasonably prudent internet user would have known of the existence of terms in the AdWords Agreement. Plaintiff had to have had reasonable notice of the terms. By clicking on "Yes, I agree to the above terms and conditions" button, Plaintiff indicated assent to the terms. Therefore, the requirements of an express contract for reasonable notice of terms and mutual assent are satisfied. Plaintiff's failure to read the Agreement, if that were the case, does not excuse him from being bound by his express agreement.

b. The AdWords Agreement is Enforceable Despite Its Lack of a Definite Price Term.

Plaintiff's argument that the Ad-Words Agreement is unenforceable because of failure to supply a definite, essential term as to price is without merit. Under California and Pennsylvania law, the price term is an essential term of a contract and must be supplied with sufficient definiteness for a contract to be enforceable.... If the parties, however, have agreed upon a practicable method of determining the price in the contract with reasonable certainty, such as through a market standard, the contract is enforceable....

The AdWords Agreement does not include a specific price term, but describes with sufficient definiteness a practicable process by which price is determined.... The premise of the AdWords program is that advertisers must bid for keywords or AdWords, and the highest bidder is placed at the top of the advertising hierarchy. Prices are determined by the market, with the keywords higher in demand garnering higher prices. Plaintiff had to have been aware of and understood the pricing process. Each time that he purchased keywords, he engaged in this process. At oral argument, Plaintiff explained the process by which price was determined and conceded that the process was outlined in the Agreement.... The court concludes that the Adwords Agreement is enforceable because it contained a practicable method of determining the market price with reasonable certainty.

Because there was an express contract covering the same conduct at issue (pay-per-click advertising under the Ad-Words program) and because the concepts of express and implied contracts are mutually exclusive and cannot co-exist, Plaintiff s argument of an implied contract is precluded as a matter of law. In addition, the Ad-Words Agreement provides that it constitutes the entire agreement between the parties, with the exception of any modifications in writing and executed by both parties....

2. The Clickwrap Agreement is not Unconscionable.

Plaintiff argues that the AdWords Agreement and in particular the forum selection clause are unconscionable. Unconscionability is a general defense to the enforcement of a contract or its specific terms.... Unconscionability has procedural and substantive components.... "The procedural component is satisfied by the existence of unequal bargaining positions and hidden terms common in the context of adhesion contracts. The substantive component is satisfied by overly harsh or one-sided results that 'shock the conscience....'" The party challenging the contractual provision has the burden to prove unconscionability....

a. The AdWords Agreement is not Procedurally Unconscionable.

Under California law, a contract or its terms may be procedurally unconscionable if it is an adhesion contract.... A contract of adhesion is a form or standardized contract prepared by a party of superior bargaining power, to be signed by the party in the weaker position, who only has the opportunity to agree to the contract or reject it, without an opportunity to negotiate or bargain....

The opportunity to negotiate by itself does not end the inquiry into procedural unconscionability. Courts consider factors such as the buyer's sophistication, the use of high-pressure tactics or external pressure to induce acceptance, and the availability of alternative sources of supply....

Plaintiff argues the AdWords Agreement was a contract of adhesion because it was not negotiated at arm's length and was offered on a "take it or leave it" basis, without an opportunity to bargain. Internet users had to agree to the terms in order to activate an AdWords account and purchase AdWords. Defendant counters that Plaintiff is a sophisticated purchaser, an attorney, who had full notice of the terms, who was capable of understanding them, and who assented to them. Plaintiff has not alleged high-pressure tactics or external pressure to accept the Agreement.

Defendant also argues that other internet providers offer similar advertising services, including MSN Search, AOL Search, Ask.com, Yahoo!, Excite, Infospace, and HotBot, and thus Plaintiff could have chosen to take his business elsewhere. Plaintiff counters that the availability of other internet service providers does not undercut the existence of an adhesion contract.... Plaintiff also asserts that only Yahoo offers comparable advertising and that Yahoo's sign up system is similar to Google's.

Plaintiff, however, has not offered any evidence in support of his assertion. As such, he has not met his affirmative burden on his summary judgment motion to make a sufficient showing that other online companies did not offer similar, competing advertising services, which lacked forum selection clauses.... On this factor in the analysis, the agreement stands up as not being procedurally unconscionable....

A contract is not necessarily one of adhesion simply because it is a form contract. Courts have recognized the prevalence and importance of standardized contracts in people's everyday lives.... Because Plaintiff was a sophisticated purchaser, was not in any way pressured to agree to the AdWords Agreement, was capable of understanding the Agreement's terms, consented to them, and could have rejected the Agreement with impunity, this court finds that the AdWords Agreement was not procedurally unconscionable.

E-signatures are also a newer problem presented by e-contracts. The individual states disagree as to how e-signatures should be used, if at all. The Uniform Electronic Transaction Act was adopted as a result.

4.9 The Uniform Electronic Transactions Act (UETA)

The Uniform Electronic Transactions Act (UETA) was passed to try to even out the different laws the states have about e-signatures, in part. The act was drafted in part by the American Law Institute, which also prepares Restatements of Law. The Act generally holds that signatures are not invalid legally just because they are electronic. For UETA to apply, both parties need to have agreed to buying/selling or licensing electronically.

Chapter Summary

Contracts are agreements that are legally enforceable. Express contracts are contracts where the terms are stated or written. Implied contracts are contracts implied by conduct. Sometimes, contracts can be voidable by one party, without that party suffering any liability for voiding it. Contracts are voidable for a variety of reasons, including duress and undue influence. On the other hand, contracts might be void because the subject matter of the contract is illegal, such as a contract to kill. Voidable contacts are different from void contracts.

There are three main types of contract law sources, which include the common law, the Uniform Commercial Code, and the Restatement of Contracts. The UCC applies to sales. The Restatement of Contracts is looked to when the other two types of law are silent on an issue.

To have a valid contract, there must be offer, acceptance, and consideration. An offer has to have some terms and be communicated to the other side. It must be accepted before it is revoked or rejected. For an acceptance, the offeree has to show through his actions or words that he agrees with the offer. For proper acceptance, the acceptance must "mirror" the offer; this is known as the mirror image concept. Whether the offeree accepts with actions or words depends upon whether the contract is a bilateral or uni-lateral contract. With a bilateral contract, each party is exchanging a promise. In a uni-lateral contract, one party is promising for the other party's performance.

In addition to offer and acceptance, there must be consideration for a legally binding contract. Consideration is something of value that is exchanged between the parties. Usually the courts will not look took closely at the actual value of the consideration.

Some contracts are required to be in writing by the Statute of Frauds. These con-tracts include ones for land, contracts that cannot be completed before one year is up, and for sales of goods valued at over or equal to five hundred dollars.

The UCC governs sales and leases of goods. If the UCC does not cover an issue, then common law will apply. Article 2 of the UCC covers the sales contracts for goods. Article 2A of the UCC covers the leasing contracts for goods. The two articles are similar.

E-contracts have raised new issues in contract law. In general, clicking the box on "I agree" to an on-line contract will be legally binding. E-signatures in contracts are one of the new issues in contract law. The Uniform Electronic Transaction Act seeks to even out state laws about electronic signatures, and states a signature is not invalid merely by being electronic.

Key Terms

Acceptance	Contract
Agreement	Counteroffer
Bilateral contract	Covenants
Capacity	Duress
"Clickwrap" agreement	E-signature
Consideration	Express contract

Forum selection clause
Fraud
Gift-giving
Goods
Implied contract
Lessee
Lessor
Merchant
Mirror image concept
Misrepresentation
Negotiation
Offer
Offeree
Offeror
Principled negotiator

Promise
Promisee
Promisor
Promissory estoppel
Quantum meruit
Specific performance
Statute of frauds
Substantial performance
Undue influence
Unilateral contract
Valid contract
Void contract
Voidable contract
Uniform Electronic Transactions
   Act (UETA)

Review Questions

1. What is necessary to form a legally binding contract?

2. When does the Uniform Commercial Code apply?

3. What is necessary to form an offer?

4. What is necessary to form an acceptance?

5. How is a bilateral contract different from a unilateral contract?

6. How are express contracts different from implied contracts?

7. Is a voidable contract automatically void?

8. When might a person not have capacity to make a contract?

9. What type of negotiator are you?

10. What are some tactics you can try in negotiation?

11. What types of contracts must be in writing?

12. What are some remedies for breach of contract?

13. Define the following: promisor, promisee, offeror, offeree, lessor, and lessee.

14. How are Articles 2 and 2A of the UCC similar and how are they different?

15. What are specific concerns raised by e-contracts?

16. What is a clickwrap agreement?

17. In the case *Feldman v. Google, Inc.*, why was the contract not considered an un-conscionable contract?

Web Links

The Uniform Commercial Code can be found online at: http://www.law.cornell.edu/ucc/ucc.table.html.

Exercises

1. Find and read a lease agreement. Identify the sections for the names of the parties, the property being leased, the time-period of the lease, and the amount of the rent.

2. Look at this website: http://hire-a-killer.com/. Be forewarned that although this website is attempting to be funny, it is offensive to some. This website is an example of illegal, or void, contracts. Let us say someone did actually wire them $8,000.00. What could potentially happen with that money?

3. Look up the table of contents for the UCC. You can use the web link above. What else does the UCC cover?

4. Attempt to draft your own employment agreement, by answering the following questions and looking up applicable clauses.

   a. Who is the employer and what is their address?

   b. What is your name and address?

   c. How long is the employment agreement for?

   d. Is the employment agreement renewable? How so?

   e. What is your position at the company going to be?

   f. What are your job duties?

   g. How many hours a week will you work?

   h. How will you be compensated?

   i. How you will be compensated for sick leave or vacations?

   j. Do you receive any benefits? For example, health insurance or a retirement plan?

   k. When and how can either party terminate the agreement?

Section III

Non-Corporate Business Entities

Chapter 5

Sole Proprietorships

Chapter Outline

Chapter Objectives

- Give the definition of sole proprietorship.

- Discuss the documents necessary for forming a sole proprietorship.

- Delineate financing for a sole proprietorship.

- Indicate that management can be an advantage or disadvantage to the sole proprietor.

- Explain how liability is the biggest disadvantage to being a sole proprietor.

- Describe another major disadvantage of sole proprietorships: continuity.

- List information about the profits, losses, and taxation of the sole proprietorship.

- Provide examples as to how the sole proprietorship is terminated.

- Introduce franchises.

5.1 Introduction to Sole Proprietorships

A sole proprietorship is a business owned by an individual, which can considered an extension of the individual. The business is not incorporated for limited liability. In fact, the sole proprietor has unlimited personal liability for the liabilities of the sole proprietorship, since essentially, the sole proprietor and the sole proprietorship are the same. The sole proprietorship is still the most common business entity as it is the easiest business entity to form, often only requiring a business license to start. While so many businesses are sole proprietorships in the United States, they do not make anywhere near the revenues that corporations do.

An example of a sole proprietorship would be The Law Offices of Emily Lynch Morissette. At one time, I had two office locations, but my law offices were owned and managed by me, a sole proprietor. I liked being a sole proprietor, as I did not want to have to deal with partners or filing quarterly, corporate taxes. I also enjoyed making all the business decisions and running my business as I saw fit. I enjoyed not having a bunch of paperwork to fill out, but just having to renew my business license every year. I reduced my liability by having legal malpractice insurance. In the state wherein I am located, I am not eligible as an attorney to be a limited liability company. In the chapter on limited liability companies, you will learn that this is a very popular business entity due to the limited liability it offers. However, some states do not allow certain professionals to form limited liability companies.

Another example of a sole proprietorship is a client of mine, a sole proprietor of a small, custom wood window business. This client was a one-man operation, who replaced windows in Craftsman homes. He worked only in one major metropolitan area. While he had enough work for himself, he did not have enough work for any partners. In addition, since he measured the windows and then built them off site, prior to installing the windows, he did not have a lot of liability. He did have liability insurance, but he did not necessarily need or want to be a limited liability company. In some states, there is a yearly fee for being a limited liability company, and for a small business, this might be cost prohibitive, especially if the business already has liability insurance and there is not a lot of liability inherent in the business.

The following case indicates that sole proprietorships are considered extensions of the individual as discussed in this section and that sole proprietorship business interests are personal property.

England v. Simmons
295 Ga. 1, 757 S.E.2d 111 (2014)

Robert Carl Haege died in December 2006. Three months earlier, Haege had made a will, in which he left his "personal assets" to his brother and sister, and in which he left his "business interests, both tangible and intangible, real or personal, connected to the business known as Traditional Fine Art, Ltd." to his brother, sister, and two longtime employees. After Haege died, questions arose about the disposition of property associated with Traditional Fine Art, Ltd., insofar as Traditional Fine Art *was a sole proprietorship and, therefore, had no legal existence separate and apart from Haege himself.* [emphasis added] The will was admitted to probate, and Sharon Haege England — Haege's sister — was appointed as executrix of his estate. England failed to distribute any property to James S. Simmons and Elery Stinson — the two longtime employees — and they filed this lawsuit against England, seeking a declaratory judgment as to the meaning of the will with respect to the property associated with Traditional Fine Art. The trial court entered a final judgment for England, concluding that, because Traditional Fine Art was only a sole proprietorship, the property associated with the business was merely the personal property of Haege, and there was, therefore, nothing to pass under the "business interests" provision of the will.

Simmons and Stinson appealed, and in a split decision, the Court of Appeals reversed. *Simmons v. England*, 323 Ga. App. 251 (746 SE2d 862) (2013). The majority of the Court of Appeals looked to the intention of the testator as evidenced by the plain terms of his will, and it concluded that Haege evidently meant to differentiate between his personal property "connected with the business known as Traditional Fine Art, Ltd." and his other "personal assets." Id. at 253–254. Noting that "the intention of the testator must prevail," and noting as well that "operation is to be given to every part of [the will] if this can be done without violating its terms or the intention of the testator," the Court of Appeals concluded that Simmons and Stinson were entitled — along with England and her brother — to share in any "business interests, both tangible and intangible, real or personal, connected to the business known as Traditional Fine Art, Ltd.," and the existence and identity of such property were "simply issues for the factfinder, which must identify the business interests." Id. (citations and punctuation omitted). Two judges dissented, reasoning as the trial court did that a sole proprietorship has no legal existence and that all property connected with the business was merely the personal property of Haege. Id. at 254–255 (Boggs, J., dissenting). On the petition of England, we issued a writ of certiorari to review the decision of the Court of Appeals, and we now affirm.

In this Court, England does not dispute the fundamental premise of the decision of the Court of Appeals — that a sole proprietor may separately dispose in his will of personal property connected with his sole proprietorship and his other personal property — and she is right not to dispute it.... Instead, England argues that Haege did not actually intend to separately dispose of any property associated with his sole proprietorship. In support of this argument, England points to the sentence of the will that immediately follows the provision leaving "business interests ... connected with the business known as Traditional Fine Art, Ltd.":

> It is specifically the intent of this provision that [James] S. Simmons enjoy, after this bequest, thirty[-]four (34%) percent of the outstanding member certificates, that Elery Stinson enjoy seventeen (17%) percent of the outstanding member certificates, [and] that James E. Haege and Sharon Haege England each enjoy twenty[-]four[-]and[-]one[-]half (24.5%) percent of the outstanding member certificates.

This sentence, England says, limits the "business interests" referenced in the preceding sentence to membership certificates evidencing ownership of Traditional Fine Art, and since it remained a sole proprietorship when Haege died, she concludes, there are no such membership certificates. The provision concerning "business interests," England argues, was meant to apply only in the event that Haege organized his sole proprietorship as a separate legal entity, which he never did.

The problem is, if Haege meant only to direct the disposition of nonexistent membership certificates, he could have done so quite simply with the sentence upon which England relies, and he could have omitted nearly all of the preceding sentence about "business interests." Moreover, that preceding sentence must refer to something more than membership certificates, insofar as the ownership interest represented by such certificates is indisputably intangible personal property, but in the preceding sentence, Haege referred to "all of my business interests, *both tangible and intangible, real or personal*, connected to the business known as Traditional Fine Art, Ltd." If such "business interests" only meant membership certificates, the references to tangible and real property would have no meaning and would, in fact, be nonsensical.

(1) Taking the will as a whole, the most natural and reasonable understanding of these provisions is that Haege left his personal property that amounted to "business interests ... connected to the business known as Traditional Fine Art, Ltd." — specifically including, but not limited to, membership certificates that he owned, if any — to Simmons, Stinson, and his brother and sister, and he left all of his other personal property to his brother and sister alone.... That is how the majority of the Court of Appeals understood the will, and it was correct to do so. We also find no error in the conclusion of the Court of Appeals that the precise identification of the property amounting to "business interests ... connected to the business known as Traditional Fine Art, Ltd." "are simply issues for the factfinder." *Simmons*, 323 Ga. App. at 254 (citation omitted). Accordingly, we affirm the judgment of the Court of Appeals.

5.2 Formation and Financing

A sole proprietorship is a popular type of business to create because it is easy to form. A sole proprietorship is begun by an individual starting to conduct business. State or federal governments do not have to provide approval for the sole proprietorship to exist. There is not a separate "sole proprietorship" form the individual has to file with the secretary of state. The tax return used is the individual's tax return, with a Schedule C (Profits and Losses of the Business) added, and not a separate tax return for the business. Some states and/or counties require a sole proprietorship to file a business license. The business license is a relatively quick and easy form to fill out with a nominal fee. If the sole proprietor has employees, he will use his Federal Employer Identification number on the tax return; otherwise, he will use his social security number. The Employer Identification Number form is found at: https:// www.irs-ein-tax-id.com/?gclid=Cj0KCQjwm9D0BRCMARIsAIfvfIbWZ2RoK9Hh HJ9X6EKJzbZPgAqHoWoIFCT7mZBgFYAzX1Q3-q4yizMaAjquEALw_wcB). If the sole proprietorship has a name different from the individual's name, then the individual should file what is known as a fictitious business name. The fictitious business name statement process can require publishing the name in a newspaper. This might also be called a "doing business as" application, depending upon the jurisdiction. Fictitious business name statements are discussed earlier in Chapter 3, but common questions asked on a fictitious business name statement are, but are not limited to the following:

- The fictitious business names;
- Location of the business;
- The mailing address of the business;
- The individual, corporation, partners names and addresses;
- What type of business it is;
- When the business first started; and
- Signatures of the responsible parties.

a. Public Document: Business License

Though there is not much paperwork, most sole proprietorships do have to fill out at least a business license. Most municipal areas require a business license in order for the sole proprietorship to be legally in business. This requirement can and often does apply to door-to-door salespeople. Information that is commonly requested on a business license application, includes, but is not limited to the following:

- Business name;
- Business address;
- Mailing address;
- Other contact information;
- A description of the business;
- An indication of what type of business it is;
- The federal identification number, social security number, or state identification number;
- Whether the business has a resale number or contractor's license;
- The names and information of the owners/partners/officers of the business; and
- Signatures of the responsible parties.

The business license is discussed further in Chapter 3, as the business license is actually a necessity of almost any type of business.

b. Private Document: An "Agreement"

There is a legal fiction that the sole proprietorship has an agreement, which is the private document that forms the sole proprietorship. Of course, it is technically impossible to form an agreement without at least two parties.

c. Financing

One of the difficulties, in starting or in growing the business, is the sole proprietor does not have unlimited capital. The sole proprietor must frequently go into debt to raise the money necessary to start or grow the business. Even when going into debt, the sole proprietor will be limited in what she can borrow, based upon her assets. Going back to the example of my business, I was lucky in that I had been working as an attorney at a few law firms prior to starting my business. Thus, when I started my business, I did not have to spend much on advertising, as I already had people referring business to me. I did have to spend money on nice office furniture, office equipment (such as computers, printers/faxes, etc.), and on rent. I tried to make sure that my rent was one that I could reasonably afford, based upon my estimate of what my income as a sole proprietor would be. Using the example of my window-making client, he did not have to spend a lot of upfront capital either, as he had been working for companies previously and was able to get referrals that way. He was able to make the windows out of his garage and he got an upfront cost from his clients so that he would be able to purchase wood for making the windows. These businesses are in contrast to a business that might take many upfront costs, such a restaurant. A restaurant needs a space large enough to seat clients, it needs a build out (a kitchen if the space does not already have one, décor, etc.), and has to hire employees in all likelihood (cooks, servers, etc.).

Of course, the sole proprietor can still use any personal funds he has. Before the housing crisis, sole proprietors frequently took loans against their houses to fund the sole proprietorship. After the economy worsened, many sole proprietors did not have a house they could borrow against, so they borrowed against their retirement funds.

5.3 Management

a. A Double-Edged Sword

The sole proprietor fully manages the business by herself. This includes decisions on whether to hire and fire employees. If the sole proprietor is a good businessperson, this is typically not a problem. However, if the sole proprietor is a bad businessperson, this becomes a major problem. In the latter instance, the sole proprietor could delegate management decisions to a manager, but the sole proprietor would still be responsible for those decisions. If a sole proprietor does not delegate management, a sole proprietor will often at least hire an accountant or a marketer who will help him with many types of decisions.

The sole proprietor also gets to make more enjoyable management decisions such as when to take a vacation or what types of new business he should pursue. Thus, you could say that a sole proprietorship's management allows for more flexibility for the sole proprietor. Management is also more flexible because the sole proprietor does not have to manage with other partners or directors.

5.4 Liability

The sole proprietor is fully liable for his own debts, incurred in the course of conducting his business. This is because the law treats sole proprietorships like the arm of the sole proprietor — they are the same, connected. Thus, when a sole proprietorship is sued, the sole proprietor is being sued. The sole proprietor is also responsible for acts committed by his employees on his behalf, if those acts were negligent. He has unlimited personal liability for those debts. Being personally liable means the sole proprietor's assets outside the business could be taken to pay his business debts, if the business debts are greater than the business assets. Thus, the proprietor's personal bank account, car, home, and even sometimes his retirement accounts could be taken to pay his business debts.

For instance, the window maker goes to a home to measure for windows. The owners have not moved vases that are in front of the windows and as the window maker is moving the vases so he can measure, he drops one and breaks it. It is a very expensive vase, worth five hundred thousand dollars. He has insurance of two hundred and fifty thousand dollars. He has fifty thousand dollars in business assets (his woodworking tools). He owns a two hundred thousand dollar condominium, which is a personal asset. This is how his insurance and assets would be utilized to pay a settlement amount of five hundred thousand dollars.

- The two hundred and fifty dollar insurance policy money would be applied to the five hundred thousand dollar lawsuit settlement first.
- The fifty thousand dollars raised by selling his business assets would be applied to the five hundred thousand dollar lawsuit second.
- Finally, the two hundred thousand dollars raised by selling his personal assets would be applied to the five hundred thousand dollar lawsuit.

Usually, unlimited personal liability is not as big of a deal as it sounds, because the sole proprietor can buy insurance to protect himself, up to at least the amount of his policy. However, if you look at the example above, although the vase is not technically related to the process of making the windows, the window maker could still be liable for breaking the vase. Thus, when a client becomes a sole proprietor, it is beneficial if the law firm reminds the client that they can have liability outside of the immediate purpose of the business. If the business is indeed highly risky, the sole proprietor may not be able to obtain insurance at all. If a client has many assets or is in a highly risky business, the client will often do better to incorporate, if possible, due to the unlimited personal liability.

Another way a sole proprietor could attempt to limit his liability is through contracts. At least between him and the other party, the sole proprietor would be able to limit some of his liability with different contractual clauses. If you have read shrink wrap agreements, those contracts are in fact usually limiting the liability of the company for liability that might result from downloading their product. However, even with a contract in place, an unanticipated disaster may arise, for which the sole proprietor would still have unlimited personal liability.

5.5 Continued Existence of Business and Transferability

One of the unfortunate aspects of being a sole proprietor is that it is not normally easy to sell the business, particularly if the business involves services. If a client hires The Law Offices of Emily Lynch Morissette, they want the services of Emily Lynch Morissette, Esq., and not Joe Schmoe, Esq. This causes difficulties in selling the business (here, other than the client list) or leaving it in a will it to heirs. In fact, usually, once the sole proprietor passes away and the business is bequeathed to a child, a new sole proprietorship needs to be created.

5.6 Profits and Losses

A sole proprietor owns the entire business, so therefore he has the right to all the profits and responsibilities for the losses of the business. Profits could include profits from the sale of services, goods, or both. For taxes, the sole proprietor is not obligated to take a mere portion of the profits or losses (as he might have to if he were part of a partnership), but instead can take one hundred percent of both on his personal taxes.

5.7 Taxation

The sole proprietorship has beneficial federal and state taxation. One of the benefits to being a sole proprietorship is the ability to add a Schedule C to the sole proprietor's regular 1040, individual income tax return. This is the federal tax return. The Schedule C indicates the profits and losses from the sole proprietorship. The losses reduce the sole proprietor's profits, on which he has to pay tax. It is common for businesses to have more losses than profits in at least the first two years of doing business. Usually, these losses can be taken against other profits.

The Schedule C, Profit or Loss from Business (Sole Proprietorship) also allows the sole proprietor to deduct certain expenses from his profits. Potentially qualifying expenses include, but are not limited to the following:

- Advertising
- Car expenses for vehicles in service for business purposes,

- Contract labor,
- Employee benefit plans if the sole proprietor has employees,
- Insurance other than health insurance (so malpractice insurance could qualify),
- Interest,
- Mortgage payments, if any,
- Legal and professional services,
- Home office expenses, if part of the home is used in business,
- Rent,
- Repairs and maintenance,
- Supplies,
- Taxes and licenses (this could include the business license),
- Travel, meals, and entertainment (might only be at fifty percent of the value),
- Travel,
- Utilities, and
- Wages.

The individual tax rate is a benefit so long as the sole proprietor is not in an extremely high tax bracket, as the profits of the business will be taxed at the individual's tax rate. Normally individual tax rates are lower than corporate tax rates so the individual tax bracket is beneficial to the sole proprietor.

In addition to these taxation rules, a sole proprietor should pay self-employment tax and FICA. FICA stands for the Federal Insurance Contributions Act and is a combination of Social Security and Medicare tax. This would have to be paid for both the sole proprietor and any employees he may hire. A sole proprietor can set up a retirement plan for himself. This would usually be a Keogh plan, which is for self-employed persons. A Keogh plan is a qualified retirement plan, which allows the sole proprietorship to have tax benefits from a retirement plan. The sole proprietor would earn interest on the amounts he contributed to the plan and then not have to pay taxes until he takes funds out of the plan, usually for retirement.

If the sole proprietor has employees, he will also need to file for a federal employer identification number, which is discussed earlier in Chapter 3.

5.8 Termination

The sole proprietor merely needs to decide to terminate the business, and then he can do so. He does not have to file any legal documents, other than filing the final Schedule C to the Form 1040. It is a good idea to notify the entity that issued him a business license that he is ceasing to do business as a sole proprietorship. He should

| SCHEDULE C
(Form 1040)

Department of the Treasury
Internal Revenue Service (99) | **Profit or Loss From Business**
(Sole Proprietorship)
▶ Go to *www.irs.gov/ScheduleC* for instructions and the latest information.
▶ Attach to Form 1040, 1040-SR, 1040-NR, or 1041; partnerships generally must file Form 1065. | OMB No. 1545-0074

Attachment
Sequence No. 09 |

Name of proprietor	Social security number (SSN)

A Principal business or profession, including product or service (see instructions)

B Enter code from instructions ▶

C Business name. If no separate business name, leave blank.

D Employer ID number (EIN) (see instr.)

E Business address (including suite or room no.) ▶
City, town or post office, state, and ZIP code

F Accounting method: **(1)** ☐ Cash **(2)** ☐ Accrual **(3)** ☐ Other (specify) ▶

G Did you "materially participate" in the operation of this business during 2020? If "No," see instructions for limit on losses . ☐ Yes ☐ No

H If you started or acquired this business during 2020, check here . . . . ▶ ☐

I Did you make any payments in 2020 that would require you to file Form(s) 1099? See instructions . . . . ☐ Yes ☐ No

J If "Yes," did you or will you file required Form(s) 1099? . . . . ☐ Yes ☐ No

Part I   Income

1	Gross receipts or sales. See instructions for line 1 and check the box if this income was reported to you on Form W-2 and the "Statutory employee" box on that form was checked . . . . ▶ ☐	1	
2	Returns and allowances	2	
3	Subtract line 2 from line 1	3	
4	Cost of goods sold (from line 42)	4	
5	**Gross profit.** Subtract line 4 from line 3	5	
6	Other income, including federal and state gasoline or fuel tax credit or refund (see instructions)	6	
7	**Gross income.** Add lines 5 and 6 . . . . ▶	7	

Part II   Expenses. Enter expenses for business use of your home **only** on line 30.

8	Advertising	8		18	Office expense (see instructions)	18	
9	Car and truck expenses (see instructions)	9		19	Pension and profit-sharing plans .	19	
				20	Rent or lease (see instructions):		
10	Commissions and fees .	10		a	Vehicles, machinery, and equipment	20a	
11	Contract labor (see instructions)	11		b	Other business property . . .	20b	
12	Depletion	12		21	Repairs and maintenance . . .	21	
13	Depreciation and section 179 expense deduction (not included in Part III) (see instructions)	13		22	Supplies (not included in Part III) .	22	
				23	Taxes and licenses	23	
				24	Travel and meals:		
14	Employee benefit programs (other than on line 19) . .	14		a	Travel	24a	
				b	Deductible meals (see instructions)	24b	
15	Insurance (other than health)	15		25	Utilities	25	
16	Interest (see instructions):			26	Wages (less employment credits) .	26	
a	Mortgage (paid to banks, etc.)	16a		27a	Other expenses (from line 48) . .	27a	
b	Other	16b		b	**Reserved for future use** . . .	27b	
17	Legal and professional services	17					

28	**Total expenses** before expenses for business use of home. Add lines 8 through 27a . . . . . . ▶	28	
29	Tentative profit or (loss). Subtract line 28 from line 7	29	
30	Expenses for business use of your home. Do not report these expenses elsewhere. Attach Form 8829 unless using the simplified method. See instructions. **Simplified method filers only:** Enter the total square footage of (a) your home: _____ and (b) the part of your home used for business: _____ . Use the Simplified Method Worksheet in the instructions to figure the amount to enter on line 30	30	
31	**Net profit or (loss).** Subtract line 30 from line 29. • If a profit, enter on both **Schedule 1 (Form 1040), line 3,** and on **Schedule SE, line 2.** (If you checked the box on line 1, see instructions). Estates and trusts, enter on **Form 1041, line 3.** • If a loss, you **must** go to line 32.	31	
32	If you have a loss, check the box that describes your investment in this activity. See instructions. • If you checked 32a, enter the loss on both **Schedule 1 (Form 1040), line 3,** and on **Schedule SE, line 2.** (If you checked the box on line 1, see the line 31 instructions). Estates and trusts, enter on **Form 1041, line 3.** • If you checked 32b, you **must** attach **Form 6198.** Your loss may be limited.	32a ☐ All investment is at risk. 32b ☐ Some investment is not at risk.	

For Paperwork Reduction Act Notice, see the separate instructions.   Cat. No. 11334P   Schedule C (Form 1040) 2020

pay all remaining liabilities and finish his business prior to termination. The sole proprietor could just decide to end the business, or he could try to sell his business. If he attempts to sell his business, then continuity problems, discussed earlier, arise. When selling the sole proprietorship, the sole proprietor is really selling two things: business assets and the goodwill of the business. The goodwill of the business is that

Schedule C (Form 1040) 2020 Page **2**

Part III   **Cost of Goods Sold** (see instructions)

33   Method(s) used to value closing inventory: **a** ☐ Cost   **b** ☐ Lower of cost or market   **c** ☐ Other (attach explanation)

34   Was there any change in determining quantities, costs, or valuations between opening and closing inventory? If "Yes," attach explanation . . . . ☐ Yes   ☐ No

35	Inventory at beginning of year. If different from last year's closing inventory, attach explanation . . .	35
36	Purchases less cost of items withdrawn for personal use	36
37	Cost of labor. Do not include any amounts paid to yourself	37
38	Materials and supplies	38
39	Other costs	39
40	Add lines 35 through 39	40
41	Inventory at end of year	41
42	**Cost of goods sold.** Subtract line 41 from line 40. Enter the result here and on line 4	42

Part IV   **Information on Your Vehicle.** Complete this part **only** if you are claiming car or truck expenses on line 9 and are not required to file Form 4562 for this business. See the instructions for line 13 to find out if you must file Form 4562.

43   When did you place your vehicle in service for business purposes? (month/day/year)   ▶   /   /

44   Of the total number of miles you drove your vehicle during 2020, enter the number of miles you used your vehicle for:

a   Business _____   **b** Commuting (see instructions) _____   **c** Other _____

45   Was your vehicle available for personal use during off-duty hours? . . . . ☐ Yes   ☐ No

46   Do you (or your spouse) have another vehicle available for personal use? . . . . ☐ Yes   ☐ No

47a   Do you have evidence to support your deduction? . . . . ☐ Yes   ☐ No

b   If "Yes," is the evidence written? . . . . ☐ Yes   ☐ No

Part V   **Other Expenses.** List below business expenses not included on lines 8–26 or line 30.

48	**Total other expenses.** Enter here and on line 27a	48

Schedule C (Form 1040) 2020

certain something that makes a consumer patronize that business over another. It is much harder to evaluate the value of goodwill than the actual business assets.

The sole proprietorship may also terminate when the sole proprietor dies. The sole proprietorship would be part of the sole proprietor's estate until a new owner takes over.

5.9 Franchises

Franchises are discussed here because many sole proprietors decide to start a business with the security of a franchise framework around them. This gives the sole proprietor the resources of a major organization. It is in between being an employee for someone else and completely owning your own business, which would use your own business concept. The sole proprietor gets the benefit of the franchise's name recognition as well. Franchises also can be other types of businesses, such as partnerships and corporations.

A franchise allows one party (here, the sole proprietor) to use the franchisor's name, trademarks, and other intellectual property to sell goods or services. The sole proprietor would be a separate business, apart from the franchisor. This allows the franchisor to avoid vicarious liability for the actions of the sole proprietor. The sole proprietor is treated like an independent contractor. The franchisor needs to be careful not to make it look like the sole proprietor is an agent of the franchisor. Issues of vicarious liability are discussed in the following case, *Kerl v. Dennis Rasmussen, Inc.* You will note that in the following case, Dennis was incorporated, and not a sole proprietor. The outcome would be the same if Dennis were a sole proprietor, though. Plaintiffs argued that Arby's was vicariously liable, as the franchisor, for the franchisee's negligent supervision of Pierce. Plaintiffs would have preferred Arby's to be liable as Arby's has deeper pockets than just Dennis Rasmussen, Inc. (DRI), the franchisee of Arby's. Pierce, an employee of (DRI), shot and killed two people. However, the court found that Arby's was not vicariously liable for this crime.

Kerl v. Dennis Rasmussen, Inc.

2004 WI 86, 273 Wis. 2d 106, 682 N.W.2d 328

This case involves a claim of franchisor vicarious liability under the doctrine of respondeat superior. At issue is whether and under what circumstances a franchisor may be vicariously liable for the negligence of its franchisee.

The issue arises in the context of a damages lawsuit stemming from a horrific crime. Harvey Pierce ambushed and shot Robin Kerl and her fiance David Jones in the parking lot of a Madison Wal-Mart where Kerl and Jones worked. Kerl was seriously injured in the shooting, and Jones was killed. Pierce, who was Kerl's former boyfriend, then shot and killed himself. At the time of the shooting, Pierce was a work-release inmate at the Dane County jail who was employed at a nearby Arby's restaurant operated by Dennis Rasmussen, Inc. ("DRI"). Pierce had left work without permission at the time of the attempted murder and murder/suicide.

Kerl and Jones' estate sued DRI and Arby's, Inc. As is pertinent to this appeal, the plaintiffs alleged that Arby's is vicariously liable, as DRI's franchisor, for DRI's negligent supervision of Pierce....

Vicarious liability under the doctrine of respondeat superior depends upon the existence of a master/servant agency relationship. Vicarious liability under respondeat superior is a form of liability without fault — the imposition of liability on an innocent party for the tortious conduct of another based upon the existence of a particularized agency relationship. As such, it is an exception to our fault-based liability system, and is imposed only where the principal has control or the right to control the physical conduct of the agent such that a master/servant relationship can be said to exist.

A franchise is a business format typically characterized by the franchisee's operation of an independent business pursuant to a license to use the franchisor's trademark or trade name. A franchise is ordinarily operated in accordance with a detailed franchise or license agreement designed to protect the integrity of the trademark by setting uniform quality, marketing, and operational standards applicable to the franchise.

The rationale for vicarious liability becomes somewhat attenuated when applied to the franchise relationship, and vicarious liability premised upon the existence of a master/servant relationship is conceptually difficult to adapt to the franchising context. If the operational standards included in the typical franchise agreement for the protection of the franchisor's trademark were broadly construed as capable of meeting the "control or right to control" test that is generally used to determine respondeat superior liability, then franchisors would almost always be exposed to vicarious liability for the torts of their franchisees. We see no justification for such a broad rule of franchisor vicarious liability. If vicarious liability is to be imposed against franchisors, a more precisely focused test is required.

We conclude that the marketing, quality, and operational standards commonly found in franchise agreements are insufficient to establish the close supervisory control or right of control necessary to demonstrate the existence of a master/servant relationship for all purposes or as a general matter. We hold, therefore, that a franchisor may be held vicariously liable for the tortious conduct of its franchisee only if the franchisor has control or a right of control over the daily operation of the specific aspect of the franchisee's business that is alleged to have caused the harm.

Here, although the license agreement between Arby's and DRI imposed many quality and operational standards on the franchise, Arby's did not have control or the right to control DRI's supervision of its employees. Summary judgment dismissing the plaintiffs' vicarious liability claims against Arby's was properly granted....

Article 6 of the license agreement addresses the issue of personnel. As to management personnel, the agreement requires a designated officer or shareholder of the licensee to attend an Arby's management training seminar. As to personnel generally, the agreement provides: "LICENSEE shall hire, train, maintain and properly supervise sufficient, qualified and courteous personnel for the efficient operations of the Licensed Business."

In February 1999, DRI hired Harvey Pierce to work at its restaurant. At the time, Pierce was a work-release inmate at the Dane County Jail. In the mid-afternoon of June 11, 1999, Pierce walked off the job without permission. He then crossed the street to the Wal-Mart store parking lot, where he lay in wait for Robin Kerl, his former girlfriend, and David Jones, her fiance, both Wal-Mart employees. When Kerl and Jones emerged from the building, Pierce shot them both in the head. He then shot himself. Jones and Pierce died of their injuries. Kerl survived but sustained serious injuries and is permanently disabled.…

A. Vicarious Liability

A person is generally only liable for his or her own torts.… Under certain circumstances, however, the law will impose vicarious liability on a person who did not commit the tortious conduct but nevertheless is deemed responsible by virtue of the close relationship between that person and the tortfeasor. The doctrine of respondeat superior ("let the master answer"), less frequently referred to as the master/servant rule, has been well-settled in the law of agency for perhaps as long as 250 years.… Vicarious liability under respondeat superior is "liability that a supervisory party (such as an employer) bears for the actionable conduct of a subordinate or associate (such as an employee) because of the relationship between the two parties.…"

"Under the doctrine of respondeat superior, a master is subject to liability for the tortious acts of his or her servant." … A prerequisite to vicarious liability under respondeat superior is the existence of a master/servant relationship.…

… This court adopted the definition of "servant" in § 220 of the Restatement (Second) of Agency: "[a] servant is one employed to perform service for another in his affairs and who, with respect to his physical conduct in the performance of the service, is subject to the other's control or right to control.…" Conversely, a "master" is "a principal who employs an agent to perform service in his affairs and who controls or has the right to control the physical conduct of the other in the performance of the service.…"

The master/servant relationship is a species of agency; all servants are agents but not every agent is a servant.… Unless an agent is also a servant, his principal will not be vicariously liable for his tortious conduct except under certain limited circumstances.

Vicarious liability is a form of strict liability without fault. A master may be held liable for a servant's torts regardless of whether the master's own conduct is tortious. Although a plaintiff who suffers a single injury may plead both vicarious and direct liability claims against a party who is asserted to be a master (as was done here), vicarious liability is a separate and distinct theory of liability, and should not be confused with any direct liability that may flow from the master's own fault in bringing about the plaintiff's harm. Vicarious liability is imputed liability. It is imposed upon an innocent party for the torts of another because the nature of the agency relationship — specifically the element of control or right of control — justifies it.

Vicarious liability under respondeat superior typically arises in employer/employee relationships but is not confined to this type of agency. A servant need not be under formal contract to perform work for a master, nor is it necessary for a person to be paid in order to occupy the position of servant.…

While a servant need not be paid in order to expose the master to liability for the servant's torts, it is well-settled that except under certain limited circumstances, a master will only be liable for torts of the servant committed within the scope of the servant's employment.... A deviation or stepping away from the master's business—a "frolic and detour" in the language of the early common law—may preclude vicarious liability. The question whether a tortfeasor was acting within the scope of employment at the time the injury was inflicted is normally for the jury to determine. This "scope of employment" question is often the main point of contention in a suit for damages predicated on a theory of vicarious liability.

A person who contracts to perform services for another but is not a servant is an independent contractor.... An independent contractor is "a person who contracts with another to do something for him but who is not controlled by the other nor subject to the other's right to control with respect to his physical conduct in the performance of the undertaking." ... The use of the label "independent contractor" in the contract between the parties is not by itself dispositive; the test looks beyond labels to factual indicia of control or right to control....

Perhaps the most commonly seen franchise is the chain-style franchise. The franchisor lets the sole proprietor make and sell the goods or services through a retail store. This would include most fast food chains. The sole proprietor or franchisee is normally allowed to select where to put the franchise and whom to hire.

The Federal Trade Commission requires franchisors to make disclosures to franchisees, prior to selling franchisees. These disclosures could include information about the franchises making a certain amount in actual sales. If the franchisor puts out information about projected sales, based upon hypotheticals, then it has to disclose the percentage of franchises that make this amount, and that these results are not a guarantee. The FTC also requires other franchisor disclosures, such as: litigation, bankruptcies, fees, estimates of costs, what goods have to be bought from the franchisor, the number of franchisees, how many franchisees have gone out of business recently, and sample contracts.

a. Franchise Agreement

The franchisor usually looks into the sole proprietor's background, through an application, to determine if this is a good fit. If it is, the parties may enter into a franchise agreement. The franchise agreement will discuss:

- how to get the goods or services up to the standards the franchisor has,
- how to train employees,
- how to not compete against the franchisor,
- how much money the sole proprietor needs to front,
- how the sole proprietor can use the franchisor's intellectual property, and
- how disputes will be resolved between the parties.

Franchise fees are numerous, and can include:

- licensing fees,
- royalties,

- assessments for advertising,

- leasing fees,

- supply fees,

- consulting fees,

- supply fees, and

- there may be an annual fee based on sales.

Fees are probably the biggest area of contention in franchise agreements. Franchises can cost a lot and the companies selling them often want a lot of the money up front. Many franchisees do not want to buy the supplies from the franchisor because it is often more expensive from buying the supplies on the open market. If the sole proprietor does not pay some or all of these fees, it can rise to wrongful termination of the franchise agreement.

Chapter Summary

In a sole proprietorship, the owner and the business are the same. The sole proprietorship is the easiest business to form, and hence they are the most common type of business entity in the United States. It is also a cheap business entity to form. In general, the only form that must be filled out as a sole proprietor is the business license. If the sole proprietor does have employees, then he will also need to obtain a Federal Employer Identification Number. If the sole proprietor does not have just his last name in the business title, then he may need to file a fictitious business name statement.

Financing the business can be difficult because the sole proprietor only has his own assets or the loan he can obtain based on his assets. The sole proprietor gets to make all the management decisions, which can be a bad thing if the sole proprietor is not a good business manager. On the positive side, as a manager, the sole proprietor gets to determine what business opportunities he should chose and when to go on vacation.

The number one disadvantage to being a sole proprietor is the unlimited personal liability the sole proprietor has for the debts and obligations of the sole proprietorship. However, the sole proprietor can seek insurance for at least some of these liabilities. Whatever insurance and business assets do not cover leaves the sole proprietor's personal assets exposed.

Another downside to the sole proprietorship is that it is difficult to bequeath or sell the business (this is known as the continuity of the business), as most consumers want to deal with the original individual who owned the business. The sole proprietor owns all the assets as well as all of the liabilities of the business. The pass-through taxation, wherein the sole proprietor can just add a schedule of the profits and losses of the business to his individual tax return is normally a benefit of doing business as a sole proprietor. In part, this is because of the ease of just filing a Schedule C but also because it is normally cheaper to pay taxes at individual, rather than corporate tax rates.

To terminate the business, the sole proprietor does not need to notify the state or federal government. However, it is a good idea for the sole proprietor to notify the entity that issued him the business license that he will no longer exist as a sole proprietorship.

Franchises are discussed in the sole proprietorship chapter because many sole proprietors decide to open up a business wherein they receive some resources, from the franchisor. However, other types of businesses can participate in a franchise. A franchise allows one party, here the sole proprietor, to use the name and intellectual property of the franchisor in selling goods or services.

In general, the franchisor and the sole proprietor will not be responsible for the other's negligence. This is because the sole proprietor will be considered an independent contractor, unless the franchisor did something to make the sole proprietor look like an agent.

The most commonly seen type of franchise is a chain-style one. In this type of franchise, the franchisor lets the sole proprietor make and sell goods or services through a retail store. A franchise agreement will probably at least discuss how to maintain the franchisor's quality standards, how to train employees, how not to compete against the franchisor, and how disputes between the parties will be resolved.

There can be many different types of fees associated with franchises, including licensing fees, royalties, assessments, leasing fees, and supply fees. If the sole proprietor does not pay these fees, he may be found to be in breach of the franchise agreement.

Key Terms

Assessment

Chain-style franchise

Doing business as (d.b.a.)

Fictitious business name (FBN) statement

Franchise

Franchise Agreement

Franchisor

Goodwill

Insurance

Personal liability

Respondeat superior

Sole proprietor

Unlimited personal liability

Vicarious liability

Review Questions

1. Why are sole proprietorships such a common business entity in the United States?

2. Although there are not many forms in starting a sole proprietorship, which one(s) may be necessary?

3. Why can flexible management be both a benefit and a hindrance to a sole proprietor?

4. What is the biggest disadvantage of being a sole proprietor? What are some ways in which a sole proprietor could limit this disadvantage?

5. What, if any, are the tax benefits of being a sole proprietor?

6. It is easy to buy and sell a sole proprietorship? Why or why not?

7. How are the taxes paid in a sole proprietorship?

8. What disclosures does the Federal Trade Commission require of franchisors to franchisees?

9. According to *Kerl v. Dennis Rasmussen, Inc.*, when can a franchisor be held vicariously liable for its franchisee?

Web Links

A great website for starting up a small business is the Small Business Administration's website: https://www.sba.gov/.

Search the Federal trade Commission's website regarding franchises. https://www.ftc.gov/.

Visit the resources available at The National Federation of Independent Business, which even has a small business "playbook": http://www.nfib.com/business-resources/.

Exercises

1. Cora is delivering cakes for her sole proprietorship, when she accidentally rear-ends the car in front of her. She has car insurance, which does cover her business, in the amount of fifteen thousand per person, thirty thousand per accident. There were four people in the car she rear-ended. Each of the four has to be rushed to the hospital and has varying degrees of injuries, which total, altogether, one hundred thousand dollars. Where will the hundred thousand dollars be taken from?

2. Find and review a franchise agreement. Circle the portions of the agreement that deal with quality standards, employee training, competition, money, intellectual property, and dispute resolution.

Chapter 6

General Partnerships

Chapter Outline

Chapter Objectives

- Provide a definition for general partnership.

- Lay out the formation of a general partnership.

- Outline how a general partnership is financed.

- Explain how a general partnership is managed.

- Describe how liability in a general partnership can be even worse than in a sole proprietorship.

- Indicate the rules regarding continuation of the general partnership.

- Go into detail about the distribution of profits and losses among partners.

- Discuss taxation of a general partnership.
- Show how a partnership is terminated.

6.1 Introduction to General Partnerships

The Uniform Partnership Act of 1914 still provides a good definition of partnership: "an association of two or more persons to carry on as co-owners of a business for profit." This definition has many different elements to it, which bear a closer look.

An association implies that the general partnership is a voluntary one. The association element makes general partnerships different from principal-agency relationships, although the two are very similar in other ways. In a principal-agent relationship, the agent is not on an equal footing with the principal and does not have an ownership interest in the business, where in a general partnership, each partner does.

The next element from this definition, though it seems very basic, is that the general partnership is inherently different from sole proprietorship as it has more than one person. General partnerships are sometimes volatile, and partners are added and deleted. If it ever gets down to one partner, it is important to remind the client that his business is no longer a general partnership.

"Persons" in this context means real or artificial persons. A real person is one you can touch. An artificial person is a business entity. Business entities are granted various levels of "human" legal rights in court. In a general partnership, business entities could be the partners, like two corporations. When Compaq and Hewlett-Packard formed a partnership, this was an example of two corporations becoming a general partnership. This is the smarter way to form a general partnership than to have two unincorporated entities form a general partnership. Like the famous anti-drunk-driving campaign, "Friends don't let friends general partnership." This is because unless the client is already protected by an underlying business entity, general partners are liable for their own acts and the acts of the other partners. This is a huge amount of personal liability, much greater than in a sole proprietorship.

The carry on element refers to an active business. An active business is one that is seeking new business, rather than attempting to wind up the business, retire, etc. As co-owners of the business, the partners share the profits and the management of the general partnership.

Finally, the goal should be to make a profit. However, this is not always the reality. The vast majority of businesses, in a normal economy, do not make any profit for at least two years. However, a business organization that does not have profit as its goal, such as a nonprofit, would be excluded from being a general partnership under this definition.

The law that mainly governs general partnership law is now the Revised Uniform Partnership Act (RUPA), which is in large part based upon the Uniform Partnership Act (UPA), which some of the states still follow. When states adopt the UPA or

RUPA, they usually put their own spin on it. In addition, partnerships are also regulated by the partnership's agreement and the common law in which state they are organized. Under RUPA, the partnership is considered separate from the partners, however, the older laws found that partnerships were merely extensions of the partners, and some of that reasoning is still prevalent. The partnership can own property in its partnership name, it can make contracts, and it can be sued or sue in the partnership's name in court.

The other major difference between UPA and RUPA, which will be discussed in detail infra, is regarding the withdrawal or leaving, by a partner, from the partnership. Very broadly, under the UPA, it was almost too easy for the partnership to be forced to dissolve, because anytime a partner left, the partnership had to dissolve. RUPA was enacted in part to help prevent all these unnecessary, and sometimes unwanted, dissolutions.

The following case is about one company attempting to argue that there is an implied partnership. While the company did not win, this case is helping to read to determine what a court looks at when determining whether an implied general partnership will be found. Pay particular attention to the court finding that there was not profit sharing, not sharing of assets, and not sharing of losses.

Big Easy Cajun Corp. v. Dallas Galleria Ltd.
293 S.W.3d 345 (2009)

Dallas Galleria Limited sued appellants on two imputed liability theories: limited partnership and single business enterprise. The trial court granted appellants a directed verdict on the limited partnership theory, but Dallas Galleria Limited obtained a jury verdict — and the trial court signed a judgment — on the single business enterprise theory. Both parties appealed the judgment on multiple grounds. For the reasons discussed below, we reverse the trial court's judgment and render judgment that Dallas Galleria Limited take nothing by its suit against appellants.

BACKGROUND

In 1999, Dallas Galleria Limited ("Galleria") entered into a lease with Big Easy Cajun — Dallas, Inc. ("BEC Dallas"), whereby BEC Dallas would operate a food-court restaurant in the Galleria mall for ten years. In 2002, BEC Dallas defaulted on the lease and abandoned the premises. Galleria sued BEC Dallas for breach of the lease. When BEC Dallas failed to answer, Galleria obtained a default judgment in the amount of $ 459,732.17, plus attorney's fees, costs, and interest (the "Default Judgment"). The Default Judgment was not satisfied.

In 2003, Galleria brought a new suit against appellants seeking to enforce the Default Judgment against them under the single business enterprise theory. Appellants include other food-court restaurants, an operating company, and a management company; all are organized as independent corporations. Subsequently, Galleria amended its petition to allege an implied partnership among appellants and BEC Dallas as another reason why they should be required to satisfy the Default Judgment.

The case was tried to a jury, but after Galleria's case in chief, the trial court directed a verdict against Galleria on its implied partnership claim. The jury returned a verdict in favor of Galleria on the single business enterprise claim and assessed Galleria's damages at $ 283,112.38. The trial court's judgment included those damages, plus attorney's fees, costs, and interest.

Both parties appealed, raising multiple issues. However, during the pendency of the appeal, the Texas Supreme Court issued an opinion on the theory of single business enterprise that controls this appeal. *See SSP Partners v. Gladstrong Investments (USA) Corp.*, 275 S.W.3d 444 (Tex. 2008). We address appellants' first issue on the viability of the theory of single business enterprise in light of *SSP Partners*. And because we conclude *SSP Partners* requires us to reverse the trial court's judgment on the single business enterprise theory of liability [removed], we review Galleria's conditional cross-point concerning the viability of its implied partnership theory of liability....

IMPLIED PARTNERSHIP

Galleria filed its own notice of appeal and included a conditional cross-point. Galleria urged that — if we reversed the jury's verdict on single business enterprise — it was entitled to a new trial on the issue of implied partnership. Galleria argues the trial court erroneously granted a directed verdict on the implied partnership issue because it produced more than a scintilla of evidence on that theory. A directed verdict is proper if there is no probative evidence raising a material fact dispute on a claim. *Prudential Ins. Co. of Am. v. Fin. Review Servs., Inc.*, 29 S.W.3d 74, 77 (Tex. 2000). In reviewing a directed verdict, we consider all of the evidence in a light most favorable to the party against whom the verdict was directed and disregard all contrary evidence and inferences; we give the losing party the benefit of all reasonable inferences created by the evidence. *Coastal Transp. Co., Inc. v. Crown Cent. Petroleum Corp.*, 136 S.W.3d 227, 234 (Tex. 2004).

A partnership is "an association of two or more persons to carry on a business for profit as owners." TEX. REV. CIV. STAT. ANN. art 6132b-2.02 (a) (Vernon Supp. 2008). We look to the following factors to determine whether persons have created a partnership:

(1) receipt or right to receive a share of profits of the business;

(2) expression of an intent to be partners in the business;

(3) participation or right to participate in control of the business;

(4) sharing or agreeing to share:

(A) losses of the business; or

(B) liability for claims by third parties against the business; and

(5) contributing or agreeing to contribute money or property to the business.

Id. art.6132b-2.03(a). The most important of these factors are sharing profits and participating in the control of the business. *Id.* Comment of Bar Comm. — 1993

("Traditionally, sharing of profits and of control have been regarded as the most important. They will probably continue to be the most important under this section.").

As to sharing of profits, Galleria argues profits of individual restaurants were "siphoned into" Big Easy Cajun — Management Corporation and Florida Operations Corporation under the guise of management fees and license fees, or royalties. Then, according to Galleria, the siphoned funds were paid out as dividends to the two men who were major shareholders of the various corporations. Even when we consider this evidence in a light most favorable to Galleria and disregard all contrary evidence and inferences, *see Coastal Transport*, 136 S.W.3d at 234, there is no probative evidence of profit sharing. Undisputed testimony in the record established the individual restaurants, including BEC Dallas, received specific administrative services in return for their management fees. These payments were compensation for services rendered and are, therefore, unrelated to the restaurant's profits. *See Schlumberger Tech. Corp. v. Swanson*, 959 S.W.2d 171, 176 (Tex. 1997). And as to the royalties, which individual restaurants paid for use of the corporate marks, the Texas Supreme Court has asserted that entitlement to a royalty based on gross receipts is not profit sharing. *See id.* Our review of the record does not yield a scintilla of evidence that any of the appellants agreed to share profits.

We next address Galleria's argument based upon participation in the control of the business. Galleria argues the Florida Operations Corporation retains control of the Big Easy Cajun intellectual property. It charges that the operations corporation "controls" the amount of license fees to be paid, and the management corporation "controls" the amount of management fees to be paid. These matters represent part of the agreement between operators of an individual restaurant and the other corporate entities. The entity that owns intellectual property safeguards its value, and the entity performing administrative tasks for one business receives payment for those services. Galleria asserts that performing those administrative tasks also represents the corporations' participation in the control of the business. Again, even when we consider this argument in a light most favorable to Galleria and disregard all contrary evidence and inferences, *see Coastal Transport*, 136 S.W.3d at 234, the record shows no evidence of a *sharing* of control in the various businesses.

Nor does the record contain evidence of the remaining partnership factors. The appellant entities did not share losses. The undisputed evidence at trial was that, once BEC Dallas was operating, individual shareholders made capital contributions to keep it running; none of the other corporate entities made such contributions. Finally, one of the majority shareholders of the corporations was asked why he organized his businesses as separate corporations. He responded that he did not want a problem at one restaurant to endanger all of his different ventures. This statement is clearly contrary to any implied agreement to share liabilities for claims by third parties against the business.

We conclude there is no probative evidence raising a material fact dispute on Galleria's claim of implied partnership. *Prudential Ins.*, 29 S.W.3d at 77. The trial court correctly granted the directed verdict on that claim.

6.2 Formation and Financing

One of the reasons there are as many partnerships as there are is that the partners do not realize they are even forming a partnership or all the liability involved in forming a partnership. If people act like partners, then the law will often treat them like partners, at least as far as third parties are involved. The law may treat them like partners even though they did not fill out a form or agreement to be a general partnership. The vast majority of partnerships are in real estate. Many partnerships are just "fallen into." If a person receives a share of business profits, this is usually an indication that they are a de facto partner. Thus, general partnerships are easy to form and comparatively inexpensive compared to corporations. In addition, partnerships do not have to have any minimum capital requirements to start, as some other business entities do. Therefore, it can be cheaper to start a general partnership, but if there are liability issues that arise, then a general partnership can become much more expensive than a business organization that limits liability.

If the partners do not have the assets to set up their partnership by themselves, it is generally easier for a partnership to obtain loans then a sole proprietor, who only has his assets to rely on. Since there are at least two partners, then both partners' assets could potentially be used as collateral for a loan. It is more difficult in a general partnership to raise funds than in a corporation, because a general partnership does not have the option of selling shares.

The name of the general partnership can be a fictitious one or it can be a combination of one or more of the partners' last names. Even if all last names were used in a general partnership's name, it would still might have to file a fictitious business name statement if those last names were different and common.

There can be state filing fees to form the general partnership. While the state filing fees and any necessary fictitious business name fees are small in comparison to forming a corporation, the partnership agreement can cost some money to draft properly. However, it really is in the best interest of the partnership to pay this fee upfront, and avoid potential, bigger expenses (especially regarding liability) in the future. Note that it is not a legal requirement that a partnership have a written agreement, and in fact, most do not, as they did not intend to form a general partnership.

a. Public Document

Many states allow general partnerships to file a public document, which gives general information about the partnership and puts the public on notice that the entity is in fact a partnership. Some states call this document a Statement of Partnership Authority. Whatever this document is called in a state, the purpose of this document is to help protect the public by requiring those responsible for the business organization to reveal their identity to at least the state's secretary of state. Thus, the questions presented on this document may include, but are not limited to, the following:

- The partnership name,
- The employer identification number,
- The address of the main office of the partnership,
- The registered agent of the partnership (if required),
- The names and mailing addresses of all the partners, and
- Those partners who have the authority to bind the partnership.

Go to the website below, read through the instructions and the form on how to prepare a Statement of Partnership Authority in the state of California. https://bpd.cdn.sos.ca.gov/gp/forms/gp-1.pdf.

b. Private Document: Partnership Agreements

One of the most important things to realize about not having a partnership agreement is that the general partnership will then be governed by either the Uniform Partnership Act (UPA) or Revised Uniform Partnership Act, which may not be the most beneficial to the partners. A partnership can be made through an oral agreement. This type of partnership can be legal, but it is not usually in the best interest of the partners, as partnership terms will be difficult to substantiate. As far as legal clients go, the attorney should encourage the clients to put their partnership agreements in writing. Remember that a partnership can even be created simply by the actions of the parties. This is frequently how partnerships are formed.

A written partnership agreement should have at least the following:

- The name of the partnership,
- The name and addresses of the individual partners,
- The general purpose of the partnership,
- The address of the principal place of business of the partnership,
- How long the partnership will last,
- What financial contributions each partner is making,
- What will happen if additional financial contributions might be necessary,
- What are the specific assets of the partnership,
- How profits and losses will be handled,
- The liability of the partners,
- Which partners will manage the partnership,
- How and when partners can be changed,
- Dissolution,
- What law applies,
- The date, and
- Signatures of the partners.

Those items that require more discussion are discussed below.

A written partnership agreement should include the names and addresses of the individual partners. The internal, and not public document, should contain the addresses of the partners, so the general partners will know where to contact each other. With the public document, the individual names of the partners are usually not revealed to the public, but are kept by a state's secretary of state. Thus, unless the private addresses of the partners were put into the partnership agreement, some of the partners might not have the other partners' addresses.

A broad purpose of the partnership should be stated. The more specific the purpose of the partnership is, then it is more likely this purpose will have to be amended if the partnership grows. Thus, it is a better practice to make the purpose initially sufficiently broad.

The principal place wherein the partnership does business should be delineated, as this is where the partnership's financial books are to be kept. The partners have rights to view the financial books, which can be important in determining whether they are receiving proper distributions of partnership assets, in accordance with their ownership percentage.

Extremely important in the written agreement is that the relative contributions of each of the partners should be listed. If this is not discussed, then no matter how much a partner contributes, he will receive an equal amount of profits as a partner who contributes much less. For example, one partner contributes an office building to a partnership. Another partner contributes minimum wage tasks to the partnership. Each will receive an equal share unless they specify otherwise in the partnership agreement. If the partners wish to change the percent of profits that each receives, based upon the percentage of their contribution, this should be discussed in depth. If the contribution is something other than cash, it should be appraised to determine its worth.

In the future, the partnership may want to require additional contributions from the partners. This should be anticipated in the partnership agreement so that it does not come as a surprise to the individual partners.

If the partnership has any property, that property should be enumerated in the agreement, as well as what percent interests in the property each partner has. If nothing is stated in the partnership agreement, it is assumed that a partner's contributions become the property of the partnership. Thus, if a partner does not want his contribution to become solely partnership property, this needs to be discussed in the partnership agreement as well.

Since partners often are not paid monthly, the accounting and financial management of the partnership should be discussed so that the partners will know when to expect any share of the profits to which they are entitled.

The management of the partnership should be discussed in the partnership agreement. It should state whether the management will be by all partners or delegated to a managing few.

If the original partners wish to make it easier than it is under RUPA to add or change a partner, they should so state in the agreement. Otherwise, a new partner or a change in partners will require unanimous approval.

A partnership can be formed with an anticipated termination date. What is more common is that the partnership continues at will until it is agreed upon by the partners to discontinue the partnership or individually withdraw. Whether the partnership plans on continuing forever, or for a limited time, it should discuss the dissolution of the partnership and how to wind up the business.

While the partnership agreement can have further additional provisions, it should at least have those above, along with the date and signature of the partners at the bottom of the agreement.

c. Financing: Contributions to the General Partnership and Property Rights

Partners do not have to contribute to the partnership in cash. Partners could contribute real, personal, or intellectual property instead or as well. The partner's work could be considered his contribution. Often, such contributions remain part of the partnership property until the partnership is dissolved. If the parties desire a different result, they should provision for it in the partnership agreement.

6.3 Management

a. Partner Authority

A general partnership allows all partners to equally manage the partnership if they so desire. In fact, unless the partnership agreement states otherwise, then each partner has an equal share in management. However, depending upon the number of partners, this may or may not be a good idea. Often, a business's success depends upon who is managing it. If you get too many partners, it is similar to having too many cooks in the kitchen. Probably three partners, equally managing, are about the ideal number of partners to share in management. If the partnership is much larger than that, it may be much better to have a managing partner(s) designated. If there are two partners, then the problem of not having a tiebreaker arises if they both have equal managerial ability. If there are two partners managing, then usually a partnership agreement will indicate that one has at least fifty-one percent managerial say so, to avoid not having a tiebreaker.

Agency law was discussed in Chapter 1. The duty of loyalty discussed in the chapter on agency applies to general partners, along with fiduciary duties. The general partner is expected to manage the general partnership to its advantage, rather than his own. In addition, the general partner is subject to the same duty of care that agents have. A general partner must use the same care and skill that a reasonable general partner would under similar circumstances. Acting negligently is not honoring the duty of care. The general partner might then usually have to pay the partnership damages for his negligence. However, in regards to a partner's negligence towards third parties, if there is no partnership agreement, each partner is responsible for the acts of his fellow partners performed in service of the partnership. Thus, if one partner acted negligently, then a third party could sue another partner for the acts of the first. This concept will be discussed more below, under liability.

Partners are agents of each other and the partnership. Thus, one partner's signature is normally enough to bind the partnership to the contract signed by that one partner. To help protect themselves, partners can file a statement of authority with their secretary of state. Supposedly, this statement gives the public notice of the authority of partners within a partnership. This can be particularly helpful when one partner is attempting to buy real estate on behalf of the partnership. In contrast to a statement of authority, a statement of denial can be filed, which denies the authority of a partner to bind the partnership. The statement of denial would list the partners without authority by name. If a third party knows that one partner does not have the authority to bind the partnership by himself, than any contract that one partner signs with that third party would not be legally binding as against the partnership. In addition, any actions that are not for carrying on the ordinary partnership business are also not legally binding upon the partnership. Unfortunately, not all members of the public who might deal with the partnership know to look up which partners have the authority to bind the partnership.

The Statement of Denial is a simpler form. It requires the name of the partnership; the fact denied, which can include denial of authority or status as a partner; and being signed under penalty of perjury. For an example, go to: https://bpd.cdn.sos.ca. gov/gp/forms/gp-2.pdf.

Luckily, there are a few things, by law, that cannot be agreed to without the unanimous consent of all the partners. These are in addition to whatever is already outlined in any partnership agreement as requiring unanimous consent. Items that normally require unanimous approval are:

- assigning property to creditors,
- selling the goodwill of the business,
- giving up the partnership's right to a jury trial, and
- acts beyond the purview of the partnership agreement.

Other than these items and unless the partnership agreement states otherwise, the partners vote on business and decisions are made on a majority basis.

6.4 Liability

The liability in a general partnership is much worse than in a sole proprietorship. In a sole proprietorship, the sole proprietor is only responsible for his own negligent acts. In a general partnership, each partner is responsible for his own negligent acts as well as the negligent acts of his partners!

Part of the reason liability is so terrible in a general partnership is because the concept of joint and several liability applies in a general partnership. The underlying reason for joint and several liability is to make it easier for the plaintiff to sue someone when initially filling out the complaint. A plaintiff might not initially know all the partners' names in a partnership. The plaintiff could put down the name of the partnership, and then just the names of some of the partners. The partnership and the named partners would be held initially responsible for one hundred percent (100%) of any recovery the plaintiff obtained. The partnership and the named partners would then seek contribution from the remaining partners for their portion of liability in the underlying incident. Note that the plaintiff could sue the partnership and/or partners in any combination, however.

There is the concept of marshaling of assets in partnership. With the marshaling of assets, before partner's personal assets can be used to pay debts or lawsuits, the partnership's assets must first be exhausted. In that scenario, if a partnership is sued and does not have enough assets in its business accounts to pay the lawsuit, then the partners would be personally liable for the remaining amount of the settlement. One way to reduce the high amount of personal liability is to buy insurance for the partnership.

6.5 Continued Existence of Business and Transferability

In general, the business continues so long as it is making a profit and the partners continue being part of the partnership. An issue may arise when a partner decides to sell his interest. In order to sell one's partnership interest, unanimous agreement of all the partners is necessary. This requirement is in place partially because the partnership is supposed to be voluntary, meaning that the partners should be able to pick their new partner. Another reason for this rule is so that the remaining partners have some forewarning that they are about to potentially lose a partner's contribution to the partnership. So long as all the partners agree, then the partner can sell his interest and the partnership can continue. Even if the partnership had to buy out the partner's interest, the partnership could continue if there was more than one partner.

6.6 Profits and Losses

There is a difference between a partner's interest in the partnership property (which will be discussed more below) and a partner's right to profits. Typically, in a partnership, partnership property is owned by the partnership, aside from personal assets of the partners. If a partner makes a contribution of property to the partnership, then absent another type of agreement it becomes the partnership's property. A partner therefore cannot sell an interest he has in partnership property without the consent of his partners. Profits made off the partnership property, such as rent from rental units, are given to the partners. The partner can spend it according to his ownership percentage. Thus, profits are typically paid out before a partner's interest, which might only occur when the partner is leaving the partnership.

a. Sharing in the Profits

RUPA states that unless there is an agreement to the contrary, the partners each get an equal portion of partnership profits. This is true no matter how much one partner puts into the partnership versus how little another partner puts into the partnership! The same is true of partnership management. Absent an agreement to the contrary, each partner gets an equal right to management, no matter what their contribution to the partnership was.

However, partners typically do not get a salary. The partners can agree to provide salaries, but unless it has been agreed to, usually the partners do not receive one. Instead, they might get a distribution at certain times delineated in the partnership agreement. This could be every six months, every year, or another time delineated by the partnership agreement.

The following are excerpts from a complaint regarding the operation of a general partnership. It involves the partners of Jacoby & Myers Legal Network, which is a famous legal network you may have seen advertised on television. The complaint is based upon Koff and Meyers not sharing the general partnership profits with Jacoby and violating their fiduciary duty towards him. As you read this, question yourself as to whether operating a legal network as a general partnership is a good idea.

LEONARD D. JACOBY, Plaintiff	COMPLAINT FOR:
vs.	1) BREACH OF PARTNERSHIP AGREEMENT;
GAIL J. KOFF; STEPHEN Z. MEYERS; AND DOES 1 THROUGH 50, INCLUSIVE,	2) BREACH OF PARTNERSHIP FIDUCIARY DUTY....
Defendants.	5) BREACH OF FIDUCIARY DUTY....

Plaintiff LEONARD D. JACOBY alleges as follows:

4. ... On or about January 1, 1984, Jacoby, Meyers and Koff (collectively, "Partners") entered into the Amended and Restated General Partnership Agreement of Jacoby & Meyers Law Offices ("Partnership Agreement"), which created the present form of the Jacoby and Meyers Law Offices, a California general partnership ("Partnership")....

6. Section 8.1 of the Partnership Agreement provides that Jacoby and Meyers each hold 40 units of participation and Koff holds 20 units of participation.

7. The Partnership Agreement provides generally for management decisions by the Management Committee on a majority basis. Specific decisions enumerated in the Partnership Agreement, however, require unanimous approval of the Management Committee, defined by Section 1.9 of the Partnership Agreement as the unanimous approval of Jacoby, Meyers and Koff.

8. Unanimous approval of the Management Committee is required in order to:

(a) change the principal office of the Partnership from Los Angeles, California;

(b) modify the procedures by which the Management Committee may act and bind the Partnership;

(c) withdraw capital from the Partnership; and

(d) distribute to partners cash available for distribution (a defined term in the Partnership Agreement), pay salaries to partners and/or permit partners to take draws from the Partnership. [tabbing added]

9. Section 10.1 of the Partnership Agreement requires that the Partnership books and records, together with all of the documents and papers pertaining to the business of the Partnership, be kept at the principal place of business of the Partnership in Los Angeles, California.

10. In the late 1970s to early 1980s, the Partners planned on growing their business to form a national law firm, with offices across the country....

13. The law firm grew from one office in California in 1972 to approximately 150 local field offices in six states by the mid-1980s. Offices were located in California, Arizona, Pennsylvania, Connecticut, New Jersey and New York. The Arizona and California offices were generally supervised directly by Jacoby and the Northeastern offices were generally supervised directly by Koff. Oversight and national responsibilities were shared by the Partners. The field offices operated as linked neighborhood law offices, specializing in providing quality personal legal services to middle-class individuals. In addition to the local field offices, the Partnership opened certain specialized "units" containing centralized groups of attorneys with particular practice skills, including personal injury units. The personal injury units, along with other specialized units, provided expertise not available in the neighborhood field offices of the Partnership. The neighborhood field offices routinely utilized the services of the specialized units for cases meriting such attention.

14. The rapid expansion in the number of field offices and the expensive creation of personal injury units unfortunately coincided with the general decline in economic conditions throughout the country. In response to these economic forces and other financial setbacks, the Partnership was forced to retreat from its expansion plans and to consolidate its offices. By the middle of 1994 the firm had closed most of its field offices and specialty units, including all of those located in California except for the personal injury units. At the present time, the firm operates eight personal injury units located in San Francisco, Sacramento, Tucson, Philadelphia, Long Island, New York City and New Jersey. It also has approximately twelve field offices located in the Northeast....

16. Rather than creating a system for dividing the day-to-day operating tasks for shared management of the firm, Meyers and Koff undertook a deliberate course of action to isolate Jacoby from the operation of the Partnership. They stopped paying rent on the principal office of the firm in Los Angeles. They refused to give pertinent financial information about the Partnership to Jacoby. They stopped paying Jacoby certain benefits traditionally provided to each of the Partners, while at the same time continuing to pay their own benefits. Jacoby had to argue with and harangue Meyers and Koff in order to receive any payment from the Partnership. Jacoby is informed and believes, and on that basis alleges, that Meyers and Koff have in the past and continue to take Partnership resources for their own individual purposes rather than legitimate Partnership expenses. Moreover, Meyers and Koff have refused to reimburse Jacoby for expenses incurred on behalf of the Partnership as part of the winding up of certain Partnership operations in the Western states, including California.

17. Meyers and Koff also forced Jacoby out of the shared control of the Partnership and refused to pay him in the same manner they paid themselves.

b. Partner's Interest in Partnership Property

There is a difference between a partnership interest and a right to profit. Remember, partnership property is usually based upon all the individual partner's contributions. Once they contribute the property, it usually becomes partnership property, and the individual partner loses the absolute right to that property. Instead, what the individual partner has is an interest in the partnership property, and he cannot use or sell the property on his own. An interest in partnership property is often based on how many partners there are; if there were three partners, they would each have a thirty-three percent interest. If there were four partners, they would each have a twenty-five percent interest. This amount could be changed by a partnership agreement. The interest in the partnership property means that once the partnership decides to dispose of that property, the individual partners might then receive thirty-three percent or twenty-five percent of the sale amount.

c. Contributing to Losses

If the partnership agreement does not cover contributing to losses, then the UPA or RUPA will apply. This means that the partners are supposed to contribute to losses in proportion to their ownership interest in the company. Thus, if a partner has a twenty-percent ownership interest in the company, then he would be required to contribute twenty-percent to cover the losses.

6.7 Taxation

One of the major benefits to a partnership is that the partnership itself does not actually pay taxes. Another benefit to a partnership is that the taxes are not much more difficult or complex than filing as sole proprietor. The partnership files its own tax return each year, known as a Form 1065. However, the partnership does not pay any tax itself. The partnership itself is not a taxable entity. The individual partners file their regular tax return and then attach a Schedule K-1 (being transitioned to Schedule K-3 in 2021), which indicates the partner's portion of partnership profits. In general, the Internal Revenue Service's Schedule K-1 (being transitioned to Schedule K-3 in 2021) looks at the beginning and ending profit, loss, and capital of each partner, as well as the partner's share of liabilities at year-end. The individual partners then pay taxes at their tax rates on their portion of partnership profits. Taxes also apply to dividends (if any) and any capital gains of the partnership. Known as pass-through taxation because it passes through the entity to the members, this avoids the double taxation of a corporation. Double taxation will be discussed more in the chapters on corporations.

6.8 Termination

Termination or dissolution of the partnership is perhaps the area wherein UPA and RUPA differ the most. Since approximately one-fifth of all states still follow UPA, UPA will be discussed. However, as you will be able to ascertain from the discussion, the numerous ways in which UPA allows for dissolution is a big reason states move from utilizing UPA to RUPA.

a. UPA

In general, under UPA, if a partner leaves the partnership, then the partnership dissolves. To dissolve means that the partnership ends or terminates. The partnership needs to wind up all of its business so that it can terminate. Winding up includes liquidating all assets into cash and distributing the necessary amounts of cash to any debts. If there is money left over, than it would be paid to the partners in accordance to their ownership interest.

Under UPA, dissolution can occur two major ways: by actions of the partners or by a court decree. These are the following actions by partners, under UPA, that cause a dissolution:

- The end of the partnership term or completion of the partnership purpose that was in the partnership agreement,
- If a partner wishes to leave,
- If all partners agree,
- If one partner is forced out per the terms of the partnership agreement,
- If it becomes unlawful for the partnership to continue,
- If a partners dies, or
- If a partner has a bankruptcy.

The partnership agreement could have provisions for the partnership to continue if there was a death, withdrawal, forced out, or bankruptcy. If the partnership does not provide for continuation though, the partnership must dissolve, per UPA, under these events. These are the following court decrees, under UPA, that cause a dissolution:

- A partner is mentally incompetent,
- A partner is incapable of performing his duties,
- A partner is violating his duties to the partnership,
- The partnership cannot make a profit, and
- If it is equitable to dissolve the partnership.

b. RUPA

Dissociation occurs when one partner leaves the partnership. Under RUPA, one partner dissociating does not necessarily mean that the partnership has to dissolve. The general rule, of which there are exceptions to, is that so long as the partnership buys out the dissociating partner, then the partnership can continue. The dissociating partner will want to file a Statement of Dissociation with the applicable secretary of state. This statement helps reduce the potential liability of the dissociating partner for the acts of the partnership. The statement can reduce the statute of limitations for liability from two years to ninety days.

6.9 Joint Ventures

A joint venture and a general partnership are different in that a joint venture is usually for one project, and a general partnership is for ongoing projects. For example, a general partnership might be for the purpose of building strip malls. A joint venture would be for the purpose of building a strip mall.

Chapter Summary

One of the best definitions of a general partnership is "an association of two or more persons to carry on as co-owners of a business for profit."[1] There are several different elements to this definition. Particularly important elements to this definition are that real and artificial people (business entities) can be partners in a general partnership. Another major element is that the partners share management and profits as co-owners of the business.

Most states follow their own version of either the Uniform Partnership Act (UPA) or the Revised Uniform Partnership Act (RUPA). Of course, a partnership agreement

---

1. UPA 1914.

can change some of defaults that apply under UPA or RUPA. If there is no written agreement changing the UPA or RUPA, then each partner will have equal rights to profits and an equal right to management, irrespective of what they contributed to the partnership.

Despite the disadvantageous of partnerships, they are still popular because they are easy to form. In fact, they are so easy to form, they are often created by accident, through the actions of the parties. Although not required, a partnership should have a partnership agreement to avoid disputes later on. Many states now allow a general partnership to file a public document, putting the public on notice about the existence of the partnership. This document or a statement of partnership authority can be helpful in letting those who are dealing with the partnership know which partners have the authority to bind the partnership. In the partnership agreement, it should cover some basic requirements:

- name and addresses of the partners,
- a broad purpose,
- the principal place of business,
- termination,
- contributions,
- management,
- adding partners, and
- so forth.

Each partner is an agent of the partnership. Thus, he has the right to bind the partnership with just his signature! Statements of authority and statements of denial can help modify each partner's ability to bind the partnership. Unfortunately, many members of the public do not know that they can often look up this information prior to dealing with a partner allegedly acting on behalf of the partnership.

The biggest disadvantage to a general partnership is the liability; it is worse than in a sole proprietorship. Each of the partners is responsible for the negligent actions of his other partners. This is part of the concept of joint and several liability. The non-responsible partner, who has to pay upfront for the cost of a lawsuit, might be able to seek contribution from the responsible partners.

Partners only have a right to profits, not a right to force the sale of their partnership interest. Once partners give assets to the partnership, the partnership owns the assets, and the partners only have an interest in the property, in accordance with their percent ownership. If the partnership does sell partnership property, then the partner may be able to get a portion of the sale in accordance with his ownership percentage.

The partnership itself does not pay taxes, although it does have to file a tax return. The taxes pass through the partnership, to the partners, and the partners pay taxes on the profits. The partnership's tax return and the partners' individual tax returns (with payment) are matched up by the Internal Revenue Service to verify profits and losses.

UPA and RUPA differ greatly in the ending of the general partnership. In general, under UPA, if a partner leaves the partnership, then the partnership ends. In general, under RUPA, if a partner leaves, the partnership does not end, so long as the partnership buys out the leaving partner's interest. Winding up happens when all non-cash assets are converted to cash, all debts are paid, and if there are any assets left over, the assets are distributed to the partners.

Key Terms

Capital	Partnership agreement
Dissociation	Pass-through tax status
Dissolution	Revised Uniform Partnership Act
Fictitious business name statement	(RUPA)
General partner	Statement of denial
Joint and several liability	Statement of partnership authority
Liquidation	Uniform Partnership Act (UPA)
Marshaling of assets	Winding up
Partnership	Wrongful dissociation

Review Questions

1. Compare and contrast a general partnership to a sole proprietorship.

2. Determine whether your state follows UPA or RUPA.

3. What documents are required to form a general partnership?

4. How is a general partnership similar to a principal-agent relationship? How is it different?

5. If there is no written partnership agreement, how is the general partnership managed?

6. Give an explanation of joint and several liability. Why is it the biggest disadvantage of a general partnership?

7. If there is no written partnership agreement, how are profits shared?

8. Discuss the taxation of the partners and the partnership.

9. What can be done to allow the general partnership to continue if dissociation is done wrongfully?

Web Links

The tax forms for a general partnership can be found at the Internal Revenue Service's website, http://www.irs.gov.

The Uniform Partnership Act and the Revised Uniform Partnership Act can be viewed in their entirety at http://uniformlaws.org/.

Exercises

1. There is no partnership agreement. If three partners contribute equally to the general partnership, then how much would each receive if the partnership profits were one hundred thousand dollars? If the partnership instead had a loss of one hundred thousand dollars, then how would those losses be allocated?

2. One of the three partners in Exercise Number 1 is unhappy in the partnership and sells his partnership interest to a third party, without speaking to the other two partners. What rights does the third party have?

3. Look on YouTube for a Jacoby & Myers commercial.

4. After reading the *Jacoby v. Koff* complaint, did you think forming the law firm as a general partnership was a good idea? Why or why not?

5. In the *Jacoby v. Koff* complaint, when was the partnership supposed to withdraw salaries from the partnership?

6. In the *Jacoby v. Koff* complaint, why do you think the complaint uses words like "isolate" and "harangue"?

7. The Internal Revenue Services' website is http://www.irs.gov. Go to this website and determine where the tax forms for a general partnership are located.

Chapter 7

Limited Partnerships

Chapter Outline

Chapter Objectives

- Distinguish a limited partnership from other types of partnerships.
- Discuss how a limited partnership is formed.
- Describe the unique financing and taxation in a limited partnership.
- Differentiate between general and limited partners within a limited partnership, particularly concerning management, liability, and profits.
- Outline the dissolution and winding-up process.

7.1 Introduction to Limited Partnerships

A limited partnership is dissimilar to a general partnership in that a limited partnership has at least one limited partner in addition to at least one general partner. Limited partners have limited liability whereas the general partners in the limited partnership do not. In fact, this type of entity was formed so that people who wanted to invest in a project could do so without having unlimited liability. In general, limited partnerships are more are more popular and numerous than general partnerships because of the limited liability and tax benefits that they offer. Projects commonly funded with limited partnerships are films, real estate investments, wildcat oil drilling, and cattle ranching. Notably, these are all areas of high risk. With the limited partnership, the investors can invest in these types of businesses without overexposing themselves to liability.

Limited partnerships are more heavily regulated by state statutes than are general partnerships. This is because limited partners are essentially investing in the risky purpose of the partnership, and they want to make sure that they are protected, despite not having management rights. General partners in a limited partnership are essentially the same as general partners in a general partnership. Thus, most of the focus in this chapter will be on limited partners.

Many states base their statutes about limited partnerships on the Revised Uniform Limited Partnership Act (RULPA). This act is very different from the Revised Uniform Partnership Act, which states that if there is no discussion about the distribution of profits in a general partnership, then the distribution will be made equally amongst the partners. In the RULPA, if distributions are not discussed in the partnership agreement, then the distributions to the partners are based upon the percentage they have contributed to the limited partnership. There are several states that utilize the Uniform Limited Partnership Act (ULPA):

- Alabama,
- Arkansas,
- California,
- Florida,
- Hawaii,
- Idaho,
- Illinois,
- Iowa,
- Maine,
- Minnesota,
- Nevada, and
- New Mexico.

The remaining states, which are the vast majority (other than Louisiana, which follows neither), follow the Revised Uniform Limited Partnership Act. As RULPA does cut down on the amount of paperwork needed to form and manage a limited partnership, it is highly likely more and more states will adopt it. Even in those states that follow RULPA, there are variations. Thus, this chapter will discuss limited partnerships in general with more of an emphasis on RULPA, but as always, verifying information with your state's statutes is important.

7.2 Formation and Financing

To form a limited partnership, there needs to be at least one general partner and one limited partner. The general partner manages the business, but may not have much money to invest in it. Movies are often financed with limited partnerships. Using the movie example, the general partner would be the director, and the limited partners would be the producers. The director has an idea of how he would like the movie to look, the actors to act, but he does not necessarily have much money, especially in an independent movie. The producers have money to invest in the movie, but are not part of the day-to-day operations of the business. The limited partner invests capital into the business. In our movie example, the director takes this money to make the movie. In addition to the documents below, remember that the eight types of paperwork common to almost any business entity (discussed in Chapter 3) also need to be reviewed to determine whether the limited partnership needs those types of paperwork or not. For example, if the limited partnership is operating under a fictitious business name, then it will also need to file a fictitious business name statement. Most partnerships, however, are named after the general partners.

a. Public Document: Certificate of Limited Partnership

To become a limited partnership, a limited partnership certificate has to be filed with the state in which the limited partnership is doing business. This document is filed with the pertinent secretary of state. Usually, partners want to put as little information as possible on the certificate of limited partnership, because it is a public document, and if there are changes that need to be made, it costs money. In general, at least this information should be on the limited partnership certificate:

- The limited partnership's name,
- The name and address of the agent for service of process of the limited partnership,
- The name and addresses of the general partner(s), and
- When the limited partnership will end.

The name of the limited partnership needs to be on the certificate, and there should be an indication that the business is a limited partnership. In general, a limited partner's last name cannot be part of the name of the limited partnership. This could mislead the public into believing that the limited partner is a general partner. However, if a general partner has the same last name, this is an exception to the rule that a limited partner cannot have his last name on the partnership. In addition, if the limited partnership was already called that name before the limited partner came on board, then that is another exception to this rule. General partners, of course, can have their last names on the partnership.

There should be an agent for service of process, which is a person or corporation designated to accept lawsuits and legal documents on behalf of a business organization. The limited partnership certificate will include the address of the agent for service of process of the limited partnership.

The certificate will include the addresses of general partners (many states allow the addresses of the limited partners to also be included), as the general partners are the partners in charge of the limited partnership.

The certificate will state how long the partnership will last or when the partnership will dissolve. This information is important to the limited partners, who invest, and want to know when they could potentially receive a return on their investment.

If the certificate does need to be amended, it can be. If there are major changes, then the certificate should be amended. This amendment generally must be approved by all partners. It is particularly important to the limited partners that the certificate of limited partnership be filed correctly, or the limited partners will not have limited liability.

b. Private Document: Partnership Agreement

Technically, a limited partnership agreement is not required by law, but many investors are smart business people, who require one before they invest. A limited partnership agreement is expensive to form, because the perceptive investors want to make sure every conceivable clause to protect them is listed in the agreement. At a minimum, the following should be discussed in a limited partnership agreement:

- The limited partnership's name;
- The names and addresses of all the partners, whether general or limited;
- Whether a partner is general or limited;
- A general purpose of the partnership;
- The principal, or main place of business of the partnership;
- When the partnership will end;
- What each partner is contributing;
- What is owned by the partnership;
- The liability of the partners;
- When profits and losses are going to be given to the partners;
- What are the duties of each partner;
- Which general partners will manage the partnership;

- How and when partners can be changed; and
- The date and signatures of all of the partners.

The items from the above bulleted list that need to be discussed in more detail are discussed below.

The names and addresses of the limited partners should be in the private document. Thus, if these partners change, it is less costly to change the names in the private document than having to change it in the public document (some states require that information about the limited partners be put into the public document though).

As with general partnerships, the purpose of the limited partnership must be stated. The purpose should be sufficiently broad so that the partnership can grow without having to change the purpose continually.

The principal place of business for the limited partnership should be designated so that the financial records can be kept there for inspection. As the limited partners are not often involved in the day-to-day business of the partnership, they will want to know where they can verify the profits and losses that they are receiving from the partnership.

If the limited partnership will only last a certain amount of time, then it can be included in the agreement, in addition to being in the limited partnership certificate. The limited partners are concerned about the end date of the limited partnership, as this might be the only time they receive any profits or losses from the business. If other distribution dates are foreseen, they should be delineated in the partnership agreement.

In a limited partnership agreement, even if the partners do not write down the contributions of each, the percentage of profits is distributed in accordance with their percentage of contributions. Unlike with general partnerships, whatever percentage the limited partner invests is the percentage of profits or losses he gets out of the partnership (if there is no partnership agreement). While limited partners are more protected by the Revised Uniform Limited Partnership Act (RULPA) than general partners under RUPA, most of the limited partners are smart enough to go ahead and make sure their contributions are also delineated in the partnership agreement.

Since limited partners are not managing the partnership and are contributing money, the agreement should indicate that they could freely sell their interest in the partnership. If a limited partner is contributing money, than it should not make much difference if that limited partner is substituted for another limited partner contributing the same amount of financial resources. Otherwise, in the absence of an agreement to the contrary, all partners must agree on a new limited partner. Below, is a sample Limited Partnership Agreement. Read through it, and look for the elements discussed above.

LIMITED PARTNERSHIP AGREEMENT

This Agreement of Limited Partnership is made effective as of _____, by and between General Partner), and Limited Partners.

IT IS HEREBY AGREED:

ARTICLE I
THE PARTNERSHIP

1.1   Name of Partnership. The name of the Partnership shall be "_____, a Limited Partnership."

1.2   Purpose of Partnership. The Partnership shall engage in the business of _____ and such activities as are related.

1.3   Principal Place of Business. The principal executive office of the Partnership shall be at _____.

1.4   Certificate of Limited Partnership. The General Partner shall immediately execute a Certificate of Limited Partnership and cause that Certificate to be filed in the office of the Secretary of State. Thereafter, the General Partner shall execute and cause to be filed certificates of amendment of the Certificate of Limited Partnership whenever required.

ARTICLE II
MEMBERS OF PARTNERSHIP

2.1   Original General Partners. The name of the General Partner is _____.

2.2   Original Limited Partners. The names of each original Limited Partner are as follows:

2.3   Admission of Additional General Partners. Subject to any other provision of this Agreement, and the Acquisition and Loan Documents, a person may be admitted as a General Partner after the Certificate of Limited Partnership is filed only with the written consent of each General Partner and the vote or written consent of fifty-one percent (51%) of all Partners.

2.4   Admission of Additional Limited Partners. Subject to the provisions of Article IX of this Agreement, governing transfers of Partnership interests, a person may acquire an interest in the Partnership directly from the Partnership and be admitted as an Additional Limited Partner only with the approval of the General Partner and fifty-one percent (51%) of all Partners. Each Partner's interest will be proportionally reduced to admit the new Limited Partner.

ARTICLE III
FINANCING

3.1   Capitalization. The Partnership shall have a total initial capitalization of up to _____. Each Partner shall contribute the sum of _____ for each _____ interest in the Partnership. The General Partner and Limited Partners shall initially contribute the amounts set forth opposite their respective names on Exhibit A.

3.2   Additional Capital Contributions.

A.   The General Partner may determine the amount of additional capital required by the Partnership and may require each Partner, General and Limited,1 to contribute a proportionate share of additional capital to the Partnership. The General Partner's determination will be binding on all Partners, unless fifty-one percent (51%) of all Partners vote otherwise. Each Partner's proportionate share of additional capital shall be defined as the product of the total amount of additional capital required by the Partnership multiplied by that Partner's "percentage interest in profits and losses" as set forth in Exhibit A. Additional capital contributions shall be made in cash by each Partner to the Partnership within ten (10) days after written notice of the amount of additional capital contributions has been delivered to each Partner.

In the event that any Partner fails to contribute any additional capital contribution required hereunder within ten (10) days after the Call Notice, then that Partner shall be in default under this Agreement. Any Partner who is in default under this Agreement for failing to contribute the additional capital contributions required hereunder shall have ninety (90) days from the date of delivery the Call Notice in which to cure that default by contributing his share of the required additional capital contribution.

So long as a Partner is in default hereunder, he shall have no voting rights but shall receive notice of any meetings.

B.   If any Partner is in default under Subsection 3.2B hereunder and fails to cure the default within ninety (90) days of the Call Notice by contributing the additional required capital then such Partner shall be in breach of this Agreement.

C.   If any Partner is in breach of this Agreement pursuant to Subsection 3.2(c), then at the option of the Partnership, his interest in the Partnership shall be terminated and he shall become an unsecured creditor for an amount equal to his original capital contribution decreased by the sum of:

1.   his proportionate share of all losses previously incurred by the Partnership (excluding depreciation);

2.   by any distributions previously made to said defaulting Partner.

3.3   Interest in Contributions. No interest shall be paid on a Partner's capital contributions.

3.4   Withdrawal and Return of Capital.

A.   No Partner may withdraw any portion of the capital of the Partnership and no Partner shall be entitled to the return of that Partner's contribution to the capital of the Partnership except upon dissolution of the Partnership.

B.   No Partner shall be entitled to demand the distribution of Partnership property other than cash as part of the return of that Partner's capital account on dissolution.

C.   No Partner shall have a priority over any other Partner as to the return of his capital account upon the dissolution of the Partnership.

ARTICLE IV
ALLOCATION AND DISTRIBUTION OF PROFITS AND LOSSES

4.1   Allocation of Profits and Losses. The net income of the Partnership shall be allocated to, and any net losses suffered by the Partnership shall be borne by, the Partners in the proportions set forth in Exhibit A attached hereto and incorporated herein by this reference.

4.2   Distribution of Cash Available for Distribution. The General Partner shall determine the amount of any distribution to the Partners and the timing of all such distributions. The General Partner's determination shall be binding upon all Partners.

4.3   Priorities Among Partners. No Partner shall be entitled to any priority or preference over any other Partner as to any distribution from the Partnership.

ARTICLE V
MANAGEMENT OF PARTNERSHIP AFFAIRS AND VOTING RIGHTS

5.1   Control and Management. Except as otherwise set forth in this Agreement, the General Partner shall have sole and exclusive control of the Limited Partnership.

5.2   Voting Rights of Limited Partners.

A.   Except as provided in Subsection 5.2(b), the Limited Partners shall not have either the obligation or the right to take part, directly or indirectly, in the active management or control of the business of the Partnership.

B.   The following Partnership actions may only be taken after approval by vote of the Partners:

1.   Veto of a call for additional capital;

2.   Admission of an additional General Partner;

3.   Admission of an additional Limited Partner;

4.   Admission of a Substituted General Partner;

5.   Amendment of the Partnership Agreement

6.   The sale or transfer of the Project;

7.   Consent to dissolution; and

8.   Election of a new general partner.

C. Except where otherwise expressly set forth in this Agreement, all of the acts listed in Section 5.2(b)(i) through 5.2(b)(ix) shall be approved by fifty-one percent (51%) vote of the interests of the Partners, each Partner having one vote for each one percent (1%) interest in profits and losses owned by that Partner with the General Partner having the same voting rights as a Limited Partner.

ARTICLE VI
PARTNERSHIP MEETINGS

6.1   Call and Place of Meetings. Meetings of the Partners at the Principal Executive Office of the Partnership may be called pursuant to the written request of any Partner.

6.2   Notice of Meeting. Immediately upon receipt of a written request stating that the Partner or Partners request a meeting on a specific date (which date shall not be less than ten (10) nor more than sixty (60) days after the receipt of the request by the General Partner), the General Partner shall immediately give notice to all Partners. Valid notice may not be given less than ten (10) nor more than sixty (60) days prior to the date of the meeting, and shall state the place, date, and hour of the meeting and the general nature of the business to be transacted. No business other than the business stated in the notice of the meeting may be transacted at the meeting. Notice shall be given by mail, addressed to each Partner entitled to vote at the meeting at the address appearing in the books of the Partnership for the Partner.

6.3   Quorum. At any duly held or called meeting of Partners, Partners holding at least fifty-one percent (51%) of the voting power who are represented in person or by proxy shall constitute a quorum for all purposes other than amending this Agreement in which case seventy-five percent (75%) of the interests of all Partners shall be required. The Partners present at a duly called or held meeting at which a quorum is present may continue to transact business until adjournment, notwithstanding the withdrawal of enough Partners to leave less than a quorum, if any action taken, other than adjournment, is approved by the requisite percentage of interests of Partners.

6.4   Meetings Not Duly Called, Noticed, or Held. The transaction of business at any meeting of Partners, however called and noticed, and wherever held, shall be as valid as though consummated at a meeting duly held after regular call and notice, if a quorum is present at that meeting, either in person or by proxy, and if, either before or after the meeting, each of the persons entitled to vote, not present in person or by proxy, signs either a written waiver of notice, a consent to the holding of the meeting, or an approval of the minutes of the meeting.

6.5   Waiver of Notice. Attendance of a Partner at a meeting shall constitute waiver of notice, except when that Partner objects, at the beginning of the meeting, to the transaction of any business on the ground that the meeting was not lawfully called or convened. Attendance at a meeting is not a waiver of any right to object to the consideration of matters required to be described in the notice of the meeting and not so included, if the objection is expressly made at the meeting. Any Partner approval at a meeting shall be valid only if the general nature of the proposal is stated in any written waiver of notice.

6.6   Proxies.

6.6.1   Every Partner entitled to vote may authorize another person or persons to act by proxy with respect to that Partner's interest in the Partnership.

6.6.2   Any proxy purporting to have been executed in accordance with this Section shall be presumptively valid.

6.6.3   No proxy shall be valid after the expiration of eleven (11) months from the date thereof unless otherwise provided in the proxy. Subject to Subsections (f) and (g) of this Section, every proxy continues in full force and effect until revoked by the person executing it. The dates contained on the proxy forms presumptively determine the order of execution, regardless of the postmark dates on the envelopes in which they are mailed.

6.6.4   A proxy is not revoked by the death or incapacitation of the person executing it, unless (except as provided in Subsection (f) of this Section), before the vote is counted, written notice of the death or incapacity of the maker is received by the Partnership.

6.6.5   Revocation of a proxy is effective by a writing delivered to the Partnership stating that the proxy is revoked or by a subsequent proxy executed by the Partner who executed the proxy or, as to any meeting, by the attendance and exercise of the right to vote at that meeting by the Partner who executed the proxy.

ARTICLE VII
ASSIGNMENT AND/OR TRANSFER OF PARTNERSHIP INTEREST

7.1   Prohibition Against Assignment, Sale, or Other Transfer. Notwithstanding any other provision of this Agreement, during the nine (9) month period after execution hereof, no Partner or his heirs, personal representative, successors, or assigns, shall have the right to assign, sell or otherwise transfer, for consideration or gratuitously, all or any portion of his interest in this Partnership, except to a bona fide resident of the State.

7.2   Assignments. A Partner may assign all or part of his interest in the profits and losses of the Partnership to any other person upon such terms and conditions as he may deem fit. The Assignee shall not be admitted as a Substituted Partner without the approval of the General Partner or, if the General Partner is the Assigning Partner, without the approval of fifty-one percent (51%) of the Limited Partners. Any assignment made to anyone, not admitted as a Substituted Partner, shall be effective only to give the Assignee the right to receive the share of profits to which the Assigning Partner would otherwise be entitled, shall not relieve the Assigning Partner from any liability under any agreement to make additional capital contributions, shall not relieve the Assigning Partner from liability under the provisions of this Agreement, and shall not give the Assignee the right to become a Substituted Partner. Neither the General Partner nor the Partnership shall be required to determine the tax consequences to any Assignee arising from the assignment of a Partnership interest. The Partnership shall continue with the same basis and capital accounts for the Assignee as was attributable to the Assigning Partner.

7.3   Transfer on Death of a Partner.

7.3.1   If any Partner dies, then his personal representative, heirs, devisees, or successors shall have an option, exercisable within sixty (60) days after the date of death to either:

7.3.1.1   elect to become Substituted Partners; or

7.3.1.2   offer to sell all but not less than all of the deceased Partner's interest to the remaining Partners.

ARTICLE VIII
DISSOLUTION OF THE PARTNERSHIP

2.1   Dissolution and Winding Up. The Partnership shall be dissolved, and its affairs shall be wound up upon expiration of the term provided for the existence of the Partnership; or when all of the assets of the Partnership have been sold or distributed by the Partnership.

ARTICLE IX
MISCELLANEOUS PROVISIONS

9.1   Entire Agreement. This Agreement contains the entire understanding among the Partners and supersedes any prior written or oral agreements between them respecting the subject matter contained herein. There are no representations, agreements, arrangements, or understandings, oral or written, between and among the Partners relating to the subject matter of this Agreement that are not fully expressed herein.

9.2   Attorneys' Fees and Costs. If any action at law or in equity, including an action for declaratory or injunctive relief, is brought to enforce or interpret the provisions of this Agreement, the prevailing party shall be entitled to reasonable attorney's fees and costs.

9.3   Governing Law. All questions with respect to the construction of this Agreement and the rights and liabilities of the parties hereto shall be governed by the laws of the State of California.

9.4   Notices. All notices shall be in writing and sent by regular United States mails. All notices to the Partners shall be sent to them at the addresses shown for them in the records of the Partnership. All notices to the Partnership shall be sent to it at its principal executive office. Notices shall be deemed to have been delivered when deposited in the United States mails.

9.5   Successors. Subject to the restrictions against assignment of partnership interests contained herein, this Agreement shall inure to the benefit of and shall be binding upon the assigns, successors in interest, personal representatives, estates, heirs, and legatees of each of the parties hereto.

9.6   Severability. If any provisions of this Agreement shall be declared by a court of competent jurisdiction to be invalid, void, or unenforceable, the remaining provisions shall continue in full force and effect.

9.7   Counterparts. This Agreement may be executed in several counterparts and all counterparts so executed shall constitute one agreement which shall be binding on all of the parties hereto, notwithstanding that all of the parties are not signatory to the original or the same counterpart.

Effective _____, 20____, at _____.

                        GENERAL PARTNER:

                        _____

                        LIMITED PARTNER:

                        _____

c. Financing

A limited partner can contribute to the limited partnership through property, services, or cash. Typically, the general partners in a limited partnership have limited funding and are seeking limited partners as investors. As many limited partnerships are in risky businesses, general partners oftentimes have to offer something special to get limited partners to invest. One of the ways in which a general partner gets a limited partner to invest in his business is that it is actually legal for the general partner to sell the limited partner his tax deductions and tax losses! An investor in a limited partnership may be looking for a loss to deduct against his profits on his taxes. Thus, in general, limited partnerships target wealthy individuals that need tax deductions to become the limited partnerships limited partners. These concepts will be discussed further in the section on taxation.

7.3 Management

In general, a limited partner is not allowed to help manage the limited partnership, or else he will lose his limited liability status. However, the limited partner can do several things without it constituting "management." As you will see, many of these items seem like a legal fiction or very beneficially worded in favor of the limited partners not being found to be general partners with unlimited personal liability. The limited partner could be an employee or independent contractor of the limited partnership. If the limited partner co-signs a loan for the limited partnership, he will have liability under the loan, but he does not become a general partner with unlimited liability to the public.

Limited partners are allowed to attend partnership meetings and to view the financial records. The rest of what a limited partner can and cannot do comes down to language. If the limited partner is merely consulting, proposing, suggesting, or advising, he has not lost his limited liability status. If the limited partner is demanding, commanding, ordering, or telling, then he has lost his limited liability status (unless he is demanding to see the financials, which he is always allowed to see). Hence, if a limited partner on a movie limited partnership fired the star of the movie, he would have become a general partner and lost his limited liability status. The limited partner essentially took away this right from the general partner and acted like the general partner himself. Only the general partners of the limited partnership are supposed to manage.

7.4 Liability

One of the main points of a limited liability partnership is that it offers limited liability to those who essentially want to gamble by investing in a risky business. Thus, the limited liability only applies to the limited partner and not the general partner, who is responsible for managing this risky business.

a. Unlimited Liability for General Partners

The general partners still have unlimited personal liability for the debts of the limited partnership. A general partner in a limited partnership will have the same type of liability as a general partner in a general partnership: unlimited personal liability for himself and the acts of his other general partners. This makes sense. The general partners have chosen an area of high risk in which to conduct business, they are responsible for managing the business, and should not be able to negate their liability away through the business entity. The general partner could still buy insurance to lessen his personal liability.

b. Limited Liability for Limited Partners

Since all the limited partner is really supposed to invest is capital (not management), his liability is limited to whatever he invested in the partnership. Thus, if he invested fifty thousand dollars, the most he can lose is fifty thousand dollars. If the limited partner invested five hundred thousand dollars, the most he can lose is five hundred thousand dollars. However, it can be hard giving up control in the management of the business when a person has a sizeable amount of money invested. Should the limited partner participate in management, he would lose limited liability status, and potentially have unlimited personal liability.

7.5 Continued Existence of Business and Transferability

Under RULPA, general partners can be admitted so long as all partners agree in writing. When a new partner is admitted, then the limited partnership certificate, which is the public document for this business entity would need to be amended.

When a general partner withdraws, to avoid the partnership's dissolution, the partnership agreement needs to have been drafted in a way that will allow the partnership to continue so long as there is at least one other general partner.

It is not as big of an impact on the partnership when limited partners withdraw from the partnership. Thus, it will not dissolve the partnership when the limited partner withdraws (unless no limited partners are left). However, because the limited partner's money will need to be replaced, limited partners typically have to provide six months' notice of withdrawal. This gives the limited partnership enough time, hopefully, to find alternate funding. At the end of the six months, then the limited partner would be able to get his capital percentage back from the partnership.

7.6 Profits and Losses

The limited partnership agreement should also address how profits and losses will be distributed between the general and limited partners. However, if it does not, RULPA holds that profits and losses are allocated based on each partner's percentage ownership in the limited partnership. Therefore, if Judy contributed four hundred thousand dollars, and this was one-tenth of the total capital contributed to the limited partnership, then she would be entitled to one-tenth of the profits or losses.

7.7 Taxation

The taxation of a limited partnership is similar to taxation in general partnerships. Taxation is pass-through, meaning that the partners are taxed at their individual tax rates. The partnership files a tax return, currently known as a Form 1065, but does not pay taxes. The IRS then matches the partnership's tax return to each of the individual partner's tax returns. The individual partners only have to add a Schedule K-1 (transitioning to a K-3 in 2021) to their regular tax return to report their partnership profits and losses.

Partners pay taxes or take losses in proportion to the amount that they originally put in. Thus, if a partner put in ten percent, he could take ten percent of the profits and have to pay taxes on that amount or take ten percent of the losses and use that to offset his other profits (if any).

The limited partner often is interested in investing in a limited partnership because of the additional tax benefits he can get. The limited partner may be looking for a loss and looking to buy tax deductions. The limited partner needs the loss and tax deductions to offset the profit he has from other sources, thus allowing him to pay less in taxes overall. Most limited partnerships have huge losses, at least in the beginning. Some losses, such as those from a limited partnership, can be taken against certain types of profits investors' have. Major tax deductions come from:

- interest payments,
- operating expenses, and
- depreciation.

Limited partnerships, even with investors, often have to take out a loan or a mortgage. These types of loans have interest and that interest is deductible for investors. Operating expenses are also deductible for investors. If the limited partnership buys a car or equipment, the car or equipment can be depreciated over time. Depreciation allows investors to deduct from income each year a certain amount, based upon that item becoming less useful.

Case Study: Movies

Many different types of film companies seek outside financing for producing movies. Small independent movie companies do so, along with larger ones, such as Scion. While Scion is an English movie company, it operates its limited partnerships for financing its movies similar to movie companies in the United States. These limited partnerships entice investors with tax deductions, tax losses, and a potential for future profit. In fact, many of these film companies openly state that because the movie making business is so speculative, it is highly likely the investor will get a percentage of the loss of making the movie. In other words, most movies fail to make any money and have tremendous losses, which investors who have many assets actually want to invest in. By investing and losing money, the investors actually save money in taxes! If you have watched the movie *The Producers*, this strange concept is exactly what that movie is discussing. Sometimes investors want a movie to be so bad that it will be highly likely the movie will lose money! In that case, the costs of making the movie are very likely to exceed the value of the film. Again, these movie companies are targeting investors in high tax rates. An example of the type of math that these film companies use is:

Initial cash investment:	$42,000.00
Tax loss and deductions:	$51,000.00
Total cash benefits:	$9,000.00
Return on cash investment:	Over 120%!

Looking at the above math, what the movie companies are indicating is that if a wealthy investor invests $42,000.00 into a bad movie, the person will lose all $42,000.00. In addition, the wealthy investor will receive $9,000.00 in tax deductions that would normally go to the general partner, but that the general partner "sells" to the limited partner to obtain his $42,000.00 investment. Hence, since the wealthy partner does not have to pay $51,000.00 to the United States Internal Revenue Service, he comes out "ahead."

7.8 Termination

Under RULPA, a limited partnership can be dissolved several ways, including the specified time limit for the partnership being expired. Thus, if the parties expected it would take three years to develop and produce a movie, they could make the expiration of the limited partnership be three years. A wiser alternative might be to say that the limited partnership expires once the movie is no longer making profits or losses. Hence, specific events being achieved can also cause the limited partnership to dissolve. If all the partners want to dissolve the partnership, they can, in writing.

Sometimes, a general partner leaving (or withdrawing from) the limited partnership will cause it to dissolve. Withdrawal can be accomplished by:

- retirement,
- dying,
- bankruptcy, or
- mental insanity.

A judge can also determine that the limited partnership should dissolve. A judge might determine that it simply is not practical to continue the business as per in the limited partnership agreement. One general partner leaving does not tend to dissolve the partnership, so long as there is one remaining. If all other partners agree in writing to continue the partnership within ninety days and there is already another general partner or they obtain one, then the limited partnership can continue.

To dissolve the limited partnership, a cancellation of the certificate of limited partnership needs to be filed with the appropriate state's secretary of state. All assets of the limited partnership need to be liquidated. Then, all creditors, including the state's tax board need to be paid. Finally, if any money is left, then it goes to the partners in their ownership percentage. This process is known as winding up.

The following case is about a dissolution requested by a general partner. Disagreements can arise when the partnership is being sold over how to evaluate the worth of the limited partnership. Pay attention to the evaluation the court finally approved.

In re Dissolution of Midnight Star Enterprises, L.P.
2006 SD 98,12, 724 N.W.2d 334, 337

Petition for dissolution of a partnership was brought by the general partner. The circuit court found the fair market value of the partnership was $6.2 million and ordered the majority partners to buy the business for that price within ten days or it would be sold on the open market. The general partner sought intermediate appeal raising two issues. Since the circuit court failed to use the hypothetical transaction standard to assess the fair market value of the partnership and ordered a forced sale, we reverse and remand.

FACTS

Midnight Star Enterprises, L.P. (Midnight Star) is a limited partnership, which operates a gaming, on-sale liquor and restaurant business in Deadwood, South Dakota. The owners of Midnight Star consist of: Midnight Star Enterprises, Ltd. (MSEL) as the general partner, owning 22 partnership units; Kevin Costner (Costner), owning 71.50 partnership units; and Francis and Carla Caneva (Canevas), owning 3.25 partnership units each. Costner is the sole owner of MSEL and essentially owns 93.5 partnership units.

The Canevas managed the operations of Midnight Star, receiving salaries and bonuses for their employment. According to MSEL, it became concerned about the Canevas' management and voiced concerns. Communications between the Canevas and the other partners broke down and MSEL decided to terminate the Canevas' employment. MSEL inquired whether the Canevas would participate in an amicable disassociation, but the Canevas declined.

MSEL then chose to dissolve Midnight Star pursuant to Article X, Section 10.1 of the Limited Partnership Agreement and brought a Petition for Dissolution. In order to dissolve, the fair market value of Midnight Star had to be assessed. MSEL hired Paul Thorstenson (Thorstenson), an accountant, to determine the fair market value. MSEL alleged the Canevas solicited an "offer" from Ken Kellar (Kellar), a Deadwood casino, restaurant, and hotel owner, which MSEL claimed was contrary to the provisions of the partnership agreement.

At an evidentiary hearing, Thorstenson determined the fair market value was $3.1 million based on the hypothetical transaction standard of valuation. Kellar testified he offered $6.2 million for Midnight Star. MSEL argued Thorstenson used the proper valuation standard and Kellar's offer did not establish the fair market value. The circuit court disagreed and found Kellar's offer of $6.2 million to be the fair market value of Midnight Star. The circuit court ordered the majority owners to buy the business for $6.2 million within 10 days or the court would order the business to be sold on the open market.

MSEL appeals. The issues are:

1. Whether Article 10.4 of the partnership agreement requires the Midnight Star to be sold on the open market.

2. Whether the circuit court erred in finding the fair market value of Midnight Star was the actual offer price and not that of a hypothetical transaction.

3. Whether the circuit court abused its discretion by ordering a forced sale of Midnight Star....

1. Whether Article 10.4 of the partnership agreement requires the Midnight Star to be sold on the open market.

Canevas claim the partnership agreement does not allow the general partner to buy out their interest in Midnight Star. Instead, the Canevas argue, the agreement mandates the partnership be sold on the open market upon dissolution. Specifically, Canevas ask this Court to interpret Article 10.4 to require the sale of the partnership. Article 10.4 provides:

> After all of the debts of the Partnership have been paid, the General Partner or Liquidating Trustee may distribute in kind any Partnership property provided that a good faith effort is first made to sell or otherwise dispose of such property for cash or readily marketable securities at its estimated fair value to one or more third parties none of whom is an affiliate of any Partner. The General Partner or Liquidating Trustee shall value any such Partnership property at its fair market value and distribution shall then proceed as if the property had been sold for cash at such value with the resulting Net Profits and/or Net Losses allocated to the Partners as provided in Article VI and subsection 10.3.2 of this Agreement.

MSEL claims the Canevas interpretation of Article 10.4 renders other provisions of the partnership agreement meaningless. MSEL points to Article 10.3.1 to demonstrate their position. Article 10.3.1 provides in part:

> Subject to 10.4 hereof, the assets of the Partnership shall be liquidated as promptly as is consistent with obtaining a fair value therefor, provided that no assets other than cash shall be sold or otherwise transferred for value to the General Partner, Liquidating Trustee, any other Partner, or any Affiliate or Related Person of any of the foregoing unless such assets are valued at their then fair market value in such sale or other transfer and fifteen (15) days prior written notice of such proposed sale or transfer is given to all Partners[.]

During oral arguments, MSEL claimed we need not interpret whether the partnership agreement provisions required a fair market valuation of Midnight Star or whether the partnership must be sold on the open market. It claimed we could merely decide whether the circuit court erred in determining the fair market value of the business. However, if the Canevas interpretation of the partnership agreement provisions is correct, there would be no need to determine the fair market value. If correct, the value of the partnership would be determined solely by the sale of Midnight Star. Therefore, we reach the question whether the partnership agreement provisions require a fair market analysis or require a forced sale.

The partnership agreement is a contract between the partners and effect will be given to the plain meaning of its words...."An interpretation which gives a reasonable and effective meaning to all the terms is preferred to an interpretation which leaves a part unreasonable or of no effect...." We must "give effect to the language of the entire contract and particular words and phrases are not interpreted in isolation...."

If we accept the Canevas' interpretation of the partnership agreement, it would mean that Article 10.4 requires the partnership to be placed on the open market and sold to the highest bidder. The plain meaning of Article 10.4 does not command that interpretation. This provision clearly states the General Partner "may distribute in kind any partnership property" if the property is first offered to a third party for a fair value.... While the General Partner may offer the property on the open market, Article 10.4 does not require it. Simply, the General Partner has to offer the property for sale if it chooses an in kind distribution of assets. Sale is not mandatory.

This interpretation is reinforced when read together with Article 10.3.1. If the Canevas' interpretation is utilized, it would render Article 10.3.1 meaningless. Article 10.3.1 instructs that "no assets other than cash shall be sold or otherwise transferred to [any partner] unless the assets are valued at their then fair market value in such sale or other transfer" and all partners receive fifteen days prior notice of the proposed sale or transfer. If Article 10.4 requires a forced sale, then there would be no need to have the fair market value provision of Article 10.3.1.

We cannot interpret one provision to render another provision meaningless. Instead, we interpret the partnership agreement to require a sale only if a partner elects to distribute in kind. However, read as a whole, the partnership agreement does not require a mandatory sale upon dissolution. Instead, the general partner can opt to liquidate using either a sale or transfer under Article 10.3.1. This gives meaning to Article 10.3.1's fair market value provision. Because MSEL decided to pursue dissolution under Article 10.3.1, we decide the correct standard for determining the fair market value of the partnership.

2. Whether the circuit court erred in finding the fair market value of Midnight Star was the actual offer price and not that of a hypothetical transaction.

MSEL claims the correct standard for appraising a business is the hypothetical transaction analysis, like the analysis employed by MSEL's expert Thorstenson. Canevas argue that the circuit court correctly concluded the offer from Kellar represented the fair market value of Midnight Star.

Fair market value is defined as, the price at which the property would change hands between a willing buyer and a willing seller when the former is not under any compulsion to buy and the latter is not under any compulsion to sell, both parties having reasonable knowledge of the relevant facts. Court decisions frequently state in addition that the hypothetical buyer and seller are assumed to be able, as well as willing, to trade and to be well informed about the property and concerning the market for such property.... MSEL argues that since the Revenue Ruling was issued in 1959, "hundreds of courts, tribunals, textbooks, and articles have reiterated the mandatory requirement for hypothetical analysis." In fact, MSEL contends that not "a single whiff of authority" can be found that supports the circuit court's decision to ignore the hypothetical transaction standard and instead apply an actual offer to determine the fair market value.

This Court has not decided a case involving this issue. However, in Priebe v. Priebe, we noted, "Revenue Ruling 59-60 represents the most substantial body of official guidance for valuing an interest in a closely held corporation ..." Moreover, other jurisdictions have employed the hypothetical transaction to arrive at the fair market value in other situations. In Heck v. Comm'r, the United States Tax Court explained the "fair market value is the standard of determining the value of property for Federal estate tax purposes...." The court went on to explain that the fair market value uses hypothetical sellers and buyers, "rather than specific individuals or entities, and their characteristics are not necessarily the same as those of the actual buyer or seller...."

Importantly, courts have noted that the fair market analysis does not contemplate actual buyers. In Estate of Jameson v. Comm'r, the court stated it was error for the lower court to "assume[ ] the existence of a strategic buyer [.]" ... The court further emphasized that "fair market value analysis depends on a hypothetical rather than an actual buyer...."

MSEL goes to great lengths in its brief to demonstrate why the hypothetical transaction valuation standard, rather than an actual buyer, is the proper standard to determine the fair market value. MSEL lists sound policy reasons why an offer cannot be the fair market value. For example, what if a partnership solicited a "strawman" to offer a low price for the business? What if a businessman, for personal reasons, offers 10 times the real value of the business? What if the partnership, for personal reasons, such as sentimental value, refuses to sell for that absurdly high offer? These arbitrary, emotional offers and rejections cannot provide a rational and reasonable basis for determining the fair market value.

Conversely, the hypothetical transaction standard does provide a rational and reasonable basis for determining the fair market value. This standard provides the basis by removing the irrationalities, strategies, and emotions from the analysis. Many articles and treatises that discuss fair market value specifically note that removing the irrationalities and biases is one of the rationales for the hypothetical transaction standard.... "[The world of fair market value] is a special world in which the participants are expected (defined) to act in specific and predictable ways. It is a world of hypothetical willing buyers and sellers engaging in hypothetical transactions...."

Finally, Section X of the partnership agreement itself requires a "fair market value" of the assets. The partnership agreement is a contract between the partners and effect will be given to the plain meaning of its words.... The partnership agreement does not provide that the value of the business upon dissolution will be the highest and best offer the partnership can obtain.

The circuit court should have used the hypothetical transaction standard in determining the fair market value of Midnight Star. This standard is backed by years of testing and numerous positive citations endorsing it. Instead of employing the hypothetical transaction standard, the court used a single offer to determine that the fair market value was $6.2 million. It was error for the circuit court to ignore this established standard....

7.9 Major Differences between General Partnerships and Limited Partnerships

To help you review, the major differences between general partnerships and limited partnerships will be synthesized here. In a general partnership, all the partners are general partners. In a limited partnership, there must be at least one general partner and at least one limited partner. There can be more than one of each type of partner.

In a general partnership, unless the partnership agreement states otherwise, all the general partners have unlimited personal liability for the other partners' actions. In a limited partnership, the general partners have unlimited personal liability for limited partnership actions and their own. The limited partners in the limited partnership do not; they can only lose up to the amount of their investment. Thus, the limited partners in a limited partnership have limited liability.

In a general partnership, if the partnership agreement does not state otherwise, then all the general partners have the right to manage equally the business. In a limited partnership, the limited partners do not have the right to manage without losing their limited liability.

In a general partnership, it is not usually necessary to file documents with the secretary of state to start the general partnership. With a limited partnership, the public documents must be filed with the secretary of state to start the limited partnership.

Chapter Summary

A limited partnership provides limited liability to its limited partners. To keep their limited liability, limited partners are not usually allowed to participate in management. To be a limited partnership, the partnership must contain at least one general partner and at least one limited partner.

The law, which is applied to limited partnerships, is the individual state's adaptation of the Revised Uniform Limited Partnership Act, also known as RULPA. Some states still do follow the Uniform Limited Partnership Act (ULPA). The limited partnership is created through the filing of a limited partnership certificate with the appropriate state's secretary of state. While a limited partnership agreement is not a requirement, it is a good idea, and many investors will want one prior to investing. If there is such an agreement, it should at least cover the partners' rights to profits and losses and admitting new partners.

The financing of a limited partnership primarily comes from the limited partners, who want a way to invest in something highly speculative, while limiting their liability exposure. Management is supposed to be solely performed by the general partner. However, there are many activities, short of management, the limited partner can partake in, without losing his limited liability status. One example includes acting as an employee of the limited partnership.

In general, the general partner retains unlimited personal liability for the limited partnership. This is similar to the liability of general partners in a general partnership. Usually, the limited partner will only be liable up to the amount of his contribution to the partnership, unless he gets involved in managing the limited partnership.

The amount of profits or losses is allocated based upon the contributions that the partners made. If a partner makes a contribution that equals twenty-five percent of all contributions, then he would be entitled to twenty-five percent of the profits or losses. The limited partner would need to then pay taxes on that twenty-five percent profit or be able to take that twenty-five percent loss against other specific types of profits.

Taxation in a limited partnership is similar to taxation in a general partnership. However, in a limited partnership, the limited partners can deduct tax losses and take tax deductions that would otherwise belong to the general partner (if the general partner gives up his tax deductions to attract investors). An example of a tax deduction a limited partner could deduct is a part of the limited partnership's mortgage interest deduction.

One general partner leaving the limited partnership does not dissolve it, if all other partners agree in writing to continue the partnership within ninety days and there is already another general partner or they obtain one.

Key Terms

Certificate of limited partnership	Limited partnership
Dissolve	Limited partnership agreement
Fair market value	Pass-through taxation
General partner	Revised Uniform Limited Partner-
Judicial dissolution	ship Act (RULPA)
Limited partner	Unlimited liability

Review Questions

1. What types of businesses are best for limited partnerships?

2. Why is it a good idea to put a minimal amount of information down on the limited partnership agreement?

3. Is a limited partnership more likely or less likely to have a partnership agreement than a general partnership?

4. How is a limited partnership better than a general partnership for purposes of raising funds?

5. How are the general partners different from the limited partners in a limited partnership?

6. How are the tax benefits treated in a limited partnership?

7. What does a limited partnership need to do if it wants to continue operations after a general partner withdraws?

Web Links

https://www.hudcos.com/film-funding/. Read the information on this website for a real-life film limited partnership and answer the exercises based upon this website.

Exercises

1. On the Hudson Entertainment website, who is the potential limited partner?

2. What law will apply to Hudson Entertainment, LP?

3. Do you think that the filming locations of Hudson Entertainment warrant a high production cost?

4. If you wanted to lose money, would you decide to invest in Hudson Entertainment, LP? What are other benefits to investing in Hudson Entertainment, LP?

5. If you are an accredited investor and do invest one thousand dollars, what is the amount of money that you can be held personally liable for?

6. After reading the case in the chapter, provide a definition for fair market value.

Chapter 8

Limited Liability Partnership

Chapter Outline

Chapter Objectives

- Compare a limited liability partnership to a general partnership and a limited partnership.

- List the elements of a registered limited liability partnership registration and a partnership agreement.

- Show that financing and management in a limited liability partnership are similar to that in a general partnership.

- Contrast liability in different states.

- Recognize that most of the attributes of a limited liability partnership, such as profits, taxation, and termination are very similar to that of a general partnership.

8.1 Introduction to Limited Liability Partnerships

Limited liability partnerships (LLPs) often consist of professionals, such as attorneys, accountants, architects, and sometimes doctors. This is because some states restrict the use of limited liability partnerships to professionals. Historically, professions have enjoyed partnerships as a business entity wherein they can readily share knowledge and management, while at least somewhat limiting their liability. In addition, limited liability partnerships are typically easier to form than corporations are, and both provide limited liability, though sometimes in differing amounts.

Limited liability partnerships are different from general partnerships in that the partners have limited liability for the acts of their other partners. This feature is one of the reasons why the number of limited liability partnerships continues to grow from year to year. Limited liability partnerships are also different from limited partnerships; in a limited liability partnership, all partners can have limited liability. As you may remember from last chapter, in a limited partnership, only the limited partners can have limited liability. However, other than the limited liability characteristic, limited liability partnerships are run surprisingly similarly to a general partnership.

8.2 Formation and Financing

The law that is normally applied to limited liability partnerships is a state's adaptation of either the Uniform Partnership Act or the Revised Uniform Partnership Act. These are the same acts that apply to general partnerships; so naturally, the two types of partnerships are formed in much the same way. In addition to the documents below, do not forget, if necessary, a fictitious business name statement and those remaining eight types of paperwork that are common to almost any business entity (i.e., professional license, sales tax permit, employer identification number, unemployment, workers' compensation, etc.).

a. Public Document: Registered Limited Liability Partnership Registration

Some states dub the public document for the limited liability partnership the registered limited liability partnership registration. Other states call the public document for the limited liability partnership the limited liability partnership registration or something similar. The public document could even be called a "Limited Liability Partnership Statement of Qualification." At a minimum, whatever this public document is called, it usually requires the following information:

- the name of the LLP, with a designation that the entity is an LLP;
- the principal place of business of the LLP;
- an agent for service of process;

- a statement regarding the limited liability of the LLP;
- the number of partners in the LLP;
- the date the LLP is formed; and
- an authorized partner's signature.

In the registered limited liability partnership registration, is it important to designate in the name of the partnership that it is, in fact, a limited liability partnership. The abbreviation LLP suffices for this requirement. The purpose of this requirement is to put the public on notice that the business is a limited liability partnership. However, it is doubtful whether the majority of the public understands that this usually means individual partners are not liable unless they participated in, or knew about, supervised negligence. Hence, this designation is probably of little value.

Similar to a limited partnership certificate, it is important that the limited liability partnership registration be filed accurately and in a timely manner. Until it has been, then the limited liability partners do not have limited liability. The registration may require a description of the business, which will normally be a professional business.

b. Private Document: Partnership Agreement

A limited liability partnership agreement can be similar to a general partnership agreement, with some exceptions. The LLP agreement would need to indicate that the agreement is for an LLP, and it would need to include language about the limited liability in an LLP. Both general partnership and limited liability partnership agreements should discuss:

- contributions,
- who receives how much of the profits and losses,
- how new partners are admitted, and
- the termination of the partnership.

For a more thorough discussion of what a general partnership and limited liability partnership agreement should cover, please review Chapter 6. General partnership agreements can be modified to suffice as limited liability partnership agreements.

If the partnership agreement does not discuss these matters, then losses/profits and management of the limited liability partnership will be held equally, despite what the individual partners contributed. This is very different from a limited partnership, which was discussed last chapter. In a limited partnership, even though there is not a limited partnership agreement discussing contributions, partners will receive a percent in the same percent they contributed.

c. Financing

Compared to a corporation, it is not as easy to obtain capital to start the limited liability partnership business. However, it is easier to obtain capital to start the business of an LLP, than with a sole proprietorship and general partnership. This is because if someone invests in an LLP, he will have limited liability.

8.3 Management

Management in an LLP is almost the same as management in a general partnership. An LLP also allows all partners to manage equally, but without full liability for each other's acts. If the partners do not want to manage equally, then this needs to be spelled out in the partnership agreement. As management can be a major reason for a business's success, it should be spelled out in the partnership agreement. For example, many law firms operate as LLPs, but not all of the partners might be good managers. The law firm should indicate which partners should manage the LLP.

As in a general partnership, the limited liability partners are agents of each other, and hence owe each other fiduciary duties, the duty of care, and the duty of loyalty. One partner can typically sign on behalf of the partnership and the partnership will be bound to uphold the contract.

Without a partnership agreement holding otherwise, then limited liability partners vote on issues on a majority basis. The UPA and RUPA will also hold, if there is no partnership agreement, that some things require unanimous approval. For example, things requiring unanimous approval would include disposing of property that is necessary to continue the limited liability partnership.

8.4 Liability

Formation, financing, and management of a limited liability partnership cannot best be discussed in general. With liability, the laws regarding liability of a limited liability partnership differ from state to state. In the past, attempts have been made to divide the states into two types, partial or full shield liability. However, what people mean by partial shield varies. The best way to look at the liability of partners in a limited liability partnership might be to look at each of the states individually.

Below are some statutes and language that show you the depth and breadth of the different language. This is not an exhaustive list of the statutes related to liability in a limited liability partnership nor is it all of the language regarding liability for partnership in an LLP in each state. Please note that many times, the language regarding liability for a limited liability partner is in a slightly different section than the majority of the language on limited liability partnerships, which has also been referenced for you. For example, most of Delaware's statutes on limited liability partnerships are located at 6 Delaware Code Sections 15-1001–15-1004. However, the section on liability in a limited liability partnership is located at 6 Delaware Code Section 15-306. Lastly, please note that the following language is all redacted from much longer code sections and a thorough reading of the entire code section on liability is probably warranted.

- **Code of Alabama Section 10-8A-3.06(c)**

"... [A] partner in a registered limited liability partnership is not personally liable or accountable, directly, or indirectly, including by way of indemnification, contribution, assessment, or otherwise, for debts, obligations, and liabilities of, or chargeable to, the registered limited liability partnership, or another partner or partners, whether arising in tort, contract, or otherwise, solely by reason of being such a partner or acting, or omitting to act, in such capacity, which such debts, obligations and liabilities occur, are incurred or are assumed while the partnership is a registered limited liability partnership." Alabama Code Sections 10-8A-10.01 to 10-8A-10.10 are the sections that speak to limited liability partnerships in Alabama, as well as foreign LLPs.

- **Alaska Statutes Section 32.06.306(c)**

"An obligation of a partnership incurred while the partnership is a limited liability partnership, whether arising in contract, in tort, or otherwise, is solely the obligation of the partnership. A partner is not personally liable, directly or indirectly, by way of contribution or otherwise, for the obligation solely by reason of being or acting as a partner. This subsection applies even if inconsistent with a partnership agreement provision that exists immediately before the vote required to become a limited liability partnership under AS 32.06.911(b)." Alaska Statutes Sections 32.06.911 to 32.06.925 has the general provisions on limited liability partnerships in Alaska and foreign LLPs.

- **Arizona Revised Statutes Section 29-1026(C)**

"Obligations incurred by a partnership or a limited partnership while the partnership or limited partnership is a limited liability partnership, whether arising in contract, tort or otherwise, are solely the obligations of the limited liability partnership. A partner is not personally liable, directly or indirectly, including by way of contribution or indemnification, for such obligations of the limited liability partnership incurred during the time the partnership or limited partnership is a limited liability partnership solely by reason of being or acting as such a partner." In general, Arizona Revised Statutes, Sections 29-1101 to 29-1109 have provisions on Arizona limited liability partnerships, as well as foreign LLPs.

- **Arkansas Code Annotated Section 4-46-306(c)**

"An obligation of a partnership incurred while the partnership is a limited liability partnership, whether arising in contract, tort, or otherwise, is solely the obligation of the partnership. A partner is not personally liable, directly or indirectly, by way of contribution or otherwise, for such a partnership obligation solely by reason of being or so acting as a partner. This subsection applies notwithstanding anything inconsistent in the partnership agreement that existed immediately before the vote required to become a limited liability partnership under § 4-46-1001(b)." This section is almost the same as the Revised Uniform Partnership Agreement language, but inserts "partnership" prior to obligation. Otherwise, Arkansas limited liability partnerships and foreign LLPs are discussed at Sections 4-46-1001 to 4-46-1105. *Id.*

- **California Corporations Code Section 16306(c)**

"... [A] partner in a registered limited liability partnership is not liable or accountable, directly or indirectly, including by way of indemnification, contribution, assessment, or otherwise, for debts, obligations, or liabilities of or chargeable to the partnership or another partner in the partnership, whether arising in tort, contract, or otherwise, that are incurred, created, or assumed by the partnership while the partnership is a registered limited liability partnership, by reason of being a partner or acting in the conduct of the business or activities of the partnership." Otherwise, California limited liability partnerships and foreign LLPs are discussed at Sections 16951 to 16962. *Id.*

- **Colorado Revised Statutes Section 7-64-306(3)**

"Except as otherwise provided in a written partnership agreement, a person is not, solely by reason of being a partner, liable, directly or indirectly, including by way of indemnification, contribution, assessment, or otherwise, for partnership obligations which are incurred, created, or assumed by the partnership while the partnership is a limited liability partnership." You can find the rest of the information on Colorado limited liability partnerships at Sections 7-64-1001 to 7-64-1010. *Id.*

- **Connecticut General Statutes Section 34-327(c)**

"[A] partner in a registered limited liability partnership is not liable directly or indirectly, including by way of indemnification, contribution or otherwise, for any debts, obligations and liabilities of or chargeable to the partnership or another partner or partners, whether arising in contract, tort or otherwise, arising in the course of the partnership business while the partnership is a registered limited liability partnership." The other sections on limited liability partnerships in Connecticut as well as foreign LLPs are located at Sections 34-406 to 34-434. *Id.*

- **6 Delaware Code, Section 15-306**

"An obligation of a partnership arising out of or related to circumstances or events occurring while the partnership is a limited liability partnership or incurred while the partnership is a limited liability partnership, whether arising in contract, tort or otherwise, is solely the obligation of the partnership. A partner is not personally liable, directly or indirectly, by way of indemnification, contribution, assessment or otherwise, for such an obligation solely by reason of being or so acting as a partner." Please note that 6 Delaware Code Sections 15-1001 to 15-1004 speak to limited liability partnerships in general, with foreign LLPs following afterword.

- **Florida Statute Section 620.8306(3)**

"An obligation of a partnership incurred while the partnership is a limited liability partnership, whether arising in contract, tort, or otherwise, is solely the obligation of the partnership. A partner is not personally liable, directly or indirectly, by way of contribution or otherwise, for such an obligation solely by reason of being or so acting as a partner." The section goes on and should be read in its entirety, though it at least starts out the same as RUPA. Florida Statutes Sections 620.8920 to 620.9902 speak to limited liability partnerships in general in Florida and foreign LLPs.

- **Official Code Georgia Annotated Section 14-8-15(b)**

"Subject to subsection (c) of this Code section and to any contrary agreement among the partners, a partner in a limited liability partnership is not individually liable or accountable either directly or indirectly by way of indemnification, reimbursement, contribution, assessment, or otherwise for any debts, obligations, or liabilities of or chargeable to the partnership or another partner, whether arising in tort, contract, or otherwise, that are incurred, created, or assumed while such partnership is a limited liability partnership, solely by reason of being such a partner or acting or omitting to act in such capacity or otherwise participating in the conduct of the activities of the limited liability partnership. Notwithstanding the provisions of this subsection, a partner may be personally liable for tax liabilities arising from the operation of the limited liability partnership as provided in Code Section 48-2-52." Otherwise, the information on Georgia limited liability partnerships is found at Sections 14-9-62 to 14-8-64. *Id.*

- **Indiana Code Annotated Sections 23-4-1-44 to 23-4-1-53** have several different areas within those sections wherein liability is discussed, along with general information on Indiana limited liability partnerships and foreign LLPs.

- **Iowa Code Section 486A.306(3)**

"An obligation of a partnership incurred while the partnership is a limited liability partnership, whether arising in contract, tort, or otherwise, is solely the obligation of the partnership. A partner is not personally liable, directly or indirectly, by way of contribution or otherwise, for such an obligation solely by reason of being or so acting as a partner. This subsection applies notwithstanding anything inconsistent in the partnership agreement that existed immediately before the vote required to become a limited liability partnership under section 486A.1001, subsection 2." Thus, it is similar to RUPA and provides full liability protection to the partners. In general, information on Iowa limited liability partnerships can be found at Sections 486A.101, and 486A.1001 to 486A.1002. *Id.*

- **Kentucky Revised Statute Section 362.220**

"**(2)** Subject to subsection (3) of this section and subject to any agreement among the partners, a partner in a registered limited liability partnership shall not be liable directly or indirectly, including by way of indemnification, contribution, assessment or otherwise, for debts, obligations, and liabilities of or chargeable to the partnership, whether arising in tort, contract, or otherwise, arising from negligence, malpractice, wrongful acts, or misconduct committed while the partnership is a registered limited liability partnership and in the course of the partnership business by another partner or an employee, agent, or representative of the partnership.

(3) Subsection (2) of this section shall not affect the liability of a partner in a registered limited liability partnership for his own negligence, wrongful acts, or misconduct."

"However, please note that Kentucky Revised Statutes Sections 362.1-931 to 363.1-932 discuss Kentucky limited liability partnerships in general.

- **Louisiana Revised Statute 9:3431(A)**

"Notwithstanding any other provisions of law to the contrary contained in Civil Code Article 2817, a partner in a registered limited liability partnership shall not be individually liable for the liabilities and obligations of the partnership arising from errors, omissions, negligence, incompetence, malfeasance, or willful or intentional misconduct committed in the course of the partnership business by another partner or a representative of the partnership." Otherwise, Louisiana limited liability partnerships are discussed in at 9:3432 through 9:3435. *Id.*

- **31 Maine Revised Statute Section 1034**

"**3. Obligation Incurred While Limited Liability Partnership.** An obligation of a partnership incurred while the partnership is a limited liability partnership, whether arising in contract, tort or otherwise, is solely the obligation of the partnership. A partner is not personally liable, directly or indirectly, by way of contribution or otherwise, for such an obligation solely by reason of being or so acting as a partner. This subsection applies notwithstanding anything inconsistent in the partnership agreement that existed immediately before the vote required to become a limited liability partnership under section 821, subsection 2."

- **Maryland Corporations and Associations Code Annotated Section 9A-306(c)**

"(c) *Limited liability partnership exception.* — Subject to the provisions of subsection (d) of this section, a partner of a limited liability partnership is not liable or accountable, directly or indirectly, including by way of indemnification, contribution, or otherwise, for any debts, obligations, or liabilities of or chargeable to the partnership or another partner, whether arising in tort, contract, or otherwise, which are incurred, created, or assumed by the partnership while the partnership is a limited liability partnership solely by reason of being a partner in the partnership or acting or omitting to act in such capacity or rendering professional services or otherwise participating, as an employee, consultant, contractor, or otherwise, in the conduct of the business or activities of the partnership.

(d) *Applicability of subsection (c).* — Subsection (c) of this section does not affect:

   (1) The liability of a partner of a limited liability partnership for debts and obligations of the partnership that arise from any negligent or wrongful act or omission of the partner or of another partner, employee, or agent of the partnership if the partner is negligent in appointing, directly supervising, or cooperating with the other partner, employee, or agent;

   (2) The liability of the partnership for all its debts and obligations or the availability of the entire assets of the partnership to satisfy its debts and obligations; or

   (3) The liability of a partner for debts and obligations of the partnership, whether in contract or in tort, that arise from or relate to a contract made by the partnership prior to its registration as a limited liability partnership, unless the registration was consented to in writing by the party to the contract that is seeking to enforce the debt or obligation."

In general, Maryland limited liability partnerships are discussed at Maryland Corporations and Associations Code Annotated Sections 9A-1001 to 9A-1016.

- **Annotated Laws of Massachusetts General Laws, Chapter 108A, Section 15(2)**

"(2) Subject to the provisions of paragraph (3), a partner in a registered limited liability partnership shall not be personally liable directly or indirectly, including, without limitation, by way of indemnification, contribution, assessment or otherwise, for debts, obligations and liabilities of or chargeable to such partnership, whether in tort, contract or otherwise arising while the partnership is a registered limited liability partnership.

(3) Paragraph (2) shall not affect (a) the liability of a partner in a registered limited liability partnership arising in whole or in part from such partner's own negligence, wrongful acts, errors or omissions, (b) the availability of partnership property to satisfy debts, obligations and liabilities of the partnership or (c) the persons on whom process may be served in an action against the partnership." Otherwise, Massachusetts limited liability partnerships are discussed at sections 45 to 49. *Id.*

- **Michigan Compiled Laws Sections 449.44 to 449.48** discuss liability in a few places.

- **Minnesota Statute Annotated Section 323A.0306(c)**

"(c) An obligation of a partnership incurred while the partnership is a limited liability partnership, whether arising in contract, tort, or otherwise, is solely the obligation of the partnership. A partner is not personally liable, directly or indirectly, by way of contribution or otherwise, for such an obligation solely by reason of being or so acting as a partner. This subsection applies notwithstanding anything inconsistent in the partnership agreement that existed immediately before the vote required to become a limited liability partnership under section 323A.1001(b)." In general, Minnesota limited liability partnerships are discussed at Sections 323A.1001 to 323A.1004. *Id.*

- **Mississippi Code Annotated Section 79-13-306(c)**

"(c) An obligation of a partnership incurred while the partnership is a limited liability partnership, whether arising in contract, tort, or otherwise, is solely the obligation of the partnership. A partner is not personally liable, directly or indirectly, by way of contribution or otherwise, for such an obligation solely by reason of being or so acting as a partner. This subsection applies notwithstanding anything inconsistent in the partnership agreement that existed immediately before the vote required to become a limited liability partnership under Section 79-13-1001(b)." In general, Mississippi limited liability partnerships are discussed in Sections 79-13-1001 to 79-13-1006. *Id.*

- **Section 358.150 Missouri Revised Statutes**

"2. Subject to subsection 3 of this section, no partner in a registered limited liability partnership shall be liable or accountable, directly or indirectly, including by way of indemnification, contribution, assessment or otherwise, for any debts, obligations and liabilities of, or chargeable to, the partnership or each other, whether in tort, contract or otherwise, which are incurred, created or assumed by such partnership while the partnership is a registered limited liability partnership.

3. Subsection 2 of this section shall not affect the liability of a partner in a registered limited liability partnership for the partner's own negligence, wrongful acts, omissions, misconduct or malpractice or the partner's liability for any taxes or fees administered by the department of revenue pursuant to chapter 143, 144 or 301, and any liabilities owed as determined by the division of employment security, pursuant to chapter 288, and any local taxes provided for in section 32.087."

In general, information about Missouri limited liability partnerships and foreign LLPs can be found at Sections 358.450 to 358.520. *Id.*

- **Nevada Revised Statutes Annotated Section 87.433(3)**

"An obligation of a partnership incurred while the partnership is a registered limited-liability partnership, whether arising in contract, tort or otherwise, is solely the obligation of the partnership. A partner is not personally liable, directly or indirectly, by way of contribution or otherwise, for such an obligation solely by reason of being or so acting as a partner. This subsection applies notwithstanding anything inconsistent in the partnership agreement that existed immediately before the filing of a certificate of registration pursuant to NRS 87.440." Other information on Nevada limited liability partnerships is located at Sections 87.440 to 87.540. *Id.*

- **New Hampshire Revised Statutes Annotated Section 304-A:15**

"II. Subject to paragraph III, a partner in a registered limited liability partnership is not liable directly or indirectly (including by way of indemnification, contribution, assessment or otherwise) for debts, obligations and liabilities of or chargeable to the partnership, whether in tort, contract, or otherwise, arising from omissions, negligence, wrongful acts, misconduct or malpractice committed while the partnership is a registered limited liability partnership and in the course of the partnership business by another partner or an employee, agent, or representative of the partnership.

III. Paragraph II shall not affect the liability of a partner in a registered limited liability partnership for the partner's own omissions, negligence, wrongful acts, misconduct or malpractice, or that of any person under the partner's direct supervision and control." Otherwise, New Hampshire limited liability partnerships and foreign LLPs are discussed at Sections 304-A:44 to 304-A:55. *Id.*

- **New Jersey Statute Section 42:1A-18(c)**

"An obligation of a partnership incurred while the partnership is a limited liability partnership, whether arising in contract, tort, or otherwise, is solely the obligation of the partnership. A partner is not personally liable, directly or indirectly, by way of contribution or otherwise, for such an obligation solely by reason of being or so acting as a partner. This subsection applies notwithstanding anything inconsistent in the partnership agreement that existed immediately before the vote required to become a limited liability partnership under subsection b. of section 47 [C.42:1A-47] of this act." New Jersey limited liability partnerships are discussed generally in Sections 42:1A-47 to 42:1A-49. *Id.*

- **New Mexico Statute Annotated Section 54-1A-306**

"(c) An obligation of a partnership incurred while the partnership is a limited liability partnership, whether arising in contract, tort or otherwise, is solely the obligation of the partnership. A partner is not personally liable, directly or indirectly, by way of contribution, indemnification or otherwise, for such an obligation solely by reason of being or so acting as a partner. This subsection applies notwithstanding anything inconsistent in the partnership agreement that existed immediately before the vote required to become a limited liability partnership under Section 54-1A-1001(b) NMSA 1978.

(d) Subsection (c) of this section shall not affect the liability of a partner in a registered limited liability partnership for the partner's own tort, including any omission, negligence, wrongful act, misconduct or malpractice, or that of any person under the partner's direct supervision and control."

- **North Carolina General Statutes Section 59-45(a1)**

"(a1) Except as provided in subsection (b) of this section, a partner in a registered limited liability partnership is not individually liable for debts and obligations of the partnership incurred while it is a registered limited liability partnership solely by reason of being a partner and does not become liable by participating, in whatever capacity, in the management or control of the business of the partnership.

(b) Nothing in this Chapter shall be interpreted to abolish, modify, restrict, limit, or alter the law in this State applicable to the professional relationship and liabilities between the individual furnishing the professional services and the person receiving the professional services, the standards of professional conduct applicable to the rendering of the services, or any responsibilities, obligations, or sanctions imposed under applicable licensing statutes. A partner in a registered limited liability partnership is not individually liable, directly or indirectly, including by indemnification, contribution, assessment, or otherwise, for the debts, obligations, and liabilities of, or chargeable to, the registered limited liability partnership that arise from errors, omissions, negligence, malpractice, incompetence, or malfeasance committed by another partner or by an employee, agent, or other representative of the partnership; provided, however, nothing in this Chapter shall affect the liability of a partner of a professional registered limited liability partnership for his or her own errors, omissions, negligence, malpractice, incompetence, or malfeasance committed in the rendering of professional services." However, please note that North Carolina General Statutes Sections 59.84.2 to 59.84.4 discuss North Carolina's limited liability partnerships in general; foreign limited liability partnerships are discussed after that.

- **North Dakota Century Code Section 45-22-08.1**

"A partner is not personally liable, directly or indirectly, including by way of indemnification, contribution, or otherwise under section 45-19-03, 45-20-06, 45-20-07, 45-21-03, or 45-21-06 or any other basis of law, for an obligation under this section solely by reason of being a partner or acting as a partner." This is clearly one of the code sections where other code sections must be referenced. Otherwise, North

Dakota's law covers North Dakota limited liability partnerships and foreign LLPs in Sections 45-22-01 to 45-22-27. *Id.*

- **Oregon Revised Statute Section 67.105**

"(3) (a) An obligation of a partnership incurred while the partnership is a limited liability partnership, whether arising in contract, tort or otherwise, is solely the obligation of the partnership. A partner is not personally liable, directly or indirectly, by way of indemnification, contribution or otherwise, for such an obligation solely by reason of being or so acting as a partner.

(b) Notwithstanding paragraph (a) of this subsection, a partner of a limited liability partnership shall continue to be liable for any obligation of the partnership for which the partner was liable before the partnership became a limited liability partnership." In general, Oregon limited liability partnerships are discussed in Sections 67.600 to 67.680. *Id.*

- **Rhode Island General Laws 1956, Section 7-12-26**

"(b) Subject to subsection (c), a partner in a registered limited liability partnership is not liable directly or indirectly (including by way of indemnification, contribution, assessment or otherwise) for debts, obligations, and liabilities of or chargeable to the partnership whether in tort, contract or otherwise, arising while the partnership is a registered limited liability partnership.

(c) Subsection (b) does not affect the individual liability of a partner in a registered limited liability partnership for his or her own negligence, wrongful acts or misconduct, or that of any person under that partner's direct supervision and control other than in an administrative capacity." See Sections 7-12-56 to 7-12-58 for information about Rhode Island limited liability partnerships in general. *Id.*

- **South Carolina Code Annotated Section 33-41-370**

"(B) Subject to subsections (C) and (D), a partner in a registered limited liability partnership is not liable directly or indirectly, including by way of indemnification, contribution, or otherwise, for debts, obligations, and liabilities chargeable to the partnership arising from negligence, wrongful acts, or misconduct committed while the partnership is a registered limited liability partnership and in the course of the partnership business by another partner or an employee, agent, or representative of the partnership.

(C) Subsection (B) shall not affect the liability of a partner in a registered limited liability partnership for his own negligence, wrongful acts, or misconduct, or that of a person under his direct supervision and control.

(D) Each individual who renders professional services on behalf of a registered limited liability partnership is liable for a negligent or wrongful act or omission in which he personally participates to the same extent as if he rendered the services as a sole practitioner. A partner of a registered limited liability partnership which renders professional services, as defined in Section 33-19-103(7), is not liable for the negligence, wrongful acts, misconduct, or omissions of other partners, agents, or employees of the registered limited liability partnership unless he is at fault in appointing, supervising, or cooperating with them." In South Carolina, the general statutes affecting South Carolina limited liability partnerships and foreign LLPS are located at 33-41-1110 to 33-41-1220.

- **Tennessee Code Annotated Sections 61-1-306**

"(c) An obligation of a partnership incurred while the partnership is a registered limited liability partnership, whether arising in contract, tort, or otherwise, is solely the obligation of the partnership. A partner is not personally liable, directly or indirectly, by way of contribution or otherwise, for such an obligation solely by reason of being or acting as a partner. This subsection (c) applies notwithstanding anything inconsistent in the partnership agreement that existed immediately before the vote required to become a registered limited liability partnership under § 61-1-1001(b).

(d) Subsection (c) does not affect the liability of a partner in a registered limited liability partnership for the partner's own omissions, negligence, wrongful acts, misconduct or malpractice, or that of any person under the partner's direct supervision and control." However, please note that Tennessee's Code Annotated, Sections 61-1-1001 to 61-1-1006 discuss limited liability partnerships overall.

- **Texas Business Organizations Code Section 152.801(a)**

"Except as provided by the partnership agreement, a partner is not personally liable to any person, including a partner, directly or indirectly, by contribution, indemnity, or otherwise, for any obligation of the partnership incurred while the partnership is a limited liability partnership." For more on Texas limited liability partnerships, please see Sections 152.801 to 152.805. *Id.*

- **Utah Code Annotated Section 48-1d-306(3)**

"A debt, obligation, or other liability of a partnership incurred while the partnership is a limited liability partnership is solely the debt, obligation, or other liability of the limited liability partnership. A partner is not personally liable, directly or indirectly, by way of contribution or otherwise, for a debt, obligation, or other liability of the limited liability partnership solely by reason of being or acting as a partner...." However, please note that Utah Code Annotated Sections 48-1-41 to 49-1-48 discuss Utah limited liability partnerships and foreign LLPs overall.

- **Virginia Code Annotated Section 50-73.96**

"A person is not, solely by reason of being a partner, liable, directly or indirectly, including by way of indemnification, contribution, assessment or otherwise, for debts, obligations or liabilities of, or chargeable to, the partnership, whether sounding in tort, contract or otherwise, that are incurred, created or assumed by the partnership while the partnership is a registered limited liability partnership." For more information on Virginia limited liability partnerships, see Sections 50-73.132 to 50-73.143. *Id.*

- **Revised Code Washington Section 25.05.125**

"Except as otherwise provided in subsection (4) of this section, an obligation of a partnership incurred while the partnership is a limited liability partnership, whether arising in contract, tort, or otherwise, is solely the obligation of the partnership. A partner is not personally liable, directly or indirectly, by way of contribution or otherwise, for such an obligation solely by reason of being or so acting as a partner. This subsection applies notwithstanding anything inconsistent in the partnership agreement that existed, in the case of a limited liability partnership in existence on June 11, 1998, and, in the case of a partnership becoming a limited liability partnership after June 11, 1998, immediately before the vote required to become a limited liability partnership under RCW 25.05.500(1)." Revised Code Washington Sections 25.05.500 to 25.05.536 discuss limited Washington liability partnerships overall.

- **West Virginia Code Section 47B-3-6(c)**

"(c) Subject to the provisions of subsection (d) of this section, a partner in a registered limited liability partnership is not personally liable directly or indirectly (including by way of indemnification, contribution or otherwise) for debts, obligations and liabilities of or chargeable to the partnership, whether in tort, contract or otherwise, arising from omissions, negligence, wrongful acts, misconduct or malpractice committed while the partnership is a registered limited liability partnership and in the course of partnership business by another partner or by an employee, agent or representative of the partnership.

(d) Subsection (c) of this section does not affect the liability of a partner in a registered limited liability partnership for the partner's own omissions, negligence, wrongful acts, misconduct or malpractice, or that of any person under the partner's direct supervision and control." Thus, New Hampshire's and West Virginia's Sections are very similar. For more information about West Virginia limited liability partnerships, read Sections 47B-10-1 to 47B-10-5. *Id.*

- **Wyoming Statute Section 17-21-306**

"(b) Except as provided by subsections (c) and (d) of this section, a partner of a registered limited liability partnership is not liable, directly or indirectly (including by way of indemnification, contribution, assessment or otherwise), for any debts, obligations or liabilities of, or chargeable to, the registered limited liability partnership or another partner or partners, whether arising in tort, contract or otherwise, solely by reason of being such a partner or acting (or omitting to act) in such capacity or otherwise participating (as an employee, consultant, contractor or otherwise) in the conduct of the other business or activities of the registered limited liability partnership, while the partnership is a registered limited liability partnership.

(c) Subsection (b) of this section shall not affect the liability of a partner in a registered limited liability partnership for the partner's own negligent or wrongful act or misconduct, or that of any person under the partner's direct supervision and control." Otherwise, Wyoming limited liability partnerships are discussed at Wyoming Statue Annotated Sections 17-21-1101 to 17-21-1107.

In general, partners in an LLP are not responsible for the torts or other types of malfeasance that the other partners commit. This is in contrast to a general partnership, wherein the major downfall was that partners were liable for the actions of their fellow partners acting on behalf of the partnership. In a general partnership, if the business assets were not enough to pay debts, then the partner's individual assets could be used to pay debts. Thus, an LLP is an improvement on the general partnership in that people can form a partnership without being worried regarding liability for acts of their partners. Remember, the partner will always be personally responsible for his own actions, just not the actions of other partners.

One of the reasons states are willing to allow this limited liability, is many states require LLPs to carry liability insurance. Examples of states that require LLPs to carry liability insurance are California, Connecticut, and Massachusetts. This helps assure that if the LLP is sued, there will be funds, other than personal funds, to cover the lawsuit.

In recent years, the discussion regarding partial shield and full shield states has become more convoluted as legal personnel mean different things when they talk about the two terms. In an effort to reduce confusion, this text provided you with specific liability statutes for each state. There are very few partial shield states left, such as Louisiana and South Carolina. Most states are full shield states. However, some states fall into a category between partial and full shield, which this text will call "limited" shield. With limited shield states, it is best to refer to the statute itself and case law (for example, New Hampshire and Pennsylvania). The trend seems to be to revise these statutes to make them full shield statutes.

a. Partial Shield versus Full Shield States

The amount of limited liability afforded to the partners depends upon whether a state is a full shield or partial shield state. If a state is a partial shield state, then a partner does have personal liability for the contractual errors his partner makes, but not the tortuous errors his partner makes. Torts include different types of negligence and personal injury actions. There are very few partial shield states left. In the majority of states, full shield is the law. Alaska's statute above is an example of a full shield state. Full shield holds that a partner does not have personal liability for the contractual errors or negligence his partner commits and is the stance of RUPA. Hence, it is typically better to be in a full shield state if you are a partner in a limited liability partnership.

b. Examples of Full versus Partial Shield States

The following are two examples illustrating the difference in liability among full and partial shield states. The first example is a tort example and the second example is a contracts example.

1. The Legal LLP

May 6th is the firm's anniversary. Every year that the anniversary falls on a weekday (or if it falls on the weekend, the closest weekday to May 6th), the firm takes the day off from work and celebrates. One year they went to a baseball game, another year they went out to eat at a fine dining establishment. This year, the firm did not go into the office at all, but instead carpooled to an amusement park. The partner in charge of the tickets, Deborah, had to race back to the office, where had she left them. May 6th is not a federal or court holiday, and mail was delivered as usual. As Deborah entered the office, she saw a piece of mail that had been delivered marked "URGENT: Must File Today. Statute of Limitations About Up!" However, she shrugged it off, because the Managing Limited Partner, Dave, specifically said, "No one shall do any work on the Firm's Anniversary." Therefore, the document was not filed within the Statute of Limitations. Who will be liable for any alleged negligence in not filing that document?

First, note that this hypothetical does not have anything to do with a contract, even though it has to do with paper. The piece of mail was an offer to contract, but since there has been no acceptance by the law firm, this is not a breach of contract. Since this is a tort hypothetical, that Deborah was negligent for not taking care of the mail, the answer will be the same whether it is a full shield state or partial shield state. Partners Deborah and Dave will both be liable, Deborah because she committed the act, and Dave because he was in charge of supervising the act. Any partners other than Deborah and Dave will not be liable, such as Tom and Harry. The LLP is liable for the actions of its members.

2. The Accountancy LLP

Lisa, a partner, is responsible for making sure that the checks are deposited every Friday. However, Lisa has been invited to happy hour by one very cute person in the next-door office. She tells herself that she will have just one quick drink, and still be able to deposit the checks by six o'clock, when the bank closes. However, several drinks later, Lisa looks up, dismayed to find that the clock reads 7:30 p.m. The checks will not be deposited in time to cover the bills the firm has paid. Who will be liable for this?

Paying bills means this is a contract issue. There is a difference, with contracts, between full and partial shield states. In either type of state, Lisa will be responsible because she is responsible for her own actions. In either type of state, the LLP will be responsible for the actions of one of its partners. The only difference between partial shield and full shield comes when discussing the liability of partners other than Lisa. In a full shield state, the other partners will not be responsible for her actions because in a full shield state, other partners are protected against the negligent and contractual wrongs of their partners. However, in a partial shield state, the other partners are only protected against the negligence of their partners. Thus, in a partial shield state, the other partners would also be liable, as this is a contracts issue.

c. "Limited" Shield

An example of a limited shield state would be New Hampshire. New Hampshire states that a partner in a limited liability partnership is not liable for other partners' acts 'whether in tort, contract, or otherwise, arising from omissions, negligence, wrongful acts, misconduct or malpractice.' The tort and contract language seems clear until the second part of the language, which seems to deal all with torts. Case law in the state of New Hampshire would need to be looked at to determine how this statute is applied.

Some states have partners retain personal liability for partnership debts, etc. This means if the partnership ran out of money to pay a partnership debt, the personal assets of the partners would be at risk. Thus, a thorough reading of the full liability statute is necessary. This may have a curtailed effect as many partnership agreements (if there is one) discuss what will happen if the partnership runs out of money. The partnership agreement typically asks the partners to contribute more.

d. Example of Arthur Anderson

Before specifically getting into Arthur Anderson, LLP, some of the background of Enron needs to be discussed.

Enron

Enron originally made its money in selling power. Then, unfortunately, Enron decided to go into communication bandwidth commodities. The communication bandwidth commodities were not nearly as lucrative as the power business. Therefore, Enron decided to inflate its profits to make it look as though the company was doing better than it was. As Enron got deeper into financial crisis, it would put its debts into offshore businesses that were not inputted in with the company's financial statements. Thus, it looked to investors that there were billions of dollars in profits; however, the executives knew there were not. Due to this deception, the stock price continued to grow, during which time, the executives unloaded their actually worthless stock.

Eventually, the company could not hide its losses anymore, and ended up filing the biggest bankruptcy in the United States, up until that time. Thousands of employees lost their jobs.

Some of Enron's executives were tried, including Kenneth Lay, the Chairman and Chief Financial Officer, as well Jeffrey Skilling, Chief Executive Officer and Chief Operating Officer. As there had never been this grandiose abuse of stealing people's retirement funds, it was difficult to prosecute them. They were tried for bank fraud, securities fraud, wire fraud, and insider trading. Lay was convicted of all the charges filed against him while Skilling was convicted of a majority of the charges filed against him.

Arthur Anderson, LLP was tried for obstruction of justice. These charges were brought due to shredding documents about the audit it performed of Enron and then did not report to the proper authorities, though they discovered fraud. Anderson himself was convicted.

As a result, dozens of lawsuits were brought against the company. Although only a few of Arthur Anderson, LLP partners and employees were involved, the LLP itself was responsible for the actions of those few. Due to the negative publicity (despite a conviction being overturned) and the tremendous amounts of lawsuits, the LLP sold off most of its businesses. At least in part, this was probably because with all the tort-related lawsuits, Arthur Anderson needed money to help pay for them. The LLP can be held liable for the acts of its partners, and probably did not have enough liability insurance to cover the lawsuits.

8.5 Continued Existence of the Business and Transferability

Like a general partnership, it is not easy to continue an LLP or to transfer the interests in an LLP. A partner in an LLP can give away her rights to profits, but cannot give over all her interests and management in the LLP without the unanimous consent of the remaining partners.

8.6 Profits and Losses

When profits or losses are made in a limited liability partnership, they are given to the partners. The profits and losses are distributed in accordance with the partnership agreement and usually do not resemble a normal paycheck, but might be paid out less frequently. The partner gets a percent of the profits or losses in an equal percent to the other partners if there is not a partnership agreement. If the partnership agreement does not spell out what this is, then the partners will all get an equal share of the profits and losses.

8.7 Taxation

Similar to the two other types of partnerships that have been discussed, general partnerships and limited partnerships, the limited liability partnership does not pay taxes itself. Rather, the tax is passed through to the individual partners, and they will pay taxes on their share of the profits or take losses on their share of the losses. Still, the limited liability partnership must file a Form 1065 and this includes an accounting of what percent of the profits/losses each partner receives. That is matched up against each partner's individual Schedule K-1, to verify the partners are being truthful and accurate.

8.8 Termination

Limited liability partnerships are usually dissolved in the same manner that a general partnership is dissolved. It will not be similar to a limited partnership, because in an LLP, all the partners can have management rights and if they withdraw, it can affect the continuation of the business. Thus, the remaining partners need to decide to continue the business after the withdrawal of limited liability partners, or it can cause dissolution. This can be provided for in the limited liability partnership agreement, if any. In the alternative, RUPA allows up to ninety days for the partnership to make this decision after the withdrawal.

The winding up process is the same as with a general partnership. The LLP should be sure to notify the secretary of state that the LLP is winding up.

Chapter Summary

Limited liability partnerships may be made up of professionals, such as accountants and attorneys. The LLP is formed by a registered limited liability partnership registration. That must be properly filed with the secretary of state, in order for the partners to have limited liability. While not required, a partnership agreement is a good idea.

Management can, and often is, equally performed by all the partners in the limited liability partnership. However, the partnership agreement can change that.

Only a full shield state fully protects one partner against all the acts of his other partners. As the limited liability partners do not have personal responsibility for the actions of their co-partners, many states require the LLP to have liability insurance. This will ensure that the lawsuits against the LLP can be paid, though through insurance, rather than personal assets. In a partial shield state, one partner is not protected against the contractual errors of his other partners. Now, there are many statutes with "limited" liability shields. Thus, it is normally better, as a limited liability partner, to be in a full shield state. To determine which type of shield your state has, it is imperative the paralegal check the full text of the liability statute in the state the LLP is located.

If the partnership agreement does not state otherwise, profits and losses will be divided equally.

Taxation and dissolution of the limited liability partnership are very similar to that in a general partnership.

Key Terms

Full shield
Limited liability partnership
Partial shield
Registered limited liability partnership

Registration
Revised Uniform Partnership Act
 (RUPA)
Uniform Partnership Act (UPA)

Review Questions

1. What are the major differences between general partnerships and limited liability partnerships?

2. What types of groups usually make up a limited liability partnership?

3. Is financing in a limited liability partnership similar to financing in a general partnership or a limited partnership?

4. Who manages an LLP?

5. Why do some LLPs have to have liability insurance?

6. Explain how a full shield and partial shield state are different.

7. How is the LLP taxed?

Web Links

Perform a search for limited liability partnerships. Note the number of law firms and accounting firms that come up. Visit some of their sites, including a legal LLP (http://www.cooley.com/index.aspx) to determine how they do business.

Exercises

1. There is also another type of partnership, which is new, and is called a limited liability limited partnership. Research whether your state allows LLLPs, and the characteristics of this type of business organization.

2. If one of the partners in an LLP, commits negligence, who is responsible? Be sure to discuss the partner's liability, the partnership's liability, and the other partners' liability, if any.

3. If one of the partners in an LLP supervises an employee, and that employee commits negligence, who is responsible?

4. If the limited liability partnership agreement does not discuss how profits will be divided, how will the profits be divided?

5. Using the statutes in the chapter, look up the full liability code section for your state. Review the statute and determine whether your state is partial, "limited," or full shield.

Chapter 9

Limited Liability Companies

Chapter Outline

Chapter Objectives

- Discuss the lack of a cohesive, nationwide set of laws for LLCs.
- Describe what a limited liability company is and how it operates.
- Outline how a limited liability company is formed.
- Point out the potential dangers of having a one-person limited liability company.
- Compare and contrast management in a member-managed limited liability company to a manager-managed limited liability company.
- Discuss the particular limited liability offered by LLCs.
- Illustrate how although this business entity has corporation characteristics, it still has pass-through taxation.
- Contrast the differences between limited liability partnerships and limited liability companies.

9.1 Introduction to Limited Liability Companies

A limited liability company is often described as a combination of a partnership and a corporation. Perhaps it is compared to a partnership because an LLC has members, which in some ways can act like partners, if they manage together. In the alternative, the members could delegate management. Another reason it is similar to a partnership is that the taxation is pass-through, which means each member will pay taxes on profits based upon his own individual tax rate. This is usually preferable to corporate tax rates, which can be much higher. The major benefit to being in an LLC is the limited liability, which is somewhat similar to the limited liability in a corporation. The members of the limited liability corporation are given limited liability for the debts of the company. As you may recall from last chapter, this is an issue with some LLPs in different states.

A limited liability company is typically not the entity to choose if the client is going to go national with their business. This is because the laws between states vary widely as to how to govern an LLC. There is a Uniform Limited Liability Company Act (ULLCA) and Revised Uniform Limited Liability Act (RULLCA), which more and more states are using in creating their own acts. However, neither the ULLCA nor RULLCA are the norm across the country as of yet. In addition, compared to other countries, such as those in Europe, the LLC is a relatively new type of business organization in the United States. There simply is not the amount of case law available for LLCs as there is for corporations. However, the LLC has become hugely popular since coming to the United States because of the tax benefits and limited liability. The number of LLCs continues to grow much faster than general partnerships and limited partnerships.

An LLC is considered separate from its members, so it has certain legal rights of its own. The LLC can represent itself in court, it can acquire property, it can obtain mortgages, make contracts, lend money, invest, pay retirement plans, and/or donate to charity. An LLC is treated like an artificial person and given many of the same rights as regular, or natural, people. The members of an LLC often do not have to be individuals, but could be corporations or partnerships.

9.2 Governing Laws of LLCs

While there is a Uniform Limited Liability Company Act (ULLCA), most states have not adopted ULLCA. Most states have adopted other laws under which their LLCs are formed. These laws vary from state to state. There is also now the Revised Uniform Limited Liability Company Act (RULLCA), and many states have not adopted it either.

In general, LLCs are regulated by state law. However, in some instances, the Securities Act of 1933 and the Securities and Exchange Act of 1934 can apply to LLCs. You will learn in more depth in later chapters that these two acts were implemented primarily to protect inactive investors. Thus, if an LLC is a small entity wherein all the members participate, then the securities acts will not apply.

Briefly, the securities acts will apply when an investment is made in a common enterprise and the investor expects to make money solely off other people's work. A common enterprise is often a common household name, such as AT&T, GE, or Starbucks. Making money solely off other people's work is what makes a security an inactive investment and regulated by the Securities and Exchange Acts of 1933 and 1934.

If the LLC does go public, and is subject to the SEC regulations, it no longer keeps its pass-through taxation. Then, it must be taxed like a corporation. Thus, there really is not a benefit to running an LLC as a publicly traded company. If a company is not going public, it is probably more beneficial to run as an LLC because of the tax benefit and because an LLC requires less formalities and meetings than a corporation does.

9.3 Formation and Financing

Many states do not allow professionals, such as certified public accountants, attorneys, and doctors to practice as LLCs. As the law has not caught up with this new business entity, it is unfortunate that it is subject to abuse. One of the ways in which states limit the abuse is to prevent many professionals from having an LLC. An LLC may not have to have capital to start, and it does not have to have liability insurance in many states, as a limited liability partnership does in many states. Thus, if a professional, such as a doctor were allowed to be an LLC, he could commit a negligent act, and the LLC might not have the assets or insurance to pay for this liability. While the doctor would still have personal liability for his own negligence, he may have shielded his personal assets. Many real estate companies, however, are operated as LLCs.

On the other hand, many states are now allowing professional limited liability companies. To prevent abuse, states that allow for professional LLCs make the individuals responsible for professional malpractice, in varying degrees. Often, too, the professional LLC can only be made up of one type of professional.

a. Public Document: Articles of Organization

The public document of an LLC may be called a charter or articles of organization, depending upon the state in which the LLC is being formed. Frequently, the LLC must also meet a state's annual reporting requirements. The LLC does this with the applicable state's secretary of state. The annual reporting requirements typically include updating the agent for service of process and updating the list of the managers. If these reporting requirements are not met, the state's secretary of state may eventually dissolve the LLC.

The articles of organization will include several basic elements:

- name,
- address of the LLC,
- agent for service of process,
- name and addresses of the organizer,

- how long the LLC will last,
- managers' names and addresses, and
- a statement regarding personal liability of members.

The name of the limited liability company must include somewhere in the name, that it is a limited liability company or an LLC. In general, this designation should be utilized when the name is utilized. This is supposed to put the public on notice of the limited liability of the company, but the public may still not understand the full implications of that limited liability. The name also has to be a name that is available in a state, and a paralegal can ascertain this by going to the applicable secretary of state's website and performing a name search.

The main office of the LLC is important so that its members can visit where the financial records of the company are supposed to be kept, and ascertain whether they are being appropriately compensated. The registered agent must be kept updated for the company, especially as there has been some abuse of the LLC business organization.

The duration of the limited liability corporation is often included in the articles, as there was a tax provision that required the LLC to designate how long it would last. Manages of the LLC should provide their names and addresses if the LLC is a manager-managed LLC.

b. Private Document: Operating Agreement

The operating agreement is a private agreement, which governs how the members in an LLC are to act in relation to each other. An LLC does not have to have annual meetings, unless the operating agreement states otherwise. Many states do not require LLCs to have a written operating agreement; however, it is a good idea to have it written down.

The operating agreement goes into detail about the management of the LLC. At a minimum, the operating agreement should probably address the following:

- the name of the LLC,
- the names and addresses of all of the members,
- the purpose of the LLC,
- the principal place of business of the LLC,
- how long with LLC will operate for,
- what the LLC can do,
- how the financial contributions to the LLC should be handled,
- how the LLC should be managed,
- whether there will be meetings, and if so, how the members will vote,
- how new members will be admitted and how members can leave the LLC, and
- termination of the LLC.

As you can see from having just read about the articles, many of the initial provisions of the LLC operating agreement are similar. It will include the names and addresses of the members so that they may contact each other, but it is placed in the agreement.

The purpose of the LLC should be broad so that the LLC does not have to keep changing the purpose of the LLC. This can save the LLC money. What the LLC can do should be discussed. For example, does the LLC have the ability to:

- sue in its own name,

- buy and/or sell property of any type, and

- loan money?

If properly drafted, the operating agreement will include a listing of the contributions each member made to the LLC, whether it is in cash, property, or services. If not cash, such assets should be appraised for value. The time when distributions will be made, including the final distributions, should be set forth to reduce conflicts later.

LLCs can be member-managed or manager-managed. If it is member-managed, the managing members can still have limited liability. Member-management typically works better in smaller LLCs than in larger ones, as all members are expected to be managers. In larger LLCs, there would be more members, and it could be more difficult to make decisions with all the members acting as managers.

With a manager-managed LLC, the managers could be certain members or could even be non-members. If the LLC was manager-managed, then only the managers would have the authority to bind the LLC.

Any meetings should be discussed. Meetings are not often required by statute statutes, so the operating agreement needs to provide for them, if so desired. The operating agreement should also contemplate what to do if members leave or want to be admitted, as well as the dissolution of the entire LLC.

c. Financing

The members of the LLC contribute to the LLC. Again, contributions can be made in cash, property, or services. If the LLC does not specify how an LLC member will receive distributions, most states hold that the distributions made should be in equal shares. An LLC has a benefit over an S Corporation (discussed in Chapter 10), which also has the beneficial tax status, in that an LLC allows for foreign investors and corporate investors.

Limited Liability Company Misuse and Beneficial Use

Fortunately, LLCs are becoming much less likely to be abused. Limited liability companies, since they did not have to typically be started with any capital, could be what is known as a shell company. In fact, the LLC was the most common type of shell company. Shell companies have little or no business and assets. Some shell companies money launder or finance terrorism. Often, shell companies just have a mailing address, but not a physical address. The shell company probably will not have employees. The LLC was a good business entity for a shell company because it could be managed anonymously. Another company or a foreign company could own the LLC.

It was particularly easy and cheap to set up a shell company because there were service providers available. The service providers could arrange the resident agent for service of process, mail forwarding services, office space, business licenses, a telephone number, voicemail, and even open a bank account! The price for these services was between one thousand and two thousand dollars a year. A service provider customer who wanted a more "established" company could buy an aged shell company. The service provider kept up all the necessary requirements for several years, which allowed for the shell company to age prior to being bought. The point of an aged company is that it looks more legitimate to lenders and consumers. Luckily, more states are tightening up on the reporting requirements of LLCs and allowing for more "piercing the corporate veil" lawsuits, which can hold LLC members personally liable in the event of fraud. Piercing the corporate veil will be discussed in more detail in regards to corporations. In addition, states are not allowing shelf LLCs either. On a positive note, LLCs are being used for good as well, through low-profit LLCs.

While a low-profit LLC still makes a profit, it has a social goal for society's good. These are often referred to as L3Cs. If there are any profits, they are distributed to the L3C's owners.

9.4 One-Person LLCs

Some states allow one person to form a limited liability company. If a person's profession is allowed to be a limited liability company, this entity would probably be greatly preferable to a sole proprietorship, because of the limited liability. However, opponents of LLCs argue that only requiring one person, along with the other lax laws on LLCs, encourages abuse. In addition, some new businesses might choose not to operate as an LLC as there are more costs to setting up the LLC than with being a sole proprietor.

9.5 Management

Typically, an LLC can decide whether to have all members participate in management or just have one or several of the members manage. In addition, the LLC could hire an outside manager. Another nice thing about the management in an LLC is that unlike with a corporation, shareholder meetings are not required. As indicated on the section on the operating agreement, an LLC can be member-managed (all members participate in management) or manager-managed (which could be specific members managing or non-members managing).

a. Flexible and Full Management

Although an LLC may be member-managed or manager-managed, some issues that come in front of the LLC must have unanimous consent of all members, unless otherwise stated in the operating agreement. Thus, in a manager-managed LLC, some things can require all members to unanimously agree. Generally, these include:

- amendments to the LLC's public documents,
- merger, and
- getting rid of almost all the LLC property.

If additional distributions are made, that would require unanimous approval. Any proposed new members, mergers, or dissolutions must be unanimously agreed to.

b. Member-Managed or Manager-Managed?

With member-managed, each of the LLC's members has an equal say in management of the LLC. This is true no matter how much each member contributed. Each member acts like an agent of the LLC and can bind the LLC, but at the same time, each member is supposed to be acting properly, as a fiduciary to the other members. Decisions would typically be made on a majority vote basis, with the exception of those items above that require a unanimous vote.

With manager-managed, the managers might be elected from within the company. Only these managers would be considered agents for the purposes of binding the company. These managers owe a fiduciary duty to the non-manager members. The managers would have equal management rights between themselves. Managers can be selected and removed by a majority vote of the members. These types of managers often are paid.

9.6 Liability

The members and managers of the limited liability company do not have personal liability for the debts (either from contracts or torts) of the limited liability company, beyond any capital contributions they may have made. Of course, if the member or manager personally commits an act leading to an injury, then he may be held personally liable. The more limited liability makes this business entity often preferred to a sole proprietorship, general partnership, or limited partnership. It can also be better than a limited liability partnership, at least if the LLP is a partial or "limited" shield state (the LLC is very similar to a full shield LLP). It also makes an LLC similar to a corporation in terms of limited liability. The members have a similar limited liability to that of shareholders of a corporation.

However, many beginning companies have to provide personal signatures to obtain capital to start the company. Thus, the members who sign this financing can be held personally liable for that debt.

The LLC itself is supposedly liable for injuries caused by its members and managers. However, many LLCs can be started with little-to-no capital. If an injured party sues the LLC, the LLC might not have any money to pay. The LLC is not always required to carry insurance, as many states require an LLP to do.

Think the Next Time You Get on That Rollercoaster!

The majority of amusement parts are operated by limited liability companies. While it is possible to buy insurance as an amusement park, it is cost prohibitive. Therefore, amusement parks often have self-insurance and/or become an LLC to limit their liability.

Examples of amusement park LLCs you may know: Legoland, Six Flags, and Magic Mountain, which is owned by Cadbury Adams USA, LLC.

Since there is not one official, nation-wide resource for monitoring accidents at amusement parks, it is difficult to assess how many injuries there are. The Consumer Product Safety Commission does a survey to attempt to estimate the number of injuries. However, this is not entirely accurate, in part because it does not cover all amusement parks, and partly because if the injury was handled on site, it is normally not reported to the CPSC. Even the states do not all require that amusement parks report injuries to them.

While many consumers assume the risk if they ride with back problems or under the height restriction, consumers are not assuming that the ride itself is faulty. In 2007, Kaitlyn Lasitter was riding the Superman Tower of Power ride at Six Flags. The cables broke during that ride, and she was severely injured.

9.7 Continued Existence of Business and Transferability

Unless changed, often for tax purposes, the LLC can continue indefinitely. If there is no specification in the articles of organization as to how long the limited liability company will last, then the LLC is known as an at-will LLC. If there is a specification in the articles of organization as to the length of time the limited liability company will last, then the LLC is known as a term LLC. As long as there is at least one member left (in states that only require one member), the LLC can continue even if other members dissociate. Many states require the dissociating members provide a six-month notice of their plan to dissociate.

Property is owned by the LLC and not the members. While a member can give away his right to profit, he cannot give away management rights by himself. To obtain a new member or substitute in a new member, usually a majority or unanimous agreement of the remaining members (depending upon the documents of the LLC) is required.

9.8 Profits and Losses

If the members do not put a clause in their operating agreement, then state law will apply as to what percentage each member receives of the LLC's profits. If the state has adopted ULLCA, then the profits would be distributed equally, even if the members contributed different capital amounts. Losses would also be shared equally. In this way, the LLC would be similar to a general partnership and a limited liability partnership.

9.9 Taxation

One reason many people prefer an LLC to a corporation is that the LLC has pass-through taxation. This means the members can pay at their individual tax rates on any profit received by them. If there is more than one member, then the members may actually report their taxes on the same forms as a partnership. The LLC would file a Form 1065, and the members would file Schedule K-1s to the rest of their taxes. Corporations typically get taxed twice or more, so this can be a substantial tax savings. If, however, the LLC wants to be taxed like a corporation, it can choose to do so. The default is that an LLC is taxed like a partnership; if the LLC wants to change that, it needs to check a box so that the IRS will tax it as a corporation. An LLC might choose to do so if the individual members are in very high tax brackets. If the LLC is a one-person LLC, then the owner of the LLC is taxed like a sole proprietor.

9.10 Termination

There are many ways in which a member can dissociate from an LLC, but this is typically not an issue so long as the LLC buys out the leaving member's interest. A member could disassociate by letting the LLC know he wants to leave, an event in the operating agreement occurs, the member is forced out, the member goes bankrupt, or the member passes away.

There are also many ways that an LLC can dissolve. These ways need to be discussed in a little more detail. Often, the LLC will state when the end date is. Thus, the articles of organization might specify that the LLC will last for twenty-five years. To prevent the LLC from dissolving after the twenty-five years, the articles could be renewed. All the members of the LLC could also agree to dissolve the LLC, usually because the LLC is not making sufficient money. A court can decide to dissolve the LLC. Even the secretary of state in the applicable state could dissolve the LLC for failure to file annual reports for two or more years. Once the LLC is being dissolved, the LLC will want to file articles of termination or articles of dissolution, depending upon the state. Before any distributions can be made to any partners, the debts of the LLC must be paid first.

Termination can happen in a new way when it comes to LLCs. If the LLC has been fraudulent, then the "veil" of the LLC may be pierced to sue the members of the LLC directly. This is the same as in a corporation, though piercing the corporate veil is not as common a remedy for LLCs as it is for corporations. Thus, piercing the corporate veil will be discussed in more detail in the corporation chapters.

9.11 Case

The following case involves a lawsuit against a limited liability company. It involves an LLC that is a medical group. In general, employees are protected when they "whistle-blow." Was Dr. Mixon correctly terminated from the LLC as a member?

Mixon v. Iberia Surgical, L.L.C.

956 So.2d 76 (2007)

STATEMENT OF THE CASE

Tynes E. Mixon, III, M.D. filed a petition for damages asserting he was wrongfully terminated from his membership in Iberia Surgical, L.L.C. (Iberia Surgical) and did not receive adequate compensation for his interest in the business. Dr. Mixon later amended his petition alleging a claim under an "abuse of rights" theory. Iberia Surgical filed motions for summary judgment. The trial court granted the Defendant's motions dismissing all claims of Dr. Mixon against Iberia Surgical. Dr. Mixon filed this appeal. For the reasons assigned below, we affirm the judgment of the trial court.

STATEMENT OF THE FACTS

Iberia Surgical was formed, in August 1998, by a group of physicians practicing in Iberia Parish for the purpose of establishing an ambulatory, out-patient surgery center. Each of the eleven physician members contributed $5000 and obtained a 9.09% interest in the business. The members executed a written Operating Agreement which provided a member may be terminated "without cause" upon unanimous vote of the membership. The contract also contained a "Buy-Out" provision in case of termination or withdrawal by one of the members. Dr. Mixon was one of the original organizers and became the managing partner.

In June 1999, Iberia Surgical, in a joint ownership venture with Iberia Medical Center, formed New Iberia Surgery Center, L.L.C., an outpatient surgical facility. Iberia Surgical owned an 80% interest and Iberia Medical Center owned a 20% interest in the new facility. The New Iberia Surgery Center was managed by a professional management company, Genesee & Associates, Inc.

Not long after the formation of Iberia Surgical, Dr. Mixon became dissatisfied with the operation of the new facility and management practices of his fellow physicians. On several occasions, he voiced concerns regarding patient care and what he perceived to be violations of federal law in the handling of medicaid patients. When the members took no action regarding his complaints, Dr. Mixon met with federal authorities to report the alleged violations. He provided documents from Iberia Surgical to federal investigators, taped telephone conversations between himself and his partners, and, at one point, placed a voice-activated recorder in the trash can of the partnership meeting room. Dr. Mixon disclosed to several partners that he had reported them to federal authorities. Soon, Dr. Mixon began to realize his behavior was not well received among the partners and he may be terminated from membership in Iberia Surgical by a vote of the organization. In fact, a proposal was circulated to amend the by-laws of the Operating Agreement to require a majority vote to terminate a member instead of a unanimous vote. Dr. Mixon perceived this proposed change to be directed against him. He requested mediation and then filed a petition in district court for declaratory judgment and injunctive relief to prohibit the members from meeting to discuss the proposed change. His fears were well founded. After months of discord, and despite his legal protests, on August 28, 2002, Dr. Mixon was terminated from Iberia Surgical by unanimous vote of the membership. Pursuant to the Buy-Out provisions of the Operating Agreement, Dr. Mixon was paid $71,356.85, over a twelve month period for his membership interest. He negotiated the checks. To date, no state or federal charges have been filed against Iberia Surgical or any of its physician members.

LAW AND DISCUSSION

Dr. Mixon contends there was no legitimate reason for his termination in Iberia Surgical since he was a productive member of the group and was, in fact, the number five producer in terms of surgical procedures. Dr. Mixon further contends he was expelled from membership in Iberia Surgical solely because he complained of and reported allegedly improper activities and violations of federal law by Iberia Surgical and New Iberia Surgery Center. This termination, he maintains, violates the Louisiana Unfair Trade Practices and Consumer Protection Law ... and the Louisiana whistleblower statute.... Additionally, Dr. Mixon asserts Iberia Surgical abused their right to terminate him from membership. He also alleges he was compensated for his ownership interest at a price far less than fair market value. We find neither the Louisiana Unfair Trade Practices and Consumer Protection Law or the Louisiana whistleblower statute provide a remedy for Dr. Mixon. Based on our review of the record, we conclude Dr. Mixon's release from membership in Iberia Surgical was done for legitimate business reasons and he was compensated, in accordance with the provisions of the Operating Agreement, which he helped draft. Each of Dr. Mixon's claims will be addressed below.

Louisiana Unfair Trade Practices and Consumer Protection Law, La.R.S. 51:1401
Louisiana Whistleblower Statute, La.R.S. 46:440.3(B)

The Unfair Trade Practices Law and Consumer Protection Law was enacted to prohibit "[u]nfair methods of competition and unfair or deceptive acts or practices in the conduct of any trade or commerce." The individuals falling within the ambit of its protection are consumers, defined under the Act as "any person who uses, purchases, or leases goods or services." A consumer transaction means "any transaction involving trade or commerce to a natural person, the subject of which transaction is primarily intended for personal, family, or household use." The statute authorizes the Attorney General to seek injunctive relief against business engaging in prohibited business practices. *Philips v. Berner* ... held this statute applies to competitors or consumers and provides a remedy for unfair or deceptive trade practices. A practice is unfair when it offends established public policy and when the practice is unethical, oppressive, unscrupulous or substantially injurious. A trade practice is "deceptive" for purposes of LUTPA when it amounts to fraud, deceit, or misrepresentation. The actions of Iberia Surgical in releasing Dr. Mixon from its membership under the terms of a contract mutually agreed upon does not amount to fraud, deceit or misrepresentation. Moreover, Dr. Mixon is not a "consumer or competitor" within the definition of the Act. We find no merit to this argument.

Louisiana Whistleblower Statute, La.R.S. 46:440.3(B)

Dr. Mixon alleges his termination from membership in Iberia Surgical was a direct result of his actions in reporting allegedly improper activities and violations of federal law by Iberia Surgical and New Iberia Surgery Center. He seeks to bring his actions within the scope of protection of Louisiana Revised Statutes 46:440.3, which provides, in relevant part:

> (B) No individual shall be threatened, harassed, or discriminated against in any manner by a health care provider or other person because of any lawful act engaged in by the individual or on behalf of the individual in furtherance of any action taken pursuant to this Part in regard to a health care provider or other person from whom recovery is or could be sought except that a health care provider may arrange for a recipient to receive goods, services, or supplies from another health care provider if the recipient agrees and the arrangement is approved by the secretary. Such an individual may seek any and all relief for his injury to which he is entitled under state or federal law.

> (2) A person aggrieved of a violation of Subsection A or B of this Section shall be entitled to exemplary damages.

This statute is part of the Louisiana Medical Assistance Programs Integrity Law adopted in 1997 and was intended to "protect the fiscal and programmatic integrity of the medical assistance programs from health care providers and other persons who engage in fraud, misrepresentation, abuse or other ill practices, as set forth in this Part, to obtain payment to which there health care providers or persons are not entitled." ... Dr. Mixon does not assert that Iberia Surgical fraudulently sought payment from the Medicaid Program to which it was not entitled. Rather, Dr. Mixon alleges Iberia Surgical was attempting to limit the number of Medicaid patients treated at the facility. Iberia Surgical's alleged effort to limit the referral of medicaid patients to the facility is not prohibited under the Louisiana Medical Assistance Programs Integrity Law. Therefore, the whistleblower provision of the statute contained in La.R.S. 46:440.3 does not apply. Moreover, the whistleblower provision under the Act is intended to protect individuals reporting violations under the statute from threats, harassment or discrimination. The actions of Iberia Surgical in terminating his membership does not rise to the level of threats, harassment or discrimination within the definition of the Act. We find no merit to this argument.

Action for Abuse of Rights

Dr. Mixon does not dispute the Operating Agreement allows for the termination of a partner by unanimous vote of the membership. Article 3.2(g) of the Operating Agreement provides:

> Termination Without Cause. A Member may be Terminated Without Cause, by unanimous vote in writing of the remaining Members of the Company. Such Termination Without Cause shall be treated as though the Member were expelled from the Company as provided in Section 3.2(e)(iv) above.

However, Dr. Mixon asserts the exercise of this contractual right by Iberia Surgical to terminate his membership was an abuse of right and violates moral rules, good faith, and elementary fairness. He also contends there was an absence of a serious or legitimate motive for the exercise of the right and, therefore, he concludes it was done to cause harm. Dr. Mixon contends the trial court erred in determining Iberia Surgical could not be subject to an action for abuse of rights.

The abuse of rights doctrine is a civilian concept which is applied only in limited circumstances because its application renders unenforceable an individual's otherwise judicially protected rights.... This doctrine applies when one of the following conditions is met: "(1) the predominant motive for exercise of the right is to cause harm; (2) there is no legitimate motive for exercise of the right; (3) exercise of the right violates moral rules, good faith, or elementary fairness; or (4) exercise of the right is for a purpose other than that for which it was granted." ... This doctrine is typically applied in situations involving the cancellation of insurance coverage. Although the insurer may have right to modify or cancel the policy, the courts have held public policy considerations may prevent the insurer from exercising this right....

We agree with the trial court that Dr. Mixon cannot support a claim for abuse of right. The members of Iberia Surgical, including Dr. Mixon, negotiated a business agreement the purpose of which was to establish a profitable out-patient surgery center. There is ample evidence in the record, including Dr. Mixon's own testimony, to establish he objected to the way the facility was being managed and had serious concerns regarding the distribution of income within the group. His views were not well received and represented the minority opinion within the organization. When the partners refused to cooperate with his suggestions, he reported them to federal authorities. Dr. Mixon then revealed to the partners that he had contacted federal investigators. Once this occurred, it became apparent that the animosity which existed between Dr. Mixon and his partners would be detrimental to the welfare of the business venture. A decision was made to buy-out Dr. Mixon's interest and sever financial ties with him. The Operating Agreement which Dr. Mixon negotiated and signed, gave Iberia Surgical the right to terminate one of its members without cause. Dr. Mixon has provided no evidence to suggest the termination was done to cause him harm or for any other reason than a legitimate business reason. The provisions of the Operating Agreement are straight-forward and provide a formula for compensation of its members in the event of a termination or withdrawal. There is no evidence to suggest the terms of the Operating Agreement violates moral rules, good faith, or elementary fairness. We find no merit to this argument.

Adequate Compensation

Dr. Mixon contends he was not adequately compensated for his interest in Iberia Surgical. The Buy-Out provisions of the Operating Agreement are contained in Article 3.3, which provides:

> Buy-Out Upon Termination of Membership; Fair Market Value Determinations. Upon termination of a Member's Interest, for any reason, there shall be no return of such Member's Capital Contribution(s). Any Member who voluntarily withdraws from the Company as provided in this Agreement shall be entitled to receive the value of such Withdrawing Member's Interest to be determined as set forth in Exhibit E, attached hereto. The value of the Withdrawing Member's Interest in the Company shall be in accordance with its "Fair Market Value" as of the most recent determination by the Company's accountant in that regard. Fair Market Value determinations as to Membership Interests shall be made by the Company's Accountant, unless otherwise unanimously agreed to in writing by the Management Committee members, all in accordance with the provisions set forth in Exhibit E.

Exhibit E, Section 1, provides:

> (c) Purchase Price and Terms. The Purchase Price of a Former Member's Interest which is sold as a result of the occurrence of a Dissolution Event, shall be determined as follows:

> ....

> (ii) The "Book Value" means the "fair market value" of a Membership Interest computed in accordance with generally accepted accounting principles, of the net equity of the Company as of the end of the last full taxable year immediately preceding the year in which the Event giving rise to the purchase and sale of the Membership Rights or Interest occurred. Notwithstanding anything contained in this Agreement to the contrary, the computation of Book Value shall be subject to the following provisions.

> (ff) Book Value shall be determined by the accountants regularly employed by the Company. The determination of the accountants shall, for the purposes of this Agreement, be binding and conclusive upon all parties.

Dr. Mixon contends "Book Value" is not synonymous with "Fair Market Value." He contends the Operating Agreement requires his membership share should be computed according to the "Fair Market Value," which he defines as the price a seller is willing to accept and a buyer is willing to pay on the open market. In support of his theory, he submits the affidavit of Chris Rainey, a certified public accountant and certified valuation analyst. Mr. Rainey testified the appropriate method to use in determining the "Fair Market Value" of Iberia Surgical is to locate a comparable in the area. His search for a comparable led him to the 1989 sale of Physicians Surgery Center in Houma. Mr. Rainey determined Physicians Surgery Center was sold for a price equal to 9.89 times its net income. He then determined the net income of Iberia Surgical for the tax year ending December 2001 was $806,062. He multiplied that number by 9.89 and concluded the fair market value of Iberia Surgical to be $7,971,953. Therefore, Mr. Rainey calculated Dr. Mixon's 9.09% equity interest, after discounting for a minority interest, was valued at $483,100.

We agree the terms "Book Value" and "Fair Market Value" are not synonymous and have generally recognized meanings in accounting in valuation. However, the Operating Agreement, Exhibit E, defines the terms interchangeably and specifically provides: "'Book Value' means the 'fair market value' of a Membership Interest computed in accordance with generally accepted accounting principles, of the net equity of the Company as of the end of the last full taxable year immediately preceding the year in which the Event giving rise to the purchase and sale of the Membership Rights or Interest occurred".... Under the agreement, the "Book Value shall be determined by the accountants regularly employed by the Company." We find the terms of the Operating Agreement clear and controlling in determining the amount owed to a member. Dr. Rainey's calculations were based on "fair market value" which was not the standard agreed upon by the parties. Under the terms of the Operating Agreement, the parties agreed to use the "book value" in determining the value of a member's interest, not fair market value. The book value of a business "has a well-defined meaning, is unambiguous, and is susceptible of only one construction. It is the value as shown by the books of the business, and no other value." ... Book value is calculated by measuring the assets of the business against its liabilities. Good will, actual value or value in the open market, is not considered in determining book value....

Iberia Surgical submitted the testimony of Caroline C. Boudreaux, the certified public accountant hired to determine the amount owed to Dr. Mixon, under the terms of the Operating Agreement. Ms. Boudreaux testified she examined the books of the business and calculated Dr. Mixon's interest to be $71,356.85. Dr. Mixon does not contend the calculations used by Ms. Boudreaux are incorrect. Instead, he contends she used "book value" instead of value in the open market or "fair market value." We find no error in the decision of the trial court finding Dr. Mixon was compensated in accordance with the terms of the Operating Agreement.

DECREE

Based on the foregoing review of the record, we affirm the decision of the trial court granting summary judgment in favor of Iberia Surgical and dismissing all claims of Dr. Mixon. All costs of this appeal are assessed to Dr. Tynes Mixon, III.

Chapter Summary

In general, an LLC is a blend of partnership and corporation laws. The people who make up the LLC are called members. One of the major benefits of an LLC is that all of the LLC members have limited liability for the debts of the LLC. All the members of the LLC can manage the LLC or the LLC can appoint managers. An LLC has most of the same rights a natural person does in a court of law, even though it is an artificial person.

Even though there is the Uniform Limited Liability Company Act, most states have not adopted that act. Therefore, the state statutes governing LLCs vary widely from state to state.

The public document of an LLC is the articles of organization and the private document is the operating agreement. The articles will contain the name of the LLC, with a designation that the business is being run as an LLC, and may also discuss how long the LLC will last. The operating agreement may include the capital contributions of the members to the LLC, and it may also discuss how do divide up the profits and losses of the company.

An LLC can be either member-managed or manager-managed. In a member-managed LLC, all the members manage equally, regardless of what amount of capital they contributed. In a manager-managed LLC, only the managers have the right to manage.

Members and managers are not liable for the LLC's debts and obligations, other than up to the amount of capital they contributed, if any. If the member or manager personally caused the debts or obligations, then they could be held personally liable. The LLC is liable for the actions of its members and managers, but because LLCs can often be run with little money, this might not be of great benefit to a plaintiff suing the LLC.

Another one of the major benefits of an LLC is that the members can choose to get the pass-through taxation, similar to a partnership, rather than being taxed like a corporation. A corporation is taxed twice, so this is normally a major tax savings.

While similar in many ways to a limited liability partnership, the LLC is probably preferable, at least in part, because liability insurance is normally not required and because there is no need to worry about partial or full shield state differences. The members are protected against the negligent or contractual errors of other members.

Key Terms

Articles of organization
At-will LLC
Limited liability
Limited liability company
Manager-managed
Member

Member-managed
Operating agreement
Term LLC
Uniform Limited Liability Company
    Act (ULLCA)

Review Questions

1. How are limited liability companies different from partnerships? How are limited liability companies different than corporations?
2. What documents are required to form an LLC?
3. Why are LLCs so easy to abuse?
4. Who manages an LLC?
5. When might a member of an LLC have personal liability?
6. What are the main advantages of doing business as an LLC?
7. How are LLCs taxed?
8. How do LLCs offer more liability protection than LLPs?
9. Was Dr. Mixon correctly terminated from the LLC as a member?

Web Links

For more information on LLCs, go to http://www.irs.gov/Businesses/Small-Businesses-&-Self-Employed/Limited-Liability-Company-LLC and https://www.sba.gov/content/limited-liability-company-llc.

Exercises

1. Janet is a member of the LLC. The LLC has not paid its rent for the building it leases. Is Janet responsible for paying the rent? What if she had personally signed the lease agreement?
2. The losses were one hundred thousand dollars this last year. There are five LLC members. There is no operating agreement. How will the losses be divided and why?
3. LLCs can be difficult to understand. Another good case to read is below.

Braucher v. Swagat Group, L.L.C.

702 F. Supp. 2d 1032 (2010)

... In the winter of 2006, Georgia Braucher and Bonnie Leiser stayed at the Comfort Inn in Lincoln, Illinois (Hotel), owned by the Defendant LLC and operated under a Franchise Agreement (Agreement) with Choice Hotels. The other Swagat Defendants were members of the LLC. Georgia Braucher and Bonnie Leiser became ill shortly after their stays at the Hotel, and both were diagnosed with Legionnaires Disease. Legionnaires Disease is a respiratory disease that presents symptoms similar to pneumonia.... On March 10, 2006, the Illinois Health Department closed the Hotel when Legionella bacteria, the bacteria that cause Legionnaires Disease, was found in the Hotel's pool and spa. Georgia Braucher died on March 19, 2006.

Bonnie Leiser and Georgia Braucher's daughter Marjorie Braucher then brought these cases against the Defendants. Choice Hotels brought cross-claims against the Swagat Defendants for indemnification. The Defendants now seek summary judgment on the Plaintiffs' claims. The Swagat Defendants also seek partial summary judgment on Choice Hotels' cross-claims for indemnification. For the reasons set forth below, the Motions to Bar are allowed, the Choice Summary Judgment Motions are allowed, and the Swagat Summary Judgment Motions and the Partial Summary Judgment Motions are allowed in part and denied in part.

STATEMENT OF FACTS

On February 15, 2001, Choice Hotels and the Swagat Defendants entered into the Agreement.... All of the Swagat Defendants were parties to the Agreement, not just the LLC. The Agreement granted the Swagat Defendants a franchise to operate the Hotel as a Comfort Inn. The Agreement gave the Swagat Defendants a license to use Choice Hotels' Comfort Inn marks, its system for operating hotels, and its reservation system. *Agreement*, § 2. The Agreement required the Swagat Defendants to pay various fees to Choice Hotels and to comply with all of the Choice Hotels' Rules and Regulations for operating the Hotel as a Comfort Inn. *Id.*, §§ 4, 6. The Agreement further authorized Choice Hotels to inspect the Hotel periodically to insure that the Swagat Defendants complied with the terms of the Agreement and Choice Hotels' Rules and Regulations. *Id.*, § 6.g.

The Agreement contained a provision entitled "Indemnification" (Indemnification Clause)....

The Agreement also contained a provision entitled "Business Relationship", which stated, in part:

> You are an independent contractor. Nothing in this Agreement makes, or is intended to make, either party an agent, legal representative, subsidiary, joint venturer, partner, employee, independent contractor or servant of the other (except that we are acting as your agent when making reservations for your Hotel)....

The Choice Hotels' Rules and Regulations stated that Choice Hotels would perform periodic inspections. The Rules and Regulations referred to such an inspection as a "Quality Assurance Review" (QAR).... The Rules and Regulations stated that the QAR:

> [I]s designed to assist you and Choice by identifying areas in which your Hotel does not meet the minimum standards of the Comfort Inn brand, as set forth in these Rules & Regulations. This review is not intended to determine whether your Hotel is in compliance with federal, state and local laws and regulations, which is your sole responsibility.

Id. A failing grade in a QAR could, at Choice Hotels' discretion, result in a notice of default and, ultimately, termination of the Agreement if the defaults were not cured within thirty days of the notice. *Id.*

The Rules and Regulations also required the Swagat Defendants to place a plaque in the lobby visible from the front desk that stated that the Hotel was independently owned and operated by the LLC. *Id.,* §828.1. The Choice Hotels provided advertising, a toll-free 800 number telephone reservation system, and a website which included an internet reservation system. The Choice Hotels' reservation system was tied directly into the Hotel's computerized reservation system. The Choice Hotels' website contained a statement on the home page that each Choice Hotel was independently owned and operated....

The Swagat Defendants began operating the Hotel as a Comfort Inn in 2001. The Swagat Defendants placed the required plaque in the lobby, stating that the Hotel was independently owned and operated. The plaque was on display in 2006 when the Plaintiffs stayed at the Hotel. The Swagat Defendants also kept copies of the current Choice Hotels' Worldwide Hotel Directory (Directory) available in the lobby. The 2006 Directory contained a statement that each hotel was owned and operated....

The Hotel participated in Choice Hotels' program that allowed guests to accumulate points toward a free stay at Choice Hotels. If a guest redeemed points for a free stay, Choice Hotels reimbursed the participating hotel for the cost of the night's stay.

The Hotel had an indoor swimming pool and spa. The Rules and Regulations required the Swagat Defendants to have either a swimming pool or a pre-approved exercise room at the Hotel.... The Rules and Regulations further stated, "Swimming pool, recreation areas and all filtration and chemical feed systems must meet all applicable local, state and federal codes...." The pool and spa area was enclosed in a separate room. The pool and spa area had a ventilation system that was separate from the rest of the Hotel, and had two exterior windows and a door that opened into an interior hallway of the Hotel....

The Hotel retained an employee of the former owner. The employee was named Wayne Filmore. Filmore handled the maintenance of the pool and spa at the Hotel until he left in 2003. Filmore showed Vasant Patel how to maintain the pool and spa.... The Illinois Department of Public Health (Department) inspector, Chad Curless, also showed Patel how to use pool test kits.... After Filmore left the Hotel, Vasant Patel maintained the pool and spa. Vasant Patel had no other training or experience in pool and spa maintenance. Choice Hotels did not provide him with any training in pool and spa maintenance.

Choice Hotels' Franchise Service Director Mark Schimmel conducted the QARs at the Hotel. He tried to conduct these reviews every seven months, usually twice a year. He said that he did not make that schedule sometimes.... The QAR included a visual inspection of the pool and spa. Schimmel would check to see that the water was clear. He would check pool records for chemical checks to determine if the franchisee was doing a minimum of maintenance on a daily basis and to determine if there were any problems. Schimmel, however, did not test the pool or spa water during the inspection. Schimmel would visually inspect the pool equipment. He would also note any chlorine smell in the pool area. Schimmel had the authority to shut down a pool if the water was cloudy. Cloudy water was a safety hazard because a person drowning at the bottom of the pool could not be seen if the water was cloudy.... If Schimmel could not see the floor drain at the bottom of the pool, he would close the pool immediately and require the franchisee to remedy the situation.

Schimmel conducted a QAR of the Hotel on November 11, 2004. This was the last QAR before the Plaintiffs' stays at the Hotel in 2006. Schimmel used a score sheet for the QAR. The sheet listed two general categories, Cleanliness (CL) and Maintenance and Capital Improvement (MCI). The Hotel started with 1000 points in each category. Schimmel assigned points for any deficiency in any listed category. These points were deducted from the initial 1000 points in one of the two categories. The Hotel received a final score in each category. A score of 750 points in each of the two general categories was passing....

In the November 11, 2004, QAR, Schimmel deducted points for deficiencies in the following aspects of the pool and spa area on the QAR checklist:

- pool area/deck dirty, furniture soiled
- algae/mildew in pool, water unclear, milky, dirty
- furniture damage/needs paint and adequate lounge furniture
- safety equipment not accessible/missing
- depth not adequately marked
- lighting inadequate/damaged/missing
- signs damage/need paint/inadequate
- fences/gates damages/inoperative/inadequate
- walls/floor/deck/ceiling damaged
- damage/needs paint, dated/aged....

The Hotel, overall, received a passing grade on this QAR....

The Department conducted periodic inspections of the pool and spa area. The Department's regulations required the Hotel to check the chlorine and pH levels in the pool and spa twice a day. The free chlorine level was supposed to be 1 to 4 parts per million (ppm) in water below 85[degree]s Fahrenheit, and between 2 to 4 ppm for water 86[degree]s and above.... The pH level was supposed to be between 7.2 and 7.6.... The Hotel was required to keep a log documenting the daily checks. The Log listed the chlorine, pH level, and water temperature determined each check....

The Department's Inspector Chad Curless conducted the inspections at the Hotel. On October 17, 2005, Curless shut down the pool and spa because the chlorine level was below 1 ppm and the pH level was greater than 8 in both the pool and spa. *Curless Deposition,* at 61–62. Curless noted on his report:

> Operational reports have been filled in for the rest of the year through 2005. This is false documentation....

Curless said that the chlorine and pH levels were all filled out for the rest of the year on the Log....

Curless discussed the proper use of pool testing kits with Vasant Patel at this time. Vasant Patel had a Taylor brand kit, but used testing chemicals that were designed to be used with a Rainbow brand testing kit. The use of the wrong chemicals could result in incorrect readings. Curless told Vasant Patel to use only the Taylor brand chemicals with the Taylor brand testing kit....

Vasant Patel called Curless on October 21, 2005, to tell him that the chlorine and pH levels were corrected in the pool and spa. Curless authorized him to reopen the pool and spa. Curless made a surprise inspection of the pool and spa on October 22, 2005. The chlorine and pH levels were within appropriate limits at that time....

Curless inspected the pool and spa again on February 8, 2006. This time he found that the chlorine level in the pool was too high at 6 ppm, there was no chlorine level in the spa, and the pH level in the spa was greater than 8. Curless closed the spa.... Curless allowed Vasant Patel to reopen the spa on February 14, 2006....

The Log stated that on February 8, 2006, the chlorine level was 3.1 and the pH level was 7.1 in both the pool and the spa. *Log.* Curless said that there was a big difference between 7.1 and 8. *Curless Deposition,* at 80. In fact, the Log stated that the free chlorine level was always between 3.1 and 3.4, and the pH level was always between 7.1 and 7.4 from January 1, 2006, until the pool and spa were closed on March 10, 2006. *Log.* Curless stated that in his experience, chlorine levels and pH levels usually would vary more than this from day to day....

On March 6, 2006, the Department received a notice of a possible outbreak of Legionnaires Disease at the Hotel. *Id.,* at 86. Curless inspected the pool and spa the next day, on March 7, 2006. This time, he found no chlorine in either the pool or spa and pH levels in excess of 8 in both the pool and spa. *Id.,* at 88. He shut both the pool and spa down and took water samples for testing. Those samples tested positive for Legionella bacteria. The Department immediately sent the Hotel notice to shut the pool and spa down....

The Log showed chlorine levels of 3.1 and pH levels of 7.3 and 7.8, respectively, on March 6, 2006, the day before Curless' inspections. Curless stated in his deposition, that in his experience, the chlorine levels would not have gone from 3.1 to 0 in one day, and pH levels would not have gone from 7.3 to more than 8 in one day....

Plaintiff Bonnie Leiser stayed at the Hotel from January 14, 2006, to January 16, 2006. She and her brother Brian Leiser stayed together in the same room. They were attending a funeral of a family member. Her brother made the reservation. Bonnie Leiser had stayed at the Hotel before. Bonnie Leiser went into the spa during her stay at the Hotel. After her stay, she became ill. She was diagnosed with Legionnaires Disease. Bonnie Leiser smoked cigarettes at the time she contracted Legionnaires Disease.

Bonnie Leiser was familiar with the Comfort Inn brand. She had seen Choice Hotels' commercials on television.... She was not aware of the fact that the LLC owned the Hotel. She testified that, at the time of her deposition, she understood that the Swagat Defendants owned the Hotel and operated it as a subsidiary of Choice Hotels.

She testified at her deposition that she assumed that Choice Hotels and the Swagat Defendants were partners. *Id.,* at 155.

Marjorie Braucher and her mother Georgia Braucher stayed at the Hotel from February 11 to February 13, 2006. Marjorie made the reservation. Georgia and Marjorie had stayed at Choice Hotels before elsewhere. Georgia Braucher did not go into the pool and spa area of the Hotel during her stay. Georgia walked down the hallway by the pool and spa area about four times during her stay, but she did not go into the area. After their stay, Georgia Braucher became ill. She was diagnosed with Legionnaires Disease and died on March 19, 2006. Georgia was 90 years old at the time....

The Department investigated the occurrence of Legionella bacteria at the Hotel pool and spa. The Department report stated that there were 160 cases of respiratory illnesses reported by people who stayed at the Hotel in early 2006.... There were five confirmed cases of Legionnaires Disease including Bonnie Leiser and Georgia Braucher.... The level of Legionella bacteria found in the water from the pool and spa was 2000 times higher than the level that would normally be found in municipal tap water.... The Department also tested water from the faucets and showers in some of the Hotel rooms.... This water had no Legionella bacteria....

The Plaintiffs' expert Dr. David Smith opined that the Hotel did not maintain the pool and spa properly. Dr. Smith is a retired United States Coast Guard Commander with extensive experience in water safety and water rescue procedures. He also has training and experience in the proper maintenance procedures for swimming pools.... He opined that Vasant Patel falsified the Log. He based his opinion on Curless' notation on the October 2005 inspection form that the records were falsified and the fact that the chlorine level and pH level on the Log stayed so uniform. He opined that the levels would have varied more widely from day to day. He noted that the Log showed that the pool and spa were regularly subjected to shock treatments designed to increase the amount of free chlorine in the pool and spa ... He said that the chlorine levels should have increased immediately after the treatments, but the Log consistently showed no change in the levels. He opined that this indicated that the Log was fabricated. Curless agreed that it was unusual for the chlorine and pH levels to stay so uniform from day to day....

The Plaintiffs' expert Dr. Carl Fliermans opined to a reasonable degree of medical certainty that Bonnie Leiser and Georgia Braucher contracted Legionnaires Disease from the bacteria in the pool and spa area of the Hotel.... Dr. Fliermans is a microbial ecologist and an expert on Legionnaires Disease.... Dr. Fliermans based his opinion on the fact that others who stayed at the Hotel contracted the disease; Bonnie Leiser and Georgia Braucher both were infected with the specific type of Legionella bacteria that was found in the pool and spa; the levels of Legionella bacteria found in the spa on March 7, 2006, were so high that the level would have been elevated when Leiser and Braucher stayed at the Hotel; the pool and spa records indicated that the pool and spa were not maintained properly; and no other cases of Legionnaires Disease were reported to the Centers for Disease Control from the Lincoln, Illinois, area generally.... He opined that under these circumstances, the source of Bonnie Leiser and Georgia Braucher's infection was the Hotel's pool and spa.

Dr. Fliermans stated that Legionnaires Disease is contracted by taking an aerosol form of contaminated water into the person's lungs. He opined that Bonnie Leiser could have breathed in the mist from the pool and spa when she used the spa. He opined that Georgia Braucher could have breathed in the mist from the pool and spa area when she walked down the Hotel hallway. He opined that the mist from the pool and spa area came into the Hotel hallway when the door to the spa and pool area was opened and closed....

Choice Hotels filed cross-claims against the Swagat Defendants.... Choice Hotels alleged cross-claims for express indemnity under the Indemnification Clause, implied indemnity, and contribution against each Swagat Defendant. The express indemnity claims asked for a judgment against each Swagat Defendant for any amount that Choice Hotels is liable to the Plaintiffs, plus attorneys fees and costs for defense of the suit.... The implied indemnity claims alleged that the Swagat Defendants were obligated to indemnify Choice Hotels if Choice Hotels was found vicariously liable for the acts of the Swagat Defendants....

ANALYSIS

The Defendants now seek summary judgment. Choice Hotels and the Swagat Defendants seek summary judgment on all of Plaintiffs' claims. The Swagat Defendants also seek partial summary judgment on Choice Hotels' Cross-Claims for express and implied indemnification....

II. *CHOICE HOTELS' SUMMARY JUDGMENT MOTIONS*

Choice Hotels moves for summary judgment on three bases. First, Choice Hotels seeks summary judgment on the Negligence Counts, the Wrongful Death Counts, the Survival Act Counts, and the Funeral Expense Counts (collectively the Duty Counts) on the grounds that it did not owe a duty to either Bonnie Leiser or Georgia Braucher to maintain the pool and spa at the Hotel. Second, Choice Hotels moves for summary judgment on the Leiser and Braucher Res Ipsa Counts (collectively the Res Ipsa Counts) on the grounds that it was not in exclusive control of the pool and spa at the Hotel. Third, Choice Hotels moves for summary judgment on the Leiser and Braucher Agency Counts (collectively the Agency Counts) on the grounds that there is no evidence that circumstances existed under which it would be responsible to either Bonnie Leiser or Georgia Braucher for the actions of any Swagat Defendant under an apparent agency theory.

At summary judgment, the movant, Choice Hotels, must present evidence that demonstrates the absence of a genuine issue of material fact.... The Court must consider the evidence presented in the light most favorable to the opponent of the motion, the Plaintiffs. Any doubt as to the existence of a genuine issue for trial must be resolved against Choice Hotels.... Once Choice Hotels has met its burden, each Plaintiff must present evidence to show that issues of fact remain with respect to an issue essential to her case, and on which she will bear the burden of proof at trial ...

The Duty Counts are all based on a theory of negligence and require evidence that Choice Hotels owed a duty to Bonnie Leiser and Georgia Braucher to maintain the pool and spa at the Hotel.... It is clear that the Agreement did not create a duty on the part of Choice Hotels toward the patrons of the Hotel, including Bonnie Leiser and Georgia Braucher. The LLC owned the Hotel. Choice Hotels provided a franchise to the Swagat Defendants pursuant to the Agreement. Under the terms of the Agreement, Choice Hotels neither owned nor operated the Hotel. The Agreement specifically provided that the Swagat Defendants were independent contractors and no agency relationship existed between them and Choice Hotels.

The face of the Agreement, however, is not controlling on the issue of duty. A franchisor may assert sufficient control of a hotel to be responsible for the operation of the pool and spa.... A franchisor, however, must make sure that the franchisee maintains the required level of quality associated with the franchised brand in order to protect trademarks.... This monitoring may include setting standards for the operation of the franchise, retaining the right to inspect the franchise operation periodically, and retaining the right to withdraw the franchise or to close an aspect of the franchise operation for failure to comply with the franchisor's standards. A franchisor will not be responsible for the operation of the franchisee hotel unless it asserts more direct control than these limited rights associated with maintaining the quality of its brand....

The Plaintiffs present no evidence that Choice Hotels went beyond these limited steps to maintain the required level of quality associated with the franchised brand. Choice Hotels made visual inspections of the pool and spa area twice a year at most, and retained the right to close the pool and spa if the water was cloudy. Choice Hotels retained the right to close cloudy pools because of the risk of drowning, not because of the risk of toxic bacteria build-up. Choice Hotels also required, in the Rules and Regulations, that the Hotel comply with the law. The Swagat Defendants had to meet these requirements anyway. Choice Hotels did not impose any additional requirements for controlling bacteria levels in the pool or spa. Choice Hotels never took any action to test the water quality in the pool and spa area. Based on the evidence presented, Choice Hotels did not exercise sufficient control over the Hotel to be considered an operator of the Hotel.

The Plaintiffs rely on *Greil v. Travelodge International, Inc.*, as authority that a franchisor may be responsible for the operation of a hotel if it only takes the limited steps that Choice Hotels did to maintain the quality of its brand.... The *Greil* decision applied California law, not Illinois law. The California cases on which the Greil court relied indicate that a franchisor may be deemed responsible for the franchisee's operations even when the franchisor only engages in limited monitoring of the franchise.... California law is inconsistent with Illinois law on this point, and Illinois law controls. The *Greil* decision, therefore, is not persuasive.

The Plaintiffs argue that Choice Hotels is liable because it voluntarily assumed the duty to maintain the pool and spa at the Hotel. Whether a party voluntarily assumed a duty is a question of law. *Castro*, 732 N.E.2d at 42. If a party voluntarily undertakes a duty, the duty is limited to the extent of the undertaking.... Here, Choice Hotels never voluntarily took on the task of maintaining the water to avoid the risk of infection. Again, Choice Hotels made visual inspections of the pool and spa area twice a year at most, and retained the right to close the pool and spa if the water was cloudy because of the risk of drowning, not because of the risk of toxic bacteria build-up. None of the evidence presented indicates that Choice Hotels assumed that duty. Choice Hotels is entitled to summary judgment on the Duty Counts alleged against it.

Choice Hotels is also entitled to summary judgment on the Res Ipsa Counts. To establish a res ipsa loquitur claim, a party must present evidence that: (1) the occurrence ordinarily does not happen in the absence of negligence, and (2) the exposure to Legionella bacteria was caused by an agency or instrumentality within the Defendants' exclusive control.... As explained above, Choice Hotels did not exert exclusive control over the pool and spa at the Hotel. Choice Hotels, at best, made limited visual inspections of the pool and spa twice a year and required the Swagat Defendants to comply with the law regulating aquatic facilities in hotels. The LLC owned the Hotel, and Vasant Patel managed the Hotel, including the pool and spa. Choice Hotels did not exert exclusive control. Choice Hotels is entitled to summary judgment on the Res Ipsa Counts.

Choice Hotels is also entitled to summary judgment on the Agency Counts. To establish an apparent agency, the Plaintiffs must present evidence that: (1) Choice Hotels held out one or more of the Swagat Defendants as having authority to act as its agent, or Choice Hotels knowingly acquiesced in one or more of the Swagat Defendants exercising the authority as Choice Hotels' agent; (2) the Plaintiffs, acting reasonably under the circumstances, assumed that an agency existed; and (3) the Plaintiffs relied on the apparent agency to their detriment....

The Plaintiffs fail to present evidence that Choice Hotels held the Swagat Defendants out as its agents. The Plaintiffs present evidence that Leiser believed that Choice Hotels operated the Hotel. She testified that she believed this based on the Choice Hotels commercial she saw on television. The Plaintiffs also present evidence that Choice Hotels operated a reservation system that used an 800 telephone number and an internet web site. Choice Hotels also operated a frequent traveler program in which customers could accumulate points that would entitle them to a free night's stay at a participating Choice Hotels.

None of this evidence demonstrates that Choice Hotels held out the Swagat Defendants as its agent. The use of the brand name shows a franchise relationship, but the existence of a franchise does not create an agency.... Bonnie Leiser does not present evidence of the content of the Choice Hotels commercials which gave her the impression that Choice Hotels operated its franchisees' hotels. In fact, the only evidence of representations regarding the relationship between Choice Hotels and the Swagat Defendants were the parties' repeated disclaimers of any agency: the plaque in the lobby of the Hotel that declared that the Hotel was independently owned and operated, the disclaimer on the Choice Hotels' website which stated that all Choice

Hotels are independently owned and operated, and the disclaimer in the 2006 Directory which stated that all Choice Hotels are independently owned and operated. The Plaintiffs fail to present evidence that Choice Hotels held the Swagat Defendants out as its agents. Choice Hotels is entitled to summary judgment on the Agency Counts as well.

The Plaintiffs rely on *Greil* and *Crinkley v. Holiday Inns, Inc.,* to support their claim of apparent agency.... Neither of these cases apply Illinois law. In addition, the *Greil* court denied summary judgment on the apparent agency theory because the franchisee hotel did not contain a disclaimer that the hotel was independently owned and operated ... The *Greil* court noted that even under California law a franchisor could avoid a claim of apparent agency by placing a disclaimer in the lobby of the franchisee hotel.... Here, the LLC displayed the disclaimer in the lobby where patrons could see it before they checked in. There is no evidence of an apparent agency. Choice Hotels is entitled to summary judgment.

III. *PARTIAL SUMMARY JUDGMENT MOTIONS*

The Swagat Defendants ask for partial summary judgment on Choice Hotels express indemnity and implied indemnity counts in the Cross-Claims. The Swagat Defendants are entitled to partial summary judgment on the implied indemnity claims, but issues of fact exist with respect to the express indemnity claims.

Indemnity clauses in contracts are enforceable in Illinois and are governed by principles of contract interpretation.... In this case, the Indemnification Clause is clear: the Swagat Defendants are obligated to indemnify Choice Hotels for all costs, including attorney fees and costs of suit, if: (1) Choice Hotels is subject to a claim for damages allegedly arising from the operation of the Hotel; (2) Choice Hotels is not at fault for the alleged damages; and (3) one or more of the Swagat Defendants is found to be at fault for the alleged injuries. The first two elements have been established: the Plaintiffs brought claims against Choice Hotels for damages allegedly arising from the operation of the Hotel, and Choice Hotels is not at fault. As discussed below, issues of fact remain with respect to whether any of the Swagat Defendants were at fault in this case. The Swagat Defendants may be obligated to indemnify Choice Hotels, and so pay its attorney fees and expenses, if one or more of the Swagat Defendants is found to be at fault for the injuries to Bonnie Leiser and the injuries and death of Georgia Braucher.

The Swagat Defendants argue that the Indemnification Clause is really a contribution clause. The Court disagrees in this situation. The clause obligated the Swagat Defendants to indemnify Choice Hotels in the limited situation in which Choice Hotels was subject to a claim, but was not at fault. If Choice Hotels had been partially at fault, then the Swagat Defendants would be correct; the clause would have imposed a contribution obligation on joint tort feasors, not an indemnification obligation. But, that did not occur here because Choice Hotels was not at fault. Thus, the Swagat Defendants are not entitled to summary judgment on the express indemnity cross-claim.

The Swagat Defendants are entitled to summary judgment on the implied indemnity claim. Choice Hotels alleged that the Swagat Defendants were impliedly obligated to indemnify it if Choice Hotels was vicariously liable for their acts. Choice Hotels is not vicariously liable for the acts of the Swagat Defendants, so there is no implied indemnity. The Swagat Defendants are entitled to partial summary judgment on this cross-claim.

IV. *SWAGAT SUMMARY JUDGMENT MOTIONS*

All of the Swagat Defendants ask for summary judgment on all of Plaintiffs' claims, both the Duty Counts and the Res Ipsa Counts. In addition, Vijay C. Patel, Himanshu M. Desai, and Vaidik International, Inc., seek summary judgment on the grounds that the LLC owned and operated the Hotel and that they, as members of the LLC, have no personal liability. Defendant Vasant Patel also seeks partial summary judgment to the extent that the Plaintiffs seek to hold him liable as a member of the LLC. The Court will address these portions of the Motions separately.

A. *The Members of the LLC*

Defendants Vijay C. Patel, Himanshu M. Desai, and Vaidik International, Inc., seek summary judgment on the grounds that they are not liable for the acts of the LLC, the owner of the Hotel. Vijay C. Patel, Himanshu M. Desai, Vasant Patel and Vaidik International, Inc., were members of the LLC. The LLC owned the Hotel. Only Vasant Patel worked at the Hotel. Defendants Vijay C. Patel, Desai, and Vaidik International, Inc. were only members. Members of limited liability companies, such as the LLC, are not liable for the tortious acts of the limited liability company.... Defendants Vijay C. Patel, Desai, and Vaidik International, Inc. are entitled to summary judgment.

The Plaintiffs argue that these Defendants are personally liable because they signed the Agreement in their personal capacities. This is clearly wrong. A member of a limited liability company who signs a contract in a personal capacity is liable on the contract, but is not thereby liable for any other obligation of the limited liability company.... These Defendants are entitled to summary judgment.

Similarly, Vasant Patel is entitled to partial summary judgment to the extent that the Plaintiffs seek to hold him liable as a member of the LLC. Vasant Patel managed the Hotel and maintained the pool and spa, and as explained below, may or may not have some personal liability for his own actions, but he is not liable simply as a member of the LLC.

B. *Res Ipsa Counts*

The LLC and Vasant Patel, personally, seek summary judgment on the Plaintiffs' Res Ipsa Counts on the grounds that the Plaintiffs failed to present evidence to establish that the pool and spa were the source of the Plaintiffs' Legionnaires Disease. To establish a res ipsa loquitur claim, a party must present evidence that: (1) the occurrence ordinarily does not happen in the absence of negligence, and (2) the exposure to Legionella bacteria was caused by an agency or instrumentality within the

Defendants' exclusive control.... The Plaintiffs have presented evidence on each of these elements. The Plaintiffs' expert, Dr. Fliermans, opined that the source of the Legionella bacteria that caused Bonnie Leiser and Georgia Braucher's Legionnaires Disease was the pool and spa at the Hotel.... The pool and spa area was in the exclusive control of the LLC and Vasant Patel, as the Hotel manager and the individual who personally maintained the pool and spa. Dr. Smith opined that the Legionella bacteria were in the pool and spa because the pool and spa were not properly maintained. Curless' inspections, when read favorably to the Plaintiffs, also support the inference the pool and spa were not properly maintained: the records were falsified at the October 2005 inspection; there was no chlorine in the spa at the February 2006 inspection; and there was no chlorine in either the pool or spa at the March 8, 2006, inspection. This evidence is sufficient to establish that issues of fact exist on the Res Ipsa Counts.

The Defendants argue that Plaintiffs failed to produce evidence that the pool and spa were the exclusive source of the Legionella bacteria because Dr. Fliermans agreed that: (1) Legionella bacteria existed in low levels in the Lincoln, Illinois, public water supply; (2) the bacteria could have theoretically multiplied in the Hotel's hot water heater; and so, (3) the Plaintiffs could have come in contact with the Legionella bacteria while taking a shower at the Hotel rather than from the pool or spa.... Dr. Fliermans, however, excluded the Lincoln, Illinois, water supply and the showers at the Hotel as possible sources of the Legionella bacteria because: (1) no cases of Legionnaires Disease from the Lincoln, Illinois, area generally were reported to the Centers for Disease Control; (2) the pool and spa were not maintained properly; and (3) the level of Legionella bacteria found in the spa area was so high on March 7, 2006, that it must have been at elevated levels at the time that Bonnie Leiser and Georgia Braucher stayed at the Hotel.... These reasons are sufficient to support the validity of his opinions for purposes of summary judgment. The Defendants may cross-examine Dr. Fliermans on these matters to point out the weakness in his opinions at trial. His opinions are sufficient to create an issue of fact.

The Defendants also ask for summary judgment on the Duty Counts. To establish the Duty Counts, the Plaintiffs must present evidence of a duty, breach of duty, injury and proximate cause.... The Plaintiffs have presented evidence on these elements. The Defendant LLC owned and operated the Hotel, and so, owed a duty to the Plaintiffs as guests. Vasant Patel, as manager and the person responsible for maintaining the pool and spa, had a duty to the Plaintiffs as guests. Dr. Smith opined that these Defendants breached their duty by failing to maintain the pool and spa properly, thereby allowing the Legionella bacteria to grow to dangerous levels. The inspections by Curless supported Dr. Smith's opinions. On the issue of proximate cause, Dr. Fliermans opined that the Legionella bacteria in the pool and spa were the source of the bacteria that caused Bonnie Leiser and Georgia Braucher to contract Legionnaires Disease. Last, Bonnie Leiser suffered injuries from her illness, and Georgia Braucher died from her illness. The Plaintiffs have presented evidence on each element.

The Defendants argue that Dr. Fliermans' opinions on causation are mere conjecture. As explained above, the Court disagrees. Dr. Fliermans had a valid basis for his conclusions that the pool and spa were the source of Legionella bacteria that caused Bonnie Leiser and Georgia Braucher's illnesses. The Defendants may attack those opinions on cross-examination at trial, but those opinions are sufficient for purposes of summary judgment.

Section IV

The Corporation

Chapter 10

For-Profit Corporations

Chapter Outline

Chapter Objectives

- Discuss the liability promoters have.

- List the reasons so many corporations decide to incorporate in Delaware.

- Provide the major steps to be taken before incorporating, including name reservation and the organizational meeting.

- Detail the requirements of the articles of incorporation and bylaws.

- Compare a regular corporation to a close corporation.

- Discuss how a regular corporation capitalizes.

- Cover the different types of financing a corporation has, particularly equity and debt financing.

- Explain the difference between common and preferred stock.

10.1 Introduction to For-Profit Corporations

Corporations are focused upon in this textbook because they make approximately eighty-five percent of all the money generated from business entities. In addition, a corporation's legal standing and how it is managed, do much to explain the financial crisis. Corporations are considered a completely separate legal entity from the shareholders. Therefore, a corporation is an artificial person, one that has many of the same rights as a natural person, such as you or me. Some of these rights include:

- the right to sue and be sued,

- to own property in the corporation's name,

- to make charitable donations in the corporation's name,

- have a corporate seal,

- make bylaws,

- mortgage property,

- make contracts,

- lend money,

- conduct business,

- elect directors and officers, and

- pay employee benefit plans, etc.

However, it is much harder to hold an artificial person to the same responsibilities as a natural person. For instance, how do you jail a corporation for stealing its employees' retirement accounts? In the past, and some might argue even now, the directors were not held personally responsible enough for the corporation's actions, though these people are often the very ones responsible for the corporation's decisions.

In general, corporations are governed by state law and are governed by the laws of the state in which the corporation is incorporated. Much of the time, the state in which the corporation is incorporated has adopted and adapted the Model Business Corporation Act, also known as the MBCA. The state's common law, or case law, will apply to the corporation if the adapted MBCA is silent on an issue. The MBCA has been revised, and most states that followed the MBCA now follow the Revised Model Business Corporation Act (RMBCA). California and Delaware are examples of states that do not follow the MBCA or RMBCA.

10.2 Preincorporation

Promoters start the corporation. This can involve:

- raising the money needed to capitalize the corporation,
- finding shareholders,
- finding directors,
- finding officers,
- finding employees (including attorneys and certified public accountants),
- drawing up a business plan, and
- determining where the corporation should be located.

During preincorporation, the promoters often make the decisions about where the corporation should be incorporated. Some states are more pro-corporation than other states. Therefore, it might not make sense to incorporate in the "home" state. Many times, because the state of Delaware is so pro-corporation, corporations will decide to incorporate there rather than in their home state, or in addition to their home state.

a. Liability of Promoters for Contracts and Expenses

To start and organize a corporation, the promoter will often have to enter into contracts on behalf of the corporation, before the corporation is formed. These are known as preincorporation contracts. The big issues in preincorporation contracts are who is liable for those contracts and for how long? Usually, promoters are liable under these contracts until the contracts are ratified by the corporation. The reasoning behind making the promoters liable is that technically, the promoter cannot be an agent of the corporation if the corporation is not formed yet. Some promoters negate this liability by writing into the contract that they are acting on behalf of the company and not themselves.

Another way the liability of the promoters is limited is that the ratification of the contract relates back to the date when the contract was made. An example of how this works is:

- Promoter Jill signs a lease agreement for Twisted Pretzels on August 6. Jill does the build out for Twisted Pretzels (prepares the space for making and selling pretzels), which takes her three months. On November 6, Twisted Pretzels has its grand opening and Jill formally passes over the keys to the store to the new owners. The new owners are now liable under the contract from August 6th.

b. Where to Incorporate?

1. Delaware: The "Gold" Standard

Some states are simply more pro-corporation than other states. Hence, corporations will sometimes forum shop. Even Delaware's Secretary of State website discusses how pro-corporation friendly the state of Delaware is. Corporations are a major source of revenue for the state. As the state did not have a tremendous amount of natural resources, it created an artificial resource for revenue. The state keeps this revenue stream by being pro-corporation. There are many reasons why Delaware is considered corporation friendly; some of the reasons are as follows:

- Delaware has protection against hostile takeovers (this will be discussed in a later chapter).
- There is limited liability for directors.
- The state does not require any minimum capital contributions to incorporate in Delaware.
- The state does not even have corporate state income tax for corporations that do not conduct business in the state (the state makes its money in filing fees and franchise board taxes based upon shares).
- The corporation can be owned anonymously.
- Service is accepted until midnight.
- Delaware has very pro-corporation laws.

Some of these benefits make a corporation incorporated in Delaware sound more like a limited liability company.

In addition, the director meetings do not have to be held in person. Shareholder meetings can be performed by a written vote, and only a majority is required to agree. Another surprisingly big factor in deciding to incorporate in Delaware is that it accepts service until midnight, Eastern Standard Time. For attorneys who are procrastinators, especially on the West Coast, this is several hours after their own Secretaries of State close.

However, the number one reason to incorporate in Delaware is the very pro-corporate laws there. Most issues on corporations have already been addressed in the court system there, on the side of the corporation. In fact, Delaware has a special court just for corporate law cases, in front of judges who have practiced corporate law.

Delaware incorporation often makes the most sense if the corporation is going to do business in multiple states. The corporation can choose to have its internal affairs governed by Delaware law. However, if the business the corporation will perform is entirely within one state, it will probably be cheaper to incorporate within the "home" state. This is especially true if the home state is also a pro-incorporation state like Delaware. For example, Nevada is considered the Delaware of the west as it enacted lenient corporate laws.

10.3 Formation and Financing

A corporation can be made up of one person (depending upon the state) or thousands of people. The corporation itself is considered an artificial person. It has many of the same rights as a natural person in a court of law. Remember that artificial people are ones that you cannot necessarily touch, such as businesses, whereas natural people are flesh and blood that you can touch. Corporations were given many of the same rights as humans under the 14th Amendment. Part of the 14th Amendment states:

> "No state shall make or enforce any law which shall abridge the privileges or immunities of citizens of the United States; nor shall any state deprive any person of life, liberty, or property, without due process of law; nor deny to any person within its jurisdiction the equal protection of the laws."

Although this is a simplified version, corporations were able to argue that they were people and should be awarded the same rights, under this amendment.

Many other business entities convert to a corporation to obtain financing more easily. Corporations can issue stock to raise money. A promoter can start the financing of the corporation even before it exists by seeking subscription agreements from investors. Once the corporation is formed, these investors become stockholders.

a. Name Availability and Reservation

Brand name recognition sells. Therefore, the corporation will likely want to reserve its brand name in all fifty states, once it finds one that meets each state's requirements and is available. Often, state requirements have to do with words that should not be included in a corporation's name unless they are true, such as an affiliation with the United States government or stating the corporation is a trust, when it is not. The corporation name should also include some indication that the entity is, in fact, a corporation.

One of the most important tasks a corporate paralegal can perform is a name availability check in each state in which the corporation wants to incorporate. You can do this by going to each Secretary of State's website. Whatever name the corporation wants to use, it should not be too similar to another corporate name.

Once the name is determined to be available, name reservation is possible. Name reservation does expire, usually within one hundred and twenty days. If the corporation is extremely concerned about name brand recognition, it might actually want to form a holding company, which serves only to hold the name. However, the corporation will need to be a bigger corporation, because the expense of holding companies is greater than name reservation.

b. Public Document: Articles of Incorporation

Not all states call the public document the articles of incorporation. Instead, they may call it the articles of organization, certificate of incorporation, or certificate of organization.

Corporations are incorporated at a state level, not a federal level. However, many states use the MBCA or RMBCA, so there is more similarity among the states as to how corporations are run than there is among the states as to how LLCs are run. Remember, however, Delaware does not use the Model Business Corporation Act, but rather has even more pro-corporation legislation.

A corporation does not legally exist until the articles of incorporation are properly filed. Proper filing consists of including the proper information in the articles, having them signed by the incorporator(s), and filing them with the secretary of state with the appropriate fee. The following can be included in the articles of incorporation:

- the corporation's name (this is required),
- the address of the corporation (this is required),
- the agent for the corporation's service of process (this is required),
- the purpose of the corporation,
- a description of the corporation's stock, including the number of authorized shares (the number of authorized shares is required),
- the names and addresses of the incorporators (this is required),
- information about the directors,
- how the corporation will be managed,
- a discussion of the liability of the shareholders and/or directors, and
- a discussion of any director indemnification.

While the items indicated above as required must be in the public document, the articles of incorporation, the rest of the information is not required to be in the articles. In fact, the corporation might prefer not to put nonrequired information in the articles as if it changes, the corporation would need to amend its articles.

The articles will also include the agent for service of process so if someone needs to sue the corporation, they know upon whom to serve the complaint. The Secretary of State will send correspondence to this address as well. Even if the corporation is not actually doing business in a state, it must still have a registered agent for service of process located there.

If the purpose of the corporation is included in the articles, this should be broadly drafted so that the corporation does not need to amend the document in case the corporation expands its business. Whatever the purpose is, the purpose has to be lawful.

The articles have to discuss how many shares and what class of shares the corporation is allowed to issue. Shares could be common or preferred. There are many more reporting requirements with a corporation than with other types of business entities. This, in turn, often increases the costs of starting and operating a corporation. After the articles and bylaws are done, the corporation still has to file annual reports with the state in which it is incorporated. It might also have to file documents to comply with securities regulations. The corporation has to file its own tax returns and pay accordingly.

1. Preemptive Rights

The details regarding shares, including preemptive rights, should be stated in the articles of incorporation. If a shareholder has a significant amount of shares, the shareholder will not want his percentage ownership in the corporation to dilute. Unless the shareholder has what is known as preemptive rights, however, every time new shares are issued, the shareholder's ownership percentage will go down.

For example, Brian owns one thousand shares in Widgets, Inc., and this represents a ten percent ownership (meaning there are ten thousand total shares). If ten thousand more shares are issued and Brian does not have preemptive rights, he would then only own five percent of the total shares (one thousand shares out of twenty thousand shares).

- Brian owns 1,000 shares = 10% ownership in Widgets.
- 10 × 1,000 means that there are currently 10,000 shares in Widgets.
- Widgets issues 10,000 more shares.
- 10,000 current shares + 10,000 newly issued shares = 20,000 total shares.
- If now there are 20,000 shares total, Brian only gets 5%.
- 1,000/20,000 = 5%.

If Brian, however, had preemptive rights, he would have the right of first refusal on newly issued shares. He would be offered an amount that would allow him to keep his initial ownership percentage. He does not have to buy these shares, but he is given the opportunity first in case he wants to. Thus, with preemptive rights, if there were originally ten thousand total shares and now an additional ten thousand are being issued, Brian would be offered another one thousand shares to add to his already held one thousand shares. Brian would then, if he bought the shares, still be a ten percent owner of shares (two thousand out of twenty thousand).

- Brian owns 1,000 shares = 10% ownership in Widgets.
- 10 × 1,000 means that there are currently 10,000 shares in Widgets.
- Widgets issues 10,000 more shares.
- 10,000 current shares + 10,000 newly issued shares = 20,000 total shares.
- Brian has preemptive rights, so he gets to buy up to 1,000 more shares.

- 1,000 current shares owned by Brian + 1,000 more shares he buys by using his preemptive rights = 2,000 shares
- 2,000/20,000 = 10%.

c. Organizational Meeting and Incorporators

After the articles of incorporation are filed, then the first meeting of the corporation is held, called the organizational meeting. The requirements for an organizational meeting can vary between each state. Usually, it will be the incorporator (often an attorney) or the directors named in the articles that hold the organizational meeting.

The purpose of an organizational meeting to take care of the final preliminaries before the corporation can truly start operating. The following is a list of the activities often conducted at an organizational meeting:

- approve the articles of incorporation,
- ratify contracts made by promoters,
- elect directors,
- appoint officers,
- adopt bylaws,
- accept and issue preincorporation stock subscriptions,
- approve the corporate seal and the look of the stock certificate,
- determine where to bank,
- determine what accounting method to use and what the corporation's fiscal year will be, and
- issue stock.

The decisions made by the promoters will typically be ratified at this meeting. The first full-term directors can be elected. Officers of the corporation can be appointed at the organizational meeting. Bylaws can be adopted. Shares may also be sold. The names of the shareholders must be recorded, along with the amount of shares, the types of shares, and the amount paid by each shareholder. How the stock certificate will look can be decided as well. If the corporation wants a specific corporate seal, the format can be agreed upon at the organizational meeting. Many more matters can be decided at the meeting, but the most important issues to be decided are the ones listed above.

d. A Study in Contrasts: Close Corporations

A close corporation is very different from a regular for-profit corporation, particularly in the lack for formalities in starting it up and running it. A close corporation, a family corporation, and a closely held corporation mean the same thing. A close corporation is one that is not publicly traded. Thus, it is privately owned. It can be thought of as sort of an incorporated partnership. Even though the corporation is privately owned, it can still be a large corporation, such as Hallmark. However, a close corporation may have stock. It is simply stock that may not be sold to outsiders (anyone other than family and/or friends that make up the close corporation). Usually, the members of the close corporation will know each other. In fact, the stock must indicate that it is close corporation stock, to let outsiders know that they will receive no value for payment on the stock and will not be allowed to be part of the corporation should they buy the stock. Thus, there is not a large market for close corporation shares. This makes it hard to get out of the close corporation if a shareholder is unhappy.

A close corporation does not require all the strict formalities of a publicly traded corporation. Most of the time, the members of the close corporation participate in running it. A close corporation does not need to have a board of directors, bylaws, or formalized shareholder meetings. Thus, the close corporation would not need to keep and maintain minutes. The close corporation does not have to abide by all the formalities a regular corporation does, and the close corporation can still keep its limited liability.

1. The Friends and/or Family Plan

A close corporation is typically limited to family and/or friends. It cannot be made up of more than fifty people. These people are the ones that run the business. To keep the business in the family, there will be restrictions on transferring shares. Before a shareholder can offer shares to someone outside the corporation, the shareholder must offer his shares to people within the corporation first. As there are limits on the number of people that can be in a close corporation, more businesses are moving to being LLPs or LLCs.

2. Formation of a Close Corporation

The close corporation does file articles of incorporation, but on those articles, the close corporation must indicate that it is a close corporation. In addition, each stock certificate must indicate that the stock is stock in a close corporation. This is to put the public on notice that even if they buy shares in the close corporation, they will not be allowed to become an actual member of the close corporation. The remaining shareholders do not want to have to manage with a new member that they did not voluntarily pick. Thus, the close corporation may even have a shareholder agreement, which states how and when a shareholder can sell his stock, or what happens to the stock when the shareholder dies.

The shareholder agreement, with transfer restrictions, serves many different purposes. If a shareholder cannot easily transfer his shares, then this makes the close corporation more stable. If a shareholder cannot easily transfer his shares, then this makes the percentage ownership of the shareholders stay the same. It also makes sure that the close corporation will not go over a certain number of shareholders. The transfer restrictions may require prior approval before a shareholder can sell his shares. The transfer restrictions could require the shareholder offer the corporation the right of first refusal.

3. Operation of a Close Corporation

In a close corporation, usually all shareholders are involved, so there is no required board of directors. In addition, there will not be formal shareholder meetings. Members of the close corporation can still act like directors or officers. Typically, all the shareholders will be involved in management. These shareholders are expecting to make their living from the corporation, and this is usually not just an investment to them.

e. Private Document: Bylaws

The private or internal document for running a regular corporation is known as the bylaws. In general, more details should be discussed in the bylaws than in the articles, because the bylaws are easier to change. Articles usually have to be changed by consent of the shareholders, while bylaws may only need consent of the directors to change. Articles have to be sent to the Secretary of State. Bylaws are also not available to the public.

Bylaws will normally cover the following:

- the name of the corporation,
- the address of the corporation,
- shareholder information,
- board of director information,
- officer information,
- stock certificate information,
- the tax year of the corporation,
- inspection of corporate records,
- how to amend the bylaws, and
- signatures.

Some of the information in the bylaws may duplicate the information in the articles, including the name, address, registered agent, and purpose of the corporation. Bylaws will discuss shareholders, directors, and officers. Shareholder meetings will be discussed in detail, particularly requirements for notice. This is because if notice is not proper, then the shareholders' meeting may not be valid. Specifically, the date, time, and place for both special and regular meetings will be addressed. The bylaws should also state how special shareholder meetings are called. One of the important things to address about shareholders' meetings is what constitutes a quorum. The bylaws should also address shareholders' voting rights and inspection rights.

Concerning directors, the bylaws will discuss the number of directors of the corporation (often an odd number), their term in office, and their required qualifications. Some qualifications might require that the director also be a shareholder or be a citizen of the state in which the corporation is located. Directors should be given the right to delegate to the officers. Since directors also appoint the officers, that should be discussed as well.

The meetings of directors will also be discussed, though not in as much detail as the shareholders' meeting. This is because the directors should know when their meetings are, as they are being paid to attend these meetings. Shareholders are not normally paid to attend meetings. Directors may not be required to attend meetings in person and may be able to attend telephonically.

Other important director provisions include the potential liability of directors, how much directors will be paid (and how that will be calculated), and the steps for removal of directors. Bylaws usually limit directors' liability, often by indemnifying the director and/or providing insurance for the director. This may seem counterintuitive, especially in light of the recent financial crisis. However, historically, corporations have been willing to indemnify and/or insure directors so that they can obtain the best candidates for the job. Well-qualified candidates are not going to want to become directors of a company where they have unlimited liability. Directors often have authority to set their salaries. However, with recent legislation, it is becoming much more public how much the top directors at corporations are making.

Officers are a big portion of the bylaws. The specific titles of officers will be delineated in the bylaws. Then, once the titles are set forth, each title's responsibilities need to be discussed, along with their compensation.

One of the more important issues for stockholders, which is discussed in bylaws, is when and if the shareholders will receive dividends on their stock. How shares are issued and transferred should be discussed.

Another big discussion in the bylaws deals with stock certificates. Often first discussed in the organizational meeting, the form of the stock certificate and the required signatures will be further delineated in the bylaws. If someone receives certificated shares, there may be a discussion as to what happens if someone's shares are misplaced, destroyed, or stolen. Other, smaller bylaws provisions might include a description of the corporate seal and the procedure for amending the bylaws.

The following is an example of basic bylaws.

Sample Bylaws of _____, Inc.
ARTICLE I
SHAREHOLDERS' MEETINGS

§ 1. TIME OF MEETING. An annual meeting for the election of directors and any other properly transacted business shall be held on the date and time as the Board of Directors (BODs) determines. In the case of a special meeting, it shall also be held on the date and time as the BODs determines.

§ 2. PLACE OF MEETING. All shareholder meetings shall be held at such place as the BODs determine. If the BODs do not set a place, then the shareholders' meeting shall take place at the principal place of business of the corporation

§ 3. CALL OF MEETING. Annual meetings can be called by the BODs, the Chairman of the Board alone, or by any officer instructed by the Directors to call the meeting. Special meetings can be called in a like manner or by a shareholder with ten percent or more of the shares of the corporation.

§ 4. NOTICE OF MEETING. There must be written notice of the shareholder meetings. Such notice must contain the location, date, and time of the meeting. If the meeting is a special meeting, then the notice must state what the special meeting is about. If the meeting is an annual meeting, then the notice must state that it is for the election of directors, and whatever other matters the BODs intends to present. The notice shall be given thirty days prior to the meeting. The notice shall be mailed, with first-class postage prepaid. The notice shall be addressed to each shareholder at their last known address. The notice shall include the names of nominees for BODs. If the meeting is adjourned, then notice of the adjourned meeting does not have to be sent out so long as the time and place are announced before the adjournment. The same business that could have transacted at the original meeting can be transacted at the adjourned meeting.

§ 5. CONSENT. If a meeting is invalid, then the shareholder can provide a consent or waiver to make the meeting valid. These consents or waivers have to be kept with the corporate records book. If a shareholder attends the meeting, even without proper notice, then he has waived his right to proper notice, unless he objects when he first arrives.

§ 6. CONDUCTING THE MEETING. The meeting shall be conducted by the President. If the President is unavailable, the meeting shall be conducted by the Vice-President. If both the President and Vice-President are unavailable, then the Secretary shall conduct the meeting.

§ 7. PROXIES. Shareholders can have proxies to represent them at the shareholders' meeting, if they are unable to attend. The proxy will expire within one year, and must be renewed for the next annual shareholders' meeting. The shareholder can revoke the proxy any time before the year is up. A proxy is a written authorization allowing someone else to vote in your stead.

§ 8. QUORUM. A majority of the voting shares will qualify as a quorum for purposes of the attendance at shareholders' meetings. So long as there is a quorum, business can be legitimately transacted. If there is not a quorum, then the meeting should be adjourned.

§ 9. SHAREHOLDERS' AGREEMENTS. Two or greater shareholders can agree in writing that they shall vote together.

ARTICLE II
BOARD OF DIRECTORS

§ 1. FUNCTIONS OF DIRECTORS. The Directors shall manage the corporation. They can delegate day-to-day operation of the corporation to officers, but the BODs ultimately maintains control and direction. Directors can set their own compensation, so long as it is lawful. Finally, directors should exercise fiduciary duties, the duty of due care, and the duty of loyalty on behalf of the corporation.

§2. QUALIFICATIONS OF DIRECTORS. Directors do not have to be shareholders in this corporation. The director should be a citizen of the United States, but does not have to be a resident in this state. The authorized number of directors constituting the Board is nine. The number of directors can be changed by amending these by-laws.

§3. ELECTION OF DIRECTORS. The initial BODs shall be elected at the organization meeting, and they shall hold office until the first annual meeting of the shareholders. From then on, directors elected at the shareholders' annual meeting shall serve until the next shareholders' annual meeting. If there are any vacancies in the meantime, those vacancies can be filled by the majority vote of the remaining directors.

§4. INDEMNIFYING DIRECTORS. This corporation can indemnify any director. This corporation shall also have the right to buy and keep insurance on behalf of a director.

§5. BOARD OF DIRECTORS' MEETINGS. The board shall fix the time and place of their meetings. Notice is not required for regular BODs' meetings. Special meetings must be noticed at least three days ahead of time by personal service. If the notice is not valid, the director can waive notice.

§6. QUORUM FOR DIRECTORS' MEETINGS. For purposes of a quorum at BODs' meetings, a majority of the directors is sufficient for a quorum. Directors need not be physically present at the meeting if there is a videoconference wherein all directors can see and hear each other.

§7. RUNNING OF THE MEETING. The Chairman of the BODs shall lead the meeting. If the Chairman is not available, the Vice Chairman of the Board may lead the meeting.

§8. REMOVING DIRECTORS. Directors can be removed by a quorum of the shareholders, with or without cause. The shareholders can vote on a replacement director at the same time.

§9. COMMITTEES OF BOARD OF DIRECTORS. One or more directors may be appointed by the board of directors to serve on a committee.

§10. WRITTEN ACTIONS BY BOARD OF DIRECTORS. An action can be taken without a meeting and if all members of the BODs consent in writing to this action.

ARTICLE III
OFFICERS

§1. OFFICERS. The officers of this corporation are the President, Vice President, Treasurer, and Secretary. One person can hold more than one office.

§2. APPOINTMENT OF OFFICERS. The BODs shall appoint officers annually. The BODs can remove the officer at any time, for any reason, but then must appoint a new officer to fill his place. Vacancies in officer positions will also be filled by appointment by the directors.

§ 3. PRESIDENT. The President, subject to the supervision by the BODs, will generally supervise and control the day-to-day business of the corporation. The President will run the shareholders' meetings.

§ 4. VICE PRESIDENT. If the President is absent, the Vice President shall fill in for the President.

§ 5. TREASURER. The treasurer must keep and maintain correct accounts of the business of the corporation, including assets, liabilities, capital, earnings, and shares. The directors shall be able to inspect said records at any time. He should distribute funds as ordered by the BODs.

ARTICLE IV
SHARES

§ 1. SHARE CERTIFICATES. Shares certificates shall have the name of the shareholder along with the number of shares, the class of shares, and the series of shares. The certificate must be signed by the President and Secretary.

§ 2. LOST SHARE CERTIFICATES. The corporation can issue new share certificates if the original share certificate is lost. The shareholder shall have to prove his right to such share certificate, through proper identification.

§ 3. RECORD DATE. Record date shall be used to determine which shareholders get notice of meetings, are able to vote at said meetings, and are entitled to dividends. The record date is the date the BODs picks thirty-to-forty days prior to the date of the shareholders' meeting.

ARTICLE V
AMENDING THE BYLAWS

The bylaws can be amended by either a quorum of shareholders or a quorum of the BODs.

ARTICLE VI
CORPORATE RECORDS

The corporation shall keep at its principal place of business originals or copies of the bylaws; accounting records; shareholder minutes; BODs minutes; and a register of all the shareholders along with their addresses, number of shares, and classes of shares.

[DATE and SIGNATURES.]

f. Capitalization

The end goal of a for-profit corporation is to make money. The starting capital for the corporation can come from shareholders or it can be borrowed. A benefit to being a creditor is that you are the first to be paid; shareholders are the last to be paid. Shareholders want to be able to sell their shares easily.

If the company does not have enough capitalization, then the corporation might not be able to pay a debt or a lawsuit settlement against them. This could potentially led to more shareholder liability than just the amount the shareholder invested. This will be discussed more in the section on piercing the corporate veil.

1. Issuance of Stock

Stock is authorized if it has been provided for in the articles of incorporation. Stock is outstanding if it has been sold. The articles must state the classes of stock, the number of authorized shares (meaning the number of shares that could be issued), and the rights of each class of stock.

Issues common to stock include:

- dividends,
- liquidation rights,
- voting rights,
- conversion rights, and
- redemption rights (preemptive rights have already been discussed earlier in the chapter).

Dividends are discussed in much more detail in Chapter 11, Investing. Liquidation rights are the rights a shareholder has, after creditors are paid, to assets leftover, in an amount equal to their ownership percentage. Voting rights of shareholders entitle shareholders to elect directors and to approve important corporate changes such as amending the articles, new classes of stock, and mergers. Conversion rights, if a shareholder has them, allows the shareholder to convert their stock into another security with the company. Redemption rights, again if the shareholder has them, allow that shareholder to make the corporation buy back his shares.

If a corporation issued all of its authorized shares and it wanted to issue more, it would need to amend the articles to include more authorized shares. Shareholder approval is necessary for amending the articles.

2. Consideration for Stock

Anything of value can be traded as consideration for stock. This includes cash, personal property, real property, intellectual property, IOUs, services, or even other securities. Many employees receive stock as part of their compensation, in addition to salary. Some individuals have made substantial amounts of money from stock options issued to them by employers.

3. Par Value

In the beginning, par value was close to the going rate for stock. The corporation could not cut a deal and sell stock to insiders at less than par. Nowadays, par value usually has nothing to do with the going rate. Some states have eliminated the concept of par value; others put par value at a nominal amount, such as a dollar. The par value is the least amount of money that the stock can sell for when it is being offered for sale.

4. Stock Certificate

Most shareholders today do not receive a paper certificate, and the records of stocks are computerized. If a shareholder does receive a paper stock certificate, it must at least have:

- the name of the company and the state it is incorporated in,
- the name of the person being issued the stock, and
- the number and type of shares.

A stock certificate needs to have the name of the company issuing the stock. The state in which the corporation is incorporated needs to be on the stock certificate. The person who is receiving the stock certificate will be named. The stock certificate will indicate what number (i.e., 100 out of 1000) the stock is. Typically, the stock certificate is signed by the president and secretary of the corporation. Finally, the stock certificate should indicate whether the stock is preferred, common, or close. Individual states may require more information on the stock certificate, but these requirements are usually the baseline requirements.

5. Transferring Stock

Stock, other than close stock, is easily bought and sold. Generally, stocks can also be assigned, pledged, and/or gifted. This makes being a shareholder in a corporation substantially different from being a partner in a partnership or a member in a limited liability company, where partners or members have to be approved.

6. Classes of Stock

Stock can comprise several classes, and within those classes, there can be a series of stock. However, if a stock is in the same series, the stockholders in that series must be treated equally. The rights that are to be the same for the shareholders in a particular series include:

- dividends,
- voting rights,
- liquidation rights,
- preemptive rights,
- conversion rights, and
- redemption rights.

These rights were discussed above, with issuance of stock.

7. Types of Stock

Types of stock include common and preferred stock (close stock was discussed earlier). In general, preferred stock gets preferential treatment when it comes to dividend payments. With common stock, the stockholder gets a percent interest in the corporation based upon the total number of shares he owns. Common shareholders typically get voting rights. However, these shareholders are paid last, after bondholders and preferred shareholders. Common stockholders can receive a part of whatever ownership is left in the company after the creditors, employees, and preferred shareholders take precedence. Common shareholders do not have an absolute right to dividends, but do have a right to participate if dividends are issued.

The rights preferred stock has over common stock are being first in line for dividends and for assets if the company dissolves — at least before the common shareholders. Preferred stockholders are paid after the bondholders. These rights are known as dividend preferences and liquidation preferences. Thus, preferred stock has more security than common stock, which makes it similar to a bond. However, because they have these rights, they may not be given the right to vote. Preferred stock does not usually gain as much value as common shares.

Preferred stock may be cumulative, which means that if the corporation was unable to pay a dividend, then before it can issue dividends to the common shareholders this year, the preferred shareholders must receive the back and current dividends first.

g. Debt Financing

While a corporation does not have to debt finance, most corporations at least partially obtain funds through debt. In debt financing, the corporation borrows money. The corporation has to pay interest on the money borrowed and to pay back the principal, usually within an agreed upon amount of time. The terms of the debt financing should be in writing, and should include at least the amount, the date the loan is due, the interest, and the collateral, if there is any. One of the biggest arguments in support of debt financing is that the interest is often tax deductible. Bondholders, who own the debt, do not have management rights in the corporation. However, bondholders are paid before stockholders, whether those stockholders are preferred or common.

1. Unsecured Debt

Unsecured debt is a promise to repay the debt. While this promise can be enforced (much more easily if it is written down), it often has to be enforced by going to court. This takes time and money, so is not the preferred type of loan. If a debt is long-term and unsecured, it might be called a debenture. A debenture may be for thirty or more years. If a debt is short-term, either secured or unsecured, it might be called a note. Notes are usually for five years or less.

2. Secured Debt

Secured debt is a promise to repay the debt that is secured by a piece of property, often the same property that the borrower took the loan out on. For example, a car loan would be secured by the car. Bonds are considered long-term debts that are secured. Bonds often have a due date, known as a maturity date, when the principal of the bond must be paid off. Mortgage bonds are bonds on a specific piece of property, which can be seized if the mortgage bond is not paid.

h. Benefits of Equity Capital versus Debt Capital

It is often more beneficial to the corporation to raise capital by issuing shares, or equity security, than by going into debt. However, shareholders prefer the corporation to raise money by going into debt. This is because most shareholders do not have preemptive rights, so when the corporation issues more shares, their ownership percentage goes down. Thus, if someone owns ten percent in the corporation, and more shares are issued when that person does not have preemptive rights, his ownership percent in the corporation will drop below ten percent. When a shareholder has less ownership percentage in a corporation, he receives less percent of the profit. In addition, sometimes shareholders receive more rights if they own more shares; if their ownership dips below a certain percentage, they could lose some of these rights.

Arguably, the government promotes corporations going into debt by providing a tax deduction for interest. Issuing shares is not tax-deductible. However, issuing shares does not cause the corporation to go into debt and is better financially for the corporation.

i. Case

The following case illustrates the issues that can arise if a corporation is not properly formed. An improperly formed corporation, also known as a de facto corporation, can still be treated like a corporation at times. A de jure corporation is a corporation that has been properly formed and is in good standing with the law. Although Alabama MBA is referred to as a limited liability company, the issues are the same as with a regular corporation. However, remember that the document similar to an LLC's operating agreement in a corporation is the bylaws.

Brown v. WP Media, Inc.

17 So. 3d 1167 (2009)

The plaintiffs below, Alabama MBA, Inc., and Hugh W. Brown, Jr., appeal from a summary judgment in favor of the defendant, W.P. Media, Inc., in this action seeking damages for breach of contract. We reverse and remand.

Facts and Procedural History

In 2001, W.P. Media and Alabama MBA executed a contract (hereinafter "the operating agreement") whereby the parties agreed to operate a joint venture named Alabaster Wireless MBA, LLC, a company intended to provide wireless Internet services to consumers. In the operating agreement, W.P. Media agreed to create a wireless network to be used by Alabaster Wireless and to provide certain technical support once the wireless network was created. Under the operating agreement, Alabama MBA was to contribute capital in the amount of $79,300 and W.P. Media was to contribute "proprietary technology" equal to the same amount. Brown signed the operating agreement on Alabama MBA's behalf as its chairman of the board.

In May 2005, Brown and Alabama MBA filed a complaint in the Jefferson Circuit Court alleging that, among other things, W.P. Media had breached the operating agreement by failing to construct a wireless network. Further, in a separate count, Brown alleged that in 2003 he had personally loaned W.P. Media $100,000 pursuant to a loan agreement and that W.P. Media had breached the loan agreement.

In December 2005, Brown moved for a partial summary judgment on the breach-of-loan-agreement claim. The trial court entered a partial summary judgment for Brown on that claim and awarded damages. The trial court also certified its judgment as final under Rule 54(b), Ala. R. Civ. P. No appeal was taken from that judgment, and that judgment is not at issue in this appeal.

In January 2007, W.P. Media moved for a summary judgment on the remaining claim that it had breached the operating agreement. Specifically, W.P. Media maintained that articles of incorporation for Alabama MBA were not filed until 2002, after the operating agreement had been executed. Thus, W.P. Media contended, the operating agreement was void because Alabama MBA lacked capacity to enter into the contract. Additionally, W.P. Media contended that Alabama MBA, as an allegedly improperly incorporated entity, was not a real party in interest and was thus due to be dismissed from the case.

The trial court denied W.P. Media's summary-judgment motion. W.P. Media subsequently filed a motion for the trial court to "reconsider" the denial of the motion, a motion to compel arbitration, and a motion for a change of venue. After a hearing, the trial court issued an order setting aside its previous order denying W.P. Media's motion for a summary judgment, entered a summary judgment for W.P. Media on the breach-of-contract claim, and held that the motions to compel arbitration and for a change of venue were moot. Brown and Alabama MBA appeal....

The issue in this case is whether Alabama MBA was properly incorporated both at the time the operating agreement was executed and at the time Alabama MBA and Brown filed the underlying action.

It is undisputed that, at the time the operating agreement was executed, the articles of incorporation for Alabama MBA had not been filed. However, Brown filed articles of incorporation for Alabama MBA in the Jefferson County Probate Court in October 2002, and the secretary of state's records indicate that Alabama MBA was incorporated at that time. The record reveals that Alabama MBA did not hold an organizational meeting, pay taxes, issue stock, or adopt bylaws until early 2007. Further, before then Alabama MBA had no bank accounts or employees; all Alabama MBA's expenses were paid by Brown personally.

In its summary-judgment motion, W.P. Media argued that because Alabama MBA was not incorporated at the time the operating agreement was executed, it lacked capacity to contract. Thus, W.P. Media maintained, the contract was "void ab initio" and no action for its breach could be maintained.

Corporate existence begins when articles of incorporation are filed, unless a later effective date is specified in the articles. Alabama Code 1975, § 10-2B-2.03, states:

"(a) Unless a delayed effective date is specified, the *corporate existence begins when the articles of incorporation are filed.*

"(b) The probate judge's filing of the articles of incorporation is *conclusive proof* that the incorporators satisfied all conditions precedent to incorporation except in a proceeding by the state to cancel or revoke the incorporation or involuntarily dissolve the corporation" (emphasis added).

There is no dispute in the record that the articles of incorporation for Alabama MBA were filed in 2002, after the operating agreement had been executed. Even so, Alabama MBA contends that it existed as a "de facto corporation" at the time the operating agreement was executed.

"[A]n improperly formed corporation can nevertheless exist as a de facto corporation. 'A de facto corporation ... can be brought into being when it can be shown that a bona fide and colorable attempt has been made to create a corporation, even though the efforts at incorporation can be shown to be irregular, informal, or even defective.' ..."

In contrast, a "de jure corporation" is "[a] corporation formed in accordance with all applicable laws and recognized as a corporation for liability purposes." ... It appears undisputed that Alabama MBA was not a de jure corporation at the time the operating agreement was executed.

Alabama MBA contends that it existed as a de facto corporation at the time the operating agreement was executed; the record, however, reveals no substantial evidence of "bona fide and colorable" attempts to incorporate Alabama MBA occurring before the execution of the operating agreement. Therefore, we hold that Alabama MBA did not exist as a de facto corporation at the time the operating agreement was executed.

Although Alabama MBA might not have existed as either a de jure corporation or a de facto corporation, Alabama MBA contends that W.P. Media is nevertheless estopped from denying Alabama MBA's corporate existence. We agree.

"Corporate action may also be established under principles of estoppel, whether or not an entity or organization qualifies as a de facto corporation. The doctrine is based on conduct by a party which recognizes an organization as a corporation or an express or implied representation by a corporation that it is a corporation. In the first instance, estoppel cannot apply to one who has not dealt with the organization or in any way recognized it as having corporate existence, or who has participated in holding it out as a corporation. In the second instance, where a party has contracted or otherwise dealt with an organization, believing it to be a corporation, there may have been no holding out of corporate status by the organization. In either instance, estoppel arises from the contract or course of dealing by the parties and is applicable in a suit by the party dealing with the organization, as well as in a suit by the organization...."

Alabama MBA, citing *City of Orange Beach v. Perdido Pass Developers, Inc.* ..., and *Bukacek v. Pell City Farms, Inc.* ..., argues that because W.P. Media treated Alabama MBA as a corporation, W.P. Media is now estopped from denying Alabama

MBA's corporate existence. In *City of Orange Beach v. Perdido Pass Developers, Inc.*, the City of Orange Beach refused to approve zoning for an island owned by Perdido Pass Developers, Inc., even though Orange Beach had entered a contract with the previous owner of the island to approve certain zoning ordinances that would allow the island to be developed. Perdido Pass and others sued Orange Beach, alleging breach of contract. On appeal, Orange Beach argued that Perdido Pass did not obtain title to the island because it was not incorporated at the time the previous owner conveyed the property and, therefore, it did not have standing to sue. We stated:

> "These arguments are also without merit.... Although Perdido Pass's articles of incorporation were filed before the signing of the deed, the evidence shows that Perdido Pass was treated as a corporation by all parties, including Orange Beach. Orange Beach received various applications from Perdido Pass, issued receipts to Perdido Pass for various payments, and issued a septic tank license to Perdido Pass for the island. We will not allow Orange Beach to deny Perdido Pass's existence as a corporation after having dealt with it as a corporation...."

In *Bukacek v. Pell City Farms, Inc.*, Bukacek entered into an agreement with others to form Pell City Farms, Inc., and he conveyed a 300-acre tract to the corporation. Subsequently, Bukacek filed an action to quiet title, alleging that Pell City Farms, Inc., was incapable of taking legal title because no articles of incorporation had been filed and it was neither a de jure nor a de facto corporation. This Court held:

> "[W]e think the fact situation here presented shows that while Pell City Farms, Inc., may not have been a corporation de jure — or perhaps even de facto — insofar as the transaction here is concerned, it should be regarded practically as a corporation, being recognized as such by the parties themselves. In other words, *the incidents of corporate existence may exist as between the parties by virtue of an estoppel.* Thus, besides corporations de jure and de facto, there can be a recognition of a third class known as 'Corporations by estoppel....'"

W.P. Media entered into a contractual relationship with Alabama MBA to operate Alabaster Wireless. The operating agreement identified Alabama MBA as a corporation, was executed in Alabama MBA's corporate name, and was signed by Brown as Alabama MBA's "chairman of the board." W.P. Media further concedes in its brief that Alabama MBA and Brown had essentially "represented" that Alabama MBA was "a viable, legal corporation" and that W.P. Media had "no reason to doubt" those representations.... Although Alabama MBA had not yet filed articles of incorporation at the time the operating agreement was executed in 2001, the articles of incorporation were subsequently filed in 2002. The record reveals that at no time during the venture did W.P. Media challenge the validity of the operating agreement until after it was sued for breaching the operating agreement. Under the facts of this case, we hold that W.P. Media's actions of entering into a contract with Alabama MBA and participating with Alabama MBA in the joint venture before and after Alabama MBA's articles of incorporation were filed estop W.P. Media from denying Alabama MBA's corporate existence for purposes of challenging the validity of the operating agreement....

WP Media also contends that Alabama MBA was not properly incorporated at the time it filed the instant action; thus, it argues, Alabama MBA was not a "real party in interest" under Rule 17, Ala. R. Civ. P., and cannot maintain this action. In support of its contention that Alabama MBA was not incorporated when the underlying action was filed, W.P. Media argues that Brown "chose not to form the corporation and [instead] treat[ed] everything personal" and that, in addition to filing articles of incorporation, Alabama MBA was *also* required to meet the prerequisites of Ala.Code 1975, § 10-2B-2.05(a). That Code section provides:

> "After incorporation the initial directors shall hold an organizational meeting, at the call of a majority of the directors, to complete the organization of the corporation by appointing officers, adopting bylaws (unless the power to adopt initial bylaws has been reserved to the shareholders in the articles of incorporation), and carrying on any other business brought before the meeting."

W.P. Media asserts, and the record supports its assertion, that Alabama MBA held no "organizational meeting" until after it and Brown filed the underlying action. W.P. Media also asserts that Alabama MBA failed to meet the record-keeping requirements of Ala.Code 1975, § 10-2B-16.01. W.P. Media argues that Alabama MBA was improperly incorporated because it failed to comply with these two Code sections after it had filed its articles of incorporation.

As started above, the plain language of § 10-2B-2.03 explicitly states that the probate judge's filing of the articles of incorporation is "*conclusive proof* that the incorporators satisfied all conditions precedent to incorporation" (emphasis added). Although § 10-2B-2.05 sets forth procedures to "complete the *organization* of the corporation" (emphasis added), that Code section explicitly states that this occurs "[a]fter incorporation." Moreover, nothing in the language of § 10-2B-16.01 requires records to be kept as a prerequisite of proper incorporation — in fact, § 10-2B-16.01 only prescribes duties of existent corporations.

As stated above, it is undisputed that Brown complied with § 10-2B-2.03 and that articles of incorporation for Alabama MBA were filed in 2002, years before the underlying action was initiated. Therefore, there is no merit in W.P. Media's argument that Alabama MBA was not properly incorporated at the time this action was filed and thus cannot be a real party in interest in this case.

Conclusion

Alabama MBA has demonstrated that W.P. Media is estopped from denying Alabama MBA's corporate existence. Therefore, the summary judgment is reversed, and the case is remanded for further proceedings.

Chapter Summary

Corporations are typically governed by state statutes, which are often based upon a version of the Model Business Corporation Act, or, more recently, the Revised

Model Business Corporation Act. Otherwise, common law, and sometimes even federal laws apply to corporations.

Corporations are often started by promoters who do all the initial work of planning and forming the corporation. Many times, the incorporator is an attorney. Promoters find investors. If the promoters sign contracts on the corporation's behalf, they are responsible for those contracts until they are taken over by the corporation.

Perhaps the best state to incorporate in, especially if the corporation is doing business in several states, is Delaware. This is because Delaware is very pro-corporation, particularly in having special courts for corporate law issues and a wide body of case law that is pro-corporation.

A corporation's name must be available in order to be procured through the Secretary of State. It also must be different from other pre-existing corporation names in that state. Once the corporation's name has been verified as available, it can be reserved. To guarantee that the name is available longer than with a name reservation, a holding company that just "holds" the name can be created, although this is option that is more expensive.

An organizational meeting helps take care of the initial business of the company. This meeting is when directors are elected, bylaws are passed, and stock is issued.

The articles of incorporation are considered the public document for the corporation. Articles of incorporation must be filed to form the corporation with the Secretary of State. The name of the company, along with address, registered agent, and stock information will be in the articles. Another item required to be in the articles of incorporation is whether stocks come with preemptive rights or not. Preemptive rights are like a right of first refusal to buy stock up to your ownership percentage in the corporation before the public has access to purchase the stock.

The bylaws are the internal rules for running the company. The bylaws go into detail about the shareholder meetings, particularly notice for the shareholder meetings. This includes how the board of directors should manage. Officer titles along with corresponding duties are delineated in the bylaws. This is a private document.

Stocks are equity financing of the corporation. Almost anything of value can be given as consideration for stock. The major types of stock are common stock and preferred stock. Common stock is riskier than preferred. Shareholders of preferred stock get dividends prior to common shareholders. However, common shareholders get to vote, whereas preferred shareholders normally do not.

Bonds are debt financing of the corporation. This is money that the corporation raised by borrowing. The debt could be unsecured, which is just a promise to repay. The debt could be secured, which is a promise to pay backed with property that may be seized if the debt is not paid. One of the benefits of debt capital is that the interest payments are tax deductible.

Key Terms

Articles of incorporation
Authorized shares
Board of directors
Bond
Buy-sell agreement
Bylaws
Certificate of incorporation
Close corporation
Common stock
Common stock certificate
Common stockholder
Corporation
Corporation by estoppel
Debenture
De facto corporation
De jure corporation
Debt securities
Dividends
Equity securities
Incorporator
Issued shares
Model Business Corporation Act
    (MBCA)
Name registration

Note
Officers
Organizational meeting
Par value
Preferred stock
Preferred stock certificate
Preferred stockholder
Preemptive rights
Preincorporation contracts
Promoter
Promoter contracts
Quorum
Registered agent
Revised Model Business Corpora-
    tion Act (RMBCA)
Secured debt
Securities
Shareholder
Shareholder agreements
Special meeting
Stock
Stockholder
Transfer restrictions
Unsecured debt

Review Questions

1. Who is responsible for preincorporation contracts?

2. Why do so many corporations incorporate in Delaware?

3. How does the public know a business is a corporation?

4. What else, other than filing articles of incorporation, does a corporation need to do to properly incorporate?

5. Who usually incorporates a corporation?

6. Discuss what happens at the organizational meeting.

7. Who runs the close corporation? Should restrictions be placed upon the transfer of shares? If so, which ones?

8. Is the close corporation limited to a certain number of people? If so, how many?

9. What purpose does putting the designation "closed" on the stock certificates have?

10. Who owns the shares in a close corporation?

11. Does the close corporation have to have annual meetings, of either shareholders or directors?

12. Who manages a close corporation?

13. If an incorporator submits articles of incorporation containing a name for the corporation that is very similar to another, already incorporated corporation's name, can the Secretary of State deny the articles?

14. Why might a shareholder want preemptive rights?

15. What information is required to be on the stock certificate?

16. What are the major types of stock, along with their characteristics?

17. Which type of debt do most lenders prefer, secured or unsecured?

18. What are the advantages of equity and debt financing?

19. What is a de jure corporation? What is a de facto corporation? How does a corporation by estoppel differ?

Web Links

You are entitled to one free credit history per year at https://www.annualcreditreport.com/index.action.

This website is one place where certain companies can look for investors: http://www.garage.com.

Exercises

1. A new corporation is forming and will just be doing business locally for several years, though it hopes to expand to other states down the line. Where should this corporation incorporate?

2. Is U.S. Armory an appropriate name for a gun corporation? Why or why not?

3. Should information about the special meetings of the board of directors be located in the articles or in the bylaws?

4. If a family owned a large dairy farm, and all the family members worked at the dairy farm, which business entity would you recommend they incorporation under?

5. A close corporation wants their shareholder agreement to indicate that shareholders can withdraw with six months' notice. What else should the transfer restrictions in the share agreement state?

6. The Solamar Resorts, Inc. has fifty thousand common shares authorized. Of these authorized shares, twenty-five thousand are issued and outstanding. If the

board holds that each stockholder should get a stock dividend of one common share for each he already owns, are there enough authorized shares to do so without amending the articles?

7. Use the sample bylaws in the chapter to answer the following questions:

   (a) Under shareholder meetings, how can an invalid meeting be made valid?

   (b) Under shareholder meetings, what constitutes a quorum?

   (c) What officers are allowed under these bylaws?

   (d) What are the qualifications of the board of directors?

Chapter 11

Investing

Chapter Outline

Chapter Objectives

- Discuss how stock options work.
- Review payment and taxation of dividends.
- Give an example of how a stock split works.
- Provide information on how the Securities and Exchange Commission registers and regulates stock.
- Review the two major statutes governing securities.
- Discuss insider trading.
- Describe state securities laws.

11.1 Introduction to Investing

The real question to be asked and answered first, in regards to investing is: Why do people want to invest? Many of us do not realize we might want to or may need to invest, because we may not realize that most of us no longer get a pension or any other type of retirement benefit from our employer, other than a 401k plan, which the employee contributes to (the employer may partially match). If we do not save, then social security might be the only retirement income we receive. Many of us do not know how much or little we are potentially going to receive from social security. Several of us might believe that social security might not be around when we retire — even more reason to consider investing! In 2015, the average a retired worker was receiving a month was approximately thirteen hundred dollars ($1,300.00). Only you know if perhaps a similar amount might be sufficient for your needs once you retire.

In addition, many of you may be thinking, that investing is too risky. However, looking at the history of the stock market, there are not many other investments that provide as much of an increase on your initial investment. That being said, one of the reasons people lost so much in the stock market during the recession, is they did not follow the traditional advice: that the closer someone gets to retirement, the more they need to convert their stocks to bonds. Bonds are less likely to lose their value, and the closer someone is to retirement, the less they can usually afford to take the time to recover from a stock market dip.

One great reason for investing is that the average life expectancy has grown over the years, and it is likely individuals will live longer than their forebears will. Approximately a one-third of one's life may be spent in retirement. When considering retirement, one common goal is to have around eighty percent of your pre-retirement income in your retirement. This is because although some expenses will decrease when you retire, others will increase. For example, you will not have to pay taxes for social security and Medicare, or expenses associated with work, once you are retired. You may face new medical expenses, such as long-term care. Medicare will not cover all your health care expenses, and many people pay for a supplemental Medicare plan. You will still need to pay for housing if you do not own a house when you retire. Eventually, you may need to consider having in home help if you are incapacitated or consider going to a paid skilled nursing facility. There are Medicare skilled nursing facilities, but it is a good idea to visit some in the area you think you might retire, as the care can vary widely, and you may decide you want to go to a paid skilled nursing facility. People need to have saved enough to meet their financial needs in retirement. Ideally, they will have enough money for activities they were looking forward to pursuing once retired, such as travel.

How do people know when they have enough for retirement? They add up any pension they will receive (they may not receive one at all), estimated social security, and projected savings. An important thing to note about Social Security is that if you were born in 1960 or later, you will not be able to retire until at least sixty-seven in order to receive the full amount of your Social Security. If the pension, social security, and projected savings are equal or greater than the expected expenses multiplied by the estimated numbers of years one will be retired, the person has enough. Many times when people are adding up what they think their retirement expenses will be, they forget things like replacing cars when they wear out. If the pension, social security, and projected savings are not equal or greater, then the person needs to make up some savings before retirement. The other main alternatives are to work longer than expected or to spend less.

Before starting any investing, one should consult a professional. Investing in the stock market may be a way in which to increase savings. A publicly traded corporation is one that is listed on a national stock exchange. The first offering of a corporation's stock to the public is known as the IPO, or initial public offering. Offering stock is a way for the corporation to make money.

Securities can be stocks or bonds. A security is determined by the following test: "the person invests his money in a common enterprise and is led to expect profits solely from the efforts of the promoter or a third party."[1] The investment must be in a common business activity as well and there must be a reasonable expectation of profits. If all of these elements or tests are met, then the investment is a security. A security can include

> "any note, stock treasury stock, bond, debenture, evidence of indebtedness, certificate of interest or participation in any profit-sharing agreement, collateral-trust certificate, preorganization certificate or subscription, transferable share, investment contract, voting-trust certificate, certificate of deposit for a security, fractional undivided interest in oil, gas, or other mineral rights, or in general, any interest or instrument commonly known as a 'security'...."[2]

This chapter focuses on equity securities, or stocks.

There are many different stock exchanges. An exchange is a group, which has a marketplace where securities can be sold and bought. Nowadays, a stock exchange can be all-online and does not need to have a physical trading "floor." Stock exchanges many people are not aware of include the Chicago Stock Exchange and the National Stock Exchange. Much more well-known stock exchanges include the New York Stock Exchange (NYSE) or the National Association of Securities Dealers Automated Quotation (NASDAQ) system. To be listed on NYSE, which is often considered the most prestigious stock exchange in the United States, a company must have earnings, before taxes, of a minimum of ten million dollars in the three years prior to being listed on NYSE. There are additional requirements as well before the stock can be listed on NYSE.

Some Issues to Consider When Purchasing Stock

1. People do not want to invest in a stock solely because they are emotionally invested in that stock. They should verify that it is a good buy before investing.

2. Consider investing in a stock that is valued at close to what it is really worth, rather than one that is priced way above what it is really worth.

---

1. *SEC v. W. J. Howey Co.*, 328 U.S. 293 (1946). Please note that this case is questioned, but has not been overturned.

2. 15 U.S.C.A. Section 77b(1).

3. Do people want to invest in a corporation whose business they do not understand?

4. How much competition does the corporation have?

5. Are the corporation's earnings healthy?

6. If the stock is out of one's price range, determine whether one can buy a fraction of the stock.

7. Assess what the future of the corporation is.

8. Does the corporation have a good business model?

11.2 Stock Options

While many corporations prefer cash for shares, a person can become a shareholder in other ways. A person can exchange knowledge or labor for shares as well. An investor might even write an IOU to obtain stock. A person might offer services to the corporation to receive stock.

Stock options are a way in which people who share knowledge, labor, or services can receive their stock. Stock options let a person buy shares from a corporation at a certain price, and usually during a set period. This price is known as the striking price. The striking price is often the same as the market price at the time the options are offered. Stock options are so named as the employee does not have to convert their options to shares; it is the employee's option to do so or not. The period could be a couple of years, but usually the employees cannot decide to buy all the shares at the end of the period. They might have to exercise their options throughout that period, for example, a quarter of the options at a time, such as in six-month increments. Typically, a person would only want to buy at that price (say, $30) if the share value had gone up or they think the stock will go up (say to $40).

For example, a company decides to give its employees stock options. It decides it will offer up to one thousand options to employees at ten dollars a share. One thousand options times ten dollars a share means that the employee will pay up to ten thousand dollars to convert the options to shares. To keep it simpler, the employee uses all the options at once, and does spend ten thousand dollars. When he is allowed to sell, the shares are selling at fifteen dollars apiece. One thousand shares times fifteen dollars each, means his shares are worth fifteen thousand dollars. As he spent ten thousand, he has a profit of five thousand dollars.

- Company offers 1,000 options at $10 a share
- $1,000 \times \$10 = \$10,000.00$
- Employee uses all options and spends $10,000.00
- When sold, shares sell for $15.00 per share
- $1,000$ shares $\times \$15.00 = \$15,000.00$
- $\$15,000.00$ sale price $- \$10,000.00$ initial cost $= \$5,000.00$ profit

11.3 Dividends

Dividends are how a corporation shares its profits with its shareholders. A dividend comes in the form of cash, shares, or property. Dividends should not come out of the capital for the company. Directors have the ultimate decision-making authority when it comes to whether the corporation should reinvest its profits or distribute the profits to the shareholders as dividends.

Typically, a company needs to pass two tests in order to issue dividends: the balance sheet and the solvency test. The balance sheet test is that the corporation must have assets equal to or greater than its liabilities, even after the dividend has been made. The solvency test is that the corporation must be able to keep paying its liabilities, or debts, once the dividend has been made. An analogy would be: can the company make and continue to make the minimum payments on its credit card? If yes, then the company can issue a dividend. However, there is obviously a lot of pressure from the shareholders to declare a dividend.

The dividend most enjoyed by shareholders is the cash dividend. The next favorite type of dividend, at least by shareholders, is the share dividend. This would provide the shareholder with more shares or a fraction of a share. The share dividend typically must be from the same class of stock as the shareholder already owns.

Property dividends are the least favored type of dividends. Often the property will be the product that the company makes. Typically, they are the least favored because they are difficult to resell, the shareholder often does not want them, and the shareholder may be required to pay taxes on them. For example, Neal owns Raisins and Nuts cereal, and receives Raisins and Nuts cereal as a property dividend. Neal hates raisins and is allergic to nuts. He owns so much of the cereal stock, he receives a pallet of individually sized Raisin and Nuts that is not labelled for resale. He is not supposed to sell it, but because he received so much of it (usually at least more than ten dollars), he is supposed to pay taxes on it! Neal has to pay taxes on a property dividend for something he invests in, but does not like, and cannot resell!

It is interesting to note that the federal government actually wants corporations to pay dividends, so it gets more taxes. To increase the likelihood that a corporation will issue dividends, the federal government instituted the accumulated earnings tax. If a corporation accumulates more money than what is reasonably necessary, it might have to pay a tax penalty of fifteen percent.

The following information is typically included in a stock quote. Stock market quotes are readily available on the internet.

How to Read a Stock Market Quote

Usually, the first two columns will look like this:

52 Weeks	
High	Low
10	2

These two columns indicate the highest and lowest the stock has sold for within a year. This will not include the current date.

The next column may be the stock's name. However, many stock market quotes now just show the symbol of the stock, which would look similar to:

Sym
ESON

The trading volume for the day might be in the next column. 100s is an abbreviation for 100,000s. Thus, a number of 562, would indicate a trading volume of 562,000 for the day.

Vol
562

For investors who are buying and selling stock in the short term, a quote will often include the high and low of the stock for that day.

High   Low
6   3

Finally, there may be a close column. The close column gives the closing price for the share for the day.

Close
5

a. Declaring

A corporation does not have to issue dividends, but once it declares them, then it owes the shareholders those dividends. If the corporation does not issue dividends, it could reinvest the money into the corporation. The board of directors has authority to declare dividends, though stock dividends may also require shareholder approval. A corporation should carefully assess whether it can truly afford to issue a dividend before declaring one. Preferred shareholders get paid dividends prior to common shareholders. Sometimes, if the corporation cannot make a dividend, due to lack of funds, for a year, the preferred shareholders will be entitled to cumulative dividends. This means that the preferred shareholders would get dividends for the prior year(s), in which dividends were not paid, as well as first year in which the corporation could again afford to issue dividends. In general, common shareholders do not have cumulative dividends. Preferred shareholders only get cumulative dividends if specifically provided for.

b. Paying

Dividends are paid to those who own shares on the record date. Remember, record date is an arbitrary date, selected by the board of directors, usually thirty days before the annual shareholders' meeting. It is a line in the sand, since shareholders are constantly buying and selling, and it would be difficult to tell exactly who owned what shares as of the time of the shareholders' meeting.

c. Taxing

A corporation is taxed twice and sometimes even three times. Corporations are taxed on their profits, and then the shareholders are taxed on dividends (or the profits that the corporation was already taxed on). If the corporation is a subsidiary, the subsidiary pays taxes, then gives the leftover profits to the parent company, the parent company pays taxes, and then gives profit to the shareholders as dividends, and finally the shareholders pay taxes on those dividends. There are tax breaks to negate some of this taxation.

The shareholder has to pay taxes on cash dividends in the year that he receives this type of dividend. This is because the Internal Revenue Service knows that technically, the shareholder has the cash to pay the taxes on the dividend. The shareholder has to pay taxes on share and property dividends in the year that he sells this type of dividend. This is because the Internal Revenue Service knows that the shareholder may not have the cash to pay the taxes on these types of dividends until they are sold.

11.4 Stock Splits

There are different types of stock splits, but this text will cover one type, in general. Stock splits are a way in which to increase the total number of shares. Do not confuse stock splits with stock dividends. Stock splits help encourage trading by reducing the price of shares. However, think of a stock split as a psychological selling mechanism. Instead of one pizza for ten dollars, the investor can have eight slices (the same as one pizza) for ten dollars. Thus, the investor is spending one dollar and twenty-five cents per share. One dollar and twenty-five cents times eight, equals ten dollars. The investor has spent the same amount of money as when it was one share for ten dollars.

- Originally, 1 share = $10.00
- Now, with the stock split, the investor can get 8 shares for $10.00
- $10.00/8 = $1.25 per share
- However, the investor has still spent $10.00
- In either instance, they have something currently worth $10.00

It makes the investor think they have received more, when the investor really has invested the same amount of money. In the alternative, the company could allow an investor to pay $1.25 per stock. Many times the value of the stock does go up after a stock split.

11.5 Securities Act of 1933

In general, if shares are sold through interstate commerce, then they are a public offering and have to be registered with the Securities and Exchange Commission (SEC). There are several exemptions, discussed below. The SEC operates under two major acts: the Securities Act of 1933 and Securities Exchange Act of 1934. The 1933 Act has to do with the original issuance of stocks in interstate commerce. It also makes it illegal to use interstate communication/transportation to sell securities without providing certain basic financial information to potential buyers. This act requires a registration of securities. It also regulates prospectuses, which are a substantial part of the registration. A prospectus contains financial information so that the investor can make a well-informed decision.

To comply with securities regulations, certain companies must file a registration statement electronically on the EDGAR system (EDGAR stands for the Electronic Data Gathering, Analysis, and Retrieval System). This system is run by the SEC. The registration statement is part of the 1933 Act, though EDGAR did not originate until much later. The registration statement requires several things. This registration includes, among many other requests for information:

- the name of the company,
- what state the company will be organized in,
- the company's principal place of business,
- risk factors,
- determination of the offering price,
- a description of the securities,
- information about the company's property,
- information about the company's legal proceedings,
- information about the directors and officers of the company,
- information about shareholders owning more than ten percent of the company,
- information about the business of the company, and
- then goes into even more detail to help investors make an informed decision.

Some of the items above are the same as required on the articles of incorporation, but the information quickly becomes much more detailed. These are companies investors are going to invest in, and they should have access to this information. The SEC promulgated Form S-1 to indicate what should be included in the registration. The form is eight pages and references many other documents. It also requires certified public accountants to certify financial statements that are included. Potential investors can look at registrations, reports, and other information about a corporation on this EDGAR system.

If a registration statement has an untrue statement of an important fact, omits important facts, or is misleading, then under the 1933 Act, the persons who signed the registration agreement, such as the directors and the accountants, can be held liable. The rule regarding the prospectus is similar.

Transactions that are exempt from some of the registration provisions include, but are not limited to:

- nonissuers,
- intrastate offerings,
- private placement, and
- small issues.

The corporations that are exempt cannot commit fraud and must give investors reports, statements, etc. Nonissuers are considered normal investors, like a person. Normal investors are not required to file registration before reselling their shares. With an intrastate offering, local businesses are raising money locally. They do not need to register. To qualify as an intrastate offering, the issuer has to be a resident of the state, and eighty percent or more of the issuer's assets have to be in the state, along with gross revenues and proceeds from the sale. With a private placement, the issuer is seeking capital from accredited investors. Accredited investors are considered especially investment perceptive, and so no registration is required. To be an accredited investor, if it is a person, the person has to have a net worth of over a million dollars and an income greater than two hundred thousand dollars a year. Different types of business organizations can sometimes qualify as accredited investors. With a small issue, this usually includes securities that will be offered in an amount of less than fifty million dollars in twelve months. There are additional requirements for small issues.

11.6 Securities Exchange Act of 1934

The Securities Exchange Act of 1934 started the Securities and Exchange Commission. The goal of the SEC, in general, is to protect investors. The SEC is run by five commissioners. The president appoints these commissioners for five-year terms; these terms do not expire all at once.

The 1934 Act:

- adopts rules regarding brokers,
- allows the SEC to make inquiries into securities fraud, and
- requires ongoing disclosures.

Section 12 companies have additional reporting requirements. Section 12 Companies have greater than ten million dollars in assets and greater than or equal to five hundred shareholders. The ongoing reporting that is required from corporations includes Section 12 companies having to file forms 10-K, 10-Q, and 8-K. A 10-K report is an annual report. It is filed electronically, within ninety days of the corporation ending its fiscal year. The information that must appear on this report is:

- information about the business,
- significant changes within the last fiscal year, and
- a general summary of the last five years.

If there are significant principal securities holders or if there have been transactions that involve a significant percent of the security, those must be indicated as well.

The 10-Q report is a quarterly report. This report will discuss:

- the finances of the corporation,
- the capitalization of the corporation,
- how much equity the stockholders own in the corporation, and
- any sales of unregistered securities during the quarter.

Quarterly reports only have to be filed for the first three quarters of the year, because the yearly report counts as the final quarterly report for the year. In general, the 10-Q should be filed within forty-five days of the end of the quarter.

The form 8-K has to be filed when there have been certain informational changes. This report should be filed within four business days of the end of the month in which the change occurs. So, what qualifies as a "certain informational change"? If the control of the corporation changes, that should be reported. If a large amount of the assets of the corporation have been added or subtracted from the corporation that should be reported. Lawsuits against the corporation should probably be reported. If changes are made in the security, it should be reported. If the security holders' rights are affected, it should be noted on the 8-K. Several other changes have to be reported as well.

11.7 Investor Protection

a. Insider Trading

The 1934 Act also includes Section 10(b). This section makes it illegal to manipulate or use deception to circumvent the regulations of the SEC. The SEC has found that insider trading is contrary to Section 10(b), although the section does not name insider trading specifically. The SEC also instituted Rule 10b-5 to supplement Section 10(b). Insider trading is trading in the open marketplace by a corporate insider who has material information, which is not available to the public. An insider includes a director, officer, and/or controller. It is considered fairer to have all investors use the same information with which to make investment decisions.

One of the most notorious examples of insider trading is Enron. A case on Enron is immediately following this paragraph. Perhaps another one of the most notorious examples of insider trading is that of Martha Stewart. The Securities and Exchange Commission (SEC) believed that Ms. Stewart was told by her friend, Sam Waksal, that his company, ImClone, had a cancer drug that was rejected by the Food and Drug Administration. This information was made known to Ms. Stewart before it was public knowledge. Martha had her broker sell her 4000 shares. Thus, she did not suffer a loss that the public suffered. She was criminally prosecuted and served jail time in the federal prison.

U.S. v. Skilling

638 F.3d 480 (2011)

Former Enron Corporation CEO Jeffrey K. Skilling was convicted of conspiracy, securities fraud, making false representations to auditors, and insider trading. After we affirmed his convictions, the Supreme Court invalidated one of the objects of the conspiracy charge — honest-services fraud — and remanded, instructing us to determine whether the error committed by the district court in submitting the honest-services theory to the jury was harmless as to any of Skilling's convictions. Because we find that the error was harmless, we affirm the convictions....

I. BACKGROUND

In May 2006, Skilling was convicted by a jury of one count of conspiracy, twelve counts of securities fraud, five counts of making false representations to auditors, and one count of insider trading. The indictment alleged several possible objects of the conspiracy, including securities fraud and honest-services fraud, and the district court's jury instructions permitted the jury to convict on any of the alleged theories of guilt. The jury returned a general verdict of guilty on the conspiracy charge without identifying the specific object of the conspiracy. The district court sentenced Skilling to 292 months of imprisonment and three years of supervised release, and assessed $45 million in restitution.

Skilling appealed, arguing, among other things, that his conspiracy conviction was premised on an improper theory of honest-services fraud. We affirmed the convictions, holding that the Government's honest-services theory was proper under Fifth Circuit case law.... We also vacated the sentence and remanded for resentencing because the district court had incorrectly applied a sentencing enhancement for substantially jeopardizing a "financial institution...."

On appeal, the Supreme Court reduced the scope of the honest-services fraud statute and invalidated the Government's honest-services theory in this case.... The Court did not, however, reverse any of Skilling's convictions, but remanded the case to us to determine whether the honest-services instruction amounted to harmless error....

III. ANALYSIS

A. *The Conspiracy Conviction*

The Government asserts that the invalid honest-services instruction was harmless with respect to the conspiracy conviction. Specifically, it argues that the evidence presented at trial proved that Skilling participated in a scheme to deceive the investing public about Enron's financial condition in order to maintain or increase Enron's stock price. If so, then we would be able to conclude beyond a reasonable doubt that absent the honest-services instruction, the jury would have convicted Skilling under a valid theory of guilt — conspiracy to commit securities fraud....

Having disposed of these two preliminary arguments, we next turn to the crux of the matter: whether, under the *Neder* standard, the evidence presented at trial proves that Skilling conspired to commit securities fraud. Based on our own thorough examination of the considerable record in this case, we find that the jury was presented with overwhelming evidence that Skilling conspired to commit securities fraud, and thus we conclude beyond a reasonable doubt that the verdict would have been the same absent the alternative-theory error.

First, the evidence overwhelmingly proved that Skilling and his co-conspirators transferred losses and the risk-management books from Enron's struggling retail division, Enron Energy Services ("EES"), to Enron's Wholesale division, which accounted for most of Enron's revenue, so that EES would appear to be more profitable than it really was. The testimony at trial established that under the mark-to-market accounting rules that EES professed to follow, it should have booked hundreds of millions of dollars in losses in the first quarter of 2001. These losses arose from bad-debt write-offs, errors in how EES had originally booked the value of its retail contracts, and unanticipated expenses that could not be passed on to EES's retail customers. According to the testimony, Skilling knew about the extent of the losses attributable to EES and approved a plan to (1) shift the losses and EES's risk-management books (and therefore most of EES's money-losing components) to Wholesale, even though the losses arose from EES's own retail contracts, not from Wholesale's business; and (2) justify this "resegmentation" as an operational change, even though it resulted in no efficiencies, Wholesale had no experience in handling retail contracts, and Wholesale and EES had different contracting procedures, origination policies, risk assessments, and marketing efforts. Dave Delainey, the CEO of EES at the time, testified that he warned Skilling that the resegmentation was fraudulent because it had no real business purpose and was designed to hide EES's losses from investors, and that Skilling approved the resegmentation anyway.

In his brief, Skilling argues that he "established through each of the government witnesses, as well as his own, that the accounting for this transaction was 'rock solid' and complied with the disclosure rules." His record citations, however, do not substantiate his claim. In fact, his argument relies almost exclusively on his own testimony at trial, which was that he has been told that the EES resegmentation adhered to generally accepted accounting principles and that he had not been told that it might be illegal. The jury, by finding him guilty, necessarily determined that his own self-serving testimony, in which he contested his liability under any theory of guilt, including the honest-services theory, was not worthy of belief. Therefore, we too decline to give Skilling's testimony any weight in our harmless-error review when unsupported by other evidence or testimony in the record.

Skilling also argues that he presented evidence at trial that EES's losses "had either not occurred, had not occurred in the way the government's witnesses described, or were only speculative losses that had to be reserved against, and that proper reserves had been taken on all accounts." The record also proves that this claim is false. The testimony at trial clearly showed that EES's losses were real, recognizable under mark-to-market accounting rules, and due to be booked. Skilling points to no evidence, other than his own say-so, that disputes this finding.

Second, the evidence overwhelmingly proved that Skilling and his co-conspirators falsely portrayed Wholesale to the investing public as a low-risk company that made sustainable profits by delivering gas and electric power to customers (i.e., a "logistics company"), even though they knew that Wholesale actually made most of its profits from its highly volatile trading operations. The evidence presented at trial proved that the majority of Wholesale's earnings in 2000 and early 2001 came from trading activities, especially from speculative trading during the California energy crisis. This trading activity created huge gains (as much as $485 million in a single day) and losses (as much as $551 million in a single day). Witnesses testified that Skilling knew about the riskiness of Wholesale's business, but falsely represented to investors and analysts that Wholesale was a "logistics company," not a "trading company."

In addition, from 1999 to the analysts conference during the first quarter of 2001, Skilling repeatedly prohibited other Enron managers from calling Wholesale a "trading company" or referring to any of Wholesale's employees as "traders," often citing the negative effect such language would have on Enron's stock price. That is, if the market perceived Wholesale to be a trading company, it would lead to a decrease in Enron's price—earnings multiplier, which, in turn, would drag its stock price down. The managers obeyed Skilling and referred to Wholesale as a "logistics company" at their own engagements with investors and analysts.

Skilling argues that he presented sufficient contradictory evidence at trial proving that Wholesale actually was a "logistics company" because it owned one of the largest pipeline and energy distribution systems in the world, which allowed Wholesale to meet supply and demand for its energy customers and cover its trading positions. Yet again, this evidence is from Skilling's own self-serving testimony. Moreover, even if we were to believe Skilling's assertions, they do not undermine the Government's proof at trial, which showed that Skilling fraudulently kept from the investing public the reality that Wholesale was driving up its profits through highly risky and volatile trading operations, not through its energy distribution system.

Third, the evidence overwhelmingly proved that Skilling and his co-conspirators used LJM and LJM2, which were two partnerships run by Andy Fastow, who also served as Enron's CFO at the time, to hide Enron's nonperforming assets and book earnings to meet its earnings targets. Specifically, the testimony showed that Skilling was intimately involved in the Enron-LJM "Cuiaba" deal involving the sale of Enron's interest in a power plant in Brazil and the Enron-LJM "Nigerian Barges" deal involving the sale of Enron's interest in power-generating barges off the coast of Nigeria. In both cases, Fastow testified that Skilling personally asked him, on behalf of LJM, to buy money-losing assets at a price that no third party would be willing to pay and, in "secret" oral side deals, guaranteed that LJM would make a certain rate of return (or at least not lose any money) while it owned the assets. Skilling also agreed that Enron would buy the assets back from LJM if a permanent buyer could not be found, which it was eventually forced to do because both assets continued to deteriorate in value. For both deals, Enron booked gains on the sales of the assets to LJM, thereby allowing Enron to meet its earnings targets, even though neither transaction was a true sale because Skilling's "secret" guarantee eliminated any risks LJM might have suffered in the transactions. This caused Enron's financial statements to be false and misleading.

Skilling makes a number of arguments about the proof at trial, none of which are especially relevant. He argues that the Government's theory at trial was (1) that the very creation of the partnerships was fraudulent; (2) that the conflict of interest inherent in the formation of the partnerships was illegal; (3) that by creating and using these partnerships Skilling was opening Enron up to excessive risk and was therefore not doing his job properly; and (4) that the deals themselves made no business sense and therefore Skilling was not doing his job properly. We disagree with Skilling's characterizations of the Government's case, although we do not need to discuss them since we do not rely on them. Rather, we find that the evidence is overwhelming that Skilling was personally involved in the Cuiaba and Nigerian Barges deals and that he used those deals to cause Enron to book fake profits and hide money-losing assets from its investors.

Nonetheless, the Government's other arguments (as characterized by Skilling) are supported by strong evidence, and this evidence, in turn, bolsters the assertion that Skilling engaged in the two deals on which we rely. Likewise, we do not rely on any of the other dozen transactions that LJM and LJM2 executed with Enron, although there is also strong evidence that Skilling and his co-conspirators committed securities fraud in relation to those transactions as well. Such evidence further bolsters the assertion that Skilling engaged in the Cuiaba and Nigerian Barges deals. For all of Skilling's many counterarguments, his personal involvement with respect to those two deals is not controverted.

Fourth, the evidence overwhelmingly proved that Skilling and his co-conspirators underreported the projected losses of Enron's broadband division, Enron Broadband Services ("EBS"), and when those losses became too large to hide within EBS, merged EBS into Wholesale. Enron had marketed EBS to the investing public as an important part of its future growth strategy, but the evidence presented at trial showed that EBS lost money in every quarter of its existence and only met its earning targets in 2000 by engaging in a series of transactions that fell outside of its core businesses: (1) the sale of part of its fiber-optic network to LJM2 at a price that no third party would pay; (2) the hedging of a gain on its investment in Avici, an Internet start-up, into the Raptor special-purpose entity, which allowed EBS to recognize the gain as earnings under mark-to-market accounting; and (3) the "monetization" of a video-on-demand contract with Blockbuster, which allowed EBS to book anticipated future earnings from the contract. Skilling knew about all of these transactions, but failed to tell investors about their impact on EBS's bottom line.

During the first quarter of 2001, EBS's managers informed Skilling that EBS was making almost no revenue from its core businesses and would likely suffer a loss of $146 million, which was well short of its first quarter target of a loss of $30 million.

After remarking that Enron was getting pressure from analysts to improve its return on invested capital, Skilling refused to adjust the unrealistic earnings target. Instead, he authorized a second monetization of EBS's contracts and approved a cost-cutting plan that included the dismissal a number of EBS employees. Again, Skilling, while selling investors on the growth potential of EBS, failed to disclose that EBS had almost no revenue from its core businesses. When EBS continued to deteriorate during the second quarter of 2001 (EBS was due to report a loss of $102 million), witnesses testified that Skilling approved a plan to merge EBS with Wholesale, knowing that, as a result, the losses attributable to EBS would be untraceable.

Again, Skilling's counterarguments are unavailing. It is not true, as Skilling claims, that the Government's theory at trial was that Skilling made bad business decisions; its argument was that Skilling hid those bad business decisions from investors. Moreover, we disagree with Skilling that the Government's case relied upon the selective editing of his statements. The record shows that Skilling's comments to investors were more than just hopeful views about a troubled new venture. Rather, given that EBS was sinking and Skilling knew it, his comments were deceitful. There was no reason for hope about EBS's prospects, and Skilling failed to disclose fundamentally important facts about EBS's problems.

Fifth, the evidence overwhelmingly proved that Skilling and his co-conspirators manipulated Enron's accounting reserves for contingent liabilities in order to hit specific earnings targets (known as "consensus estimates"). The evidence showed that Skilling knew that missing the consensus estimate by even a small amount would have a significant negative effect on Enron's stock price and, conversely, that exceeding the consensus estimate would have a significant positive effect on the stock price. Toward the end of the fourth quarter of 2002, Delainey told Skilling that Wholesale, which was making huge profits from its speculative trading, "had a couple of quarters [of reportable earnings] in its pocket." Skilling was pleased to hear this news and later said at an Enron management committee meeting that Enron had significant reserves that were available to meet its earnings targets for 2000. In fact, Wholesale set aside $873 million in trading income as reserves for contingent liabilities, which the testimony showed was a significant over-reservation. After the end of the accounting year, but before Enron had reported earnings, Wholesale told Richard Causey (Enron's Chief Accounting Officer at the time), who then told Skilling, that Wholesale had extra reserves available. Skilling, through Causey, communicated to Wholesale that it should shift as much reserves to earnings as was necessary to report 41 cents per share, which was 7 cents more than the fourth quarter earnings target of 34 cents per share. Wholesale shifted the money from a "gas and power valuation" contingent-liabilities reserve account, even though there had been no changes in the circumstances associated with the reserve account. Enron then produced a document for its outside auditors that falsely stated other reasons for the reserve transfer. Enron's stock price went up after Enron reported earnings for that quarter.

In response, Skilling argues that there was extensive evidence at trial that the final reserve amount accurately reflected contingent liabilities and that any differences were immaterial from an accounting perspective. We disagree that the record shows this. A Wholesale accountant testified that, on Skilling's command, he released money from the reserve account in order to make earnings go up, without consideration of the correct reserve amount. Such an act is fraudulent: when a company establishes reserves based on the earnings it wants, its investors do not know if the reserve accounts accurately reflect the contingent liabilities facing the company, and they do not know that the company is meeting or exceeding its earnings targets only by moving reserves from one bucket to another. Further, the amount transferred from reserves to earnings was not immaterial, since the transfer allowed Enron to exceed its earnings targets and caused Enron's stock price to increase.

Lastly, we note that we do not rely on the Government's allegation that Enron fraudulently misstated earnings for the fourth quarter of 1999 and fraudulently transferred contingent-liability reserves to beat the consensus estimate for the second quarter of 2000. Although there is strong evidence for a conviction on these allegations, there is not sufficient evidence to find harmlessness. Nonetheless, both allegations show that Enron executives had a pattern of manipulating earnings targets.

These five fraudulent schemes, which formed a large part of the basis for the Government's proof at trial, all represent efforts by Skilling and his co-conspirators to manipulate Enron's reported earnings or conceal Enron's losses from the investing public with the intent and result of affecting Enron's stock price. Because they are supported by overwhelming evidence, we find that the honest-services instruction was harmless error beyond a reasonable doubt....

More recently, the United States Attorney's office, the main enforcer of insider trading rules, had a long winning streak of convicting people of insider trading. However, the Second Circuit Court of Appeals ruled differently on one case. The United States Supreme Court has been asked to hear the case and determine whether the ruling should stand. The ruling makes it more difficult to convict people of insider trading, especially if the information is third hand. This is because the Second Circuit Court of Appeals found that an individual has to have direct knowledge of the corporate insider giving the material information and know that he was in violation of law.

b. Short-Swing Profits

Section 16 of the Securities and Exchange Act of 1934 regulates short swing profits. Thus, any profits made by buying or selling stocks by a director, officer, or ten percent or more shareholder, in less than six months is recoverable by the corporation. There is a presumption that any profits made in six months are illegal, whether or not someone actually had material information not available to the public. The SEC cannot always tell when nonpublic information is used improperly; thus, the presumption.

c. State Securities Laws

State security laws try to prohibit fraud and often require further registration. These laws usually apply to intrastate offerings. State regulations of securities laws are referred to as "blue sky laws." This references a desire in making laws to prevent investors from buying a valueless part of the blue sky (kind of like selling someone swampland in Florida).

Blue sky laws do apply to securities that are also regulated by federal law. Federal laws do not prevent blue sky laws. A majority of states do follow the Uniform Securities Act in instituting their own blue sky laws. Still, most states vary widely in what is required for registering the security within the state.

Chapter Summary

Public companies are corporations with stocks on a national securities exchange; examples of such stock exchanges are the New York Stock Exchange and the NASDAQ. The first time stock is offered by a corporation, it is called an IPO, or initial public offering.

Stock options are a way in which employees can capitalize on additional benefits provided by a corporation, other than salary. If a person does not work for a corporation and receive stock options, that person can still invest separately. Some stocks offer dividends, which is a way to make a profit from stock without having to sell it. Directors should not declare stock dividends if the corporation cannot afford to distribute them, i.e. the dividends come out of the corporation's capital. There are three types of dividends: cash, share, and property. With cash dividends, the taxes on those dividends must be paid in the year the dividend was received. With share and property dividends, the taxes on those dividends must be paid in the year the dividend was sold.

The Securities and Exchange Act of 1933 requires companies to file registrations. The registration requires basic information about the business and the security. However, there are different types of companies that are excluded from having to make these registrations. They include nonissuers, intrastate offerings, private placements, and small issues. Nonissuers are just regular investors; they do not have to register before reselling their shares. If a business is performing a securities offering within a state, then that business will be governed by blue sky laws within the state and not have to file a registration with the SEC. If a stock is sold to sophisticated investors, then it does not need to be registered; these types of investors include people who have over a million dollars in net assets, and make more than two hundred thousand dollars a year. Small issues are usually securities offered in less than fifty million dollars in twelve months.

The Securities and Exchange Commission regulates securities. The SEC was begun with the Securities and Exchange Act of 1934. It contains Section 10(b). This is utilized to prevent using deception to sell securities. This same section also covers insider trading. Insider trading is when an insider makes money off buying or selling shares, based on material information not known to the public. Short-swing profits are slightly different. Directors, officers, and ten percent or more shareholders are not allowed to keep profits on buying and selling stocks within six months, whether they had insider information or not.

Key Terms

Accredited investor
Accumulated earnings tax
Blue sky laws
Cash dividend
Distribution
Dividend
Electronic Data Gathering, Analysis, and Retrieval (EDGAR) system
Equity insolvency test
Going public
Initial Public Offering (IPO)
Insider
Property dividend

Prospectus
Registration statement
Securities Act of 1933
Securities and Exchange Commission (SEC)
Securities Exchange Act of 1934
Security
Seller
Share dividend
Short-swing profits
Solvency
Stock split

Review Questions

1. What are the advantages, for the corporation, of going public?

2. When must the taxes on share dividends be paid? What about on cash dividends?

3. How does a stock split work?

4. When was the Securities and Exchange Commission created?

5. What main documents does the Securities Act of 1933 require?

6. What is required by form 8-K?

7. Prior to Sarbanes-Oxley, it was harder to criminally convict a person for unethical accounting. What were the charges Mr. Skilling was convicted of?

8. What evidence was provided that Skilling participated in deceiving the public about Enron's financial condition to increase the stock's price?

9. Research what mark-to-mark accounting is.

10. How did Wholesale actually make most of its profits?

11. While Skilling was telling investors EBS had growth potential, was it making money from its core businesses?

12. Explain insider trading.

13. What is meant by the term "blue sky laws"?

Web Links

Go to the Social Security Administration's website (http://www.ssa.gov) and check on the current rate of Social Security you will be paid, based upon your past work history.

The Securities and Exchange Commission's EDGAR database is located at http://www.sec.gov/edgar/searchedgar/webusers.htm.

Exercises

1. Scientists at Cancer Corporation believe that they are about to determine a cure to all cancers. The corporation's management sends an email to all employees involved that they may not discuss this outside of work. The Cancer Corporation is publicly traded and its stock price does go up when Cancer Corporation officially announces this information. If one of the employees tells his girlfriend about the advancement prior to it being made public, and his girlfriend buys the stock, what has she just committed?

2. If a corporation is not able to pay all its bills, should it declare a dividend?

3. When would an employee most likely exercise his stock options?

4. Research whether or not the United States Supreme Court heard the Second Circuit Court of Appeals case on insider trading.

Chapter 12

Directors and Officers

Chapter Outline

Chapter Objectives

- Define the role directors play in a corporation.
- Explain how directors are elected, for how long, and how they are removed.
- Outline when directors can take action without a meeting.
- Review the duties of officers and directors.
- Compare indemnification to insurance as ways in which to protect directors from liability.
- Discuss the business judgment rule.
- Clarify that directors delegate the day-to-day management of the business to officers.

12.1 Introduction to Directors and Officers

The bylaws discussed in Chapter 10, For-Profit Corporations, reviewed some of the requirements regarding directors and officers of the corporation. In this chapter, the requirements are discussed in detail. The directors govern the corporation. These directors get their power from the articles of incorporation, the bylaws, and from state statutes. However, for such an important position, there are not many statutory requirements to be a director. Some states require directors to be a certain age or older and to live in the state. They are elected by the shareholders and can be removed with or without cause by the shareholders.

Officers serve at the desire of the directors, meaning they are appointed by the directors, and they are removed by the directors. They are agents for the corporation. They are high-level employees, to whom the directors delegate day-to-day operations of the business. The duties that apply to directors also apply to officers.

12.2 Role

The directors oversee the corporation. In general, they are supposed to act collectively. In a small to mid-size company, a director might also be an officer and/or shareholder. In a larger company, there will normally be a requirement that at least some of the directors cannot be shareholders.

The directors make the decisions about the corporation. They manage the corporation. However, the directors do have some limits on how they manage the corporation. Directors may need shareholder approval to:

- amend the articles or bylaws,
- issue stock,
- dissolve the company,
- merge with another company, or
- sell some of the corporation's assets.

Things that are typically the role of the directors include declaring and paying dividends to shareholders. Directors also have to approve major decisions of the corporation. Directors are responsible for appointing, managing, and firing officers. Directors may also be called upon to authorize more shares or obtain bonds for further financing of the corporation. Even when the directors delegate some of these tasks to the officers to effectuate, the directors still have to oversee the actions of the officers.

Officers of a corporation must prepare the minutes of both the shareholders' and board of directors meetings. In addition, officers have to keep track of the corporations' records. Officers can also perform other duties as dictated by the directors.

Officer titles may include, but not be limited to:

- President,
- Vice President,
- Secretary, and
- Treasurer.

The President runs the shareholder meetings. He is the head of the officers. The Vice President fills in for the President when the President is not present. However, sometimes companies will have Vice Presidents of different parts of the company, such as a Vice President of Marketing and the Vice President of Manufacturing. The Secretary needs to keep the minutes. The Secretary may also prepare the notices of meetings and the prospectus for the corporation. Many of these jobs can overlap. The Treasurer looks after the corporation's finances.

12.3 Election and Appointment

Directors are elected by the shareholders. There needs to be a board of directors at all times at a regular corporation. Nowadays there can be a one-person board of directors, but historically, there were a minimum of three directors on the board. The number of directors for a given corporation will probably be in the bylaws. This number will often be an odd number to avoid a tie when the directors vote.

The very first board of directors for a corporation is typically appointed by the incorporators at the organizational meeting, as discussed in Chapter 10. This board typically serves until the first shareholders' meeting, wherein the shareholders vote for the directors though a majority vote or a quorum. Directors can be voted in by using either straight voting or cumulative voting. Straight voting is one share equals one vote. Cumulative voting is multiplying the shareholder's number of shares by the number of open positions on the board of directors. Thus, if a shareholder has five hundred and forty shares, and there are two open positions on the board, then the shareholder would have five hundred and forty shares times two, which would equal one thousand and eighty votes to cast.

- In cumulative voting, the number of shareholders is multiplied by the number of open positions.
- If there are 540 shares and 2 open positions, $540 \times 2 = 1080$ votes.

People often confuse cumulative voting by looking at the number of directors running for the open positions, rather than the number of open positions.

a. Term

The term of office for a director is usually one year, but sometimes can be longer. The reason for having a longer term would be to provide stability to the board. Also, directors can be reelected as many times as allowed by the bylaws.

Officers can either be voted on by the board of directors or appointed. Officers are appointed by the directors, and they can be removed at any time by the directors. If an officer is doing a poor job, directors typically look at officer positions at the annual directors' meeting. However, officers can be removed by the directors at any time.

b. Vacancies

Vacancies in the board of directors might arise due to death or resignation. Sometimes, the remaining directors can appoint a new director to serve until the next election, and sometimes, the shareholders must have a special meeting to elect a new director. Special meetings cost more money, as a new meeting must be properly noticed, and are typically avoided.

Vacancies of an officer are often filled by a majority vote of the board of directors.

c. Removal

To remove directors, the shareholders can decide not to reelect a director, and they do not have to have a reason for not reelecting the director. Directors can be removed for cause, even when it is not a shareholders' meeting, if this is provided for in the bylaws and/or approved by the shareholders. Cause includes fraud or failure to uphold a duty required of the directors. Sometimes, the other directors can remove a director for cause. Occasionally, it may be necessary to ask a judge to step in to remove a director. This normally occurs when it would be in the best interests of the corporation.

With officers, the removal procedure is different. The board of directors can remove officers at any time, and do not even need to have cause.

12.4 BOD Meetings

Annual meetings of the board of directors are held to replace officers and to ratify the past year's actions taken by the officers. At the same time, dividends might be approved, the financials may be reviewed, and annual reports may be filed. Directors may have other regular meetings, usually on at least a quarterly basis.

Annual reports to the shareholders typically include:

- financial statements,
- a summary of the business conducted over the course of the year,
- perhaps some information on the corporation's products,
- information about the directors and some officers,
- as well as the price of stock, and
- any dividends.

Directors are not required to be given notice of such meetings unless provided for in the governing documents of the corporation; this is particularly true for annual meetings, which the directors should already know about. This is less true for special meetings, which require some notice. Notice could be in writing, by email, fax, and/or phone. If the notice is improper, the director could cure that defect by waiving notice. A special meeting might be held in order to discuss whether or not to approve or suggest a merger with another company.

The concept of quorum is important to a board meeting, but has a broader definition that goes beyond just application to the board meeting. A quorum is the minimum number of people necessary to legitimately transact business. Depending upon the state, a quorum could be anywhere from one-third to fifty-one percent. If a quorum of directors is not present at a meeting, then the meeting cannot be legitimately held. If a quorum of the directors is present, then typically, the directors get one vote per director.

Minutes must be complete and truthful and must be taken at each meeting of the board. The Secretary should sign the minutes, and then file the minutes in the corporation's minutes book. Notice should also accompany the minutes in the minutes book. A very basic format of minutes of the annual meeting of the board of directors is provided below.

Minutes of Annual Meeting of Board of Directors of
_____, Inc.

The annual meeting of the Board of Directors of _____, Inc., took place on _____ at the principal place of business for the company, located at_____.

Present at the meeting were the following board members:_____.

With _____ percent of the board members being present, a quorum was declared.

ELECTION OF OFFICERS

The chairperson stated that the appointment of the new officers would take place. The board then appointed new officers. The following persons were duly appointed to the corporate offices:

NAME   OFFICE

[insert name and office]

[The rest of the minutes go in here.]

The Board then reviewed the actions of the officers and directors for the past year, and adopted and approved them.

There being no further business to come before the meeting, the meeting was adjourned.

Submitted: Approved:

_____   _____

Secretary   President

a. Action without Meeting

Directors, unlike shareholders, cannot vote by proxy. They can, however, have a meeting without having to physically meet. This is usually accomplished through videoconferencing and counts as "meeting." The board of directors can act without meeting or even videoconferencing, through unanimously agreeing in writing to act without meeting. Unanimous agreement among directors is often easier to obtain than unanimous agreement between shareholders as there are likely fewer directors.

12.5 Duties

These duties, which were discussed in agency relationships, apply to directors:

- fiduciary duty,
- duty of care, and
- duty of loyalty.

The very same duties also apply to officers. Recall that the fiduciary duty is one of being in a position of trust and confidence. This duty is owed to the corporation.

Directors show the duty of due care by diligent management. Typically, the diligent management that would have been expected of an ordinarily prudent director is what is required of the director. Officers must also use due care in their job. The duty of due care requires both directors and officers must exercise good faith in carrying out their tasks for the corporation. The director's attendance at board meetings is indicative of whether the director exercised due care. Both directors and officers should make informed decisions. While at the board meetings, the directors should participate. The director should investigate further if there are signs of potential embezzlement. Illegal acts by directors are typically not acceptable under the duty of due care, even if the director or officer meant to benefit the corporation.

The duty of loyalty requires that the director and officer be true to both the corporation and its shareholders. This means that the director or officer must put the interests of the corporation above his own interests. The duty of loyalty is also known as the duty not to compete or to not have a conflict of interest. Insider trading is considered a violation of the duty of loyalty.

Taking a corporate opportunity for one's self is a violation of the duty of loyalty. This is known as self-dealing and can be either on behalf of the director/officer or another company that a director is a part of. Self-dealing is only acceptable if the noninterested members of the board approve this transaction. In the alternative, the shareholders who do not have an interest could approve it. The transaction should be fair to the company.

Self-dealing means that the directors should not compete against the corporation either. In the following case, Mr. Guth was a director and President of Loft, Inc. Loft had candy stores in which the stores sold Coke. Megargel of Pepsi tried to promote Pepsi when it was not well known and wanted Guth to buy it and put it into the Loft stores. However, Guth bought Pepsi Company himself (when it went into bankruptcy), without first offering it to Loft. Note in the following case the reasons Mr. Guth was found to have taken the corporate opportunity for himself.

Guth v. Loft, Inc.

5 A.2d 503, 23 Del. Ch. 255 (1939)

... As stated by the appellants, there were certain questions before the Chancellor [Judge] for determination:

(1) Was Guth at the time the Pepsi-Cola opportunity came to him obligated, in view of his official connection with Loft, to take the opportunity for Loft rather than for himself? On this point the appellants contend no finding was made.

(2) Was Guth, nevertheless, estopped from denying that the opportunity belonged to Loft; and was he rightfully penalized to the extent of his whole interest therein, merely because resources borrowed from Loft had contributed in some measure to its development; and did Loft's contributions create the whole value behind the interests of Guth and Grace in Pepsi, thereby constituting Loft the equitable owner of those interests? These questions were answered in the affirmative; and because of the answers, the Chancellor, it is said, did not answer the last question before him, that is, upon what theory and to what extent should Loft share in the proceeds of the Pepsi-Cola enterprise?

... In these circumstances of contention, certain questions suggest themselves for consideration, and some of them for answer: Did the Chancellor make an explicit finding that the Pepsi-Cola opportunity belonged in equity to Loft, and if so, was such finding justifiable in fact and in law? If the Chancellor made no such explicit finding, should he have done so, or should this court make such finding? Assuming that the Chancellor made no explicit finding and that this court should not feel justified in making such finding, was, and is, the doctrine of estoppel properly invocable in favor of the complainant?

... I am of the opinion that under such circumstances as are disclosed in this case, Guth is estopped by what he subsequently caused Loft to do, to deny that when he embraced the Megargel offer he did so in behalf of Loft. The offer cannot be viewed in any light other than an expectancy that was Loft's. Guth is estopped to contend to the contrary. The case of Bailey v. Jacobs ... cite at an earlier point in this opinion, is a pertinent and persuasive authority in support of that view....

Manifestly, the Chancellor found to exist facts and circumstances from which the conclusion could be reached that the Pepsi-Cola opportunity belonged in equity to Loft.

Corporate officers and directors are not permitted to use their position of trust and confidence to further their private interests. While technically not trustees, they stand in a fiduciary relation to the corporation and its stockholders. A public policy, existing through the years, and derived from a profound knowledge of human characteristics and motives, has established a rule that demands of a corporate officer or director, peremptorily and inexorably, the most scrupulous observance of his duty, not only affirmatively to protect the interests of the corporation committed to his charge, but also to refrain from doing anything that would work injury to the corporation, or to deprive it of profit or advantage which his skill and ability might properly bring to it, or to enable it to make in the reasonable and lawful exercise of its powers. The rule that requires an undivided and unselfish loyalty to the corporation demands that there shall be no conflict between duty and self-interest. The occasions for the determination of honesty, good faith and loyal conduct are many and varied, and no hard and fast rule can be formulated. The standard of loyalty is measured by no fixed scale.

If an officer or director of a corporation, in violation of his duty as such, acquires gain or advantage for himself, the law charges the interest so acquired with a trust for the benefit of the corporation, at its election, while it denies to the betrayer all benefit and profit. The rule, inveterate and uncompromising in its rigidity, does not rest upon the narrow ground of injury or damage to the corporation resulting from a betrayal of confidence, but upon a broader foundation of a wise public policy that, for the purpose of removing all temptation, extinguishes all possibility of profit flowing from a breach of the confidence imposed by the fiduciary relation. Given the relation between the parties, a certain result follows; and a constructive trust is the remedial device through which precedence of self is compelled to give way to the stern demands of loyalty....

The rule, referred to briefly as the rule of corporate opportunity, is merely one of the manifestations of the general rule that demands of an officer or director the utmost good faith in his relation to the corporation which he represents.

It is true that when a business opportunity comes to a corporate officer or director in his individual capacity rather than in his official capacity, and the opportunity is one which, because of the nature of the enterprise, is not essential to his corporation, and is one in which it has no interest or expectancy, the officer or director is entitled to treat the opportunity as his own, and the corporation has no interest in it, if, of course the officer or director has not wrongfully embarked the corporation's resources therein....

On the other hand, it is equally true that, if there is presented to a corporate officer or director a business opportunity which the corporation is financially able to undertake, is, from its nature, in the line of the corporation's business and is of practical advantage to it, is one in which the corporation has an interest or a reasonable expectancy, and, by embracing the opportunity, the self-interest of the officer or director will be brought into conflict with that of his corporation, the law will not permit him to seize the opportunity for himself. And, if, in such circumstances, the interests of the corporation are betrayed, the corporation may elect to claim all of the benefits of the transaction for itself, and the law will impress a trust in favor of the corporation upon the property, interests and profits so acquired....

As stated in 3 Fletcher Cyclopedia, Corporations, § 862, an authority seemingly relied on by the appellants,

> "There is a vast field for individual activity outside the duty of a director, yet well within the general scope of the corporation's business. The test seems

to be whether there was a specific duty, on the part of the officer sought to be held liable, to act or contract in regard to the particular matter as the representative of the corporation — all of which is largely a question of fact."

Duty and loyalty are inseparably connected. Duty is that which is required by one's station or occupation; is that which one is bound by legal or moral obligation to do or refrain from doing; and it is with this conception of duty as the underlying basis of the principle applicable to the situation disclosed, that the conduct and acts of Guth with respect to his acquisition of the Pepsi-Cola enterprise will be scrutinized. Guth was not merely a director and the president of Loft. He was its master. It is admitted that Guth manifested some of the qualities of a dictator. The directors were selected by him. Some of them held salaried positions in the company. All of them held their positions at his favor. Whether they were supine merely, or for sufficient reasons entirely subservient to Guth, it is not profitable to inquire. It is sufficient to say that they either wilfully or negligently allowed Guth absolute freedom of action in the management of Loft's activities, and theirs is an unenviable position whether testifying for or against the appellants.

Prior to May, 1931, Guth became convinced that Loft was being unfairly discriminated against by the Coca-Cola Company of whose syrup it was a large purchaser, in that Loft had been refused a jobber's discount on the syrup, although others, whose purchases were of far less importance, had been given such discount. He determined to replace Coca-Cola as a beverage at the Loft stores with some other cola drink, if that could be accomplished. So, on May 19, 1931, he suggested an inquiry with respect to desirability of discontinuing the use of Coca-Cola, and replacing it with Pepsi-Cola at a greatly reduced price. Pepsi-Cola was the syrup produced by National Pepsi-Cola Company. As a beverage it had been on the market for over twenty-five years, and while it was not known to consumers in the area of the Loft stores, its formula and trademark were well established. Guth's purpose was to deliver Loft from the thraldom of the Coca-Cola Company, which practically dominated the field of cola beverages, and, at the same time to gain for Loft a greater margin of profit on its sales of cola beverages. Certainly, the choice of an acceptable substitute for Coca-Cola was not a wide one, and, doubtless, his experience in the field of bottled beverages convinced him that it was necessary for him to obtain a cola syrup whose formula and trademark were secure against attack. Although the difficulties and dangers were great, he concluded to make the change. Almost simultaneously, National Pepsi-Cola Company, in which Megargel was predominant and whom Guth knew, went into bankruptcy; and Guth was informed that the long established Pepsi-Cola formula and trademark could be had at a small price. Guth, of course, was Loft; and Loft's determination to replace Coca-Cola with some other cola beverage in its many stores was practically co-incidental with the opportunity to acquire the Pepsi-Cola formula and trademark. This was the condition of affairs when Megargel approached Guth. Guth contended that his negotiation with Megargel in 1931 was but a continuation of a negotiation begun in 1928, when he had no connection with Loft; but the Chancellor found to the contrary, and his finding is accepted.

It is urged by the appellants that Megargel offered the Pepsi-Cola opportunity to Guth personally, and not to him as president of Loft. The Chancellor said that there was no way of knowing the fact, as Megargel was dead, and the benefit of his testimony could not be had; but that it was not important, for the matter of consequence was how Guth received the proposition.

It was incumbent upon Guth to show that his every act in dealing with the opportunity presented was in the exercise of the utmost good faith to Loft; and the burden was cast upon him satisfactorily to prove that the offer was made to him individually. Reasonable inferences, drawn from acknowledged facts and circumstances, are powerful factors in arriving at the truth of a disputed matter, and such inferences are not to be ignored in considering the acts and conduct of Megargel. He had been for years engaged in the manufacture and sale of a cola syrup in competition with Coca-Cola. He knew of the difficulties of competition with such a powerful opponent in general, and in particular in the securing of a necessary foothold in a new territory where Coca-Cola was supreme. He could not hope to establish the popularity and use of his syrup in a strange field, and in competition with the assured position of Coca-Cola, by the usual advertising means, for he, himself, had no money or resources, and it is entirely unbelievable that he expected Guth to have command of the vast amount of money necessary to popularize Pepsi-Cola by the ordinary methods. He knew of the difficulty, not to say impossibility, of inducing proprietors of soft drink establishments to use a cola drink utterly unknown to their patrons. It would seem clear, from any reasonable point of view, that Megargel sought to interest someone who controlled an existing opportunity to popularize his product by an actual presentation of it to the consuming public. Such person was Guth, the president of Loft. It is entirely reasonable to infer that Megargel approached Guth as president of Loft, operating, as it did, many soft drink fountains in a most necessary and desirable territory where Pepsi-Cola was little known, he well knowing that if the drink could be established in New York and circumjacent territory, its success would be assured. Every reasonable inference points to this conclusion. What was finally agreed upon between Megargel and Guth, and what outward appearance their agreement assumed, is of small importance. It was a matter of indifference to Megargel whether his co-adventurer was Guth personally, or Loft, so long as his terms were met and his object attained.

Leaving aside the manner of the offer of the opportunity, certain other matters are to be considered in determining whether the opportunity, in the circumstances, belonged to Loft; and in this we agree that Guth's right to appropriate the Pepsi-Cola opportunity to himself depends upon the circumstances existing at the time it presented itself to him without regard to subsequent events, and that due weight should be given to character of the opportunity which Megargel envisioned and brought to Guth's door.

The real issue is whether the opportunity to secure a very substantial stock interest in a corporation to be formed for the purpose of exploiting a cola beverage on a wholesale scale was so closely associated with the existing business activities of Loft, and so essential thereto, as to bring the transaction within that class of cases where the acquisition of the property would throw the corporate officer purchasing it into competition with his company. This is a factual question to be decided by reasonable inferences from objective facts.

It is asserted that, no matter how diversified the scope of Loft's activities, its primary business was the manufacturing and selling of candy in its own chain of retail stores, and that it never had the idea of turning a subsidiary product into a highly advertised, nation-wide specialty. Therefore it had never initiated any investigation into the possibility of acquiring a stock interest in a corporation to be formed to exploit Pepsi-Cola on the scale envisioned by Megargel, necessitating sales of at least 1,000,000 gallons a year. It is said that the most effective argument against the proposition that Guth was obligated to take the opportunity for Loft is to be found in the complainant's own assertion that Guth was guilty of an improper exercise of business judgment when he replaced Coca-Cola with Pepsi-Cola at the Loft stores. Assuming that the complainant's argument in this respect is incompatible with its contention that the Pepsi-Cola opportunity belonged to Loft, it is no more inconsistent than is the position of the appellants on the question. In the court below, the defendants strove strenuously to show, and to have it believed, that the Pepsi-Cola opportunity was presented to Loft by Guth, with a full disclosure by him that if the company did not embrace it, he would. This, manifestly, was a recognition of the necessity for his showing complete good faith on his part as a corporate officer of Loft. In this court, the Chancellor having found as a fact that Guth did not offer the opportunity to his corporation, it is asserted that no question of good faith is involved for the reason that the opportunity was of such character that Guth, although Loft's president, was entirely free to embrace it for himself. The issue is not to be enmeshed in the cobwebs of sophistry. It rises far above inconsistencies in argument.

The appellants suggest a doubt whether Loft would have been able to finance the project along the lines contemplated by Megargel, viewing the situation as of 1931. The answer to this suggestion is two-fold. The Chancellor found that Loft's net asset position at that time was amply sufficient to finance the enterprise, and that its plant, equipment, executives, personnel and facilities, supplemented by such expansion for the necessary development of the business as it was well able to provide, were in all respects adequate. The second answer is that Loft's resources were found to be sufficient, for Guth made use of no other to any important extent.

Next it is contended that the Pepsi-Cola opportunity was not in the line of Loft's activities which essentially were of a retail nature. It is pointed out that, in 1931, the retail stores operated by Loft were largely located in the congested areas along the Middle Atlantic Seaboard, that its manufacturing operations were centered in its New York factory, and that it was a definitely localized business, and not operated on a national scale; whereas, the Megargel proposition envisaged annual sales of syrup at least a million gallons, which could be accomplished only by a wholesale distribution. Loft, however, had many wholesale activities. Its wholesale business in 1931 amounted to over $ 800,000. It was a large company by any standard. It had an enormous plant. It paid enormous rentals. Guth, himself, said that Loft's success depended upon the fullest utilization of its large plant facilities. Moreover, it was a manufacturer of syrups and, with the exception of cola syrup, it supplied its own extensive needs. The appellants admit that wholesale distribution of bottled beverages can best be accomplished by license agreements with bottlers. Guth, president of Loft, was an able and experienced man in that field. Loft, then, through its own personnel, possessed the technical knowledge, the practical business experience, and the resources necessary for the development of the Pepsi-Cola enterprise.

But, the appellants say that the expression, "in the line" of a business, is a phrase so elastic as to furnish no basis for a useful inference. The phrase is not within the field of precise definition, nor is it one that can be bounded by a set formula. It has a flexible meaning, which is to be applied reasonably and sensibly to the facts and circumstances of the particular case. Where a corporation is engaged in a certain business, and an opportunity is presented to it embracing an activity as to which it has fundamental knowledge, practical experience and ability to pursue, which, logically and naturally, is adaptable to its business having regard for its financial position, and is one that is consonant with its reasonable needs and aspirations for expansion, it may be properly said that the opportunity is in the line of the corporation's business.

The manufacture of syrup was the core of the Pepsi-Cola opportunity. The manufacture of syrups was one of Loft's not unimportant activities. It had the necessary resources, facilities, equipment, technical and practical knowledge and experience. The tie was close between the business of Loft and the Pepsi-Cola enterprise.... Conceding that the essential of an opportunity is reasonably within the scope of a corporation's activities, latitude should be allowed for development and expansion. To deny this would be to deny the history of industrial development.

It is urged that Loft had no interest or expectancy in the Pepsi-Cola opportunity. That it had no existing property right therein is manifest; but we cannot agree that it had no concern or expectancy in the opportunity within the protection of remedial equity. Loft had a practical and essential concern with respect to some cola syrup with an established formula and trademark. A cola beverage has come to be a business necessity for soft drink establishments; and it was essential to the success of Loft to serve at its soda fountains an acceptable five cent cola drink in order to attract into its stores the great multitude of people who have formed the habit of drinking cola beverages. When Guth determined to discontinue the sale of Coca-Cola in the Loft stores, it became, by his own act, a matter of urgent necessity for Loft to acquire a constant supply of some satisfactory cola syrup, secure against probable attack, as a replacement; and when the Pepsi-Cola opportunity presented itself, Guth having already considered the availability of the syrup, it became impressed with a Loft interest and expectancy arising out of the circumstances and the urgent and practical need created by him as the directing head of Loft.

As a general proposition it may be said that a corporate officer or director is entirely free to engage in an independent, competitive business, so long as he violates no legal or moral duly with respect to the fiduciary relation that exists between the corporation and himself. The appellants contend that no conflict of interest between Guth and Loft resulted from his acquirement and exploitation of the Pepsi-Cola opportunity. They maintain that the acquisition did not place Guth in competition with Loft any more than a manufacturer can be said to compete with a retail merchant whom the manufacturer supplies with goods to be sold. However true the statement, applied generally, may be, we emphatically dissent from the application of the analogy to the situation of the parties here. There is no unity between the ordinary manufacturer and the retailer of his goods. Generally, the retailer, if he becomes dissatisfied with one supplier of merchandise, can turn to another. He is under no compulsion and no restraint. In the instant case Guth was Loft, and Guth was Pepsi. He absolutely controlled Loft. His authority over Pepsi was supreme. As Pepsi, he created and controlled the supply of Pepsi-Cola syrup, and he determined the price and the terms. What he offered, as Pepsi, he had the power, as Loft, to accept. Upon any consideration of human characteristics and motives, he created a conflict between self-interest and duty. He made himself the judge in his own cause. This was the inevitable result of the dual personality which Guth assumed, and his position was one which, upon the least austere view of corporate duty, he had no right to assume. Moreover, a reasonable probability of injury to Loft resulted from the situation forced upon it. Guth was in the same position to impose his terms upon Loft as had been the Coca-Cola Company. If Loft had been in servitude to that company with respect to its need for a cola syrup, its condition did not change when its supply came to depend upon Pepsi, for, it was found by the Chancellor, against Guth's contention, that he had not given Loft the protection of a contract which secured to it a constant supply of Pepsi-Cola syrup at any definite price or for any definite time.

It is useless to pursue the argument. The facts and circumstances demonstrate that Guth's appropriation of the Pepsi-Cola opportunity to himself placed him in a competitive position with Loft with respect to a commodity essential to it, thereby rendering his personal interests incompatible with the superior interests of his corporation; and this situation was accomplished, not openly and with his own resources, but secretly and with the money and facilities of the corporation which was committed to his protection.

Upon a consideration of all the facts and circumstances as disclosed we are convinced that the opportunity to acquire the Pepsi-Cola trademark and formula, goodwill and business belonged to the complainant, and that Guth, as its president, had no right to appropriate the opportunity to himself....

12.6 Compensation and Indemnification

The board of directors sets directors' compensation if it is not otherwise provided for in the articles of incorporation or bylaws. However, that compensation must be discussed, usually in the bylaws, and should be reasonable. Part of the compensation may include stock. It will often consist of both an annual amount as well as bonuses for attending meetings.

Many times, as mentioned, a director will be indemnified from liability so that the corporation can attract the best qualified candidate for the job. In indemnification, the corporation would pay for the expense of a lawsuit and any settlement on behalf of the director. This indemnification is limited in that it usually does not include breaches of duty, fraud, or a transaction wherein the director receives a financial benefit to which he is not entitled.1 Further limiting this indemnification is that often the director has to be successful in defending himself in litigation or have acted with justification. Indemnification is different from insurance. While the corporation might pay the insurance premiums to insure a director, if there is a payout, it is made by the insurance company and not the company.

Officer compensation is determined by the directors.

SAMPLE INDEMNITY AGREEMENT

This Indemnity Agreement, effective as of _____, is made by and between corporation with executive offices located _____ and the Director _____ (the "Indemnitee").

RECITALS

A. The Company is aware that competent and experienced persons are increasingly reluctant to serve as directors or officers of corporations unless they are protected by comprehensive liability insurance or indemnification, due to increased exposure to litigation costs and risks resulting from their service to such corporations, and due to the fact that the exposure frequently bears no reasonable relationship to the compensation of such directors and officers;

B. The Company believes that it is unfair for its directors and officers and the directors and officers of its subsidiaries to assume the risk of large judgments and other expense that may be incurred in cases in which the director or officer received no personal profit and in cases where the director or officer was not culpable;

C. It is necessary for the Company to contractually indemnify its officers and directors and the officers and directors;

D. Section 145 of the General Corporation Law of Delaware, under which the Company is organized ("Section 145"), empowers the Company to indemnify by agreement its officers, directors, employees and agents,;

E. The Company, has determined that the liability insurance coverage available to the Company and its subsidiaries as of the date hereof is unreasonably expensive. The Company believes, therefore, that the interest of the Company's stockholders would best be served by a combination of such insurance as the Company may obtain, and the indemnification by the Company of the directors and officers of the Company and its subsidiaries;

AGREEMENT

NOW, THEREFORE, the parties hereto, intending to be legally bound, hereby agree as follows:

1. Agreement to Serve. The Indemnitee agrees to serve and/or continue to serve as an agent of the Company, at its will (or under separate agreement, if such agreement exists), in the capacity the Indemnitee currently serves as an agent of the Company, so long as he or she is duly appointed or elected and qualified or until such time as he or she tenders his resignation in writing or he or she is removed from such position.

2. Mandatory Indemnification. The Company shall indemnify the Indemnitee from:

(a) *Third Party Actions.* If the Indemnitee is a person who was or is a party or is threatened to be made a party to any proceeding (other than an action by or in the right of the Company) by reason of the fact that he or she is or was an agent of the Company, or by reason of anything done or not done by him or her in any such capacity, against any and all expenses and liabilities of any type whatsoever actually and reasonably incurred by him or her in connection with the investigation, defense, settlement or appeal of such proceeding if he or she acted in good faith and in a manner he or she reasonably believed to be in or not opposed to the best interests of the Company; and

(b) *Derivative Actions.* If the Indemnitee is a person who was or is a party or is threatened to be made a party to any proceeding by or in the right of the Company to procure a judgment in its favor by reason of the fact that he or she is or was an agent of the Company, or by reason of anything done or not done by him or her in any such capacity, against any amounts paid in settlement of any such proceeding and all expenses actually and reasonably incurred by him or her in connection with the investigation, defense, settlement, or appeal of such proceeding if he or she acted in good faith and in a manner he or she reasonably believed to be in or not opposed to the best interests of the Company; and

3. Partial Indemnification. If the Indemnitee is entitled under any provision of this Agreement to indemnification by the Company for some or a portion of any expenses or liabilities of any type whatsoever incurred by him or her in the investigation, defense, settlement or appeal of a proceeding but not entitled, however, to indemnification for all of the total amount thereof, the Company shall nevertheless indemnify the Indemnitee for such total amount except as to the portion thereof to which the Indemnitee is not entitled.

4. Interpretation of Agreement. It is understood that the parties hereto intend this Agreement to be interpreted and enforced so as to provide indemnification to the Indemnitee to the fullest extent now or hereafter permitted by law.

5. Severability. If any provision or provisions of this Agreement shall be held to be invalid, illegal or unenforceable for any reason whatsoever, (i) the validity, legality and enforceability of the remaining provisions of the Agreement (including, without limitation, all portions of any paragraphs of this Agree-

ment containing any such provision held to be invalid, illegal or unenforce-able, that are not themselves invalid, illegal or unenforceable) shall not in any way be affected or impaired thereby, and (ii) to the fullest extent possible, the provisions of this Agreement (including, without limitation, all portions of any paragraphs of this Agreement containing any such provision held to be invalid, illegal or unenforceable, that are not themselves invalid, illegal or unenforceable) shall be construed so as to give effect to the intent man-ifested by the provision held invalid, illegal or unenforceable.

6. Modification and Waiver. No supplement, modification or amendment of this Agreement shall be binding unless executed in writing by both of the parties hereto. No waiver of any of the provisions of this Agreement shall be deemed or shall constitute a waiver of any other provision hereof (whether or not similar) nor shall such waiver constitute a continuing waiver.

7. Governing Law. This Agreement shall be governed exclusively by and con-strued according to the laws of the State of _____, as applied to contracts between _____ residents entered into and to be per-formed entirely within _____.

The parties hereto have entered into this Indemnity Agreement effective as of the date first above written.

CORPORATION

By: _____

Its: _____

INDEMNITEE:

_____

12.7 Liability

Directors and officers can be held responsible for torts or crimes which they or their supervised employees commit. Directors can also be subject to what is known as a derivative lawsuit by the shareholders, which will be discussed in Chapter 13.

There is a rule that helps protect directors and officers from liability. This rule is known as the business judgment rule. So long as the director made a decision in good faith, then he cannot be held personally liable for damages arising out of that decision. In the past, this has meant that courts have a hands-off approach in inves-tigating violations of the duty of care. Good faith here means acting without a conflict of interest, acting as an ordinarily prudent director in the situation, and in a manner in the best interest of the corporation. The business judgment rule protects the man-ager and the decision made by the manager. This means the director will not be in trouble and that decision will stay in place. Justifications for the business judgment rule include that it allows the directors to take risks, it prevents the courts from becoming overly involved, and it allows directors to do their jobs. However, this may be slowly eroding due to the recent violations of directors' duties made public in the national news.

Directors and officers also use another concept to limit their liability: reliance upon others. Directors, under this rule, are allowed to rely upon reasonable information given to them by those immediately involved in the corporation's business. This is usually how corporate attorneys run into potential malpractice issues; the director will state that he relied upon the corporate attorney to his detriment. To use the "reliance on others" argument, the director or officer will have to rely on an employee who is believed by the director or officer to be competent. Another way to use the reliance on others argument is for the director or officer to rely on attorneys, certified public accountants, etc., so long as that information is within their professional knowledge. Finally, a director can rely on a committee of other board members, so long as the director believes them to be competent. Whomever the director relies on, the reliance must be to the director's detriment.

Directors and officers can still be held personally responsible for negligence, fraud, or a breach of one of their duties. However, often, the corporation will have purchased D & O insurance, or directors and officer insurance, which may cover the director. This type of insurance usually excludes self-dealing acts, dishonesty, fraudulent compensation, or crime. There is a difference between insurance and indemnification. With indemnification, the corporation pays the lawsuit settlements on behalf of the directors. With insurance, the corporation pays the insurance premiums, but the insurance company pays the lawsuit settlements.

12.8 Delegation to Officers

Directors can and do delegate tasks to officers. Thus, the officers actually take care of the day-to-day carrying out of the directors' decisions. The directors have to continue to supervise the officers. The directors maintain responsibility for the actions of the officers in carrying out the duties given to them by the directors. Some responsibilities may not be delegated, for example, if they are substantially management of the corporation.

Chapter Summary

Part of the directors' roles are:

- to declare and pay dividends,
- approve major corporate decisions,
- oversee the officers, and
- determine if the corporation needs further financing though shares or bonds.

Some of these duties may be delegated to the officers. The role of officers is that they are appointed by the directors. Sometimes, a person can be both a director and officer.

When the corporation first starts, typically, the board of directors has been appointed by incorporators. Thereafter, directors are elected at the shareholder meetings. Most directors now serve one-year terms, though it can sometimes be longer. The corporation can request certain qualifications in its bylaws for its directors. Directors can set their own compensation, but, this must be discussed in the bylaws. Vacancies can be filled by a majority of the remaining directors. For officers, the directors appoint a new officer. Removal of directors can be with or without cause by the shareholders. Removal of the officers is done by the directors.

At the board of directors' meetings, minutes must be taken. Notice normally is not required for regular meetings, but is required for special meetings of the board of directors. At the meeting, a quorum of the directors must be present in order to legitimately conduct the meeting. Most directors have one vote, and often a majority vote is sufficient to pass an issue. Written action, without a meeting, is uncommon.

Both directors and officers have to uphold fiduciary duties, the duty of care, and the duty of loyalty. The duty of care requires both directors and officers to act in good faith and to use reasonable business judgment in their tasks on behalf of the corporation. The duty of loyalty requires that the directors and officers will not put their own interests first and will not act in conflict with the corporation's interest. While directors and officers can be held responsible for committing a tort or crime, sometimes the business judgment rule can prevent other liability. To use the business judgment rule, the director will have to show that he acted in good faith, and this normally will not protect him against a criminal charge. Another argument a director officer might use to defend themselves from liability is reliance on others.

Key Terms

Annual meeting
Annual report
Annual shareholders' meeting
Board of directors
Business judgment rule
Competing with the corporation
Corporate officer
Cumulative voting
Directors
Directors and officers insurance
    (D & O insurance)
Duty of care

Duty of loyalty
Minutes
Proxy
Officers
Quorum
Regular meeting of the board of
    directors
Reliance on others
Self-dealing
Shareholder
Shareholders' meeting

Special meeting of the board of
  directors

Straight voting
Written consent

Review Questions

1. How is the role of directors and officers different?

2. Can directors be shareholders as well?

3. How long do most directors serve?

4. Give the definition of a quorum.

5. What are the duties of directors and officers, respectively?

6. Why was Mr. Guth, in *Guth v. Loft, Inc.* found to have taken a corporate opportunity for himself?

7. What is expected of a director or officer when they have a conflict of interest with the corporation?

8. Explain how the business judgment rule works.

9. Who is normally relied upon in a "reliance upon others" argument?

10. How are indemnification and insurance different?

Web Links

Go on the internet and research the discussions on the *Guth v. Loft, Inc.* case. There are many different commentaries on this case.

Exercises

1. Since the indemnification of directors and officers is becoming more and more limited, what types of behavior would be indemnified?

2. Research a company you are interested in and determine the salaries of the board of directors.

Chapter 13

Shareholders

Chapter Outline

Chapter Objectives

- Provide the role or functions of shareholders, particularly regarding voting and shareholder lawsuits.

- Emphasize the right of shareholders to inspect the financial records of the corporation.

- Define quorum again, as it also deals with shareholders.

- Differentiate between direct and derivative lawsuits.

- Describe piercing the corporate veil.

- Detail shareholder meetings, including notice, consent, proxy, and action without a meeting.

13.1 Role

Shareholders elect the directors. They also can vote on certain corporate issues and may help make changes to the bylaws. Even though shareholders are often called owners of the corporation, they do not manage. The board of directors manage the corporation, and the officers carry out the orders of the directors. Shareholders have one obligation to the company, and that is to pay for the stock. To be a shareholder, a shareholder only needs one stock in the corporation. A shareholder could be a person or another business entity.

If the corporation is found liable, usually the most the shareholder's liability will be is the amount he invested in that stock. Typically, shareholders are not agents of the corporation, and their actions cannot bind the corporation.

13.2 Rights

Shareholders do have certain rights and those include rights to vote, a liquidation right, and a right to sell their shares. Some shareholders have an additional right, that of preemptive rights. Preemptive rights give a current shareholder the choice to purchase enough newly issued shares to keep their ownership interest in the corporation. This means if new shares are issued, the shareholder has the opportunity to keep his ten percent ownership in the corporation by buying up to ten percent of the newly issued shares. If he decided not to, or did not have preemptive rights, then his ownership percentage of ten percent would decrease below ten percent if new shares were issued. The original percentage the shareholder owned does not have to be ten percent; it could be more or less. Notice however, that one of the rights listed was not an absolute right to dividends. Shareholders are often confused about this. Shareholders only have a right to participate in dividends if dividends are in fact declared.

The liquidation right is the right to a portion of any proceeds left after the corporation has dissolved and paid all its creditors first. The shareholder would receive a portion of the liquidation rights that equates to his ownership percentage. For example, if La Plume Corporation was dissolving, and after they paid their creditors, they had ten thousand dollars left. If a shareholder had an ownership percentage of five percent, the shareholder would receive five hundred dollars.

- La Plume Corporation has $10,000.00 after dissolving to distribute to the shareholders.
- A shareholder owns 5%.
- The shareholder will receive 5% of $10,000.00, which is $500.

The right to sell shares just indicates that the general rule is shareholder can freely sell his shares. This is not true of a close corporation, which was discussed earlier in this text. In a close corporation, shares are limited to friends and family, so if an outsider buys a share, they will have rights to profit, but not managerial rights.

a. Inspecting

As investors, shareholders always have the right to inspect the financial records of the corporation. This can include annual reports, balance sheets, and income statements. The reports should be audited by an accountant. In addition, the shareholders are also normally allowed to look at the minutes and shareholder records. This also includes the corporation's articles of incorporation, bylaws, and shareholder's lists. Shareholder lists can be viewed in order to allow a shareholder to seek others to vote with or to seek votes from.

At first glance, the right to inspect may not seem like an important right. However, it is an important right, and one that is often litigated. A shareholder might not know how much they should be getting paid in dividends, unless they can look at the financial records of the corporation.

b. Voting

One of the purposes voting serves for shareholders is that they get to control who manages the corporation. However, many shareholders do not research the managers before they vote, or they do not vote at all. Instead, it seems shareholders now rely more on litigation to fix problems with their directors after the fact, rather than carefully vetting them before they are elected. Shareholders do have the power to remove directors prior to their term being up, and this can be with or without cause. If removal of a director does not take place at an annual meeting, it can be expensive to notice a special meeting to remove a director.

Shareholders are also given opportunities to vote on other corporate issues. Issues shareholders might vote on include items set forth by the board of directors. An issue could be a fundamental corporate change, such as amending the articles of incorporation, a merger, a sale of the majority of assets, or a voluntary dissolution. In the alternative, the shareholders might be called upon to vote on whether a conflict of interest the director has with the corporation is fair to the corporation or not. Shareholders might also vote on items set forth by other shareholders. Sometimes, shareholders do have the power to amend the bylaws.

Unless otherwise stated, one share equals one vote. This is known as straight voting. As it is difficult to get shareholders to vote, many corporations are seeking alternatives to get more shareholders to vote. If there is not a quorum at the meeting, then the meeting must be recalled, which is expensive. Thus, corporations are trying internet voting, telephone voting, and even text voting.

Sometimes a corporation will have what is known as cumulative voting. Cumulative voting is only for voting in directors. Cumulative voting occurs when a shareholder's shares are multiplied by the number of open positions on the board of directors. The shares are not multiplied by the number of directors running. Thus, if there are two open positions on the board, three directors are running, and a shareholder has fifty shares, that shareholder will get one hundred votes.

- 2 open positions, 3 directors running, shareholder has 50 shares
- Cumulative voting means 2 × 50 shares = 100 votes

c. Actions

1. Direct

A direct action occurs when one shareholder or just a few shareholders sue the corporation for an injury the corporation caused to that shareholder. The shareholder(s) literally claims to have been directly injured. Examples of direct actions include interference with or being denied voting rights and inspection rights, or not receiving a dividend when other shareholders did. The inspection lawsuits would be regarding the corporation's failure to let the shareholder look at the shareholders' lists and corporate records. There are still other reasons a direction action can be brought, for example, for a contract violation or personal injury. A direct action is run just like a regular lawsuit.

2. Derivative

A derivative action occurs when a representative shareholder sues to enforce a right of the corporation. The shareholder has to do this as the directors of the corporation are not enforcing the right themselves. The right to sue is still the corporation's right, and the shareholder steps into the corporation's shoes. In this type of action, if the shareholder wins, then any winnings go to the corporation. The shareholder does get reimbursement for expenses and attorneys' fees and might see an increase in her share value because of the lawsuit settlement. The corporation would pay these fees.

The two major types of derivative lawsuits are when the shareholder sues to enforce the corporation's rights against the board of directors (who will not sue themselves) or when the shareholder sues to enforce the corporation's rights against third parties (though this is less likely). A shareholder might sue because the director or officer used corporate assets improperly or mismanaged the company. The board of directors manage the corporation, and this includes being able to bring lawsuits in the corporation's name. If derivative actions were not allowed, then it would not be as easy to hold the fiduciaries liable. This is because a fiduciary, or director, is very unlikely to agree to sue himself if he is mismanaging.

The shareholder that brings the derivative action will usually be someone who is representative of the interests of the corporation. The shareholder is treated like the plaintiff and any wrongdoers are treated like defendants.

There are three requirements of a shareholder in order to bring a derivative action:

- The shareholder has to have been a shareholder when the negative act occurred,
- As indicated above, the shareholder has to appropriately represent the interests of the corporation, and

- The shareholder has to have made a written demand on the company, requesting that the company take action and the corporation must have failed to meet the demand for at least ninety days.

This last requirement gives the corporation one more opportunity to take care of the issue itself. If the corporation does not take this opportunity, it is usually because the wrongdoing was caused by a director or officer. If a director or officer did commit the wrongdoing, then this notice requirement is waived. If a majority of the non-wrongdoing directors finds that the lawsuit is not in the best interest of the corporation, however, then the court could dismiss the derivative suit.

The following case illustrates the NASDAQ delisting a security. Read the case and determine whether the facts could have also given rise to a shareholder derivative suit.

Fog Cutter Capital Group, Inc. v. Securities and Exchange Commission
474 F.3d 822 (2007)

The National Association of Securities Dealers (NASD) delisted Fog Cutter Capital Group's public stock from Nasdaq. The Securities and Exchange Commission dismissed Fog Cutter's petition for review.... The issue in this petition for judicial review is whether the Commission's dismissal was "arbitrary, capricious, an abuse of discretion, or otherwise not in accordance with law," 5 U.S.C. § 706(2)(A).

The NASD is a registered "national securities association" under the Securities Exchange Act of 1934, 15 U.S.C. § 780-3(b). At all times relevant to this case, the NASD operated Nasdaq, an electronic securities exchange. As a self-regulatory organization, the NASD must maintain rules to protect investors and the public interest.... One of these rules, approved by the Commission, stated that the NASD "will exercise broad discretionary authority over the initial and continued inclusion of securities in Nasdaq in order to maintain the quality and public confidence in its market." ... To that end, the NASD will delist securities if, in its "opinion," events occur that render it "inadvisable or unwarranted" to continue listing the securities "even though the securities meet all enumerated criteria for" listing....

For Fog Cutter, the disqualifying events centered on the criminal investigation, indictment, and conviction of its Chief Executive Officer and Board Chairman, Andrew Wiederhorn, and the manner in which the company dealt with this development. Wiederhorn founded Fog Cutter in 1997 and, with family members, controlled approximately fifty-three percent of the company's stock. The company operated a national restaurant chain and engaged in banking, financing, and real estate investment activities.

In March 2001, federal prosecutors informed Wiederhorn and Lawrence Mendelsohn, a former president of Fog Cutter, that they were targets of a grand jury investigation into the collapse of Capital Consultants, LLC, an investment adviser for union pension plans. Other than the fact that Wiederhorn and Mendelsohn were investigated for actions unrelated to Fog Cutter, the details of the criminal case are un-necessary to recount. Mendelsohn pleaded guilty and agreed to cooperate with the government. Wiederhorn later entered into a plea agreement and pleaded guilty to a two-count indictment charging him with giving an illegal gratuity and filing a false tax return, both felonies. The district court sentenced him to eighteen months in prison and ordered him to pay a $25,000 fine and $2 million to the Capital Consultants receiver.

On June 2, 2004, the day before Wiederhorn entered into the plea deal, he finalized a leave-of-absence agreement with Fog Cutter. The agreement acknowledged Wieder-horn's plea agreement and imminent incarceration, and provided that during his ab-sence he would retain his titles and responsibilities. Fog Cutter agreed to pay Wiederhorn his $350,000 annual salary, bonuses, and other benefits while he was imprisoned. The company also agreed to pay him a $2 million "leave of absence pay-ment" to retain his "good will, cooperation and continuing assistance, and in recog-nition of Wiederhorn's past service to the Company, to help avoid litigation and for ... other reasons." Fog Cutter knew Wiederhorn would use the $2 million payment to pay the restitution his plea agreement ordered. In its filings with the Commission, Fog Cutter disclosed this information and the $4.75 million cost of its agreement with Wiederhorn.

In July 2004, NASD staff decided that it was contrary to the public interest for Fog Cutter to remain listed on Nasdaq with Wiederhorn exercising substantial in-fluence over the company while incarcerated.... An NASD Panel determined that the Board's willingness to amend Wiederhorn's employment agreement, acquiescence to Wiederhorn's demands for financial support during his imprisonment, payment of his court-ordered restitution, and retention of him in his executive and director positions during his imprisonment were contrary to the public interest. The NASD Listing and Hearing Review Council affirmed the Panel's decision "in order to protect the quality of and public confidence in The Nasdaq Stock Market, and to protect in-vestors and the public interest." ... Fog Cutter applied to the Securities and Exchange Commission for review of the Council's decision. The Commission dismissed the application for review, focusing, as had NASD, on Wiederhorn's status as a convicted felon and the Board's actions supporting and retaining Wiederhorn on the Board and in management.

Fog Cutter's main complaint is that the Commission failed to take into account the company's sound business reasons for acting as it did. The decision to enter into the leave-of-absence agreement was, Fog Cutter argues, in the best interest of its shareholders. The company tells us that Wiederhorn's continuing commitment to the company and his return to an active role in the company after his incarceration were essential to preserving Fog Cutter's core business units.

The company focuses on its 2002 purchase of a majority interest in George Elkins Mortgage Banking Co., Inc. (GEMB). The Stock Purchase Agreement conditioned Fog Cutter's majority interest in GEMB upon Wiederhorn's serving as either a mem-ber of the Board or as CEO of Fog Cutter. If he occupied neither position, the minority shareholders had an option to repurchase their interest in GEMB, unless Wiederhorn's absence was due to his death or disability. Fog Cutter claims such a repurchase would be at "fire sale" prices, and that keeping Wiederhorn on board was therefore essential.

The company has presented nothing to support the likelihood that the options would be exercised. Nor has the company ever specified how much it would have lost from the exercise of the options. All we have is Fog Cutter's obscure assertion, without any citation to the record, that GEMB was "potentially valued at up to $ 10 million." … Even if we put aside the "potentially," we are still left with no information about the difference between the option price and the fair market value — or potential value — of Fog Cutter's GEMB stock. What we do know is that Fog Cutter made a deal with Wiederhorn that cost the company $ 4.75 million in a year in which it reported a $ 3.93 million net loss. We know as well that Fog Cutter handed Wiederhorn a $2 million bonus right before he went off to prison, a bonus stemming directly from the consequences of Wiederhorn's criminal activity.

Under Section 19(f) of the Exchange Act, 15 U.S.C. § 78s(f), the Commission must dismiss an application for review of an NASD delisting order if (1) the "specific grounds" "exist in fact," (2) the decision was in accordance with NASD rules, (3) the rules are and were applied in a manner consistent with the Exchange Act, and (4) the decision imposes no unnecessary or inappropriate burden on competition under the Act. Whether the Commission acted arbitrarily, capriciously, or unlawfully depends on whether its review of the NASD's decision complied with Section 19(f).

Here there was ample evidence supporting the NASD's grounds for taking action against Fog Cutter: Wiederhorn's guilty plea, the leave of absence deal and its cost to the company, the Board's determination that Wiederhorn should retain his positions with Fog Cutter, and the concern that Wiederhorn would continue to exert influence on company affairs even while he was in prison. The decision was in accordance with NASD rules giving the organization broad discretion to determine whether the public interest requires delisting securities in light of events at a company. That rule is obviously consistent with the Exchange Act, and NASD's decision did not burden competition.

Fog Cutter claims that it had to pay Wiederhorn and retain him because if it fired him in light of his guilty plea, it would have owed him $6 million. This scarcely speaks well for the company's case. The potential obligation is a result of an amendment the Board granted Wiederhorn in 2003 while he was under investigation. Wiederhorn's employment agreement stated that if terminated "for cause," he was entitled only to his base salary through the date of termination and payment of unreimbursed business expenses. If it terminated Wiederhorn without cause, Fog Cutter would have owed him three times his annual salary, three times his largest annual bonus from the last three years, unreimbursed business expenses, and accrued but unpaid base salary and bonuses — which Fog Cutter estimates would amount to $6 million — all as a lump-sum payment within ten days. Before the amendment to Wiederhorn's employment agreement in 2003, termination "for cause" included the conviction of *any* felony other than a traffic offense. In the 2003 amendment, the relevant provision allowed the Board to terminate Wiederhorn "for cause" upon conviction of a felony *involving Fog Cutter.* The Board had known about the investigation of Wiederhorn in connection with Capital Consultants for more than two years when it agreed to this amendment.

Fog Cutter thinks NASD's action was "unfair." But it was the company that bowed to Wiederhorn's demand for an amendment to his employment agreement, knowing full well that it was dramatically increasing the cost of firing him. Now it argues that terminating Wiederhorn would have been too expensive. One is reminded of the old saw about the child who murders his parents and then asks for mercy because he is an orphan. The makeup of Fog Cutter's Board was virtually unchanged between the time it amended the employment agreement and entered into the leave-of-absence agreement.... It was, to say the least, not arbitrary or capricious for the Commission to find that Wiederhorn exercised thorough control over the Board, and to find this troubling. We agree that the Board provided little or no check on Wiederhorn's conduct, and that the Board's actions only aggravated the concerns Wiederhorn's conviction and imprisonment raised.

That Fog Cutter did not itself violate the securities laws and that it disclosed the relevant events does not demonstrate any error in the delisting decision. The NASD's rules state that it may apply criteria more stringent than the minimum standards for listing.... Fog Cutter's disclosure of its arrangements with Wiederhorn did not change the nature of those arrangements, which is what led the NASD to find that the company's actions were contrary to the public interest and a threat to public confidence in the Nasdaq exchange.

Fog Cutter points to the continued listing of two companies — Steve Madden and Martha Stewart Living Omnimedia — in spite of the fact that Steve Madden and Martha Stewart, the chief executives of the companies, were convicted and imprisoned. This amounts to a selective prosecution argument, and it goes nowhere. To prove selective prosecution, a claimant must be part of a protected class under the Equal Protection Clause, U.S. CONST. amend. XIV, § 1, and show not only that prosecutors acted with bad intent, but also that "similarly situated individuals [outside the protected category] were not prosecuted."

... Fog Cutter clearly cannot prove all, if any, of these factors. As the Commission points out, Martha Stewart Living Omnimedia is listed on the New York Stock Exchange, not Nasdaq. And it is the NASD, not the Commission, that institutes the delisting investigations and renders delisting decisions. The Commission's role is as a reviewing body, not an initiator.

In delisting Fog Cutter, the NASD was concerned with the integrity and the public's perception of the Nasdaq exchange in light of both Wiederhorn's legal troubles and the Board's ongoing acquiescence to his demands. The Commission amply supported these concerns and was well within its authority to dismiss Fog Cutter's application for review of the NASD's delisting decision. We therefore deny Fog Cutter's petition for judicial review.

13.3 Liability

Typically, in a corporation, shareholders are only liable up to the amount of their investment. In other words, the shareholders' personal assets are usually not subject to being seized during a lawsuit. However, there are exceptions to this general rule, which fall under the doctrine of piercing the corporate veil or making a personal guarantee in order to secure a loan to finance the corporation.

a. Piercing the Corporate Veil

In general, shareholders do not have any liability for the corporation's debts other than what the shareholder invested in his stock. However, a major exception to this general rule is known as piercing the corporate veil. The limited liability the shareholder typically has is caused by a veil between third parties such as creditors and the shareholders that does not normally let the creditors of the corporation go after the shareholders. The corporation itself acts as the "veil" between the two. However, sometimes, this veil can be pierced. Usually the veil can be pierced when the shareholders are:

- treating the corporation's bank accounts like their own (known as commingling of assets),
- not holding meetings or taking minutes (known as lack of formalities), or
- not properly funding the corporation (known as inadequate capitalization).

Commingling of assets is when the shareholders do not have separate bank accounts from those of the corporation's bank accounts. A shareholder might improperly use the corporation's bank accounts to pay the shareholder's individual bills. Corporate formalities include:

- annual shareholders meetings,
- regular board of directors' meetings,
- corporate records, and
- minutes.

Inadequate capitalization is when a corporation does not have enough money in its bank accounts to pay debts. Not keeping this much money in the corporation's bank accounts implies that the corporation is not legitimate because it cannot pay its obligations.

13.4 Meetings

There are two types of shareholder meetings, and those are annual and special meetings. The bylaws should discuss, in detail, the annual meeting. Annual meetings of the shareholders need to take place yearly. Often, the meeting will be held at the corporation's principal place of doing business. Annual shareholder meetings often follow a format. Directors are elected, independent auditors might be voted on, as well as any other issues. The votes of shareholder proxies are tallied. The corporation executives might give a speech on the company's performance and answer questions. As most of the votes have already been provided by proxy, the shareholders' meeting just formalizes the vote.

For a shareholder meeting to be valid, there must be a quorum of shareholders at the meeting. Again, the minimum number of people necessary to legitimately transact business is the definition of a quorum. A quorum can be anywhere from one-third to fifty-one percent, depending upon the state. Out of that quorum at the meeting, a sufficient number of people need to actually vote. A sufficient number of votes must normally be a majority of the quorum.

Special meetings are for unusual items that did not come before the annual meeting. Perhaps there has been some misconduct by directors or the company is thinking about merging. The board, or shareholders with over ten percent of the shares, may call a special meeting.

a. Notices and/or Written Consents

Record date is used to determine which shareholders are entitled to notice of the meeting. Record date is a line drawn in the sand. The corporation arbitrarily picks a date, often one month before the meeting and states that whoever owns stock on that day shall get notice of the meeting. Since shareholders are constantly buying and selling stock, this solves the issue of who gets notice.

The notice must include the place, time, and date of the meeting. It is beneficial if the time of the meeting indicates the time zone as well. The notice will normally also include the purpose of the meeting. The meeting often includes an "et cetera" clause, meaning a clause that allows for any proper business that needs to, to come before the meeting. If this clause is not in the notice, then only the list itemized can come before the meeting. The notice will indicate the record date. It is signed by the secretary of the corporation. If any shareholders are not properly given notice, then the shareholder could cure this defect by either signing a written waiver or coming to the meeting without objecting.

b. Proxies

A proxy is basically an absentee ballot. A proxy gives another person authorization to exercise rights owned by the first person. Most minority shareholders cannot afford to go to the corporation's shareholder meetings, and this is how they are represented at the meeting. The proxy statement will often be written and indicate who has authority to vote for the signed shareholder. The proxy will probably indicate that it is only good for a certain shareholders' meeting. The proxy votes the shareholder's shares as directed by the shareholder. Most of the time, the proxy will specifically indicate who the proxy should vote for on behalf of the shareholder, but sometimes, it does not. When it does not, the proxy might be authorized to vote at his own discretion. The proxy is signed by the shareholder.

Only those who are shareholders on the record date are allowed to vote at the shareholders' meeting. The proxy documents are sent by the corporation to the shareholders and include an annual report, a disclosure statement, the proxy, and an envelope to return this information in to the company. This is done at the corporation's expense. The packet will usually be mailed several weeks before the annual shareholders' meeting. As it is difficult to get sufficient response rate to obtain a quorum, many corporations are experimenting with email, fax, text, etc.

Proxy statements are regulated by the Securities and Exchange Commission. The SEC states that the proxy must indicate what the shareholders are voting upon. If the proxy is for the election of directors, a shareholder must have the ability to abstain from voting on one or more directors. For all other issues, the shareholders must be allowed to vote individually, if desired. There are many other requirements to the proxy statement as well, some of which include:

- The date, time, and location;
- The right to revoke the proxy;
- Directors and officers; and
- Voting procedures.

A proposed proxy statement should be sent to the SEC no less than ten days before it is mailed to the shareholders.

An example of some of the wording of a proxy may be something like as follows:

"The undersigned, revoking prior proxies, appoints _____, to vote all shares of ABC, Inc. stock as indicated above which the undersigned is entitled to vote at the Annual Meeting. The undersigned acknowledges prior notice."

c. Minutes Book, Stock Book, and Seal

Minutes are kept in the minutes book, which is maintained at the corporation and may also be kept at the corporate attorney's office (if offsite). Notice of both shareholders' and directors' meetings should be included. Any consents (i.e., waivers of notice) should be included. It is a good idea to also provide a copy of the articles of incorporation and the bylaws, as well as the organizational meeting minutes. This minutes book is then open for inspection by the shareholders.

It is a requirement that minutes of the shareholders' meetings be taken and be accurate. The secretary will normally take and sign the shareholder minutes. Along with these minutes should be indicators of how notice was sent to all the shareholders, or if it was not sent that those shareholders waived notice, and whether shareholders voted by proxy.

The following is an example of a simple Corporate Minutes Questionnaire. The larger the corporation, the longer the questionnaire will most likely be, or the company may reuse prior minutes in preparing future ones. The paralegal would either attend the meeting and fill in the questionnaire there, or meet with the client after the meeting and fill in the questionnaire based upon the client's responses.

Corporate Minutes Questionnaire

Corporation's Name: _____

Address, including city, state, and zip: _____

Tax Year End of Corporation: _____

Date and Time of Annual Meeting: _____

Location of Annual Meeting: _____

Directors: _____

Shareholders: ____   _____

Incoming

Name	Number of Shares Held

[add lines as necessary]

1. Were any other persons attending the shareholders' meeting?

2. Did the Corporation change from one bank to another? Did the corporation add another bank?

3. Current Bank Signors:

President	
Secretary	

4. Did the Corporation borrow any money during the year? If so, indicate the amount, from whom, as well as the interest rate and time in which the loan must be repaid. Include leases in your answer, whether of cars, equipment, or real property.

5. Did the Corporation open or renew any Lines of Credit? If so, please provide details.

6. Did the Corporation lend money to anyone? If so, state name and amount. Please provide details.

7. Did the Corporation make any large cash purchases (over $5,000) of property (automobile, equipment, furniture, etc.)? If so, please specify.

8. Did the Corporation make any contributions to pension or retirement plans? If so, where and how much?

9. Did the Corporation employ a new Certified Public Accountant? If so, please specify.

10. Please list any other matters that need to be included in the minutes.

Questionnaire completed by:_____, paralegal

    Once the paralegal has filled out the Corporate Minutes Questionnaire, if the client is utilizing one, she would then use the response from that questionnaire to create the minutes for the shareholders' meeting. The following is a basic format for the minutes for the shareholders' meeting.

Minutes of Annual Meeting of Shareholders of
_____, Inc.,
A _____ [indicate state] Corporation

The annual meeting of the shareholders of _____, Inc., a _____ [indicate state] Corporation, was held at _____ on _____ at _____.

The following shareholders were present at the meeting representing the voting shares as set forth below:

NAME OF ISSUEE   NO. OF SHARES HELD

[input information]

The president announced that a quorum of the voting shareholders were present and the meeting was called to order.

ELECTION OF DIRECTORS

The president then announced that the election of the directors was in order. The Directors were then elected to serve until the next annual meeting of shareholders, and until the successors are duly elected and qualified. Upon motion duly made and seconded, the following persons were elected:

[Insert pertinent information from client questionnaire].

After discussion on motion duly made, seconded and carried, the shareholders received the financial reports for the year prior.

After discussion on motion duly made, seconded and carried, the actions of the Board of Directors in the operation of the business of the corporation for the year prior were approved and ratified.

There being no further business to come before the meeting, on motion duly made, seconded, and adopted, the meeting was adjourned.

_____

Secretary's Signature
ATTEST:

_____

President's Signature

d. Action without a Meeting

If the shareholders give written consent, then they could act without having a meeting. It would be treated the same as if there was a meeting. Depending upon the state, the number of shareholders required to give consent will either be a majority or a unanimous vote. Due to many corporations having a larger number of shareholders, it can be very difficult to get a majority or unanimous vote of the shareholders to have an action without a meeting.

Chapter Summary

At the shareholders' meeting, the shareholders elect the directors. This occurs at the annual meeting, though there can also be special shareholders' meeting in order to discuss issues that arise. The meetings must be noticed, which includes the place, date, and time of the meeting. If a shareholder cannot physically attend a shareholders' meeting, he can have another who is there vote for him by means of a proxy. The shareholder does this by signing a written document that authorizes another person to vote for him.

Shareholders have the right to inspect. Inspection rights include looking at the financial records and the corporate documents such as bylaws, minutes, and articles. They may also have preemptive rights. This gives a current shareholder the right to buy new shares to keep his ownership interest in the corporation. A shareholder can have a right to participate in a dividend, if one is issued, but does not have absolute right to a dividend. A shareholder also has a right to sell his shares and a right to liquidation money, in accordance with his ownership percentage, if there is any money remaining after paying creditors.

Shareholders have the right to vote. Only shareholders that own shares on the record date are allowed to vote in a shareholders meeting. In addition, there must be quorum of shareholders for the meeting to be properly transacted. Directors can be elected through straight voting or cumulative voting. Straight voting is one share equals one vote. Cumulative voting is when one share is multiplied by the number of open positions on the board of directors and then that is the total number of votes that shareholder has.

Shareholders have two types of lawsuits that can be brought against the corporation: direct and derivative actions. A direct action is when a shareholder has been directly injured. A derivative action is one a shareholder can bring against a wrongdoer that has harmed the corporation, if the board of directors fails to bring suit themselves. The right to do so derives from the right of the corporation to sue, but the corporation is not suing, so the shareholder gets involved.

In general, shareholders themselves have limited liability, and can only lose the amount they invested in their stock. There is a major exception to this rule: piercing the corporate veil. Shareholders can be sued under this doctrine when assets are commingled, formalities are not observed, or the corporation is not adequately capitalized.

The rules regarding the noticing of shareholder's meetings are strict. If a shareholder does not receive proper notice, then the corporation might have to re-notice the meeting, which costs time and money. To fix this defective notice, the shareholder could sign a written waiver. If the shareholder cannot afford or does not want to attend the shareholders' meeting himself, then he could use a proxy to vote for him. He signs a proxy card, giving another the authority to vote for him. Actions without a shareholders' meeting rarely occur, because it takes a majority or even a unanimous vote from the shareholders to agree to it.

Key Terms

Annual Meeting of the Board of
   Directors
Annual shareholders' meeting
Bylaws
Commingling of assets
Cumulative voting
Derivative action
Direct action
Distribution rights
Directors
Dividends
Inadequate capitalization
Inspection rights
Limited liability
Minute book

Minutes
Notice of shareholders' meeting
Piercing the corporate veil
Preemptive rights
Proxy
Record date
Quorum
Shareholder
Shareholders' list
Shareholder meetings
Special shareholders' meeting
Stock certificates
Straight voting
Voting rights

Review Questions

1. Who is arguably the owner of the corporation? What does this person actually own?

2. What items does a shareholder have a right to inspect?

3. Do shareholders have an absolute right to dividends?

4. Who is responsible for electing or the board of directors?

5. Explain why a shareholder might want preemptive rights.

6. What are the differences between a direct and a derivative action?

7. Argue that piercing the corporate veil is a moral rule as well as a legal rule.

8. What is a proxy?

9. What does the Securities and Exchange Commission require to be in the proxy statement?

10. Are actions without a meeting common for shareholders?

Web Links

Look online for a case regarding piercing the corporate veil.

For more details on piercing the corporate veil go to: http://www.hfw.com/Piercing-the-Corporate-Veil-Dec-2012.

Exercises

1. If a corporation's articles and bylaws do not discuss how directors are elected, how are the directors elected? If a shareholder has three hundred shares, then how many votes would that shareholder receive?

2. If a quorum is a third in a state, and one hundred and twenty-five thousand shares vote out of four hundred and fifty thousand, has a quorum been meet for purposes of the shareholders' annual meeting?

3. If the annual shareholders' meeting is set for September 7 and the record date is thirty days before, what is that date?

4. Derivative actions are difficult to understand. Another great case to help you is below.

Perlman v. Feldmann
219 F.2d 173 (1955)

This is a derivative action brought by minority stockholders of Newport Steel Corporation to compel accounting for, and restitution of, allegedly illegal gains which accrued to defendants as a result of the sale in August, 1950, of their controlling interest in the corporation. The principal defendant, C. Russell Feldmann, who represented and acted for the others, members of his family, was at that time not only the dominant stockholder, but also the chairman of the board of directors and the president of the corporation. Newport, an Indiana corporation, operated mills for the production of steel sheets for sale to manufacturers of steel products, first at Newport, Kentucky, and later also at other places in Kentucky and Ohio. The buyers, a syndicate organized as Wilport Company, a Delaware corporation, consisted of end-users of steel who were interested in securing a source of supply in a market becoming ever tighter in the Korean War. Plaintiffs contend that the consideration paid for the stock included compensation for the sale of a corporate asset, a power held in trust for the corporation by Feldmann as its fiduciary. This power was the ability to control the allocation of the corporate product in a time of short supply, through control of the board of directors; and it was effectively transferred in this sale by having Feldmann procure the resignation of his own board and the election of Wilport's nominees immediately upon consummation of the sale.

The present action represents the consolidation of three pending stockholders' actions in which yet another stockholder has been permitted to intervene. Jurisdiction below was based upon the diverse citizenship of the parties. Plaintiffs argue here, as they did in the court below, that in the situation here disclosed the vendors must account to the non-participating minority stockholders for that share of their profit which is attributable to the sale of the corporate power. Judge Hincks denied the validity of the premise, holding that the rights involved in the sale were only those normally incident to the possession of a controlling block of shares, with which a dominant stockholder, in the absence of fraud or foreseeable looting, was entitled to deal according to his own best interests. Furthermore, he held that plaintiffs had failed to satisfy their burden of proving that the sales price was not a fair price for the stock per se. Plaintiffs appeal from these rulings of law which resulted in the dismissal of their complaint.

The essential facts found by the trial judge are not in dispute. Newport was a relative newcomer in the steel industry with predominantly old installations which were in the process of being supplemented by more modern facilities. Except in times of extreme shortage Newport was not in a position to compete profitably with other steel mills for customers not in its immediate geographical area. Wilport, the purchasing syndicate, consisted of geographically remote end-users of steel who were interested in buying more steel from Newport than they had been able to obtain during recent periods of tight supply. The price of $ 20 per share was found by Judge Hincks to be a fair one for a control block of stock, although the over-the-counter market price had not exceeded $ 12 and the book value per share was $ 17.03. But this finding was limited by Judge Hincks' statement that 'what value the block would have had if shorn of its appurtenant power to control distribution of the corporate product, the evidence does not show.' It was also conditioned by his earlier ruling that the burden was on plaintiffs to prove a lesser value for the stock

Both as director and as dominant stockholder, Feldmann stood in a fiduciary relationship to the corporation and to the minority stockholders as beneficiaries thereof. . . . His fiduciary obligation must in the first instance be measured by the law of Indiana, the state of incorporation of Newport. . . . Although there is no Indiana case directly in point, the most closely analogous one emphasizes the close scrutiny to which Indiana subjects the conduct of fiduciaries when personal benefit may stand in the way of fulfillment of trust obligations. In Schemmel v. Hill, 91 Ind.App. 373, 169 N.E. 678, 682, 683, McMahan, J., said: 'Directors of a business corporation act in a strictly fiduciary capacity. Their office is a trust.... Directors of a corporation are its agents, and they are governed by the rules of law applicable to other agents, and, as between themselves and their principal, the rules relating to honesty and fair dealing in the management of the affairs of their principal are applicable. They must not, in any degree, allow their official conduct to be swayed by their private interest, which must yield to official duty. In a transaction between a director and his corporation, where he acts for himself and his principal at the same time in a matter connected with the relation between them, it is presumed, where he is thus potential on both sides of the contract, that self-interest will overcome his fidelity to his principal, to his own benefit and to his principal's hurt.' And the judge added: 'Absolute and most scrupulous good faith is the very essence of a director's obligation to his corporation. The first principal duty arising from his official relation is to act in all things of trust wholly for the benefit of his corporation.'

In Indiana, then, as elsewhere, the responsibility of the fiduciary is not limited to a proper regard for the tangible balance sheet assets of the corporation, but includes the dedication of his uncorrupted business judgment for the sole benefit of the corporation, in any dealings which may adversely affect it.... Although the Indiana case is particularly relevant to Feldmann as a director, the same rule should apply to his fiduciary duties as majority stockholder, for in that capacity he chooses and controls the directors, and thus is held to have assumed their liability.... This, therefore, is the standard to which Feldmann was by law required to conform in his activities here under scrutiny.

It is true, as defendants have been at pains to point out, that this is not the ordinary case of breach of fiduciary duty. We have here no fraud, no misuse of confidential information, no outright looting of a helpless corporation. But on the other hand, we do not find compliance with that high standard which we have just stated and which we and other courts have come to expect and demand of corporate fiduciaries. In the often-quoted words of Judge Cardozo: 'Many forms of conduct permissible in a workaday world for those acting at arm's length, are forbidden to those bound by fiduciary ties.... A trustee is held to something stricter than the morals of the market place. Not honesty alone, but the punctilio of an honor the most sensitive, is then the standard of behavior. As to this there has developed a tradition that is unbending and inveterate. Uncompromising rigidity has been the attitude of courts of equity when petitioned to undermine the rule of undivided loyalty by the 'disintegrating erosion' of particular exceptions....' The actions of defendants in siphoning off for personal gain corporate advantages to be derived from a favorable market situation do not betoken the necessary undivided loyalty owed by the fiduciary to his principal.

The corporate opportunities of whose misappropriation the minority stockholders complain need not have been an absolute certainty in order to support this action against Feldmann. If there was possibility of corporate gain, they are entitled to recover. In Young v. Higbee Co., supra, 324 U.S. 204, 65 S.Ct. 594, two stockholders appealing the confirmation of a plan of bankruptcy reorganization were held liable for profits received for the sale of their stock pending determination of the validity of the appeal. They were held accountable for the excess of the price of their stock over its normal price, even though there was no indication that the appeal could have succeeded on substantive grounds. And in Irving Trust Co. v. Deutsch, supra, 2 Cir., 73 F.2d 121, 124, an accounting was required of corporate directors who bought stock for themselves for corporate use, even though there was an affirmative showing that the corporation did not have the finances itself to acquire the stock. Judge Swan speaking for the court pointed out that 'The defendants' argument, contrary to Wing v. Dillingham (5 Cir., 239 F. 54), that the equitable rule that fiduciaries should not be permitted to assume a position in which their individual interests might be in conflict with those of the corporation can have no application where the corporation is unable to undertake the venture, is not convincing. If directors are permitted to justify their conduct on such a theory, there will be a temptation to refrain from ex-erting their strongest efforts on behalf of the corporation since, if it does not meet the obligations, an opportunity of profit will be open to them personally.'

This rationale is equally appropriate to a consideration of the benefits which New-port might have derived from the steel shortage. In the past Newport had used and profited by its market leverage by operation of what the industry had come to call the 'Feldmann Plan.' This consisted of securing interest-free advances from prospective purchasers of steel in return for firm commitments to them from future production. The funds thus acquired were used to finance improvements in existing plants and to acquire new installations. In the summer of 1950 Newport had been negotiating for cold-rolling facilities which it needed for a more fully integrated operation and a more marketable product, and Feldmann plan funds might well have been used toward this end.

Further, as plaintiffs alternatively suggest, Newport might have used the period of short supply to build up patronage in the geographical area in which it could com-pete profitably even when steel was more abundant. Either of these opportunities was Newport's, to be used to its advantage only. Only if defendants had been able to negate completely any possibility of gain by Newport could they have prevailed. It is true that a trial court finding states: 'Whether or not, in August, 1950, Newport's position was such that it could have entered into 'Feldmann Plan' type transactions to procure funds and financing for the further expansion and integration of its steel facilities and whether such expansion would have been desirable for Newport, the evidence does not show.' This, however, cannot avail the defendants, who—contrary to the ruling below—had the burden of proof on this issue, since fiduciaries always have the burden of proof in establishing the fairness of their dealings with trust prop-erty....

Defendants seek to categorize the corporate opportunities which might have ac-crued to Newport as too unethical to warrant further consideration. It is true that reputable steel producers were not participating in the gray market brought about by the Korean War and were refraining from advancing their prices, although to do so would not have been illegal. But Feldmann plan transactions were not considered within this self-imposed interdiction; the trial court found that around the time of the Feldmann sale Jones & Laughlin Steel Corporation, Republic Steel Company, and Pittsburgh Steel Corporation were all participating in such arrangements. In any event, it ill becomes the defendants to disparage as unethical the market advantages from which they themselves reaped rich benefits.

We do not mean to suggest that a majority stockholder cannot dispose of his controlling block of stock to outsiders without having to account to his corporation for profits or even never do this with impunity when the buyer is an interested customer, actual or potential, for the corporation's product. But when the sale necessarily results in a sacrifice of this element of corporate good will and consequent unusual profit to the fiduciary who has caused the sacrifice, he should account for his gains. So in a time of market shortage, where a call on a corporation's product commands an unusually large premium, in one form or another, we think it sound law that a fiduciary may not appropriate to himself the value of this premium. Such personal gain at the expense of his coventurers seems particularly reprehensible when made by the trusted president and director of his company. In this case the violation of duty seems to be all the clearer because of this triple role in which Feldmann appears, though we are unwilling to say, and are not to be understood as saying, that we should accept a lesser obligation for any one of his roles alone.

Hence to the extent that the price received by Feldmann and his codefendants included such a bonus, he is accountable to the minority stockholders who sue here.... And plaintiffs, as they contend, are entitled to a recovery in their own right, instead of in right of the corporation (as in the usual derivative actions), since neither Wilport nor their successors in interest should share in any judgment which may be rendered.... Defendants cannot well object to this form of recovery, since the only alternative, recovery for the corporation as a whole, would subject them to a greater total liability.

The case will therefore be remanded to the district court for a determination of the question expressly left open below, namely, the value of defendants' stock without the appurtenant control over the corporation's output of steel. We reiterate that on this issue, as on all others relating to a breach of fiduciary duty, the burden of proof must rest on the defendants.... Judgment should go to these plaintiffs and those whom they represent for any premium value so shown to the extent of their respective stock interests.

The judgment is therefore reversed and the action remanded for further proceedings pursuant to this opinion.

Chapter 14

Remaining Issues Related to For-Profit Corporations

Chapter Outline

Chapter Objectives

- Outline the unique issues of double taxation with a corporation.

- Compare S corporations' special taxation to regular corporations' taxation.

- Review how to become a nonprofit, which is not taxed.

- Discuss why and how the articles of incorporation are amended.

- Detail the various ways in which corporate changes can be made, including mergers, shares purchases or exchanges, asset purchases, and hostile takeovers.

- Delineate the types of dissolution, whether it is voluntary, administrative, or involuntary.

- Give the requirements for qualifying in a foreign jurisdiction.

- Make clear that while most corporations attempt to avoid the additional costs of doing business in foreign jurisdictions, it can sometimes be more costly not to do so.

14.1 Introduction to the Remaining Issues Related to For-Profit Corporations

Corporations are unique in that their profits are usually taxed two or three times, depending upon whether the corporation is a subsidiary or not. Using tax deductions or otherwise attempting to avoid taxes then becomes a big issue with corporations.

One of the biggest remaining issues regarding for-profit corporations is that of changes in the corporate structure. These changes include, but are not limited to:

- mergers,
- share exchanges,
- consolidations,
- the sale of assets or shares, and
- hostile takeovers.

Unfortunately, sometimes a corporation needs to terminate. This can be a voluntary or involuntary undertaking. Hopefully, the situation was not caused by the directors' inappropriate behavior, and preferably, the liquidation will not have to be judicially supervised.

For each foreign state that the corporation is legally allowed to transact business, it needs to qualify to do so. However, once it is qualified, there are costs associated. Thus, many corporations would prefer not to have to qualify, which they might not have to do if they are not considered to be conducting business within that state. However, if they are found to be conducting business and didn't first qualify, then they can be fined.

14.2 Taxation

Corporations use IRS Form 1120 to report their earnings. Corporations usually pay at a different rate of tax than for a regular person. However, corporations may also be able to get different tax deductions than a regular person would, such as salaries and making retirement contributions to employees.

When a corporation does make a profit, it can either go ahead and distribute the profits as dividends, or retain the profits, known as retained earnings. Typically, retained earnings are invested by the company and bring about higher profits in the future, which cause the stock's price to go up. Shareholders would still benefit because the share price would be higher if the shareholder decided to sell his stock. However, the government, through the Internal Revenue Service (IRS), does not like it when a corporation does not give out dividends, but hangs on to its profits, because then the IRS does not get to tax the dividends more immediately. Therefore, the IRS instituted the accumulated earnings tax to encourage corporations to distribute dividends.

The accumulated earnings tax states if the corporation has earnings beyond what is reasonable, and its purpose is to avoid having shareholders pay taxes on dividends, then the corporation can be subject to this tax. The tax is fifteen percent or more (depending on the year) of the accumulated taxable total that is above two hundred and fifty thousand dollars. The current amount of the tax is approximately twenty percent.

a. Double

The Internal Revenue Service subjects corporate profits to double taxation. When a corporation makes a profit, it pays taxes on the profit. This is the first tax. When the corporation declares a dividend (thus giving the shareholders part of the profits), then the shareholders have to pay income tax on those profits. This is the second or double tax. The corporation does not receive any type of tax deduction for issuing dividends. If a corporation is a subsidiary, it may have to pay even more taxes overall.

This is because if when the subsidiary makes a profit, it pays taxes. Then the remainder of the profit goes to the parent company, who pays taxes on all its profits. Finally, the parent company may issue dividends, and the dividends would be taxed as well. There are ways in which to avoid all these taxes and many corporations have major tax deductions or tax breaks that reduce their taxes.

b. State

Corporations also usually have to pay state taxes. This might be revenue-based or a flat tax. There is also the "pleasure of doing business" fee, which is a tax for using the state's highways and emergency system. There might be property and or sales tax. Corporations must collect state sales taxes on goods sold on the Internet.

c. S Corporations: A Specially Taxed Type of Corporation

With an S Corporation, the corporation receives special tax benefits not available to a regular publicly held company. However, an S Corporation still has limited liability. With S Corporation taxes, all the profits and losses of the corporation pass-through to the shareholders of the corporation. The shareholders pay their share of the profits and losses at their individual tax rate. Thus, an S Corporation is not subject to double taxation like a publicly held corporation.

In order to receive these tax benefits, the Internal Revenue Service puts several restrictions on S Corporations. The S in S corporation refers to Subject S Revision Act of the IRS code.[1] The S refers to how the corporation will be taxed. S Corporations can:

- only have one class of stock;
- have no more than one hundred shareholders;
- shareholders have to be an individual, estate, charity, pension fund, or trust (meaning the shareholders cannot be partnerships or corporations);
- shareholders cannot be nonresident aliens (if they were, then the IRS would not get the individual shareholder's taxes); and
- there has to be unanimous agreement among all the shareholders to have S status (however, there only has to be a majority of shareholders to revoke S status).
- The corporation cannot usually be a bank.
- The corporation cannot usually be an insurance company.

If the S Corporation does not maintain these requirements, then it will no longer get the benefits of S Corporation taxation and will be taxed like a regular corporation.

---

1. 26 U.S.C. Sections 6242 et seq.

As an LLC has the same benefits as an S Corporation — limited liability and pass-through taxation — many times people elect for an LLC instead. The LLC does not have the requirements above.

1. Formation of S Corporations

S Corporations form like a regular corporation and then make an election to become an S Corporation later. The board of directors decides that S status should be selected, and this is approved by the shareholders. C Corporations are regular corporations, but people usually drop the C and just say corporation.

2. Taxation of S Corporations

To obtain the beneficial tax status for the year, the S election has to be done before fifteen days before the third month in the corporation's annual year. Recall that the corporation's annual year does not need to be January 1st to December 31st. The form used to elect is Form 2553. If election is taken back, then the corporation cannot elect it again for five years.

A shareholder may particularly like an S Corporation, because if there are losses, then the shareholder gets to use a portion of that loss to offset some of his other profits. The taxation, in general, will be pass-through. Thus, this is a benefit, so long as the shareholders' tax brackets are less than the corporate tax bracket would be. This avoids double taxation as well.

The S Corporation has to report to the IRS, with the income and losses of the corporation and the shareholders' percent of each. The shareholders also report their own percent of income and losses on their tax return.

3. Termination of S Corporation

While termination can be performed voluntarily, termination of the S Corporation often happens involuntarily, by allowing over one hundred shareholders. The S Corporation is losing popularity as the limited liability company becomes more prevalent. The limited liability company has far fewer formalities to uphold, and has pass-through.

d. Nonprofit Corporations: A Corporation That Has to Qualify in Order Not to Be Taxed

Nonprofits are corporations that seek not to be taxed. To avoid taxes, the nonprofits have to meet certain requirements. Nonprofits are supposed to perform a public benefit, a mutual benefit, or a religious benefit. More specific examples of nonprofits include some hospitals, schools, and religious institutes. Public benefit nonprofits benefit the public, so a hospital could fall under public benefit. A mutual benefit nonprofit is for the mutual benefit of its members, so a private school could fall under mutual benefit. Religious benefit can include several different types of religions, including, but not limited to the Catholic Church, Unitarian Church, Jewish Synagogues, Muslim temples, Scientology, etc. One of the reasons nonprofits often want to be a corporation or an LLC is that these types of business entities can help the nonprofit avoid at least some liability.

1. Formation of Nonprofits

First, the nonprofit should determine what type of nonprofit it will be. If it is a public benefit corporation, then it should be for science, medicine, teaching, or the like. If it is a mutual benefit one, than the goal of the nonprofit is to be for the benefits of its members, such as a paralegal alumnae association. However, mutual benefit could even be a sorority or a fraternity. Lastly, the nonprofit could be religious.

States regulate how nonprofits within their state should be formed. In general, a nonprofit does still have to file articles of incorporation, upon which it will indicate that it is a nonprofit. Sometimes, a state entity, such as the state's attorney general may have to approve the nonprofit.

Merely incorporating as a nonprofit does not automatically mean a corporation can avoid paying taxes to the Internal Revenue Service (IRS). The tax exemption is a separate application with the IRS. The qualification to become a nonprofit is regulated under Internal Revenue Code Section 501(c).

2. Operation of Nonprofits

A nonprofit does have a board of directors and is guided by its bylaws. Any profits made by the nonprofit cannot be issued as dividends. Instead, the profits should be reinvested into the purpose of the nonprofit. Thus, if a nonprofit is formed for the purpose of finding a cure for cancer, and the nonprofit makes a profit, that profit cannot be issued as a dividend, as it would be able to with a regular C Corporation. Rather, the profit must be reinvested back into preventing cancer, perhaps by funding cancer research. There are no stocks and stockholders in a nonprofit.

3. Taxation of Nonprofits

The IRS has to agree that the nonprofit is not required to pay federal taxes. After the nonprofit forms, then it does a separate tax exemption application with the IRS. The IRS agrees through a ruling or letter. Nonprofits also have to file yearly paperwork to indicate that they are still nonprofits. Nonprofits also typically do not have to pay state taxes such as property or income taxes.

14.3 Amending the Articles of Incorporation

The regular corporation may want to amend the articles of incorporation if material changes have been made to the corporation. If the amendment will affect the rights of the shareholders, then the shareholders should approve the amendment. Sometimes though, the board of directors can amend the articles without shareholder approval. This would include any time up until shares are issued. If the amendment is for a routine matter after the issuance of shares, then the board of directors can usually amend without shareholder approval.

When shareholder approval is required, the board of directors will frequently first adopt the amendment and recommend it to the shareholders. The majority of shareholders would then be required to approve the amendment in order for it to pass. If a shareholder does not agree to the amendment, then that shareholder might be bought out. This is known as an appraisal right.

The paperwork amending the articles is often called the Articles of Amendment. These articles will require:

- the name of the company,
- the amendments,
- what will happen if there are share changes,
- when the amendment was adopted, and
- how the amendment was adopted (i.e., by board of directors or by shareholders).

If the adoption is by the shareholders, the corporation may need to record how many shareholders adopted the amendment.

a. Must Amend If Any Changes to Stock

The articles of incorporation must be amended if there are any changes to stock. This includes preemptive rights, if they are added, and changes to stock include adding new classes of stock. If the stock originally had par value, and that par value has changed, then the articles should be amended. If the corporation wants to increase the number of shares it is authorized to issue, so that it can raise more money, then it should amend the articles.

b. Other Reasons

One of the reasons to amend the articles, other than dealing with shares, is any issue that was left out of the original articles of incorporation should be added once it is discovered it was left out. Another reason to amend the articles, which does not have to do with stock, is if the corporation wants to change its name.

14.4 Corporate Combinations

When control is transferred in a corporation, those who have rights in the corporation are affected. These transfers can come from:

- mergers,
- share exchanges,
- consolidations,
- purchase of assets,

- purchase of stock, and/or
- hostile takeovers.

During some of these combinations, shareholders may have voting rights or liquidation rights. During combinations, the board of directors still has duties.

In general, to get approval for these types of changes, both the directors and shareholders must agree. After the change is approved by both, then articles of amendment will most likely need to be filed. In approving a change, the board of directors should be considering whether the change is in the best interests of the corporation. Shareholders typically have to approve the change by a majority vote, though some states require a higher percentage of approval. If shareholders do not agree, then they may be entitled to have their shares bought back at fair market value.

a. Merger

A merger is when company A combines with company B, and only company A survives. Company A would be dubbed the surviving corporation. Company B would be the merging corporation. Company A takes over all the assets, but also takes over all the liabilities of Company B. Company A would be a single corporation after the merger. A merger might help a company move into a new part of the United States. A merger might also expand Company A's product line.

A merger might be between a parent company and a subsidiary of that parent. When the subsidiary merges back into the parent company, this is called an upstream merger. If the parent company owns ninety percent or more of the stocks, then it is not required to obtain shareholder approval for the merger. The reason that it does not have to be approved by either corporation is that the parent owns so much stock that a vote is unnecessary. This is known also as a short-form merger. When the parent company merges into the subsidiary, this is called a downstream merger.

In conducting a merger, the corporation must comply with both state and federal laws. This generally requires some sort of negotiation at the start. If a deal is reached, then it is frequently written down as a letter of intent, which just indicates the parties' understanding. Next, the step is to draft a plan of merger. The plan will have a date, information about both companies' stock, and information about the surviving corporation (such as the name, location, and directors). There will be a discussion about whose shares will be converted. The merging corporation must let the surviving corporation know of all known assets and liabilities and discuss how the merging corporation will be dissolved.

Company B's shareholders normally get shares in Company A. Company B shareholders would then be Company A shareholders. In the alternative, Company A could just buy out all Company B's shareholders, meaning that Company B shareholders would not become shareholders of Company A, but would receive money for their previous stocks. Company A's articles of incorporation will need to be amended to include any changes from the articles of merger.

In addition, the plan of merger must typically be approved by both the board of directors and the shareholders for the merging and surviving corporations. Shareholders may be able to opt out of the merger. If the shareholder was entitled to vote on the merger, and was against it, he may be able to get an appraisal right, which is the fair value of his stock in cash. Appraisal rights depend upon the state. The following case is about such appraisal rights. Pay attention to the reasons this award was not limited to appraisal rights.

Williams v. Stanford

977 So.2d 722 (1st. Dist. 2008)

This case calls upon us to navigate the relatively uncharted terrain of a recently revised portion of Florida's statutory corporations law. We decide here whether minority shareholders who object to a total transfer of corporate assets, and who allege that the majority shareholder has engaged in a course of conduct involving improper self-dealing and malfeasance over time, are limited to the statutory remedy of offering up their shares for a fair price. We conclude that Florida law does not so constrain minority shareholders' rights in the limited cases where such shareholders raise facially sufficient and serious allegations of unfairness. In such cases, minority shareholders may seek remedies beyond appraisal. Accordingly, we partially reverse the summary judgments entered in appellees' favor and remand for further proceedings; we affirm without comment the grant of summary judgment as to appellants' claim for trade name infringement. Quite obviously, we express no view on whether appellants will ultimately be entitled to the remedies they seek.

BACKGROUND

These two consolidated appeals reflect a soured business relationship between appellants Paul and James Williams ("the Williams brothers") and appellee John C. Stanford. The Williams brothers together held a thirty percent stake in Brown and Stanford, Inc. ("B & S"), at one time a successful construction company in Jacksonville; Mr. Stanford held the remaining seventy percent of the close corporation's shares. The Williams brothers worked as carpenters for B & S from 1997 until 2002.

At some point, the Williams brothers began to harbor suspicions about Mr. Stanford's management of B & S finances. When, despite increasing revenues, the once-profitable company recorded a net loss for calendar year 2001, the Williams brothers asked Mr. Stanford to permit them to examine B & S's financial records. Mr. Stanford initially made limited records available, but two days later, on May 6, 2002, he summarily fired the brothers.

Subsequent investigation—much of it in the form of discovery—procured evidence that Mr. Stanford and his wife had charged numerous personal expenses to the company's credit card (including charges totaling approximately $48,000 to a popular home-shopping network), and had used B & S funds to build a 3,200-square-foot home for themselves and to improve property belonging to Mr. Stanford's father. The Williams brothers allege that, in all, the Stanfords misappropriated at least

$250,000 in corporate funds and credit and, either intentionally or not, concealed those expenditures by hiding them in existing customers' accounts over a period of years.

On July 31, 2002, the Williams brothers demanded that Mr. and Mrs. Stanford, as B & S's directors, initiate a suit to recover the corporate funds they used for personal benefit. Not surprisingly, the Stanfords balked at such a suit. On October 23, 2002, the Williams brothers filed a shareholder-derivative action on behalf of B & S, naming the Stanfords as defendants. As this controversy matured, the Williams brothers added numerous claims and amended their complaint several times. The complaint ultimately included two counts — a claim that the Stanfords breached their fiduciary duty by paying personal expenses with company monies, and a claim that they breached their common law duty of loyalty — which are not on appeal.

In July 2003, the Stanfords retained appellee Henderson Keasler, a Florida law firm, to represent themselves individually and to represent B & S in defense of the derivative action. Sometime afterward, Mr. Stanford apparently expressed his desire to stop working for B & S, in counsel's words, as "an indentured servant to [the Williams brothers,] who had accused him of stealing and pilfering his own company." On the advice of his attorneys, he resigned as B & S's qualifying agent in October 2003, but continued to collect B & S paychecks. Mr. Stanford's resignation as B & S's qualifying agent prevented B & S from conducting continued business as a construction company. Consequently, on October 31, 2003, B & S shut down its operations.

Henderson Keasler and the Stanfords, with the consult of B & S's accountant, evaluated several strategic options to effectuate Mr. Stanford's goals, including filing for bankruptcy and dissolving B & S. The Stanfords and their counsel determined, based on a 2002 appraisal that considered the company's financial situation at the time, but did not account for corporate funds used for the Stanfords' benefit, that B & S's assets were roughly equal to its liabilities. They then decided upon a transaction by which the Stanfords would form a new company, appellee J.C. Stanford & Son, Inc., and transfer B & S's assets to Stanford & Son in exchange for the latter's assumption of B & S's liabilities. The asset transfer, which appellees have loosely characterized as a merger, began on November 1, 2003; the Williams brothers happened upon the news of the asset transfer during a November 24, 2003, deposition of Mr. Stanford, at which time the transaction was well under way. Mr. Stanford, through counsel, notified appellants by letter dated December 4, 2003, that the company would purchase each brother's B & S stock for $25,000, and that appellants had a statutory right to have their shares appraised. The asset transfer to Stanford & Son, which Mr. Stanford solely owned, was completed by December 31, 2003. Stanford & Son forged ahead, commencing on November 1, 2003, the day after B & S shut down, conducting the business known as J.C. Stanford & Co., just as B & S had done up until the merger. The company maintained the same location, the same telephone number, and the same staff, equipment, and vehicles as previously used by B & S.

Appellants were now faced with a dilemma. They could exercise their appraisal rights as to all their shares (twenty-one each) and thereby seek compensation, but in the process they would divest their holding in B & S and would lose standing to maintain their derivative action. They could, in the alternative, forego their appraisal rights and risk defeat in the derivative action. The brothers chose a middle course, fashioning what they termed a "conditional election of appraisal rights." Each brother tendered twenty of his twenty-one shares with the contention that twenty shares were worth $125,000, substantially more than the $25,000 price Mr. Stanford offered for all twenty-one. In a subsequent declaratory action filed by appellees, the trial court ruled in May 2004 that the Williams brothers' "conditional" exercise of their appraisal rights was a nullity — that a shareholder entitled to appraisal must elect appraisal as to all or none of the shareholder's interest. Appellants do not challenge that ruling in this appeal.

Meanwhile, in the still-pending derivative action, the Williams brothers, having learned of the asset transfer, moved to disqualify Henderson Keasler, citing the firm's conflicted representation of B & S and the Stanfords individually. The trial court granted the motion as to Henderson Keasler's representation of B & S.

On February 26, 2004, appellants filed a verified amended complaint, alleging the following claims: (I) breaches of fiduciary duty by the Stanfords, stemming from their alleged personal use of corporate assets and corporate funds; (II) breaches of fiduciary duty by the Stanfords in conjunction with their transfer of B & S's assets to Stanford & Son; (III) breaches of common law duty of loyalty by the Stanfords; (IV) trade name infringement by the Stanfords, stemming from the use of B & S's trade name by Stanford & Son; (V) breaches of fiduciary duty by Henderson Keasler, which, as B & S's corporate counsel, improperly facilitated the transfer of B & S's assets to Stanford & Son. In a second amended complaint filed in 2005, appellants added Stanford & Son as a defendant as to count II, and two Henderson Keasler lawyers as individual defendants as to count V. Appellants filed a third amended complaint in 2006, adding a sixth count for rescission and cancellation of the transfer of B & S's assets to Stanford & Son.

On March 27, 2006, the trial judge granted the defendants' motions for partial summary judgment as to counts IV and V, and granted their motion to strike the prayer for relief in count II, the claim against the Stanfords and Stanford & Son for breach of fiduciary duty stemming from the asset transfer and which sought imposition of a constructive trust on Stanford & Son's profits. On June 21, 2006, the trial court granted summary judgment as to count VI, the rescission claim, and, without further hearing, granted the Stanfords' and Henderson Keasler's motions for attorney's fees pursuant to section 57.105, Florida Statutes (2006), on the ground that counts IV and V were essentially frivolous. The court also granted appellees' motion pursuant to section 607.1331(2)(b), Florida Statutes (2006), for attorney's fees that accrued during the declaratory action regarding appellants' appraisal rights.

Appellants have appealed the summary judgments as to counts IV, V, and VI, the trial court's decision to strike the demand in count II for imposition of a constructive trust,' and the awards of attorney's fees. We affirm the summary judgment as to the trade name infringement claim, but, for the reasons that follow, we reverse the trial court's rulings as to the other claims presented on appeal and remand for further proceedings.

ANALYSIS

I.

Permeating the causes of action advanced here are the Williams brothers' specific allegations (though as yet unproven) of unfair dealing and breaches of fiduciary duty on the Stanfords' part, which culminated from several years of alleged value-destroying activities. Although appellants present numerous issues for review, the essential issue is whether Florida's "appraisal rights" statute thwarts the Williams brothers in their efforts to obtain judicial scrutiny of the transfer of B & S assets from B & S to J.C. Stanford & Son, a company Mr. Stanford created with the admitted intention of withdrawing from the business relationship with the Williams brothers. The Williams brothers also seek recovery against Henderson Keasler, alleging the law firm served the Stanfords' interest at the expense of B & S, the firm's corporate client. We conclude that appellants raise allegations which, if true, are sufficient to trigger remedial rights beyond mere appraisal. Accordingly, these allegations withstand appellees' motions for summary judgment.

A.

Section 607.1302, Florida Statutes (2003) — Florida's "appraisal rights" statute — generally requires minority shareholders who dissent from a major transaction or disposition of assets to seek the remedy of tendering their shares for appraisal and buy-back at a fair price:

> (1) A shareholder is entitled to appraisal rights, and to obtain payment of the fair value of that shareholder's shares, in the event of any of the following corporate actions:
>
> .... (c) Consummation of a disposition of assets pursuant to s. 607.1202 if the shareholder is entitled to vote on the disposition, including a sale in dissolution but not including a sale pursuant to court order or a sale for cash pursuant to a plan by which all or substantially all of the net proceeds of the sale will be distributed to the shareholders within 1 year after the date of sale;
>
> (d) Any other amendment to the articles of incorporation, merger, share exchange, or disposition of assets to the extent provided by the articles of incorporation, bylaws, or a resolution of the board of directors, except that no bylaw or board resolution providing for appraisal rights may be amended or otherwise altered except by shareholder approval....

Appraisal must determine the "fair value" of the dissenting shareholder's shares.... "'[F]air value' means the value of the corporation's shares determined: (a) Immediately before the effectuation of the corporate action to which the shareholder objects." ... The trigger here is Mr. Stanford's disposition of all B & S assets....

In most cases, the statute denominates appraisal as a dissenting shareholder's exclusive remedy.... The exclusivity rule does not apply, however, where the minority shareholder has alleged that the challenged transaction "[w]as procured as a result of fraud or material misrepresentation." … The Williams brothers argue their allegations of corporate malfeasance on the Stanfords' part fall under the ambit of subsection (4)(b) and constitute facially sufficient allegations that raise factual issues for resolution by a finder; of fact. The argument has force. Pending a factfinder's determination as to the truth of the Williams brothers' allegations, the brothers suggest they have shown "fraud or material misrepresentation" entitling them, in their shareholder-derivative stance, to rescission or such other curative remedies as might restore the parties to the status quo ante. We reject the concept, implicit in appellees' argument, that a buy-back at the fair value of the stock immediately before the Stanfords' disposition of corporate assets would suffice as a complete remedy.

B.

To date, no Florida court has had occasion to interpret the governing provisions of section 607.1302 in its 2003 form. As is often true, however, Delaware case law provides guidance to our construction of the statute.… Our review of pertinent Delaware cases supplies principles of corporate law that ought to control in this case. The most significant of these holds that dissenting minority shareholders should be entitled to remedies beyond appraisal when challenging corporate transactions as allegedly not entirely fair, and certainly where such transactions have fraudulently devalued the stock.

In *Weinberger v. UOP, Inc.,* the Delaware Supreme Court sketched, in broad strokes, the principle that a shareholder can challenge a corporate transaction premised on unfair dealing by exercising rights beyond mere appraisal.… The *Weinberger* court wrote, in the context of a proposed merger between a parent and its subsidiary:

> The concept of fairness has two basic aspects: fair dealing and fair price. The former embraces questions of when the transaction was timed, how it was initiated, structured, negotiated, disclosed to the directors, and how the approvals of the directors and the stockholders were obtained. The latter aspect of fairness relates to the economic and financial considerations of the proposed merger, including all relevant factors: assets, market value, earnings, future prospects, and any other elements that affect the intrinsic or inherent value of a company's stock.

… The court held that, in some cases where transactions raise questions of procedural unfairness, appraisal should not constitute a dissenting shareholder's sole remedy:

> [W]hile a plaintiffs monetary remedy ordinarily should be confined to the more liberalized appraisal proceeding…, we do not intend any limitation on the historic powers of the Chancellor to grant such other relief as the facts of a particular case may dictate. *The appraisal remedy we approve may not be adequate in certain cases, particularly where fraud, misrepresentation, selfdealing, deliberate waste of corporate assets, or gross and palpable overreaching are involved.…*

The Delaware court elaborated on the *Weinberger* approach two years later, holding in *Rabkin v. Philip A Hunt Chemical Corp.* that appraisal would be an inadequate remedy for dissenting minority shareholders who alleged that corporate directors and officers, *inter alia,* manipulated the timing of a merger to artificially depress the cash-out price that minority stockholders would be paid for their shares post-merger.... Because the plaintiffs in *Rabkin* alleged specific acts of unfair dealing — the defendant-directors of the acquiring company were "charged with bad faith which goes beyond issues of 'mere inadequacy of price'" — the court concluded that summary judgment in the defendants' favor was inappropriate and that, if their claims of unfair dealing were true, the plaintiffs would have been entitled to equitable remedies beyond an appraisal of their shares....

Beyond the Delaware Supreme Court's exposition of persuasive common law tenets, we note that a Delaware chancery court has now applied the *Weinberger-Rabkin* framework to its own construction of the 2003 version of section 607.1302(4)(b), Florida Statutes (2003).... The Delaware chancellor interpreted the Florida statutory phrase "fraud or material misrepresentation" as implicating the same entire-fairness analysis contemplated in *Weinberger* and *Rabkin.*... We are inclined to align our interpretation of section 607.1302(4)(b) with that of the *Berger* court, which interpreted the phrase "fraud or material misrepresentation" in the statute essentially synonymously with "unfair dealing ..."

C.

In the present case, the Williams brothers alleged sufficient acts of unfair dealing to withstand appellees' motion for summary judgment, which the trial court should have denied. Appellants alleged that Mr. Stanford suddenly and secretively transferred B & S assets to a newly, created company — J.C. Stanford & Son, Inc. — with, admittedly, the intention of effectuating a squeeze-out of the Williams brothers. Shortly before the disposition of B & S assets, Mr. Stanford resigned as B & S's qualifying agent, depriving B & S of its ability to conduct an ongoing construction business. The complaint raises more than a specter that, at the time appraisal rights would have arisen, the Williams brothers' shares could not have been worth much.

In cases such as the present controversy, involving dissenting shareholders who seek more than appraisal of their shares in the wake of objectionable transactions, courts must balance the principle that an adequate remedy should exist for a dissenting shareholder in an unfair transaction against the consideration that courts should not become bogged down in a wide range of disputes over the fairness of cash-out prices offered to minority shareholders who object to corporate transactions. We have no question that, in the present case, we are not dealing with "a fair price complaint artfully disguised in the camouflage of procedural unfairness." ... As appellants' counsel pointed out during oral argument, the Williams brothers' complaint over the fairness of the transfer of B & S assets stems from the fact that, at the time appellants' statutory appraisal right crystallized, the company's treasury — and thus the corresponding value of their shares — had been all but eviscerated through several years of the Stanfords' alleged misappropriations and mismanagement of corporate funds, activities the Williams brothers did not detect until the company recorded a net loss in 2001. Contingent upon proof of the allegations, appraisal at the time of the November 2003 transfer of B & S assets, effectuated after years of allegedly value-destroying activities on the Stanfords' part, would not have afforded the Williams brothers adequate recourse in this particular case. We find the allegations of the Stanfords' various activities analogous to those advanced against the defendants in *Rabkin,* who allegedly manipulated the timing of a merger to reduce the cash-out price paid to minority shareholders upon appraisal....

Appellants' right to appraisal would have been as of the November 2003 asset transfer; we find nothing in the statute that would allow a valuation before the November 2003 transfer of assets from B & S to Stanford & Son. We thus reject any suggestion that the appraisal remedy would allow appellants to recoup the diminished value represented by the alleged wrongful transactions over a period of time before the assets transfer. Moreover, we are unable to conclude that appellees' alleged mismanagement and misappropriations of corporate funds, followed by a de facto merger, not only triggered the appraisal right, but also cemented that right as the Williamses' sole remedy.... Because the appraisal must be conducted with regard to the shares' value "[i]mmediately before the effectuation of the corporate action to which the shareholder objects," Section 607.1301(4)(a), Florida Statutes (2003), appraisal would likely have yielded an inequitable result. The 2003 asset transfer represents precisely the type of transaction contemplated in *Rabkin* and *Weinberger* — one so procedurally and structurally unfair that a fair price would be unattainable without independent equitable relief outside an appraisal proceeding.

D.

We interpret the "fraud or material misrepresentation" exception in section 607.1302(4)(b) to mean that a minority shareholder who alleges specific acts of "fraud, misrepresentation, self-dealing, [or] deliberate waste of corporate assets," *Weinberger,* 457 A.2d at 714, may be entitled to equitable remedies beyond an appraisal proceeding if those allegations are proven true and if the alleged acts have so besmirched the propriety of the challenged transaction that no appraisal could fairly compensate the aggrieved minority shareholder. We adopt the entire fairness analysis developed in *Weinberger* and *Rabkin* to assess whether a corporate transaction avails aggrieved minority shareholders of rights beyond appraisal. The trial court erred in granting summary judgment as to appellants' claim for rescission of the transfer of assets; we reverse summary judgment and remand for factual determinations as to the truth of appellants' allegations of fraud, misrepresentation, and breaches of fiduciary duty on the Stanfords' part.

II.

Resolution of the remainder of appellants' claims on appeal largely flows from our resolution of the threshold issue above. Because we conclude that appellants alleged facts sufficient to withstand summary judgment and that, if true, entitle them to remedies other than appraisal, we also conclude the trial court erred in dismissing their claim against the Henderson Keasler law firm for breach of fiduciary duty to B & S. Citing the fact that the Stanfords waived Henderson Keasler's conflict between the firm's representation of them and its representation of B & S, the trial court relied on *Rudolf v. Gray,* a case from the Fifth District in which all shareholders collectively waived the conflict of interest for corporate, counsel to continue its representation of individual shareholders.... Assuming *Rudolf* supplies the controlling rule, we find the present case distinguishable, in that only the Stanfords, instead of all shareholders, acting for B & S, approved the conflict waiver. Any conflict of interest that arose from Henderson Keasler's representation of the Stanfords individually and its concomitant representation of B & S was therefore not properly waived, and the trial court should not have dismissed appellants' claim against the firm alleging breach of fiduciary duty.

We likewise reverse the trial court's decision to strike the Williams brothers' demand that Stanford & Son place its profits in a constructive trust for the benefit of B & S. A constructive trust is an equitable remedy available in cases dealing with breaches of fiduciary duty; such an instrument restores property to its rightful owner and prevents unjust enrichment.... In particular, a court may impose a constructive trust when property is acquired through fraud.... Because appellants have established that genuine issues of material fact existed which cast a pall upon the transfer of B & S assets to Stanford & Son, they advanced a viable claim for the imposition of a constructive trust. The trial court dismissed their claim in part because he believed appellants sought the imposition of a trust pursuant to their claim for trade name infringement, when in actuality they sought the trust in conjunction with their claim alleging breach of the Stanfords' fiduciary duty to B & S. Accordingly, we reverse and remand with instructions that the trial court consider both appellants' claim against Henderson Keasler and their demand for the imposition of a constructive trust in light of their allegations of fraud and unfair dealing surrounding the transfer of B & S assets....

CONCLUSION

In light of the foregoing, we AFFIRM the summary judgment for appellees on the Williams brothers' claim for trade name infringement. We REVERSE, however, the summary judgments entered on appellants' claim for rescission of the asset transfer and appellants' claim against Henderson Keasler for breach of fiduciary duty. We also REVERSE the order striking appellants' demand for the establishment of a constructive trust for the benefit of B & S, as well as the trial court's assessment of attorney's fees against appellants with respect to the declaratory action and counts IV and V of their complaint in the shareholder-derivative action. Appellants shall enjoy the benefit of a trial on the merits of their facially sufficient claims. The cause is REMANDED for further proceedings consistent with this opinion.

If the plan of merger is adopted, then articles of merger are filed with the applicable secretary of state.

b. Share Exchanges

In a share exchange, the buying corporation will buy many or even all of the shares of the target corporation. The shareholders of the target could get stock in the buying corporation, a third corporation, or they could just be bought out.

In conducting a share exchange, state and federal laws must be complied with. A plan of exchange, under these laws, is often required as this is similar to a merger. Typically, a share exchange must be approved by the directors and shareholders of both companies. Often both companies will still exist, but the company whose shares were bought out might be a subsidiary of the buying corporation.

c. Consolidation

Consolidations occur when Company A combines with Company B, and Company C is formed from those two corporations. Both Company A and B disappear. Company C starts its existence as a new corporation. Usually, it makes better financial sense for one of the original corporations to survive, so you will not see as many consolidations occurring today. In general, the same rules that are applicable to mergers are applicable to consolidations. This includes Company C being responsible for all the liabilities as well as the assets of both Companies A and B.

d. Purchase of Assets

Purchase of assets occurs when one company is going to purchase all or most of the assets of another. It is typically based upon a letter of intent, which is made after negotiations. There will then be an agreement regarding the asset purchases. It will include:

- the name of the parties,
- the description of the assets undergoing change in ownership,
- the amount of money to be paid for those assets,
- whether any liabilities will be assumed by the purchasing company,
- the date of the agreement,
- signatures of the parties, and
- when the transfer will take place.

Depending upon the state, there may or not be shareholder approval required by the buying corporation. Typically, there is shareholder approval required only by the corporation whose assets are being sold, and not the acquiring corporation. One of the benefits of a purchase of assets is that the acquiring corporation may not become responsible for the liabilities of the selling corporation. There are exceptions to this general rule, however, especially when the purchase really does equate to a merger. Generally, the buying corporation just picks what it wants and leaves the rest, which are usually liabilities. The buying corporation does not have to give shares to the selling corporation's shareholders. The buying corporation does not usually have to make a public filing either.

When a purchase of assets occurs, the selling corporation must typically have its shareholders agree to it, in particular if the sale would leave them unable to continue in business. This is because, often, a purchase of assets will require the selling corporation to dissolve afterward. A corporation is made up of its assets, so if it sells them, then usually it has nothing left. If the corporation stays in business, then it will probably be a shell company.

If shareholders do not agree, they are known as dissenting shareholders and have appraisal rights. This means they can get the fair market value of their shares. The shareholders should be notified of the appraisal rights before the purchase of assets is voted on. To obtain the appraisal rights, the dissenters must give a written notice of their appraisal rights to the corporation and not vote for the purchase of assets. This general dissenting procedure applies to mergers, share exchanges, purchase of assets, and purchases of stock.

e. Purchase of Stock

The buyer of the stock takes over all the rights and responsibilities of the stock when he purchases it. The agreement will include the buying price for the stock and how this amount will be paid. If there are liabilities of the corporation, including litigation, than the seller corporation needs to disclose those. The seller will have to make warranties that he has the authority to sell and that he has complied with securities laws. The buyer will have to warrant that he can in fact buy the stock.

f. Hostile Takeovers

A hostile takeover is a nonconsensual taking over of another company by going over the heads of that company's management. Thus, this type of change is performed without the board of directors' approval. There are two major ways in which to effectuate a hostile takeover: through a tender offer or a proxy contest. To take over using a tender offer, the aggressor usually starts by buying stocks on the sly, but only up to 4.9%. The aggressor is normally going to offer prices which are currently above the market price to obtain this initial 4.9%. At 5%, the Securities and Exchange Commission makes the aggressor disclose the tender offer. Then, the aggressor tries to buy a majority of shares. If the aggressor is unable to buy a majority of shares, then all the shares are returned and the aggressor gets his money back.

The Williams Act regulates tender offers and lays out these rules. The Williams Act also requires that there not be fraud or manipulation in tender offers. If there is, this can bring on either criminal or civil charges.

The second way a hostile takeover can be performed is through a proxy contest. A proxy contest occurs when the aggressor corporation tries to get the target's shareholders to vote for its management team. The aggressor usually does this by stating that its management gets its shareholders better dividends, raises stock values more, etc.

An example of a hostile takeover is in 2009, when Kraft Foods tried a hostile takeover of Cadbury. It was so contentious that the United Kingdom changed its hostile takeover rules as a result. At the time Kraft attempted the hostile takeover, it was the second largest food conglomerate world-wide. Cadbury fought the hostile takeover for months and then made an agreement with Kraft. Cadbury was not for sale at the time of the hostile takeover. Cadbury told its shareholders the deal was not a good one. Cadbury tried to convince its shareholders that the business model of Kraft, being a conglomerate, was against Cadbury's more personal business model.

Cadbury also told shareholders that being bought out by another candy company, any candy company, would be better than to become part of Kraft. Cadbury also had the government state that it would oppose a hostile takeover that did not respect the company. However, Cadbury eventually agreed that the majority of its shareholders would sell. This agreement was approved by over seventy percent (70%) of the shareholders. Investors were given cash and shares in Kraft. In 2012, Kraft split into Kraft Food Groups and Mondelez. In 2015, Heinz gave shareholders shares and cash in Heinz Kraft.

There are many different ways in which a target corporation can attempt to stave off a hostile takeover. The board of directors may not be able to use some of these types of takeover defenses without shareholder approval, including poison pills, and courting white knights. Some of defensive takeovers are:

- **Poison pill**

In a poison pill, the board may grant an additional right to each common share that is issued and outstanding. The poison pill would be triggered during the tender offer. This right might be greater voting rights or the ability to buy more shares. The point of a poison pill is to make it more difficult for the aggressor to buy the target company.

- **To court a white knight**

To court a white knight is to seek out another company to which the target would prefer to merge with than the aggressor corporation. In general, the target is hopeful that the new company, or white knight, will allow the current management at the target to stay in place. White knights are friendly to the target corporation.

- **To buy another company**

To buy another company is just as it sounds. Do not get it confused with to court a white knight, which is to merge with another company. To buy another company may not be feasible, because the target corporation is often in a weakened position. The target company is already susceptible to a takeover, so it may not have the money to buy another company to make it stronger and able to avoid a hostile takeover.

- **Golden parachute**

A golden parachute is the concept that if high-level managers are forced to leave the corporation, then the aggressor has to pay them an extreme amount of money. This amount would normally be in the millions of dollars. As such, it makes it much more expensive for the aggressor to hostilely takeover.

- **Pac-Man**

The Pac-Man is a reverse tender offer. The target corporation would then do a tender offer on the aggressor. This may not be feasible, as if the target corporation was weak enough to be takeover, they may not be able to turn around and try to take over the aggressor.

- **Suicide pact**

A suicide pact occurs when the managers of the target corporation are fired. Even if only one of them is fired, the rest all agree to resign. The target is hoping that all of them quitting will leave the aggressor without stable management, but since oftentimes the aggressor is attempting to replace the target's management, this may be of limited value.

- **Crown jewels**

When the corporation has a profitable asset, it can try to sell that asset to make itself less attractive to the aggressor, and thus hopefully avoid being taken over. The profitable asset is known as a crown jewel. It can be dangerous to sell the crown jewel(s), as it might make the target so weak it goes under anyway. For example, a target corporation has three crown jewels: valuable real estate, a "secret" recipe for cinnamon rolls that it sells, and a terrific chief financial officer. Selling off the valuable real estate probably would not weaken the company so much that it would need to dissolve. Selling off the recipe for the cinnamon rolls that is sells would almost certainly cause the company to be so weak it needed to dissolve.

Many states allow corporations to protect themselves against hostile takeovers. An example of one such state would be Delaware. Although there was some controversy over whether such state laws were constitutional or not, the United States Supreme Court ruled they were constitutional.[2]

14.5 Termination

To begin a discussion of termination, the different broad categories in termination should be defined. Dissolution occurs when the corporation formally ends its legal existence. Liquidation and winding up are used interchangeably. The process for either one is the corporation converts all assets to cash, pays creditors, and gives any remaining assets to the shareholders. Winding up helps protect creditors. Unknown

---

2. *CTS Corp. v. Dynamics Corp. of Am.*, 481 U.S. 69 (1987).

claims can be brought against a dissolved corporation, so it is in the corporation's best interest to go ahead and pay all claims possible. In addition, the corporation should retain funds for any unknown claims. If it does not and there are unknown claimants, they may seek to get their money from the former shareholders.

a. Voluntary Dissolution

To be voluntary, the board of directors and the shareholders have to approve the dissolution. Both the board of directors and shareholders might agree on dissolution for reasons such as:

- the corporation is no longer making a profit,
- a merger, and/or
- the sale of most of its assets or stock.

Typically, the board and then the shareholders vote on the dissolution. A special shareholders' meeting might be called for the shareholders to vote on the dissolution, however, if the corporation is in dire financial straits, this may not be possible. If shareholders do not agree to the dissolution, they can attempt to get appraisal rights for their shares.

The majority of shareholders should approve the dissolution. The shareholders could even unanimously approve the dissolution. However, if the corporation needs to be dissolved prior to its starting business, then only the board of directors needs to approve the dissolution.

After the approval, the corporation should file articles of dissolution. Then, the corporation can liquidate. Again, liquidate means turning everything that is not cash into cash. The next step would be to pay off any creditors. If there is any money left, the remaining money should go to the shareholders, preferred and then common.

b. Administrative Dissolution

In an administrative dissolution, the secretary of state dissolves the corporation. This makes sense because the state is essentially who gave the corporation life, so it can also take it away. The secretary of state might administratively dissolve the corporation because:

- it has not paid its state income taxes,
- has not filed its annual reports with the secretary of state, or
- has not maintained its registered agent for service of process.

The corporation's period for existence could have also expired.

c. Involuntary Dissolution

Three different groups of people can make the corporation involuntarily dissolve:

- creditors,
- the secretary of state, or
- the shareholders of the corporation.

Administrative dissolution as involuntarily dissolution has already been discussed above.

With an involuntary dissolution, the court will frequently appoint a liquidator to watch over the dissolution and winding up process. This may be because the court does not trust the corporation to do so ethically. The liquidator will be someone not directly involved in the corporation.

Most of the time, an involuntary dissolution would have to be sought by a majority, rather than a minority of the shareholders. Reasons shareholders ask for involuntary dissolutions include the directors committing fraud and/or the corporation going bankrupt. Other reasons include procuring the articles of incorporation through fraud, violating state criminal laws, not starting the business, or abandoning the business after starting up. Still further reasons include the directors being deadlocked for two years or corporate assets being misused by the board.

A creditor could bring about an involuntary dissolution if the creditor was unable to get its debt paid back by the corporation. This happens when the corporation is not doing well financially. Specifically, the creditor must show that the corporation owes it money and that the corporation is insolvent. If the court forces the corporation into liquidation, this should force the corporation to try to raise money to pay its creditors. The following case is regarding dissolution for failure to pay creditors. However, what was the other reason given for promoting the dissolution?

Sartori v. S & S Trucking, Inc.
2006 MT 164 (2006)

Justin Sartori sued his business partner, Tony Stacy, for breach of corporate fiduciary duty with regard to their corporation, S & S Trucking, Inc. ("S & S"). Stacy answered the complaint and asserted a counter-claim. Although the District Court concluded that Sartori breached his fiduciary duties to S & S, the court did not grant damages and/or attorney fees to Stacy, and because the corporation's loan was under Sartori's name, the court ordered S & S dissolved unless Stacy paid off or refinanced the loan within a set time.

We restate the appeal issues as follows:

1. Did the District Court err in ordering corporate dissolution when it did not find that the corporation had been injured?

… In 2003, Stacy, who worked as a truck driver, approached his friend, Sartori, also a trucker, about purchasing a hauling business. Sartori expressed interest in the proposal, and the two men applied for a business loan with First Interstate Bank in Eureka in order to make the purchase. Because Sartori had a good credit history and Stacy did not, the bank agreed to loan Sartori the money. The bank finalized the loan listing "JUSTIN M. SARTORI DBA: S & S TRUCKING" as the borrower. The loan was for a term of years in the amount of $78,493.68. Although the bank did not list Stacy as a borrower on the loan, he nonetheless pledged his logging truck and trailer as collateral. Sartori pledged twenty acres of real property that he owned with his wife.

On August 23, 2003, Stacy and Sartori signed the articles of incorporation for S & S, which the Secretary of State approved. While stock certificates were never actually issued, Stacy and Sartori agreed that they would be the only shareholders and would each own an equal number of shares. The partners designated Stacy as President and Sartori as Secretary/Treasurer, and hired Tanya Pluid as the office manager.

Within weeks after forming the corporation in September 2003, Stacy and Sartori began to realize that they had incompatible working styles. Several incidents occurred in which Sartori did not show up when or where Stacy expected. Stacy came to believe that Sartori was not pulling his weight and therefore proposed some changes in the way the parties initially agreed to pay out earnings from the company's income. Sartori refused to approve the changes and the relationship further deteriorated. Both men contacted attorneys to see about disentangling from the corporation. Eventually, Stacy scheduled a meeting for November 22, 2003, to iron out the parties' differences, but Sartori refused to attend once he decided the notice was for a board of directors meeting and that Stacy failed to notify him sufficiently in advance per the bylaws.

Prior to the November 22, 2003, meeting, Sartori engaged in a number of actions to undermine S & S, including incorporating a new trucking company, Brimstone Enterprise ("Brimstone"), on October 31, 2003. In addition, Sartori contacted the Eureka Post Office to have S & S's mail forwarded to Sartori's mail box; he transferred S & S's Department of Transportation ("DOT") number to Brimstone; he cancelled or transferred S & S's vehicle licenses; he contacted S & S's suppliers and cancelled or attempted to cancel S & S's accounts; he closed S & S's bank account; and he attempted to transfer S & S's insurance to Brimstone. Sartori also contacted businesses with whom S & S worked in an effort to transfer their business to Brimstone. For example, when Eureka Pellet Mill told Sartori that it was obligated to honor its contract with S & S, Sartori started getting up early in the morning and hauling sawdust to the Eureka Pellet Mill — on behalf of Brimstone — before Stacy arrived at work. S & S could no longer do interstate business until it received a new DOT number, as Sartori had transferred S & S's number to Brimstone. Sartori's actions caused S & S to incur other losses and expenses, including trailer rent, trailer repairs, trip permit fees, and cell phone fees.

On December 18, 2003, Sartori sued Stacy for breach of corporate fiduciary duty and demanded judicial dissolution of S & S. Stacy answered the complaint and filed a counter-claim alleging that Sartori engaged in deceit, intentional interference with a business contract, intentional interference with prospective economic advantage, defamation, and breach of fiduciary duty. The District Court conducted a bench trial and found that "Sartori did everything in his power to sabotage S & S after he quit the company on November 17, 2003," and therefore had breached his fiduciary duty to the business. Although the District Court stripped Sartori of his interest in the company and his positions as a director and an officer, the court rejected Stacy's proposal to keep S & S in business under its current corporate identity. The court disagreed with Stacy's contention that the loan should stay in place under Sartori's name until S & S paid it in full, because, while the court explicitly found that Sartori's actions were "tortious," it did not believe "tying up Sartori's credit and property for the next five years" was an appropriate remedy. Thus, the court ordered Sartori removed as a shareholder and director of S & S, and awarded him no compensation for his interest in the corporation. Further, the court held that unless Stacy and/or S & S paid off or refinanced the bank loan by July 1, 2005, action would be taken to dissolve the corporation.

The court grounded its decision in § 35-1-938, MCA, which provides that a corporation is subject to judicial dissolution in a proceeding by a shareholder if a deadlock exists. The court noted that neither Stacy nor Sartori disputed that the requisites for judicial dissolution had been met....

1. Did the District Court err in ordering corporate dissolution when it did not find that the corporation had been or was threatened with injury?

The District Court dissolved S & S pursuant to § 35-1-938(2), MCA, which states that a district court may dissolve a corporation in a proceeding by a shareholder if it is established that:

> (a) the directors are deadlocked in the management of the corporate affairs, the shareholders are unable to break the deadlock, and *irreparable injury to the corporation is threatened or being suffered* or *the business and affairs of the corporation can no longer be conducted to the advantage of the shareholders generally because of the deadlock*;
>
> (b) the directors or those in control of the corporation have acted, are acting, or will act in a manner that is illegal, oppressive, or fraudulent;
>
> (c) the shareholders are deadlocked in voting power and have failed, for a period that includes at least two consecutive annual meeting dates, to elect successors to directors whose terms have expired; or
>
> (d) the corporate assets are being misapplied or wasted.

... The District Court determined that dissolution of S & S was appropriate pursuant to subsection (a).

Stacy maintains on appeal that, rather than dissolving the corporation, the District Court, using its power under § 35-1-939, MCA, should have simply removed Sartori as a shareholder and director of the corporation. While Stacy appears to concede that he and Sartori were unable to break their management deadlock as to corporate affairs, he argues that the court failed to find any harm to the corporation per the statutory language. Stacy stresses the fact that S & S is now a twelve-employee company that has thrived in the wake of Sartori's departure. Since there has been no corporate injury, Stacy argues, there can be no dissolution.

In making this argument, Stacy ignores relevant statutory language. Section 35-1-938(2)(a), MCA, provides that the court may order dissolution if "irreparable injury to the corporation is threatened or being suffered or *the business and affairs of the corporation can no longer be conducted to the advantage of the shareholders generally because of the deadlock*." ... Stacy and Sartori were S & S's only shareholders. Although the corporation may not have suffered irreparable injury, the District Court found that the management deadlock led Sartori to take numerous steps to sabotage the corporation. As a result, the business and affairs of S & S could no longer be conducted to the advantage of the shareholders, Stacy and Sartori. The court properly exercised its statutory authority when it dissolved S & S.

In dismissing Stacy's argument, we note that he cites cases that apply § 35-1-921(1)(a)(i), MCA, the predecessor to § 35-1-938, MCA, to support his contention that the District Court only had authority to dissolve the company if it found corporate injury. The earlier statute provided that a corporation can be dissolved in an action "by a shareholder" when it is established that:

> the directors are deadlocked in the management of the corporate affairs and the shareholders are unable to break the deadlock and that irreparable injury to the corporation is being suffered or is threatened by reason thereof. ...

While the earlier rendering includes similarities to the present statute, the two differ in key respects. First of all, under the former statute, irreparable injury is a prerequisite to dissolution. Under the present statute, irreparable injury is listed in the disjunctive and is thus not necessary. Further, the older version does not provide that a "court" may dissolve a corporation because "the business and affairs of the corporation can no longer be conducted to the advantage of the shareholders generally because of the deadlock." In light of these differences between the two statutes, Stacy's references to cases discussing the predecessor statute are not pertinent to our analysis.

We hold that the District Court correctly ordered dissolution of S & S pursuant to § 35-1-938(2)(a), MCA....

d. Articles of Dissolution

Once the corporation is liquidated, then it should file the articles of dissolution. These articles will probably contain:

- the name of the corporation,
- the address,
- the dissolution date,
- agreement by the shareholders for the dissolution,
- acknowledgement that the creditors are paid, and
- statements that the shareholders have received any money left.

The corporation will probably also have to show that it does not owe any more state taxes, with a statement from the state's tax board.

e. Liquidation

If the dissolution is voluntary, then a court will not often be involved in overseeing the liquidation, which is converting all the assets into cash. Sometimes, a shareholder will ask for the court to oversee liquidation in a voluntary dissolution case.

After the creditors have been paid, the shareholders will receive a portion of any money left over according to their pro rata interest, with preferred shareholders being paid first, before common shareholders.

1. Judicial

Judicial liquidation occurs when dissolution is activated by the creditors, state, or shareholders. This would normally occur when the directors have acted improperly. The court does not feel that it can trust the directors to conduct the liquidation honestly or ethically. Therefore, the court appoints someone to handle the liquidation. This person is known as a liquidator, or sometimes as a receiver.

2. Nonjudicial

Nonjudicial liquidation can be brought about by a dissolution that is voluntary or even one that is sometimes administrative. In these instances, the court does trust the directors and other managers of the corporation to run ethically the liquidation process. Therefore, no liquidator is appointed.

3. What Does the Company Do about Potential Claims?

The corporation should attempt to notify all known creditors of its dissolution. The notice should be mailed to the last known address and state that the creditor must take action within one hundred and twenty days or be barred from making that claim.

With unknown claims, the corporation may have to take out ads in newspapers to let potential unknown claimants know about the dissolution of the company. Then, these claimants might have as much as three years in which to make a claim. Thus, the corporation would rather send notice to as many people as possible, because this can limit liability to one hundred and twenty days instead of three years.

14.6 Qualification in Foreign Jurisdictions

A corporation has existence in the state where it is domiciled. In the state wherein it is domiciled, it is known as a domestic corporation. If it wants to "exist" outside of this state, it must seek permission from each other state wherein it wishes to exist. In these other states, it will be known as a foreign corporation.

If a corporation is doing business in another state from the one in which it incorporated, then the corporation has to qualify in that other state as a foreign corporation or:

- it can be fined,
- lose the privilege of using that state's courts, and
- the directors and officers can be opened up to personal liability.

However, most corporations do not want to be considered as doing business in another state unless they actually are because doing business in another state means paying additional filing fees, taxes, and/or the additional expense of defending lawsuits in a far-away location.

a. When Required

To determine whether the corporation should go ahead and qualify in a foreign state, it should be determined just how much and how long the corporation plans to do business in that state. In addition, it must be determined if what the corporation is doing in that state really constitutes doing business for purposes of having to qualify. If what the corporation is doing in that state does not qualify as doing business, then it will normally be cheaper for the corporation not to qualify in that state. Finally, the management of the corporation should consider what would be the effects of failing to qualify in that state if the corporation was found to be conducting business in that state. The corporation may receive substantial penalties.

Whenever a business moves into a foreign state, it can potentially subject itself to that state's courts. Typically, the corporation must have at least minimum contacts with the state in order to be subject to the court's jurisdiction in that state. Once the corporation is doing business in a foreign state, the corporation is required to have an agent for service of process that can receive litigation paperwork on behalf of the corporation. If the corporation fails to do this or does not keep its registered agent current, then the secretary of state will accept service on behalf of the corporation.

1. Requirements

To qualify, the corporation will probably need to obtain a certificate of authority from the foreign state (though rules vary from state to state). This is obtained by filing an application for it. It will need to be the application that is used in that state. Hopefully, the same name of the corporation in the domicile state is available to it in the foreign state. If not, the corporation may need to change its name in the foreign state. If the corporation wants to keep a substantially similar name, it could add a qualifier to its name such as "Blue Cross of California." "Of California" would be the qualifier in this instance. Another alternative would be to get the permission of the corporation with the name in the foreign state to use it. This might require paying the company that has precedence over the name in the state. In some way, the corporation will need to indicate that it is a corporation; the qualifier of "Corp." or "Inc."

would satisfy. The foreign state may also require a certificate of good standing from the domicile state before allowing the corporation to qualify.

b. What Constitutes Transacting Business?

In general there are several things that do not constitute transacting business, that the layperson might think do constitute doing business. For example, a corporation can participate in a lawsuit in a foreign state without that constituting business. The corporation can also decide to have a meeting in a foreign state without that constituting business. The corporation can open a bank account in a foreign state. This will not constitute the transacting of business. The corporation can sell through independent contractors and this will not constitute the transacting of business. Also, mail orders do not constitute doing business in a foreign state. There are very large loopholes in what does and does not constitute doing business, so many companies solely sell through independent contractors and/or mail order. The corporation can own property in a foreign state without it being considered doing business. An isolated transaction that is finished within thirty days and is not an action in the course of repeated transactions is also not considered doing business. So, this begs the question, just what is transacting business? It is conducting regular and continuous business of a similar nature in the foreign state for over thirty days.

c. Rights

The corporation that qualifies in a foreign state will in general be governed by the laws of its domicile state, except when those contradict those of the foreign state. The internal affairs of the corporation may still be governed by the domicile state. The foreign corporation will get service of process in the new state. It has to pay fees and taxes to the new state. The foreign corporation has to file annual reports with the new state.

d. Maintaining Good Standing as a Foreign Corporation

To maintain good standing, the corporation has to file:

- annual reports,
- pay the fees, and
- pay its taxes.

If the corporation does not, then the corporation could find its qualifications revoked in the foreign state. The corporation may even be given a warning about its failure to maintain good standing, and at that time should correct any deficiencies.

1. Negative Effects of Failing to Maintain Good Standing

One of the possible negative effects from failing to qualify is that the corporation may not be able to maintain or defend itself in a lawsuit in the state. In addition, the corporation can also be penalized monetarily for not being in good standing or properly qualifying. Other consequences could be holding that the corporation's contracts are not enforceable and its directors and officers may be subject to more liability.

e. Withdrawal as a Foreign Corporation

If the corporation was doing business in the state, the corporation should formally seek a withdrawal from the secretary of state in the foreign state if it no longer conducts business in that state. The withdrawal will end the corporation having to pay taxes or make reports in that state. In the form for withdrawal, the corporation will give a forwarding address. To obtain the withdrawal, the corporation must have paid all its taxes and fees that were owed.

Chapter Summary

Corporations are notably different from other types of business entities in that they are doubly taxed. First, if the corporation makes a profit, it pays a tax on that profit. If the corporation issues some of that profit to the shareholders as dividends, then the shareholders pay a second tax on that profit.

When there are material changes in the corporation, it may need to file an amendment to its articles. In particular, if there are changes to the stock, then the articles of incorporation need to be amended. This amendment should be filed with the secretary of state, and if shareholder consent is necessary, that should be garnered first.

Merger happens when two or even more corporations combine and one or more corporations cease to exist and one survives the merger. A majority of shareholders usually have to agree to a merger or share exchange, especially if the company is ending its existence or having its shares exchanged. If a shareholder does not agree, then he may be bought out, which is known as appraisal rights.

Share exchanges occur when one corporation buys all the shares of another corporation. Both corporations will legally exist. Usually, the corporation whose shares were bought becomes a subsidiary of the parent (or buying corporation).

Consolidation occurs when two companies combine, to form one new company, and neither one of the older companies survives the consolidation. The new company has all the assets and liabilities of the companies that started it.

Purchase of assets happens when a corporation buys all or a most of the assets of a selling corporation. The buying corporation does not typically have to get its own shareholders' approval, but the selling corporation does. A purchase of stock occurs when the buying corporation obtains a significant amount of shares of the selling corporation.

A hostile takeover can be attempted with either a tender offer or proxy contest. A tender offer happens when the aggressor goes over the head of the target's management, straight to the shareholders, and tries to get control of the target's shares. The Williams Act governs tender offers. A proxy contest occurs when the aggressor corporation attempts to have the target's shareholders vote for its management team. Hostile takeovers can be fended off with a variety of defenses. Ways in which to attempt to fend off a hostile takeover include poison pills, selling crown jewels, courting white knights, and conducting a Pac-Man defense.

Dissolution of the corporation is the corporation ceasing to exist. It can happen voluntarily, by the state dissolving it, or by a court dissolving it. In liquidation, all the corporation's assets are converted to cash and used to pay off creditors.

The location where a corporation is originally incorporated is known as the corporation's domicile. This holds true even if the corporation ends up doing most of its business in another state. A corporation is a foreign corporation for purposes of every state other than its state of domicile. To conduct business as a foreign corporation, the corporation must get a certificate of authority from each foreign state wherein it plans to conduct business. Once a corporation is seen as having at least minimum contacts with the foreign state, then it is subject to that state court's jurisdiction.

Key Terms

Accumulated earnings tax
Administrative dissolution
Aggressor corporation
Amendment of articles
Appraisal rights
Articles of dissolution
Articles of merger
Articles of share exchange
Consolidation
Crown jewels
Dissenting shareholder
Dissolution
Domestic corporation
Double taxation
Foreign corporation
Foreign state
Formalities
Golden parachute
Hostile takeover
Involuntary dissolution
Judicial liquidation
Known claim
Letter of intent

Liquidation
Liquidator
Merger
Nonjudicial liquidation
Nonprofit corporation
Pac-Man
Parent corporation
Plan of merger
Poison pill
Proxy contest
Purchase of assets
Receiver
Registered agent for service of
    process
S corporation
Share exchange
Short-form merger
Subsidiary
Suicide pact
Surviving corporation
Target corporation
Tender offer
To court a white knight

Transacting business   Voluntary dissolution
Unknown claim   Williams Act

Review Questions

1. How can a corporation avoid double taxation?

2. Explain how taxation works in an S Corporation.

3. What is required before a business can become an S corporation?

4. What percent of the shareholders have to agree to elect "S" status?

5. How is "S" status revoked?

6. Should the S Corporation have limitations on transferability? If so, why?

7. Why is the S Corporation as a business entity no longer as popular as it once was?

8. How is an S Corporation different from a C Corporation?

9. What are the main types of nonprofits?

10. If the nonprofit does make money for the year, what must it do with that money?

11. Is tax exemption automatic in a nonprofit? If not, then how is it obtained?

12. Does a nonprofit have a board of directors as well as bylaws?

13. Does a nonprofit have stock?

14. What are reasons to amend the Articles of Incorporation?

15. What are the major corporate changes?

16. Who typically has to approve major corporate changes?

17. What are the differences between merger and consolidation?

18. What are the differences between a purchase of assets and a merger?

19. What can a shareholder, who does not agree with a merger or purchase of assets, do?

20. Explain the concept of a hostile takeover.

21. What are some ways in which the target corporation can attempt to avoid a hostile takeover?

22. How does a corporation voluntarily dissolve?

23. Can a creditor force a corporation to dissolve?

24. What does the registered agent for service of process, in the foreign state, do for the corporation that qualifies to do business in that state?

25. Can the registered agent in the foreign state have a post office box as an address?

Web Links

For tax forms particular to nonprofits and S Corporations, go to http://www.irs.gov.

Go online and find a current article about a hostile takeover attempt. Determine what happened to the attempt.

You can also go directly to the Securities and Exchange Commission's website at http://www.sec.gov to check on their laws on corporate changes.

Exercises

1. ABC Corporation has not issued dividends in three years because it wants to put aside five hundred and fifty thousand dollars to grow its business. What is the issue with doing this?

2. Lady is a shareholder at the Palomino, Inc. This corporation wants to merge with Arabian Horses, Inc. Lady is not happy about the thought that Palominos and Arabian Horses could be interbred at the new merged corporation. However, she is in the minority of shareholders. What rights does she have?

3. Two corporations merge. Only one survives, Corporation B. A creditor of the nonsurviving corporation, Corporation A, sues Corporation B for Corporation A's debt. Does Corporation B legally have to pay?

4. If a corporation is solely selling through the internet, does it need to qualify in other states in order to sell via the internet?

5. Identify what type of corporate combination each of the following is:

   a. Stampco, Inc. and Labels 'R' Us combine their company and only Stampco, Inc. survives.

   b. Stampco, Inc. and Labels 'R' Us combine their companies, dissolve, and form a new corporation.

6. Why was the award in *Williams v. Stanford* not limited to appraisal rights?

Section V

The Business Entity as a Litigant

Chapter 15

The Business Entity as Defendant

Chapter Outline

Chapter Objectives

- Discuss the general rule on duty and breach of duty.
- Explain causation in negligence.
- Explain compensatory, punitive, and nominal damages.
- Differentiate between contributory and comparative negligence.
- Give the defenses to negligence.

- Outline three theories under which a products liability case can be brought.
- Overview employment discrimination, particularly the differences between disparate treatment and disparate impact.
- Introduce monopolies along with the relevant laws.

15.1 Introduction to the Business Entity as Defendant

In the chapter on agency, respondeat superior was discussed. A business entity can be held liable for the negligence of its employees while in the course and scope of their employment. A business can also be held responsible for the defective products it makes. Other issues the business entity may face as a defendant are employment discrimination and claims of being a monopoly. While there are other lawsuits against business entities, these are some of the main categories. An understanding of the types of litigation a business entity faces as a defendant is helpful if you plan to go into this area of law.

Behavior that is unreasonable, and leads to a compensable injury, is negligence. To prove negligence, a plaintiff would need to show that the business entity defendant had a duty to the plaintiff, the business entity breached that duty, this caused the injury, and there were damages. Each of these elements, as well as defenses will be discussed in more detail below.

15.2 Negligence

a. Duty

The first element of negligence is duty. A business entity must owe a duty to the plaintiff to use reasonable care. The duty of reasonable care requires the business entity to use the same amount of care that a reasonable business entity uses under the same circumstances, or similar circumstances. The duty is only owed to plaintiffs who foreseeably could be injured.

b. Breach

The next element of negligence is a breach of that duty. Was the business defendant a reasonable business entity to the plaintiff? If not, then there has been a breach. A reasonable business entity does not cause an accident by failing to pay attention. The business entity is judged upon the knowledge it had at the time of the injury.

There are two main tests for determining whether reasonableness has been breached. These are the Learned Hand[1] formula and the risk-utility formula. With

---

1. Learned Hand was the proper name of a judge who came up with this formula for breach of duty.

the Learned Hand formula, the test looks at whether the burden of taking precautions weighs more than the likelihood and possible severity of the harm. If the burden is high, then it is unlikely the defendant has breached his duty under this test. The risk-utility test is similar. If the enormity of the risk is greater than the utility of the action, then the defendant has breached his duty under this test.

c. Causation

Causation is another element of negligence. The business entity's actions must be the cause of the plaintiff's injury; otherwise, the business is not liable for negligence. There are two types of causation, both of which are required: actual and proximate cause.

The but-for and substantial factor tests are used to determine actual causation. The but-for test is that the plaintiff would not have been injured but for the defendant's negligence. If that is so, then the defendant actually caused the injury. The substantial factor test applies when there is more than one defendant and the other defendant's negligence contributed to the plaintiff's injury. Thus, the substantial factor test asks whether a defendant was a substantial factor in bringing about the harm to the plaintiff. If so, then the defendant is found liable. If one of the defendants cannot prove which defendant is most at fault, then they will each be found at fault.

Proximate cause is whether the plaintiff was a foreseeable plaintiff or not. Proximate cause looks at how closely connected the business entity defendant's actions were to the plaintiff's injuries. If the connection is a close one, then the business entity defendant will be liable. Proximity holds that it is not fair for a business entity defendant, to be found negligent if it is not reasonable that it should know its actions might cause harm.

d. Damages

The final element of negligence is damages. A damage is something that the plaintiff has lost, usually money, because of the incident. The point of damages is to try to restore the plaintiff as closely as possible to the place he was in before the injury.

There are compensatory damages, which are further divided into economic and non-economic damages, punitive damages, and nominal damages. In negligence though, compensatory damages are the most common and so will be discussed; punitive and nominal damages are uncommon in negligence, and thus, will not be discussed here.

Compensatory damages are the damages that try to put the plaintiff back into the place he would have been had the injury not happened. Thus, they will cover past and future medical bills, loss of wages, and sometimes pain and suffering, loss of consortium, or emotional distress. Economic damages are usually out-of-pocket damages, and can include medical bills, property loss, and lost earnings. Non-economic damages are pain and suffering, which are harder to prove. Loss of consortium is the damage one spouse may be entitled to by having his spouse injured and not receiving the benefits of marriage.

e. Defenses

Even if the plaintiff is able to prove all four elements of negligence, the defendant may have a defense. The major defenses to negligence, which are available to a business entity defendant, are contributory negligence, comparative negligence, assumption of the risk, and statutes of limitations. While not a full defense, the defendant may also argue that the plaintiff did not mitigate damages, which might reduce the damages the defendant has to pay. Under mitigation of damages, plaintiffs have a duty to seek prompt medical treatment and perform other tasks, which will lessen their potential injuries and reduce costs. Plaintiffs are expected to do this within reason.

Contributory negligence holds that if the plaintiff contributed in some way to her own injury, then she is not allowed to recover damages from the defendant. This is an extreme approach and not widely used anymore, other than in a few states. To abate some of the harshness of this rule, the last clear chance doctrine was implemented. This doctrine states that if the defendant could have avoiding harming the plaintiff at the last minute, then the defendant can be found liable. The plaintiff has to prove that the defendant had a last clear chance not to injure her, and he did not take it. Another doctrine, which abates some of the harshness of contributory negligence, is the sudden emergency doctrine. If there is a sudden emergency, then the plaintiff is not held to as high of a standard of care not to injure herself.

The vast majority of states now use some type of comparative negligence. Comparative negligence finds that even if the plaintiff did contribute to her injury, she may be able to recover against the defendant. The plaintiff's recovery would be reduced by the amount of her own negligence, depending on whether the state is a pure or modified comparative negligence state.

There are a few types of comparative negligence. Pure comparative negligence is one of the types. In pure comparative negligence, the plaintiff's damages against the defendant are reduced by the percentage of the plaintiff's own negligence, so long as she is ninety-nine or less percent at fault. Another type of comparative negligence is modified comparative negligence. In modified comparative negligence, the plaintiff has to be equally (50%) or less than equally (49%) negligent compared to the defendant in order to recover.

Another defense to negligence is assumption of the risk. If the plaintiff understands the dangers and willingly goes ahead and partakes in a dangerous activity, then she has assumed the responsibility for the outcome of her actions. Note that this particular plaintiff must both understand the danger and voluntarily accept it.

Assumption of the risk can be express or implied. Express would be the plaintiff signing a written waiver or stating that she assumes the risk. Implied assumption of the risk occurs when the plaintiff, through conduct, shows she accepts the risk.

Still another defense to negligence is that the plaintiff has not filed the cause of action within the applicable statute of limitations. Statutes of limitations are regulations on the length of time a plaintiff has in which to file a lawsuit. If the plaintiff does not bring her lawsuit within that time, then she is barred from bringing it.

15.3 Products Liability

Manufacturers and sellers of goods can be sued for injuries caused by those goods to a person. This is known as products liability. The manufacturer can still be held liable under products liability even if he was careful and used safety precautions. This is much more like strict liability than negligence. Part of the reason for this is that it the manufacturer of the product typically has more money to absorb the lawsuit than the consumer does.

a. The Parties

Before getting more into the different types of products liability, the parties in products liability should identified. Manufacturers make the product that causes the injury. Sellers put the defective products into the economy, for sale to the public. The person injured by the product is the ultimate user of the product. However, this is not always the same as the person who originally bought the product.

b. Recovery Theories

The three main types of products liability are negligence, breach of warranty, and strict liability. For negligence, the plaintiff will have to prove the four elements of negligence, discussed above, in regards to the defective product. However, this is not an easy way in which to prove products liability. The plaintiff has to show that the manufacturer or seller breached the duty of reasonable care, which may not be the case.

It is easier to bring a products liability case as a strict products liability case, because then the plaintiff does not have to show that the duty of reasonable care was breached. To prove a strict products liability case, the plaintiff has to show that the product's defect makes it unreasonably unsafe. Then, the plaintiff has to prove the element of the seller or manufacturer being in the business of selling these types of products. The third element the plaintiff has to show is that the product was not substantially altered from the time it left the manufacturer or seller until it reached the ultimate user. Although the plaintiff does not have to show breach of duty, he still has to show proximate cause. The fourth element of a strict products liability case is the product defect must have proximately caused the injury to the plaintiff. Last, but not least, the plaintiff has to prove that she used the product properly to recover under strict products liability. The Third Restatement of Torts instead bases products liability on the type of defect, such as warning, design, or manufacturing defects.

c. Breach of Warranty

Breach of warranty is the third way in which a plaintiff can sue in products liability. This is also strict liability. When a product is put up for sale, there are implied warranties such as the warranty of merchantability and the warranty of fitness of the product for a limited purpose. The warranty of merchantability just implies that the item has to be usable and safe for the ordinary purpose of the item. If it is not, then the plaintiff may be able to recover under breach of the warranty of merchantability. The warranty for fitness for a limited purpose is different; it applies when a consumer needs the product to work in a way for which it was not normally intended. The warranty comes when the seller tells the consumer that the product can be used in that new way. Thus, the seller must understand the purpose for which the consumer is going to use the product and the consumer must be relying on the seller's knowledge that the product can be used that way.[2]

In addition to implied warranties, there can also be express warranties with a product. An express warranty occurs when the seller makes representations to the consumer about the product. An assertion can be a representation, such as "these tires are safe." The seller could also make an express warranty when describing the product or when using samples of the products to demonstrate it. To be an express warranty, these representations have to be made before or during the sale, and not after the sale.

d. Restatement (Third) of Torts

There is also the Third Restatement of Torts approach to products liability, which the courts are moving towards, and so is discussed. The Restatement (Third) of Torts looks at products liability from a defects standpoint: design, manufacturing, or warning defects. A design defect occurs at the design of the product. Thus, all the products would be defective. To prove a design defect case, the plaintiff has to prove that the risk of the defective design is greater than the benefit of that design, as well as that there was a reasonable alternative to the bad design. With a manufacturing defect, one of the products, during the manufacturing process did not conform to the rest of the products. That nonconformity makes that particular product defective. With a warning defect, the plaintiff is stating that there were not sufficient warnings or directions for the products. The warnings are only required for unobvious dangers of the product. The warning has to be a reasonable size and use the appropriate language or symbols to show a reasonable user of the product what the dangers are.

e. Defenses

Contributory negligence is not a defense to products liability, but assumption of the risk can be. Product misuse by the ultimate user is a defense particular to products liability. If the ultimate user misused the product substantially, in an unreasonably unforeseen manner, then she is not entitled to recover under products liability. An act of a third person can also be a defense to products liability. For instance, if the third party greatly abused the product, especially when contrasted to the original defect, then the manufacturer or seller may not be found liable. Finally, statutes of limitations are also a defense to product liability cases.

---

2. Uniform Commercial Code, Section 2-315.

15.4 Employment Discrimination

Title VII of the Civil Rights Act of 1964 can be utilized against employers with fifteen or greater employees. It can also sometimes cover labor unions. It covers all employment agencies, local and state governments with more than fifteen employees, and federal agencies.

The goal of Title VII is to stop job discrimination due to "race, color, religion, national origin, or sex."[3] Unless there were bona fide occupational qualifications, then it is against the law to discriminate on these traits. Discrimination in the job due to these traits could include firing, not hiring, not paying appropriately, or not giving equal working conditions. It could also include promoting or demoting, benefit payments, job training, and referrals. With religion, an employer (unless religiously affiliated), must make reasonable accommodation for the religious beliefs of its employees. There can also be other exceptions for military veterans.

The employee has to prove several things to win a lawsuit under the Civil Rights Act, Title VII, including that the employer had an illegal discriminatory basis. The employee must also show that he was not treated the same, or that there was what was known as disparate treatment. This must be intentional. The employer can try to rebut the disparate treatment by showing that there was a business necessity to it. Another way the employee can show discrimination is through proving there was retaliation. The employer is not allowed to fire the employee for making a discrimination claim.

The agency that is supposed to enforce this is the Equal Employment Opportunity Commission, also known as the EEOC. The statute of limitations for bringing a Title VII private complaint is within one hundred and eighty to three hundred days of the discrimination.

The states may still have their own fair employment laws. In 1991, the Civil Rights Act made it possible to get compensatory and/or punitive damages against an employer, up to three hundred thousand dollars per employee. The employee may be able to get his job back as well as any back pay owed him.

Another area of concern in discrimination is age discrimination. The Age Discrimination in Employment Act prohibits discrimination based on age. This protection is for employees forty or more years old. Typically, these employees cannot be forced to retire mandatorily.

a. Disparate Treatment Discrimination

When a person is treated less well than others are because of race, color, nationality, gender, or religion, then that is considered disparate treatment discrimination. The employer must be intentionally discriminating against the victim. To win a disparate treatment discrimination case, the disparately treated party has to prove several things. The party has to prove that they are in a protected class under Title VII. The

---

3. http:// www.eeoc.gov/ laws/ statutes/ index.cfm.

party has to prove both that they applied for and were qualified for the job. The party has to prove that they were not selected despite applying and being qualified. Finally, the party has to prove that even though they applied and were qualified, the employer kept trying to fill the position with other applicants who had the same qualifications.

b. Disparate Impact Discrimination

The point of disparate impact discrimination laws is that they are supposed to prevent disparate effect, even when a policy does not have an intent of being discriminatory. Even when a neutral sounding employment qualification is used, if this discriminates against a whole class of protected people, then this is known as disparate impact discrimination. Since the discrimination is against a class of people, this type of lawsuit will often be brought as a class action.

There might be statistical information about whom the employer hires, which could help prove the disparate impact discrimination. However, if a protected class were represented in an equal percentage to that in which it shows up in the United State population, then this would not be disparate impact discrimination.

To defend itself from a disparate impact discrimination allegation, the employer just has to show a reasonable factor other than the reason alleged was the reason behind the disparate impact discrimination.

c. Federal Laws Prohibiting Age and Disability Discrimination

The ADEA stands for Age Discrimination in Employment Act. This act was instituted to prohibit age discrimination in hiring, promotions, pay, etc. To be covered under the ADEA, an employer must not be a federal employer and must have twenty or more employees. Labor unions are also covered under the ADEA if they have twenty-five or more employees. Employment agencies are subject to the ADEA. Local and state government workers are covered for the most part, and some federal employees are covered.

The ADEA prevents discrimination toward people forty-years and older. The EEOC also regulates age discrimination. The following case gives the prima facie information necessary for an ADEA claim. After making the prima facie case, once the employer proffers a nondiscriminatory reason, the plaintiff only has to show that whatever other reason given for firing the plaintiff is only a pretext and that age was a determining factor, to prove liability under the ADEA.

Cash Distributing Co. v. Neely
947 So. 2d 286 (2007)

James A. Neely sued his former employer, Cash Distributing Company, Inc. ("Cash"), claiming he was dismissed because of federally prohibited age discrimination. The jury returned a verdict in Neely's favor, and Cash appealed, urging us to either set aside the verdict because Neely failed to rebut every nondiscriminatory reason offered at trial for the dismissal, or to allow a set-off for the amount of retirement benefits paid to Neely subsequent to his termination. Neely cross-appealed, claiming he was entitled to additional damages.

A sharply divided Court of Appeals affirmed the trial court's decision as to Cash's appeal and affirmed in part and reversed and remanded in part as to Neely's cross-appeal.... Although we find the Court of Appeals reached the correct conclusion in this case, we granted certiorari to address the appropriate allocation of the burdens of proof (both production and persuasion) to be followed in our trial courts in employment discrimination cases.

BACKGROUND FACTS AND PROCEEDINGS

Cash, is a regional Mississippi beer wholesale distributorship for Anheuser-Busch products, with offices in Starkville, Columbus, and Tupelo. The distributorship is a family-owned business founded in Columbus by the late Marvin and Emily Cash, whose grandson, Danny Cash ("Danny"), currently serves as CEO and equity owner. Cash operates pursuant to its distributorship agreement with the brewery, Anheuser-Busch ("the Brewery") in St. Louis, Missouri.

In 1973, Marvin hired Neely, who began a twenty-seven-year climb up the ladder at Cash. In 1996, Neely — who had served for ten years as Sales Manager — was considered for promotion to General Manager of Cash's Columbus operations. Marvin and his son, Mike Cash, who was the executive vice-president, voted in favor of promoting Neely, and Danny, who had just been named vice president, cast the sole dissenting vote.

According to Danny, when his grandfather hired Neely, there was a casual attitude at Cash, and the rules set by the Brewery were often relaxed or ignored. However, in 1997, the Brewery began a new approach to raise its wholesalers up to a minimum standards level. The new approach involved "assessments" which included a visit to the wholesaler by a Brewery representative each spring. At the conclusion of the visit, the Brewery representative provided a list of deficiencies to be addressed. The Brewery then followed up with another visit in the fall to determine whether the identified problems had been addressed and alleviated.

In April 1997, the Brewery's market manager visited Cash's Columbus operation for an assessment and provided a list of issues and problems to be addressed. Immediately after this visit, Danny issued a three-page, single-spaced memorandum to Neely pointing out these issues and demanded that Neely address them before the Brewery's follow-up visit in the fall. The topics listed included customer survey, employee survey, community involvement, standard operating procedures, employee training jacket, assessment manual main books, and steering team. The memo also addressed the need for a market plan.

The following year, Marvin died, and Danny became Cash's CEO. He announced that, due to the new requirements imposed by the Brewery upon its distributors, he intended to strictly enforce the policies and rules. These changes included strict documentation requirement in preparation for the Brewery's periodic assessments and evaluations of Cash's operations.

Danny began to require Neely to submit daily call sheets disclosing where he had been and what he had done each day, and to submit regular written evaluations of the employees who worked for him in the Columbus operation. Danny also instituted a "ride-with" policy, requiring managers (such as Neely) to ride in the truck and visit customers with Cash's salespersons. At trial, Neely testified he understood that the Brewery required these and other technological changes.

Neely frequently failed to timely complete his duties as assigned by Danny, often refusing to complete them at all. In fact, Neely freely admitted at trial that he refused to do tasks for Danny that he often happily did for Marvin. Danny's father, Mike, testified that Neely simply did not want to take orders from Danny. Despite being ordered to provide monthly evaluations on employees, Neely refused to do so. Neely testified that he might have submitted three evaluations on one of the employees from June 14, 1996, to March 3, 2000. Danny abandoned his efforts to obtain the required monthly evaluations, and he directed Neely to provide quarterly evaluations. These Neely also refused to complete. He also declined to use the required tracking forms to prevent out-of-date beer from being sold by Cash's customers.

Danny's evaluations of Neely included both criticism and praise. For instance, in the January evaluation, Danny told Neely he needed to work with team leaders on setting up on-premises promotions. In Neely's February evaluation, Danny stated, "[k]eep up the great job of reducing expenses." Danny's August 1998 evaluation of Neely began with praise: "The accounts I did visit looked really good. We really dominated the cooler displays and other aspects of the business. The trucks have looked good rolling down the road and the warehouse has been clean each time I visited." However, later in the memo, Danny stated, "[i]n order to provide more value vs. 'twenty years of service' the positions need to keep adding abilities, not seniority. This is not a social security system."

In the "game plan" for 1999—while Neely was the general manager of Cash's Columbus operations—Danny stated, "I'm very pleased with the overall direction the impact has given the Columbus operation." Then, in a document Danny prepared called "Jim Neely Time Line," when referring to an employee named Tony Carley who worked for Cash, Danny noted, "[h]e was later promoted to supervisor and actually did most of the work for the other too [sic] much older supervisors that were riding their time out."

In early 2000, Neely rode with one of his salesmen, Mickey Lewis, to visit his accounts. After the visits, neither Lewis nor Neely reported finding any out-of-date product at the customer locations. Soon thereafter, on March 3, 2000, Danny called Neely into a conference and terminated his employment with Cash, replacing him with Carley who, at that time, was 38 years old.

Neely filed suit against Cash in the Circuit Court of Lowndes County, alleging violation of the Age Discrimination in Employment Act ... and at the conclusion of the trial, the jury returned a verdict for Neely and awarded him $120,000.00 in back pay. The jury also found that Cash's violation of the ADEA was not willful....

Cash timely perfected its appeal, claiming it was entitled to judgment notwithstanding the verdict because Neely failed to rebut all of the nondiscriminatory reasons Cash presented at trial for his dismissal, and that, in any case, the verdict should be offset by $208,896.66 in retirement benefits paid to Neely after he was terminated. Neely cross-appealed, claiming as error the trial court's refusal to grant him an additur or new trial on damages, front pay, prejudgment and post-judgment interest, costs, and attorney fees.

In a majority opinion written by Judge Irving on behalf of a five-judge majority, the Court of Appeals affirmed the trial court on Cash's direct appeal and affirmed in part Neely's cross-appeal, conditioned on Cash's acceptance of an additur in the amount of $58,754; however the majority reversed and remanded on the trial court's failure to grant prejudgment interest.

In 1967, the United States Congress passed the ADEA, which "prohibit[s] arbitrary age discrimination in employment." ... Specifically, the ADEA makes it "unlawful for an employer to ... discharge any individual ... because of such individual's age...."

A plaintiff wishing to establish an employer's liability for violation of the ADEA may bring the claim in state or federal court.... When a plaintiff brings an ADEA claim in our state courts, we are bound to apply the law as interpreted by the United States Supreme Court....

In setting forth the standard of review for this case, we borrow the following from the Court of Appeals:

> When reviewing the denial of a motion for judgment notwithstanding the verdict, we consider the evidence in a light most favorable to the non-moving party (in this case, Neely). We also give the non-moving party the 'benefit of all favorable inference [sic] that may be reasonably drawn from the evidence.'... We will reverse only if the evidence 'points so overwhelmingly in favor of the moving party [in this case, Cash] that reasonable jurors could not have found in favor of the non-moving party....

In bringing an ADEA claim, the plaintiff must follow a precise scheme, or allocation, of the burdens of proof (both production and persuasion). Our analysis of these burdens and their application in this case must begin with a review of United States Supreme Court precedent.

In *McDonnell Douglas Corp. v. Green,* ... the Supreme Court squarely addressed what it called the "critical issue" of "the order and allocation of proof in a private, non-class action challenging employment discrimination." The *McDonnell Douglas* Court explained that "[t]he complainant in a Title VII trial must carry the initial burden under the statute of establishing a prima facie case of racial discrimination.... The burden then must shift to the employer to articulate some legitimate, nondiscriminatory reason for the employee's rejection." If that burden is met, the employee must then "be afforded a fair opportunity to show that [the employer's] stated reason for [the employee's] rejection was in fact pretext...."

Eight years later, the Supreme Court provided additional explanation in *Texas Department of Community Affairs v. Burdine*.... The *Burdine* Court began by restating its holding in *McDonnell Douglas*:

> First, the plaintiff has the burden of proving by the preponderance of the evidence a prima facie case of discrimination. Second, if the plaintiff succeeds in proving the prima facie case, the burden shifts to the defendant 'to articulate some legitimate, nondiscriminatory reason for the employee's rejection.'... Third, should the defendant carry this burden, the plaintiff must then have an opportunity to prove by a preponderance of the evidence that the legitimate reasons offered by the defendant were not its true reasons, but were a pretext for discrimination....

... The *Burdine* Court then clarified *McDonnell Douglas* by explaining that

> [t]he nature of the burden that shifts to the defendant should be understood in light of the plaintiff's ultimate and intermediate burdens. The ultimate burden of persuading the trier of fact that the defendant intentionally discriminated against the plaintiff remains at all times with the plaintiff. The *McDonnell Douglas* division of intermediate evidentiary burdens serves to bring the litigants and the court expeditiously and fairly to this ultimate question....

Where a plaintiff establishes a prima facie case, discrimination is presumed unless the employer provides a nondiscriminatory explanation for the adverse employment action. This is so because the acts establishing the prima facie case, "if otherwise unexplained, are more likely than not based on the consideration of impermissible factors...."

The *Burdine* Court went further to state that "[i]f the trier of fact believes the plaintiff's evidence, and if the employer is silent in the face of the presumption, the court must enter judgment for the plaintiff because no issue of fact remains in the case." ... However, where the employer does "carr[y] [its] burden of production, the presumption raised by the prima facie case is rebutted, and the factual inquiry proceeds to a new level of specificity."

The foregoing is a fair statement of the United States Supreme Court's guidance on the subject as of 1981. The question which remained unanswered, however, was whether a Title VII plaintiff who presented a prima facie case, but offered no rebuttal to nondiscriminatory reasons offered by the employer, could nonetheless prevail. We find the confusion related to this question arises from some courts' misreading of the Supreme Court's holdings in *McDonnell Douglas* and *Burdine*. There appears to be an inconsistent understanding and application of the concept of rebutting the employer's nondiscriminatory explanation for terminating the aggrieved employee.

III.

We do not read *McDonnell Douglas* and *Burdine* to require a Title VII (or ADEA) plaintiff to rebut with specific evidence each and every nondiscriminatory reason offered by an employer for the termination. We do read them to say that "the plaintiff must then have an opportunity to prove by a preponderance of the evidence that the legitimate reasons offered by the defendant were not its true reasons, but were a pretext for discrimination".... Requiring courts to provide this opportunity is, we think, quite different from saying that the plaintiff must present specific rebuttal evidence as to each nondiscriminatory reason for the dismissal.

The confusion, as demonstrated by the briefing provided to us in this case, arises from *Wallace v. Methodist Hospital System*.... In *Wallace,* the United States Court of Appeals for the Fifth Circuit held that, once an employer provides evidence of a nondiscriminatory reason for the plaintiff's termination, "'the plaintiff must produce substantial evidence of pretext.'" *Wallace* next states that "[t]he plaintiff must put forward evidence rebutting each of the nondiscriminatory reasons the employer articulates." *Wallace* cites two additional Fifth Circuit cases and one case from the Court of Appeals for the Seventh Circuit for the proposition that a plaintiff "'must present facts to rebut each and every legitimate non-discriminatory reason advanced by [her employer] in order to survive summary judgment....'"

We note that the Fifth Circuit's minority position that the employee rebut "each and every" nondiscriminatory reason proffered by the employer has been adopted by three other courts of appeals. However, we are unable to find any statutory support for the proposition, nor do we find it espoused or approved by any decision of the United States Supreme Court.

While this Court often defers to Fifth Circuit decisions interpreting federal law, we are under no obligation to do so.... We will not hesitate to take a different path where we conclude it is necessary to comport with controlling precedent from the United States Supreme Court.

IV.

We find the plaintiff's burden of rebutting the employer's nondiscriminatory reasons for termination is clearly described by the following statement in *Burdine*:

> A satisfactory explanation by the defendant destroys the legally mandatory inference of discrimination arising from the plaintiff's initial evidence. Nonetheless, this evidence and inferences properly drawn therefrom may be considered by the trier of fact on the issue of whether the defendant's explanation is pretextual. Indeed, there may be some cases where the plaintiff's initial evidence, combined with the effective cross-examination of the defendant, will suffice to discredit the defendant's explanation.

... We are also persuaded by another United States Supreme Court decision which found the Fifth Circuit approach too restrictive. In *Reeves v. Sanderson Plumbing Products, Inc...*, the Supreme Court explained that the Fifth Circuit concluded that petitioner 'very well may be correct' that 'a reasonable jury could have found that [respondent's] explanation for its employment decision was pretextual.' Nonetheless, the court held that this showing, standing alone, was insufficient to sustain the jury's finding of liability: 'We must, as an essential final step, determine whether Reeves presented sufficient evidence that his age motivated [respondent's] employment decision.' And in making this determination, the [Fifth Circuit] ignored the evidence supporting petitioner's prima facie case and challenging respondent's explanation for its decision.... [T]he [Fifth Circuit] proceeded from the assumption that a prima facie case of discrimination, combined with sufficient evidence for the trier of fact to disbelieve the defendant's legitimate, nondiscriminatory reason for its decision, is insufficient as a matter of law to sustain a jury's finding of intentional discrimination. In so reasoning, the [Fifth Circuit] misconceived the evidentiary burden borne by plaintiffs who attempt to prove intentional discrimination through indirect evidence.

... The Court went on to specifically stress

'[t]he factfinder's disbelief of the reasons put forward by the defendant (particularly if disbelief is accompanied by a suspicion of mendacity) may, together with the elements of the prima facie case, suffice to show intentional discrimination. Thus, rejection of the defendant's proffered reasons will *permit* the trier of fact to infer the ultimate fact of intentional discrimination.'

... Cash argues that Neely failed to rebut every nondiscriminatory reason offered for his termination. We take Cash's argument to mean that Neely had to offer proof that each of the events Cash claims led to his dismissal did not actually happen. For instance, under Cash's view of the rebuttal requirement, once Cash asserts it terminated Neely because he refused to fill out certain forms, Neely must come forward with some proof that he actually did fill out the forms. It is this view of the rebuttal requirement that we find unduly restrictive and without foundation in any employment discrimination decision from the United States Supreme Court. Indeed, the language quoted above from *Reeves* that "[t]he fact finder's disbelief of the reasons put forward by the defendant" does not require the factfinder to disbelieve a particular event occurred, but rather requires the factfinder to find that — *even if it did occur* — it was not the *motivating reason* for the dismissal. The jury in this case could very well have found that all of Danny's testimony about Neely's insubordination, while true, was not the real reason for Neely's dismissal....

It is not enough, of course, for Neely simply to make the claim. He must produce some proof which persuades the jury that the true reason for his termination was impermissible age discrimination. And because Neely did exactly that in this case, that is, he produced evidence which persuaded the jury that the real motivation for his dismissal was impermissible age discrimination rather than the reasons proffered by Cash, we must leave the jury verdict undisturbed unless we find that, viewing the evidence in the light most favorable to Neely, no reasonable, rational juror could have reached the same conclusion....

V.

In light of this precedent, we decline to follow the Fifth Circuit's view that an ADEA plaintiff must specifically rebut each and every nondiscriminatory reason offered by the employer its adverse employment action. Instead, we shall now fulfill our duty to set forth the test to be used in our state courts for determination of ADEA claims. This test is not new, but is simply a restatement of the test as pronounced and discussed in the United States Supreme Court precedent cited herein, and a rejection of the test set forth by the Fifth Circuit in *Wallace*.

First, an ADEA plaintiff must establish a prima facie case by showing (1) he or she was a member of the class protected by the ADEA ("individuals who are at least 40 years of age,"…, (2) he or she was otherwise qualified for the position, (3) he or she suffered an adverse employment action, and (4) he or she was replaced by a substantially younger person.…

Once an ADEA plaintiff establishes a prima facie case (assuming the factfinder believes the facts establishing the prima facie case are true), a presumption arises that the employer engaged in impermissible discrimination, and absent some response by the employer, judgment must be entered for the plaintiff.

If the employer responds by proffering nondiscriminatory reasons for the employment decision, the employee must be afforded an opportunity to submit additional evidence that the nondiscriminatory reasons offered by the employer were pretextual, and that the employment decision was motivated by impermissible discrimination.… In responding to a particular nondiscriminatory reason proffered by the employer, the plaintiff may claim either that the event never happened at all, or that the event did, in fact, happen, but was not the true reason for the adverse employment decision.…

The plaintiff may, of course, offer additional evidence of discrimination, such as the employer's verbal or written comments indicating a discriminatory animus. The plaintiff may also offer additional evidence of pretext, such as evidence that the reason offered by the employer for the adverse employment decision also applied to other employees who were not subjected to the same punishment.

The jury must consider all of the evidence submitted at trial and determine whether the motivating factor for the employer's action was impermissible discrimination. In other words, even though several factors may have contributed to the adverse employment action, if the jury finds that the employee would not have been terminated or subjected to the adverse employment decision absent impermissible discrimination, the plaintiff should prevail.…

VI.

Cash does not contest that Neely established a prima facie case of discrimination under the ADEA. Instead, Cash claims it discharged Neely for the nondiscriminatory reasons of insubordination and his failure to discover and report out-of-date product on a particular occasion while riding with a salesman. Neely might have claimed that this event never happened at all, which would have served as evidence to rebut Cash's proffered reason for termination. Had this happened, the jury would have been free to believe whichever version of the facts it found credible, and the matter would have proceeded to verdict.

Instead, Neely did not deny that most of the events claimed by Cash occurred. However, Neely offered substantial evidence that these events were not the reason for his termination. For instance, Neely offered evidence that despite Cash's claims of insubordination and poor performance, his operation in Columbus received perfect scores following several evaluations by the Brewery. Neely also offered evidence that out-of-date product was fairly common and that the extremely meticulous audit of his territory was unprecedented, amounting to (according to another witness) a "witch hunt."

Additionally, Neely offered evidence showing that Danny possessed discriminatory animus toward him. This and other evidence of discrimination offered by Neely is fairly set forth in Judge Irving's majority opinion submitted on behalf of the Court of Appeals....

The jury in this case obviously credited Neely's account of his dismissal and the evidence supporting it over explanations supplied by Cash. This Court has no basis to disturb that decision on appeal. The jury was free to find that even if, as Cash claimed, Neely had been insubordinate, that justification was pretextual based on evidence of unequal treatment, age-related statements made by Cash's CEO, and the impeachment of Cash's witnesses. As Judge Irving stated, "[t]he responsibility of determining what evidence is credible and what is not is the proper province of the jury." ... A motion for judgment notwithstanding the verdict must be denied where "there is substantial evidence in support of the verdict, that is, evidence of such quality and weight that reasonable and fair-minded jurors in the exercise of impartial judgment might have reached different conclusions." ... Such is the case here....

The Americans with Disabilities Act was instituted in 1990 to help stop disability discrimination. Towards this end, employers cannot normally require a pre-employment medical examination or ask about the prospective employee's medical past. Note that once the job has been offered, then the employer can require the employee to undergo either of these. An employer can ask about whether an applicant can perform the tasks that are required by the job, prior to employing the applicant.

So what exactly does the ADA prevent? Employers cannot discriminate against employees with a current disability, a past disability, or a perceived disability. The employer must have more than fifteen or more employees and it cannot discriminate regarding hiring, promoting, firing, paying, training, etc.

What is considered a disability? The Americans with Disabilities Act states that a disability is "any physical or mental impairment that substantially limits one or more of an individual's major life activities." To be disabled, the person must have this type of impairment, have historical evidence of the impairment, and be viewed as having the impairment. Physical or mental impairment could come from disease, amputation, psychological problems, mental problems, etc. The major life activities include walking, talking, learning, breathing, and working. Drug and alcohol abusers are not protected under the ADA.

In addition, employers should make reasonable accommodations so that qualified disabled (those who could perform the essential job functions with or without reasonable accommodation) can work. Reasonable accommodations could include providing more handicapped access or even training. If the employer would suffer undue hardship (i.e. through expense), then it may not have to provide the accommodation. If the employer violates reasonable accommodations, then the employer may have to hire, reinstate, pay back pay, and/or pay compensatory/punitive damages.

The EEOC also regulates the ADA. To file, the injured party has to file with the EEOC first. The EEOC can decide to sue the employer itself, or to let the employee do it.

d. Defenses to Employment Discrimination

To defend itself against an employment discrimination case, the employer will first claim the plaintiff failed to prove discrimination happened. Defenses to employment discrimination include bona fide occupational qualifications, merit, and seniority. A bona fide occupational qualification is a necessary job qualification. An example of a bona fide occupational qualification is that a women's fashion magazine might only use female models to show off the clothes.

15.5 Antitrust Law

Before we can discuss antitrust law, we need to understand what a trust is. A trust is a monetary or fiduciary relationship regarding property. One person in the relationship is known as the trustee. The trustee has title to the property, but has to use the property for the benefit of the beneficiary of the trust.

Courts look at two main things when applying antitrust law (this is in addition to the Sherman or Clayton Acts). The court will look at what is known as the rule of reason and per se illegality. In the rule of reason, courts can only hold contracts in restraint of trade are illegal if the contract in restraint has *undue* or *unreasonable* restraints. Whether a contract is reasonable or not depends upon the nature and circumstances surrounding the contract. In essence, if the contract helps destroy competition, it will be held illegal.

Some contracts are so anticompetitive on their face that they are presumed illegal. This is known as illegal per se. Contracts may be held illegal per se wherein the contracts between competitors discuss pricing and territories where each company can sell. This means that those violations are considered automatic violations.

a. Monopoly

In the past, corporations could use a trust to create a monopoly. The trust would let all or most of the stock of many companies be transferred to a trustee. The trustee could then control all of these companies. The trustee could set the price of the products. Hence, because the price was controlled, there really was not an open or free marketplace. A monopoly is illegal if it is obtained using wrongful tactics.

b. Activities Prohibited by the Sherman Act and Clayton Act

Anti-trust laws break up these monopolistic trusts. The Sherman Act was enacted in 1890. In essence, the Sherman Act promotes competition in the marketplace. The Sherman Act forbids contracts that restrain trade or commerce. The Sherman Act also forbids monopolies. The fact that there is a monopoly is not enough to hold the company responsible. Sometimes a monopoly is not sought, but just happens. So long as the company does not try to enforce or widen the monopoly, it is usually not found in violation of the Sherman Act. The monopoly must normally be a deliberate action to be illegal. The question then becomes, what is deliberative action? Predatory conduct constitutes this type of action. In predatory conduct, the company wants to get more market share and does so by injuring current or future competitors. The injury has to be caused by something other than the predatory company's improved performance. Sometimes this can be indicated by selling products for too low an amount.

The Sherman Act legislates price fixing. Price fixing happens when competitors agree to charge the same amount of money for their similar products. To violate the Sherman Act, the actions must have occurred in or have a substantial effect on interstate commerce. Other major types of lawsuits under the Sherman Act are territorial contracts and concerted actions.

When competitive companies make a contract to fix prices, this is dubbed horizontal price fixing. It does not matter if the price was reasonable. The Sherman Act also applies to providers of services. If accountants in an area have an agreement to charge a set price, this can be price fixing. However, there are exclusions to this. Price-fixing is considered a per se violation of the Sherman Act.

On the other hand, there is vertical price fixing. This occurs when the manufacturer tries to control the resale price of its manufactured goods. This is when there is an agreement between the manufacturer and the seller of the goods. If there is coercion in doing so, then this will be illegal; otherwise, the practice is normally held as legal. In addition, it is okay to charge a lesser price if the costs are lower for servicing this buyer or the seller is trying to match prices with his competition. However, if the goods are the same and the price discrimination does cut out competition, then it will be illegal.

Territorial agreements occur when competitors try to fix trade within a geographical area. These can either be horizontal or vertical trade agreements. When competitors agree to exclusive territories amongst themselves, this is known as horizontal territorial agreement. When a manufacturer and distributor agree to a distributor having an exclusive territory, it is known as a vertical territorial agreement. A vertical territorial agreement is not automatically against the law. It would be subject to the rule of reason, which looks at whether the restraint on trade is unreasonable or not.

Still, there can be more permanent measures taken between companies to effect a monopoly, which includes mergers and joint ventures. An important thing to note however, is that not all businesses are subject to the Sherman Act. Insurance companies may be excluded as may be investment companies. There are other exclusions as well, such as activities required by the state.

However, the Sherman Act had several major failings, among them that it was not a very clear act. Thus, in 1914, the Clayton Act was added as an amendment to the Sherman Act. The Clayton Act went through more revisions as well. The Clayton Act and the Sherman Act overlap substantially, as the Clayton Act, in part, was instituted to make the Sherman Act clearer. At the same time as the Clayton Act, Congress instituted the Federal Trade Commission Act. The FTC and the Justice Department can enforce antitrust laws, but only the Justice Department can bring criminal charges. Individuals can sue for damages. The overall effect of the Clayton Act was to outlaw actions that could substantially lessen competition or actions which tend to cause a monopoly. Some of the specific things the Clayton Act looks at are price discrimination, special arrangements, and mergers/ acquisitions.

Price discrimination is illegal if different prices are charged to different buyers of goods when that lessens competition substantially or tends to cause a monopoly. However, it still allows for discrimination in pricing if due to the different quality or quantity sold.

If a company has many assets, then it should let the Federal Trade Commission know it plans to merge. What punishment is imposed if a company violates the Sherman Act or its amendment, the Clayton Act? There are several different options. First, there can be criminal fines and even prison time. This crime carries a stiff penalty, as it is a felony. The maximum fine is one million dollars and the maximum jail time (which can be in addition to the fine) is ten years. This is if the illegal act is performed by an individual. If the act is performed by a company, the fine can be as much as ten million dollars. There can be an injunction. The purpose of the injunction here is to stop the violations of the Acts. It is easier to get an injunction in this instance than criminal penalties. There can be a form of punitive damages in that the injured company may get triple damages. Finally, property owned in violation and moving in interstate commerce can be taken by the United States government.

The Robinson-Patman Amendment was added to the Clayton Act in the 1930s. The purpose of this amendment was to try to lessen the advantage large purchasers have in bulk buying over smaller purchasers. This would then aid small stores against large retail chains. However, this amendment only applies to interstate commerce, not intrastate; it also only applies to the sale of goods. In addition, the government has not been heavily enforcing the Robinson-Patman Act. The Federal Trade Commission has the authority to regulate this. The Robinson-Patman Amendment also made predatory pricing illegal. Predatory pricing occurs when the price is lower than the marginal cost. The company that sells below that price is willing to take the hit to drive out competition. There are certainly many exceptions to this, such as cutting prices due to seasonal changes, when goods are about to go bad, or discontinued items. A seller can also choose to price match.

The amendment also covers special arrangements such as reciprocal dealing and exclusive dealing. Reciprocal dealing occurs when a buyer and seller agree to buy each other's goods. Exclusive dealing happens when one party agrees to buy only from the other party.

The following case is about an alleged monopoly due to driving up the price of a good.

Weyerhaeuser Co. v.
Ross-Simmons Hardwood Lumber Co.
127 S.Ct. 1069 (2007)

Respondent Ross-Simmons, a sawmill, sued petitioner Weyerhaeuser, alleging that Weyerhaeuser drove it out of business by bidding up the price of sawlogs to a level that prevented Ross-Simmons from being profitable. A jury returned a verdict in favor of Ross-Simmons on its monopolization claim, and the Ninth Circuit affirmed. We granted certiorari to decide whether the test we applied to claims of predatory pricing in *Brooke Group Ltd. v. Brown & Williamson Tobacco Corp.,* ... also applies to claims of predatory bidding. We hold that it does. Accordingly, we vacate the judgment of the Court of Appeals.

I

This antitrust case concerns the acquisition of red alder sawlogs by the mills that process those logs in the Pacific Northwest. These hardwood-lumber mills usually acquire logs in one of three ways. Some logs are purchased on the open bidding market. Some come to the mill through standing short- and long-term agreements with timberland owners. And others are harvested from timberland owned by the sawmills themselves. The allegations relevant to our decision in this case relate to the bidding market.

Ross-Simmons began operating a hardwood-lumber sawmill in Longview, Washington, in 1962. Weyerhaeuser entered the Northwestern hardwood-lumber market in 1980 by acquiring an existing lumber company. Weyerhaeuser gradually increased the scope of its hardwood-lumber operation, and it now owns six hardwood sawmills in the region. By 2001, Weyerhaeuser's mills were acquiring approximately 65 percent of the alder logs available for sale in the region....

From 1990 to 2000, Weyerhaeuser made more than $75 million in capital investments in its hardwood mills in the Pacific Northwest.... During this period, production increased at every Northwestern hardwood mill that Weyerhaeuser owned.... In addition to increasing production, Weyerhaeuser used "state-of-the-art technology," ... including sawing equipment, to increase the amount of lumber recovered from every log.... By contrast, Ross-Simmons appears to have engaged in little efficiency-enhancing investment....

Logs represent up to 75 percent of a sawmill's total costs.... And from 1998 to 2001, the price of alder sawlogs increased while prices for finished hardwood lumber fell. These divergent trends in input and output prices cut into the mills' profit margins, and Ross-Simmons suffered heavy losses during this time.... Saddled with several million dollars in debt, Ross-Simmons shut down its mill completely in May 2001....

Ross-Simmons blamed Weyerhaeuser for driving it out of business by bidding up input costs, and it filed an antitrust suit against Weyerhaeuser for monopolization and attempted monopolization under §2 of the Sherman Act.... Ross-Simmons alleged that, among other anticompetitive acts, Weyerhaeuser had used "its dominant position in the alder sawlog market to drive up the prices for alder sawlogs to levels that severely reduced or eliminated the profit margins of Weyerhaeuser's alder sawmill competition." ... Proceeding in part on this "predatory-bidding" theory, Ross-Simmons argued that Weyerhaeuser had overpaid for alder sawlogs to cause sawlog prices to rise to artificially high levels as part of a plan to drive Ross-Simmons out of business. As proof that this practice had occurred, Ross-Simmons pointed to Weyerhaeuser's large share of the alder purchasing market, rising alder sawlog prices during the alleged predation period, and Weyerhaeuser's declining profits during that same period....

II

In *Brooke Group,* we considered what a plaintiff must show in order to succeed on a claim of predatory pricing under §2 of the Sherman Act. In a typical predatory-pricing scheme, the predator reduces the sale price of its product (its output) to below cost, hoping to drive competitors out of business. Then, with competition vanquished, the predator raises output prices to a supracompetitive level.... For the scheme to make economic sense, the losses suffered from pricing goods below cost must be recouped (with interest) during the supracompetitive-pricing stage of the scheme.... Recognizing this economic reality, we established two prerequisites to recovery on claims of predatory pricing. "First, a plaintiff seeking to establish competitive injury resulting from a rival's low prices must prove that the prices complained of are below an appropriate measure of its rival's costs." ... Second, a plaintiff must demonstrate that "the competitor had ... a dangerous probabilit[y] of recouping its investment in below-cost prices...."

The first prong of the test — requiring that prices be below cost — is necessary because "[a]s a general rule, the exclusionary effect of prices above a relevant measure of cost either reflects the lower cost structure of the alleged predator, and so represents competition on the merits, or is beyond the practical ability of a judicial tribunal to control." ... We were particularly wary of allowing recovery for above-cost price cutting because allowing such claims could, perversely, "chil[l] legitimate price cutting," which directly benefits consumers.... Thus, we specifically declined to allow plaintiffs to recover for above-cost price cutting, concluding that "discouraging a price cut and ... depriving consumers of the benefits of lower prices ... does not constitute sound antitrust policy...."

The second prong of the *Brooke Group* test—requiring that there be a dangerous probability of recoupment of losses—is necessary because, without a dangerous probability of recoupment, it is highly unlikely that a firm would engage in predatory pricing. As the Court explained in *Matsushita*, a firm engaged in a predatory-pricing scheme makes an investment—the losses suffered plus the profits that would have been realized absent the scheme—at the initial, below-cost-selling phase.... For that investment to be rational, a firm must reasonably expect to recoup in the long run at least its original investment with supracompetitive profits.... Without such a reasonable expectation, a rational firm would not willingly suffer definite, short-run losses. Recognizing the centrality of recoupment to a predatory-pricing scheme, we required predatory-pricing plaintiffs to "demonstrate that there is a likelihood that the predatory scheme alleged would cause a rise in prices above a competitive level that would be sufficient to compensate for the amounts expended on the predation, including the time value of the money invested in it...."

We described the two parts of the *Brooke Group* test as "essential components of real market injury" that were "not easy to establish." ... We also reiterated that the costs of erroneous findings of predatory-pricing liability were quite high because "'[t]he mechanism by which a firm engages in predatory pricing—lowering prices—is the same mechanism by which a firm stimulates competition,'" and therefore, mistaken findings of liability would ""'chill the very conduct the antitrust laws are designed to protect....'"""

III

Predatory bidding, which Ross-Simmons alleges in this case, involves the exercise of market power on the buy side or input side of a market. In a predatory-bidding scheme, a purchaser of inputs "bids up the market price of a critical input to such high levels that rival buyers cannot survive (or compete as vigorously) and, as a result, the predating buyer acquires (or maintains or increases its) monopsony power." ... Monopsony power is market power on the buy side of the market.... As such, a monopsony is to the buy side of the market what a monopoly is to the sell side and is sometimes colloquially called a "buyer's monopoly...."

A predatory bidder ultimately aims to exercise the monopsony power gained from bidding up input prices. To that end, once the predatory bidder has caused competing buyers to exit the market for purchasing inputs, it will seek to "restrict its input purchases below the competitive level," thus "reduc[ing] the unit price for the remaining input[s] it purchases." ... The reduction in input prices will lead to "a significant cost saving that more than offsets the profit[s] that would have been earned on the output." ... If all goes as planned, the predatory bidder will reap monopsonistic profits that will offset any losses suffered in bidding up input prices....

Predatory-pricing and predatory-bidding claims are analytically similar.... This similarity results from the close theoretical connection between monopoly and monopsony.... The kinship between monopoly and monopsony suggests that similar legal standards should apply to claims of monopolization and to claims of monopsonization. . . .

Tracking the economic similarity between monopoly and monopsony, predatory-pricing plaintiffs and predatory-bidding plaintiffs make strikingly similar allegations. A predatory-pricing plaintiff alleges that a predator cut prices to drive the plaintiff out of business and, thereby, to reap monopoly profits from the output market. In parallel fashion, a predatory-bidding plaintiff alleges that a predator raised prices for a key input to drive the plaintiff out of business and, thereby, to reap monopsony profits in the input market. Both claims involve the deliberate use of unilateral pricing measures for anticompetitive purposes. And both claims logically require firms to incur short-term losses on the chance that they might reap supracompetitive profits in the future. . . .

More importantly, predatory bidding mirrors predatory pricing in respects that we deemed significant to our analysis in *Brooke Group*. In *Brooke Group*, we noted that "'predatory pricing schemes are rarely tried, and even more rarely successful.'" . . . Predatory pricing requires a firm to suffer certain losses in the short term on the chance of reaping supracompetitive profits in the future. . . . A rational business will rarely make this sacrifice. The same reasoning applies to predatory bidding. A predatory-bidding scheme requires a buyer of inputs to suffer losses today on the chance that it will reap supracompetitive profits in the future. For this reason, "[s]uccessful monopsony predation is probably as unlikely as successful monopoly predation. . . ."

And like the predatory conduct alleged in *Brooke Group*, actions taken in a predatory-bidding scheme are often "the very essence of competition." . . . Just as sellers use output prices to compete for purchasers, buyers use bid prices to compete for scarce inputs. There are myriad legitimate reasons — ranging from benign to affirmatively procompetitive — why a buyer might bid up input prices. A firm might bid up inputs as a result of miscalculation of its input needs or as a response to increased consumer demand for its outputs. A more efficient firm might bid up input prices to acquire more inputs as a part of a procompetitive strategy to gain market share in the output market. A firm that has adopted an input-intensive production process might bid up inputs to acquire the inputs necessary for its process. Or a firm might bid up input prices to acquire excess inputs as a hedge against the risk of future rises in input costs or future input shortages. . . . There is nothing illicit about these bidding decisions. Indeed, this sort of high bidding is essential to competition and innovation on the buy side of the market.

Brooke Group also noted that a failed predatory-pricing scheme may benefit consumers. . . . The potential benefit results from the difficulty an aspiring predator faces in recouping losses suffered from below-cost pricing. Without successful recoupment, "predatory pricing produces lower aggregate prices in the market, and consumer welfare is enhanced." . . . Failed predatory-bidding schemes can also, but will not necessarily, benefit consumers. . . . In the first stage of a predatory-bidding scheme, the predator's high bidding will likely lead to its acquisition of more inputs. Usually, the acquisition of more inputs leads to the manufacture of more outputs. And increases in output generally result in lower prices to consumers. Thus, a failed predatory-bidding scheme can be a "boon to consumers" in the same way that we considered a predatory-pricing scheme to be....

In addition, predatory bidding presents less of a direct threat of consumer harm than predatory pricing. A predatory-pricing scheme ultimately achieves success by charging higher prices to consumers. By contrast, a predatory-bidding scheme could succeed with little or no effect on consumer prices because a predatory bidder does not necessarily rely on raising prices in the output market to recoup its losses.... Even if output prices remain constant, a predatory bidder can use its power as the predominant buyer of inputs to force down input prices and capture monopsony profits....

The general theoretical similarities of monopoly and monopsony combined with the theoretical and practical similarities of predatory pricing and predatory bidding convince us that our two-pronged *Brooke Group* test should apply to predatory-bidding claims.

The first prong of *Brooke Group's* test requires little adaptation for the predatory-bidding context. A plaintiff must prove that the alleged predatory bidding led to below-cost pricing of the predator's outputs. That is, the predator's bidding on the buy side must have caused the cost of the relevant output to rise above the revenues generated in the sale of those outputs. As with predatory pricing, the exclusionary effect of higher bidding that does not result in below-cost output pricing "is beyond the practical ability of a judicial tribunal to control without courting intolerable risks of chilling legitimate" procompetitive conduct.... Given the multitude of procompetitive ends served by higher bidding for inputs, the risk of chilling procompetitive behavior with too lax a liability standard is as serious here as it was in *Brooke Group*. Consequently, only higher bidding that leads to below-cost pricing in the relevant output market will suffice as a basis for liability for predatory bidding.

A predatory-bidding plaintiff also must prove that the defendant has a dangerous probability of recouping the losses incurred in bidding up input prices through the exercise of monopsony power. Absent proof of likely recoupment, a strategy of predatory bidding makes no economic sense because it would involve short-term losses with no likelihood of offsetting long-term gains.... As with predatory pricing, making a showing on the recoupment prong will require "a close analysis of both the scheme alleged by the plaintiff and the structure and conditions of the relevant market...."

Ross-Simmons has conceded that it has not satisfied the *Brooke Group* standard....

c. Federal Agencies Enforcing Antitrust Laws

The agency in charge of enforcing the Clayton act is the Federal Trade Commission or FTC. The Federal Trade Commission has a lot of discretion. It has to determine whether actions are unfair methods of competition. To do so, it looks at whether consumers will be harmed substantially; if the acts are against public policy; and if the acts are unethical or oppressive. The main goal of the FTC is prevention. It can issue cease and desist orders.

Chapter Summary

Defendants are required to use reasonable care not to injure the plaintiff, otherwise, they can be found liable for negligence. The four elements of negligence are duty, breach of that duty, causation, and damages. The duty the defendant has is a reasonable person duty. The defendant needs to act as a reasonable person would towards the plaintiff. The defendant must have actually caused the plaintiff's injury, which can be judged either by using the but-for test or the substantial factor test. But-for the defendant's negligence, the plaintiff would not have been harmed. With the substantial factor test, there were two or more acts, which caused the harm to the plaintiff. This test asks: Was the defendant a substantial factor in causing the harm to the plaintiff? There also needs to be proximate cause to show causation. Was it reasonable for the defendant to believe he might have injured this plaintiff? If yes, then there is proximate cause.

The main damages recovered in negligence cases are compensatory damages, which are meant to compensate the plaintiff for the injury. Compensatory damages can be broken down into further categories of general and special damages. General damages are damages that occur naturally as a result of this type of injury. Special damages are damages that are specific to this particular plaintiff.

While products liability is a difficult subject matter to master, many manufacturing business entities are finding themselves subject to lawsuits of this nature. There are three main parties in products liability: the manufacturer, the seller, and the ultimate user. If a strict products liability case is instituted, then the plaintiff will have to show the product is defective, the defect makes the product unreasonably unsafe, the manufacturer or seller was in the business of selling that product, the product was not substantially changed, there is proximate cause, and the ultimate user did not misuse the product.

Products liability cases can also sue under breach of warranty, such as the warranty of merchantability or the warranty of fitness for a limited purpose. The first warranty holds that the product has to be safe for ordinary use. The second warranty states that if the seller tells the buyer that the product can be used for a specific purpose, then the product must be useable for that purpose.

The Restatement (Third) of Torts handles products liability cases differently. It looks at design, manufacturing, and warning defects. Design defects are at the design level and all products in that line have the same defect. Manufacturing defects are at the manufacturing level and only that product in the line has the defect. Warning defects deal with whether there were proper warnings or instructions on how to use the product.

The Civil Rights Act of 1964 holds that there should not be job discrimination based upon race, color, religion, gender, or nationality. Employers with greater than fifteen employees are typically covered, as are employment agencies, labor unions, local and state government, and federal government. These employees should not be discriminated against in hiring, promoting, demoting, compensation, benefits, and training. There are two types of Civil Rights Act of 1964, Title VII actions: disparate treatment discrimination and disparate-impact discrimination. Disparate treatment discrimination happens when an employer treats one person poorly due to their race, color, religion, gender, or nationality. Disparate impact discrimination occurs when the employer discriminates against an entire class of people that fits under a particular race, color, religion, gender, or nationality. Defenses to these types of actions include bona fide occupational qualifications (BFOQ), merit, and seniority. A BFOQ is a qualification that is required for the job. The Age Discrimination in Employment Act (ADEA) protects job applicants and employees who are forty years old or older.

There are two major types of violations of antitrust laws: per se ones and rule of reason violations. Per se violations are considered automatic. Rule of reason violations are illegal if they are anticompetitive.

Horizontal price fixing is illegal, at least when selling goods. Competitors should not try to agree on a low price or a high price, as both are illegal. Price-fixing is known as a per se violation of the Sherman Act. The Clayton Act regulates anti-competitive mergers.

The Robinson-Patman Agreement holds that it is illegal to sell the same goods to buying competitors at different prices, unless there are different costs in servicing differing buyers. However, this only applies to goods moved within interstate commerce. It is illegal for a competitor to try to remove the competition by selling at very low prices.

Key Terms

Actual cause
Affirmative action
Age Discrimination in Employment
    Act (ADEA) of 1967
Americans with Disabilities Act
    (ADA)
Assumption of risk
Bona fide occupation qualification
    (BFOQ)
Breach of duty
Breach of warranty
Business necessity defense
But-for test
Civil Rights Act of 1964
Clayton Act
Comparative fault
Compensatory damages

Contributory negligence
Defective warning
Design defect
Disparate impact
Disparate treatment
Employment discrimination
Equal Employment Opportunity
    Act of 1972
Equal Employment Opportunity
    Commission (EEOC)
Express assumption of the risk
Express warranty
Foreseeability
Foreseeable plaintiff
Foreseeable use
Horizontal price fixing
Horizontal territorial agreement

Implied assumption of the risk
Implied warranty
Intended use
Last clear chance
Learned Hand formula
Loss of consortium
Manufacturer
Manufacturing defect
Manufacturing warranty
Mitigation of damages
Modified comparative negligence
Monopoly
Out-of-pocket expenses
Pain and suffering
Per se illegality
Predatory pricing
Price fixing
Products liability
Protected class
Proximate cause
Punitive damages
Qualified individual with a disability
Reasonable accommodation

Reasonable care
Reasonable person standard
Reciprocal dealing
Restatement of Torts
Restraint of trade
Risk-utility test
Reverse discrimination
Rule of reason
Seller
Sherman Act
Substantial factor test
Title VII of the Civil Rights Act of
  1964
Ultimate or end user
Unreasonably dangerous
Vertical price fixing
Vertical territorial agreement
Warning defect
Warranty
Warranty of fitness for a particular
  purpose
Warranty of merchantability

Review Questions

1. What are the elements of negligence?

2. Who is a reasonable person?

3. What is the risk-utility formula?

4. Explain loss of consortium.

5. Why is contributory negligence sometimes considered harsh?

6. What are proper defenses to products liability?

7. What is the difference between state antidiscrimination laws and federal antidiscrimination laws?

8. What is the prima facie case for an ADEA claim?

9. What agency is responsible for regulating antitrust laws?

10. Are territorial agreements always illegal?

11. In *Weyerhauser Co. v. Ross-Simmons Hardwood Lumber Co.*, what are the prerequisites to get damages for predatory pricing?

Web Links

Visit the Equal Employment Opportunity Site to learn more about the EEOC; http://www.eeoc.gov. Specifically, go to http://www.eeoc.gov/facts/accommodation.html for information on how small employers need to handle the ADA.

Exercises

1. An employment agency only hires Filipinos. The agency has eleven employees, who work across the country. Is this a violation of the 1964 Civil Rights Act, Title VII?

2. If a women's clothing store will not hire male salespeople, who would attend customers in the women's dressing room, is this a violation of Title VII?

3. If a group of dealers finds that a manufacturer sells to competitors cheaper, is this in violation of the Robinson-Patman Act?

Chapter 16

The Business Entity as Plaintiff

Chapter Outline

Chapter Objectives

- Differentiate between suretyship and guaranty.

- Provide remedies outside of bankruptcy that the creditor can use.

- Discuss secured transactions in personal property.

- Delineate the bankruptcy process.

- List the priority in which creditors are paid.

- Outline the major business torts.

16.1 Introduction to the Business Entity as Plaintiff

Businesses can also find themselves as plaintiffs in lawsuits. Two of the biggest areas in which a business can be a plaintiff in (other than intellectual property, which was discussed in Chapter 3) are bankruptcy and business torts such as:

- misrepresentation,
- interference with contract,
- interference with prospective business advantage, and
- unfair competition.

If you are going into this area of law, it is of benefit to understand the instances when a business entity might be a plaintiff.

16.2 Suretyship and Guaranty

Suretyship and guaranty are involved when a third party agrees to pay on behalf of another, and then does not pay. Specifically a surety is a third person who agrees to be liable for the debt. The creditor can sue the third person for repayment of the loan. In a guaranty, the third party is secondarily liable after the person who incurred the debt. Thus, the creditor can only go after the guaranty once he has gone after the primary debtor. In either event, the surety or guarantor has a right of reimbursement from the debtor. However, if the creditor was unable to get the money, the surety or guarantor will be unlikely to as well.

In the following case, is Kennedy treated more like a surety or a guaranty?

JSV, Inc. v. Hene Meat Co., Inc.

794 N.E.2d 555 (2003)

… On August 30, 1999, JSV, Inc. ("JSV") signed a lease to rent a portion of a building in Indianapolis from Hene. Kennedy signed the lease on behalf of JSV as one of that corporation's officers. In addition, Kennedy signed a document simply denominated "GUARANTY." Appellant's App. p. 30. The document indicated that it was "an absolute and unconditional guaranty" of the lease's performance by JSV and that the guaranty would not be affected by any modifications or alterations of the lease.… Kennedy's printed name and signature on the document are not followed by any corporate officer designation.

JSV stopped paying rent to Hene in September 2000. On June 5, 2001, Hene sued both JSV under the lease and Kennedy under the guaranty. Hene mailed a summons and copy of the complaint to Kennedy's last known address in Georgia, and also sent a process server to Georgia who posted the summons and complaint at that address.

On April 16, 2002, Hene moved for summary judgment. Kennedy's first response to this motion came on August 27, 2002, when he attempted to file designated evidence that included affidavits by himself and JSV's president, Joseph S. Vuskovich. At the summary judgment hearing conducted on September 3, 2002, the trial court granted Hene's motion to strike this response. On September 9, 2002, the trial court denied Kennedy's motion to dismiss Hene's complaint, which had alleged, inter alia, that he had never been properly served. On that same day, the trial court also granted Hene's summary judgment motion and entered judgment against both JSV and Kennedy personally for the sum of $75,041.07. Kennedy alone now appeals....

III. Grant of Summary Judgment

The final argument of Kennedy's that we address is whether the trial court erred in granting summary judgment in favor of Hene on its claim that Kennedy was personally liable under the guaranty he executed. Our standard of review of the grant or denial of a motion for summary judgment is the same as that used in the trial court: summary judgment is appropriate only where the evidence shows that there is no genuine issue of material fact and that the moving party is entitled to judgment as a matter of law.... All facts and reasonable inferences drawn from those facts are construed in favor of the nonmoving party.

"The interpretation of a guaranty is governed by the same rules applicable to other contracts." ... Absent ambiguity, the terms of a contract will be given their plain and ordinary meaning and will not be considered ambiguous solely because the parties dispute the proper interpretation of the terms...."Generally, construction of a written contract is a question of law for the trial court for which summary judgment is particularly appropriate." ... Whenever summary judgment is granted based upon the construction of a written contract, the trial court has either determined as a matter of law that the contract is not ambiguous or uncertain, or that the contract ambiguity, if one exists, can be resolved without the aid of a factual determination....

We conclude that the guaranty Kennedy executed was unambiguously a personal guaranty, notwithstanding the fact that the word "personal" does not appear in the document. It is axiomatic under Indiana law that a guaranty agreement must consist of three parties: the obligor, the obligee, and the surety or guarantor.... Here, Hene as landlord under the lease was the obligee and JSV as the tenant was the obligor; the disputed issue is the identity of the guarantor. Kennedy claims he signed both the lease *and* the guaranty as an officer of JSV.

However, there would have been no point in Hene's obtaining Kennedy's guaranty of the lease if he was doing so only in his official capacity as an officer of JSV. Such an action would have been equivalent to JSV guaranteeing JSV's performance of the lease and to JSV being both the obligor under the lease and the guarantor under the guaranty. As we have previously held in a factually similar case, such a result would be paradoxical and untenable.... In *Kordick,* we concluded that where a corporate officer executed a guaranty with respect to credit extended to the corporation, the guaranty was a personal one and the officer personally was the guarantor despite the fact that the officer placed his corporate title after his signature on the guaranty.... We further concluded that this was apparent as a matter of law and summary judgment on the issue was appropriate.... In this case, the guaranty is even more clearly a personal one than was the case in *Kordick* because Kennedy's signature thereon is not followed by any corporate officer designation. The trial court did not err in concluding that the guaranty Kennedy executed was a personal one as a matter of law and in granting summary judgment against Kennedy personally.

Conclusion

The trial court did not err in striking Kennedy's untimely summary judgment.... Additionally, it properly concluded that Kennedy was personally liable to Hene on the guaranty he executed for any breach of the underlying lease by JSV. We affirm.

16.3 Creditors' Remedies/Collecting Debts

Creditors have the right to take possession of collateral. The creditor can hold onto the collateral, waiting for payment, or may turn around and sell the collateral. The creditor does not have to use the courts to get the collateral so far as he obtains the collateral peacefully. To do so peacefully, the creditor cannot:

- trespass,
- commit assault or battery, and
- cannot break or enter onto property.

If the creditor does not do so peacefully, he may be prevented from seeking the collateral in the future. In addition, the creditor needs to have a legal contract.

The holder of a mortgage can foreclose on the real property if the mortgagee does not pay. Depending upon the sale price of the property, this may more than satisfy the debt, just cover the debt, or not satisfy the debt.

The creditor has other rights he may exercise if he does not want to resort to forcing a bankruptcy. The creditor could put a lien against property. One of the more common types of liens is a mechanic's lien. This type of lien deals with labor or materials that were utilized in improving land/homes. If the creditor is not paid, then he can file for a mechanic's lien against the real property. Another common type of lien is a judicial lien. If the debtor does not pay, and the creditor successfully applies to the court, then the court will award the debt and costs to the creditor. To satisfy this debt, then the creditor will need to seek a writ of attachment, which would allow him to seize property to pay off the debt. Yet another common type of lien is known as garnishment. Garnishment deals with collecting property of the debtor that is in the hands of a third party. Wage garnishment is probably the most known type of garnishment. In the following case, note the leeway a creditor has in wage garnishment.

Indiana Surgical Specialists v. Griffin

867 N.E.2d 260 (2007)

Indiana Surgical Services ("Indiana Surgical") appeals the small claims court's decision that the earnings Helen Griffin received as an independent contractor for MDS

Courier Services ("MDS") could not be garnished. Although Griffin was an independent contractor, she received periodic payments for her personal services, which payments were earnings that could be garnished. – ISSUE

FACTS AND PROCEDURAL HISTORY

In March 2001, Indiana Surgical obtained a default judgment against Griffin. In 2005, Indiana Surgical learned Griffin worked for MDS. It filed a motion for proceedings supplemental and named MDS as garnishee-defendant. MDS did not respond to the motion or answer interrogatories included with the motion. On December 16, 2005, after MDS failed to appear, the small claims court issued a Garnishment Order. The order required MDS to "withhold from the earnings of" Griffin, (App. at 12), the appropriate amount until the total debt was paid.

On December 29, 2005, MDS responded to the order in a letter to the clerk of the court:

> JMB-MDS Courier Services, Inc. employs drivers on a "contract" basis, therefore, drivers are not actual employees, but rather "contracted" to do a particular job. Because of this, we are not responsible for any payroll deductions including garnishments.

It is therefore the sole responsibility of the individual to make such restitutions....

On June 23, 2006, Indiana Surgical sought to have MDS held in contempt because it had not garnished its payments to Griffin. At a hearing in July 2006, Dawn Klingenberger, the manager of the local MDS office, testified Griffin was a subcontractor of MDS and MDS called her as needed. Griffin was compensated per job at "thirty-five percent of whatever she does," (Tr. at 7), and paid on a bi-weekly basis. After the hearing, the small claims court entered the following order: ."The Court finds that [MDS] is not in contempt of the previously issued Garnishment Order. [MDS] presented evidence that the judgment debtor is a subcontractor, and not an employee. [Indiana Surgical] may pursue and [sic] Order of Attachment against [MDS]." (App. at 19.) · RULE

DISCUSSION AND DECISION

Indiana Surgical argues the trial court erred by declining to enforce the garnishment order issued to MDS on the ground Griffin was a "subcontractor" and not an employee of MDS. Indiana Surgical asserts the trial court's "distinction between wages subject to withholding and other earnings" is not supported in law.... Under the facts of this case, we agree.

Garnishment refers to "any legal or equitable proceedings through which the earnings of an individual are required to be withheld by a garnishee, by the individual debtor, or by any other person for the payment of a judgment." ... The "garnishment of the earnings of an individual," ... is addressed in Ind. Code ch. 24-4.5–5.

Earnings are "compensation paid or payable for personal services, whether denominated as wages, salary, commission, bonus, or otherwise, and includes periodic payments under a pension or retirement program." … In discussing the federal counterpart to the Indiana statute, the Supreme Court stated: "There is every indication that Congress, in an effort to avoid the necessity of bankruptcy, sought to regulate garnishment in its usual sense as *a levy on periodic payments of compensation* needed to support the wage earner and his family on a week-to-week, month-to-month basis.…"

Griffin received "periodic payments of compensation" for her personal services as a courier. These payments were earnings that could be garnished through a garnishment order. The trial court erred to the extent it held otherwise. We reverse and remand for further proceedings including, but not limited to, a determination of MDS's liability for payments made to Griffin after Indiana Surgical acquired an equitable lien upon service of process in proceedings supplemental. In light of our holding, the trial court should also determine whether MDS should be held in contempt of the garnishment order. · - conclusion

Reversed and remanded.

16.4 Secured Transactions in Personal Property

A secured debt is simply one that is guaranteed by personal property owned by the debtor. Thus, a security interest is an interest in that personal property. The Uniform Commercial Code, Section 9, deals with secured transactions. To understand secured transactions better, it is important to know some definitions used in this area of law. A secured party just has a security interest in the debtor's personal property that is being used as collateral. A debtor is the person who owes money. Collateral is the personal property (or other property) that holds the security interest. Sometimes, creditors will file a statement to give the public notice that they have an interest in the collateral.

If a creditor has a secured debt, then he can recoup the debt through obtaining possession of the personal property securing the debt, such as a car that secures a car loan. In addition, this creditor has priority over other creditors who have rights in the same personal property.

To have a legitimate security interest, the creditor has to either have possession of the personal property or have a security agreement that discusses the security interest in the personal property. The secured party has to have given originally the debtor something of value; going back to the car loan, this would be the car. The debtor has to have rights to the collateral.

A creditor is going to want to perfect his security interest to protect it against other creditors who claim rights to the same collateral. This is done by filing a statement, which puts the public on notice. This is one of the more common ways to perfect, though it can sometimes be performed without filing, for example, by possession.

16.5 Bankruptcy

Paralegals need to know a little about bankruptcy if they go into corporate law. Often, when the corporation is dissolving, it is because the corporation is going bankrupt. The paralegal would then be expected, in all likelihood, to help with this process. Bankruptcy is handled entirely in the federal courts and not state courts.

It is important to realize that there are many different types of bankruptcy. The major types are Chapter 7, Chapter 9, Chapter 11, Chapter 12, or Chapter 13. Chapter 7 is liquidation and is usually for individuals. Chapter 9 is for cities that file for bankruptcy, and since this is not a common type of bankruptcy for a corporate paralegal to practice, it will not be discussed here. Chapter 11 allows a company, typically, to reorganize. Chapter 12 applies to family farmers, and since this is also not a common type of bankruptcy for a corporate paralegal to practice, it will not be discussed here. Finally, Chapter 13 is an individual's reorganization. A debtor may have more than one chapter available to him under which to file or he may even change which chapter he is filing under after he has already filed.

Bankruptcy allows debts to be discharged. This means the debtor does not have to pay those debts anymore. However, some types of debts cannot be discharged in Chapter 7:

- student loans given by the government;
- some taxes;
- debts that were not listed on the petition;
- alimony;
- child support;
- drunk driving injuries, etc.

In addition to these types of debts that a debtor cannot discharge, there are other reasons why a debtor may not be able to discharge a debt. If a business entity continues to stay open after its bankruptcy, it has to pay the debts it tried to discharge in bankruptcy. If a debtor was fraudulent, then the bankruptcy court can revoke the bankruptcy charge for up a year after the discharge. Once a debtor has filed for Chapter 7 or Chapter 11 and received a discharge, he cannot obtain another discharge under Chapter 7 for eight more years.

a. Priority Disputes among Creditors

The bankruptcy court looks at the parties and then the claims in order to determine payment. A party who has a perfected security interest is going to be paid first, over an unsecured creditor and an unperfected secured party. If there are two or more perfected security interests, then the bankruptcy court typically will give money to the first one to perfect priority.

In attempt to be fair, the bankruptcy court pays claims in a certain order: secured claims first, priority claims second, and unsecured claims third. There are seven subsets of priority claims, as indicated below. These prioritized claims are paid out in order from one to seven. There are three types of unsecured claims, but they are all treated equally: secured claims for the current value of the security that are less than what is owed; priority claims that are over the priority limits are allowed; and all other unsecured claims. The prioritized claims are:

1. Alimony and child support;

2. Administrative expenses incurred in bankruptcy;

3. Gap expenses incurred in running a business until the order for relief;

4. Employee wages up to ten thousand, nine hundred and fifty dollars and employee benefits;

5. Consumer deposits, meaning refunds for deposits made to a going bankrupt business;

6. Taxes; and

7. Drunk driving injuries.

b. Debtor Protection

People filing for bankruptcy protection get to keep some exempt assets. Each state can decide what exempt property it will let individuals keep. Some states follow the federal exemptions that would allow the debtor to exempt twenty-two thousand, nine hundred and twenty-five hundred dollars of the value of her home. If the home is worth more, then the house could be sold and the debtor will obtain the twenty-two thousand, nine hundred and twenty-five hundred in cash. Many states allow the debtor to keep his home, household items, automobiles, disability benefits, and alimony.

As part of debtor protection, the debtor can ask for an accounting of his unpaid debt to verify that the amount of the debt is accurate. The creditor or secured party has to comply with this request, or can be liable for damages. In addition, once the debtor has paid off the debt, then he is supposed to be given a termination statement.

c. Steps in a Bankruptcy Proceeding

Bankruptcy starts with a petition. The petition can be voluntary, meaning it is filed by the debtor, or it can be involuntary, meaning it could be filed by the debtor's creditors. Any person or business entity that either resides, conducts business, or owns property in the U.S. can file under Chapter 7. Other chapters are not so inclusive. Bankruptcy Court is federal district court. The petition is assigned a bankruptcy judge.

A person who files for bankruptcy has to undergo credit counseling before filing. To file Chapter 7, a person has to earn less than the median income in the state he lives in. There are requirements that must be met for a creditor to file an involuntary petition. One of these is the debtor must owe equal to or greater than a certain amount in unsecured claims to the creditor who filed.

Once either a voluntary or an involuntary petition is filed, then the judge goes ahead and produces an order for relief. A bankruptcy trustee collects the debtor's assets and divides them among the creditors. There is a meeting of creditors, and the debtor or bankrupt party must attend and answer questions posed to him. Unsecured creditors, after the meeting, must file a proof of claim. An automatic stay starts once the petition is filed. The debtor's property now becomes part of the bankruptcy estate, which is separate from the debtor.

d. Liquidation Proceedings

Liquidation does not necessarily require a bankruptcy. Chapter 7 is the step to take when the debtor cannot work out a plan under Chapter 11 or 13. The debtor's assets, where possible, will be converted to cash and the creditors will be paid out of that. However, after the debtor's current assets are liquidated, the debtor does not have to pay any further on the debts. In *Hebbring*, the plaintiff was not allowed to claim payments made to a retirement plan were exempt from being liquidated. Why is that?

Hebbring v. U.S. Trustee
463 F.3d 902 (2006)

We must decide whether a debtor seeking protection under Chapter 7 of the Bankruptcy Code may ever include voluntary contributions to a retirement plan as a reasonably necessary expense in calculating his disposable income. We hold that the Bankruptcy Code does not disallow such contributions per se, but rather requires courts to examine the totality of the debtor's circumstances on a case-by-case basis to determine whether retirement contributions are a reasonably necessary expense for that debtor. In this case the bankruptcy court did not clearly err in finding that Lisa Hebbring's voluntary retirement contributions are not a reasonably necessary expense based on her age and financial circumstances, and thus that she has sufficient disposable income to repay her creditors. We therefore affirm the district court's decision affirming the bankruptcy court's dismissal of Hebbring's petition on the ground that allowing her to proceed under Chapter 7 would be a substantial abuse of the Code.

… Lisa Hebbring filed a Chapter 7 bankruptcy petition in the United States Bankruptcy Court for the District of Nevada on June 5, 2003, seeking relief from $11,124 in consumer credit card debt. Her petition and accompanying schedules show that Hebbring owns a single-family home in Reno, Nevada valued at $160,000, on which she owes $154,103; a 2001 Volkswagen Beetle valued at $14,000, on which she owes $18,839; and miscellaneous personal property valued at $1,775. Hebbring earns approximately $49,000 per year as a customer service representative for SBC Nevada.

Her petition reports monthly net income of $2,813 and monthly expenditures of $2,897, for a monthly deficit of $84. In calculating her income, Hebbring excluded a $232 monthly pre-tax deduction for a 401(k) plan and an $81 monthly after-tax deduction for a retirement savings bond. When she filed for bankruptcy Hebbring was thirty-three years old and had accumulated $6,289 in retirement savings.

The United States Trustee ("Trustee") moved to dismiss Hebbring's petition for substantial abuse, *see* 11 U.S.C. § 707(b), arguing that she should not be allowed to deduct voluntary retirement contributions from her income and that her recent paystubs showed that her gross income was higher than she had claimed. As a result, the Trustee contended, Hebbring's monthly net income was actually $3,512, leaving her $615 per month in disposable income, sufficient to repay 100% of her unsecured debt over three years.

Opposing the Trustee's motion, Hebbring argued that her recent paystubs were not representative of her monthly income because they included overtime and pre-mium wages received during a one-time sales promotion. She further stated that her petition mistakenly omitted veterinary expenses and homeowner's association and insurance fees, and under-reported her monthly food expense by $200 to $250. She included receipts to corroborate these claims, but she never amended her expense schedule.

The bankruptcy court granted the Trustee's motion to dismiss, stating in relevant part:

> [Hebbring's retirement contributions] wouldn't be meaningful if she owed fifty thousand dollars. But she doesn't owe that much.... She only owes a small amount of money.... She's not an older person. She's a young person.... I have consistently held that putting away money in 401[k]'s is inconsistent with what you're trying to do.... You can't be looking after yourself and sav-ing money at the expense of your creditors.... [S]he has disposable income that she's otherwise trying to save through different plans; [a]nd she is also using part of her money to support her animals; [a]ll of which, I think she can pay something on account of her creditors.... I think it would be an abuse of Chapter 7 for her to be able to discharge all these debts and not pay something to these creditors.... [a]nd so I am going to grant the motion to dismiss unless within thirty days she files a Chapter 13 and agrees to pay ... a meaningful amount to the creditors.

Hebbring appealed the dismissal to the Ninth Circuit Bankruptcy Appellate Panel. The Trustee transferred the appeal to the United States District Court for the District of Nevada, which affirmed the bankruptcy court. Hebbring filed this appeal chal-lenging, *inter alia,* the bankruptcy court's finding that her contributions to her 401(k) plan and savings bond are not a reasonably necessary expense....

The purpose and structure of the Bankruptcy Code, as well as our precedent, com-pel the conclusion that voluntary contributions to a retirement plan may be a rea-sonably necessary expense for some debtors. Courts must therefore conduct a fact-specific inquiry to determine whether a debtor who saves for retirement at the expense of his creditors may nevertheless proceed under Chapter 7. The bankruptcy court erred in suggesting that voluntary retirement contributions are per se not reasonably necessary. However, the bankruptcy court's alternative finding that Hebbring's retirement contributions are not reasonably necessary based on her age and financial circumstances, and that she is therefore capable of paying her unsecured debts, is not clearly erroneous; nor did it abuse its discretion in dismissing her Chapter 7 petition. We therefore affirm.

A

At the time Hebbring filed her petition, 11 U.S.C. § 707(b) provided that a court "may dismiss a case filed by an individual debtor under this chapter whose debts are primarily consumer debts ... if it finds that the granting of relief would be a substantial abuse of the provisions of this chapter." In determining whether a petition constitutes a substantial abuse of Chapter 7, we examine the totality of the circumstances, focusing principally on whether the debtor will have sufficient future disposable income to fund a Chapter 13 plan that would pay a substantial portion of his unsecured debt.... To calculate a debtor's disposable income, we begin with current monthly income and subtract amounts "reasonably necessary to be expended ... for the maintenance or support of the debtor or a dependent of the debtor...."

Neither the Bankruptcy Code nor the Code's legislative history defines "reasonably necessary." Some courts, including the Third and Sixth Circuits, have employed a per se rule that voluntary contributions to retirement plans are never a reasonably necessary expense.... These courts typically emphasize that allowing debtors to exclude retirement contributions from disposable income at the expense of unsecured creditors is unfair.... In contrast, other courts, including the Second Circuit, have adopted a case-by-case approach, under which contributions to a retirement plan may be found reasonably necessary depending on the debtor's circumstances....

We believe this latter approach better comports with Congress's intent, as expressed in the language, purpose, and structure of the Bankruptcy Code. By not defining the phrase "reasonably necessary" or providing any examples of expenses that categorically are or are not reasonably necessary, see 11 U.S.C. § 1325(b)(2), the Code suggests courts should examine each debtor's specific circumstances to determine whether a claimed expense is reasonably necessary for that debtor's maintenance or support.... We find no evidence that Congress intended courts to employ a per se rule against retirement contributions, which may be crucial for debtors' support upon retirement, particularly for older debtors who have little or no savings.... Where Congress intended courts to use a per se rule rather than a case-by-case approach in classifying financial interests or obligations under the Bankruptcy Code, it has explicitly communicated its intent.... Congress's decision not to categorically exclude any specific expense, including retirement contributions, from being considered reasonably necessary is probative of its intent....

Requiring a fact-specific analysis to determine whether an expense is reasonably necessary is sound policy because it comports with the Code's approach to identifying substantial abuse of the Chapter 7 relief provisions. We have consistently held that § 707(b) does not include a "bright line test" for substantial abuse, but rather "commit[s] the question of what constitutes substantial abuse to the discretion of bankruptcy judges within the context of the Code...." "Congress chose neither to define 'substantial abuse' in the 1984 Act nor to leave specific guidance in legislative history. Congress thus left a flexible standard enabling courts to address each petition on its own merit." ... That Congress granted courts the discretion to identify substantial abuse necessarily suggests it intended courts to have the discretion to answer the subsidiary question of whether particular expenses are reasonably necessary.

In light of these considerations, and in the absence of any indication that Congress sought to prohibit debtors from voluntarily contributing to retirement plans per se, we conclude that bankruptcy courts have discretion to determine whether retirement contributions are a reasonably necessary expense for a particular debtor based on the facts of each individual case.... In making this fact-intensive determination, courts should consider a number of factors, including but not limited to: the debtor's age, income, overall budget, expected date of retirement, existing retirement savings, and amount of contributions; the likelihood that stopping contributions will jeopardize the debtor's fresh start by forcing the debtor to make up lost contributions after emerging from bankruptcy; and the needs of the debtor's dependents.... Courts must allow debtors to seek bankruptcy protection while voluntarily saving for retirement if such savings appear reasonably necessary for the maintenance or support of the debtor or the debtor's dependents....

We are not dissuaded by cases endorsing a per se rule.... The Bankruptcy Code and congressional intent control how courts should identify reasonably necessary expenses. A per se rule is inappropriate in the face of Congress's delegation of discretion to bankruptcy courts to evaluate expenses on a case-by-case basis.

Nor do we believe that "the case by case approach ... is potentially difficult to apply and may lead to disparate results even before the same judge." ... The case-by-case approach we adopt should be no more difficult to apply to retirement contributions than to other forward-looking expenses that bankruptcy courts must evaluate for reasonableness, such as life insurance premiums ... ; private school tuition for debtors' children ... ; or home maintenance costs....

Here, the bankruptcy court suggested that it employed a per se rule against retirement contributions, but also found, in the alternative, that Hebbring's retirement contributions are not a reasonably necessary expense based on her age and specific financial circumstances. This finding is not clearly erroneous. When she filed her bankruptcy petition, Hebbring was only thirty-three years old and was contributing approximately 8% of her gross income toward her retirement. Although Hebbring had accumulated only $6,289 in retirement savings, she was earning $49,000 per year and making mortgage payments on a house. In light of these circumstances, the bankruptcy court's conclusion that Hebbring's retirement contributions are not a reasonably necessary expense is not clearly erroneous....

Hebbring also challenges the bankruptcy court's ruling on three bases that require little discussion. She contends that the bankruptcy court should have held an evidentiary hearing; that it erred in finding, based on schedules she submitted, that she had the ability to fund a Chapter 13 plan; and that it erred in concluding that the Trustee met his burden of demonstrating substantial abuse by a preponderance of the evidence.

A

The bankruptcy court was not required to hold an evidentiary hearing because there were no disputed issues of material fact.... Although in her opposition to the Trustee's motion to dismiss Hebbring argued that her expenses were higher than she had stated in her expense schedule, she never filed an amended schedule.... In *Harris,* unlike here, the bankruptcy court concluded that the debtors' expenses were unreasonable and dismissed their Chapter 7 petition for substantial abuse without making any factual findings or taking any evidence regarding the reasonableness of the disputed expenses....

The bankruptcy court did not err in concluding that Hebbring has the ability to fund a Chapter 13 plan. The court calculated Hebbring's income and expenses from the very schedules Hebbring submitted to support her petition for relief from her debts. These uncontested schedules demonstrate that, including her voluntary retirement plan contributions, Hebbring has $172 per month in disposable income, sufficient to repay 56% of her unsecured debt over three years or 93% over five years (not including interest on the debt). Even subtracting attorneys' and trustee fees for a Chapter 13 plan from Hebbring's disposable income, she can still pay 27% over three years or 65% over five years (not including interest on the debt). The bankruptcy court thus did not err in finding that Hebbring is able to fund "a substantial portion of the unsecured claims" in a Chapter 13 plan....

For the foregoing reasons, the district court's order affirming the bankruptcy court's order dismissing this case is AFFIRMED.

e. Reorganizations

Chapter 11 is when a debtor, whether an individual or a company reorganizes to hopefully make their financial situation stronger. With a Chapter 7 bankruptcy, a company must dissolve at the end. With a Chapter 11 bankruptcy, a company does not have to dissolve at the end. An individual will often reorganize under Chapter 13, rather than Chapter 11, because Chapter 13 is specifically for individuals who wish to reorganize. Chapter 11 bankruptcy is very similar in many ways to Chapter 7. There are some differences, such as in Chapter 11, a bankruptcy trustee is not required. The debtor acts as a trustee by being a debtor in possession. A debtor in possession continues to run the business through the Chapter 11 and comes up with a plan for reorganizing the business. If the debtor in possession is unable to do so, then a trustee might still be used. When there is not a trustee, the creditors' committee plays a much more influential role.

A debtor needs to make a plan for reorganization that the creditors will agree to. A disclosure statement is sent to the creditors and shareholders so that they can make an informed decision.

16.6 Business Torts

a. Misrepresentation

In order for misrepresentation to be found, the defendant must have:

- made a false statement, intending to deceive the plaintiff;
- the defendant must know that the statement he is making is untrue;
- the plaintiff has to rely upon that untrue statement to his own detriment; and
- there must be damages.

If there is misrepresentation, then the plaintiff may be allowed to:

- cancel the agreement,
- seek monetary damages, or
- seek any financial gain the defendant obtained based upon the misrepresentation.

b. Interference with Contract

It is a business tort to interfere intentionally with a contract. To prove interference with a contract, the plaintiff has to show that:

- he had a contract with a third party;
- the defendant knew about the contract;
- the defendant made it impossible for the contract to be performed or caused the third party, wrongfully, to breach the contract; and
- there must be damages.

c. Unfair Competition

Unfair competition is made up of case law, state statutes, federal statutes, and Federal Trade Commission regulations. It can be equated to intellectual property because unfair competition is mainly about using a business's goodwill, rather than personal or real property. Part of the Lanham Act protects against unfair competition, and this act is an intellectual property act. In unfair competition, it is common for a competitor to act as if another's product is his own. False advertising is a component of unfair competition. A competitor could act as if another's product is his own when he puts the other's trademarks on his own product or when he uses a trademark that is confusingly similar. Counterfeiting would fall under this.

False advertising is using a description to describe goods or services falsely. Examples would be not publishing additional charges along with an advertised price or claiming that a product is better than another product when this cannot be proven. It can also occur when a product is advertised as being from a part of the world it is not. For example, champagne can only come from the Champagne region in France. Otherwise, it must be called something else. States also have false advertising laws, but these laws differ greatly from state to state. Thus, it can be more effective to use the Lanham Act to prosecute false advertising, as this is the federal act. It is interesting to note that under this act, anyone who likely will be injured by the false advertising can recover. This would not only be the competitor who is using the false advertising, but it could also include the buyers of the products.

One of the reasons it can be difficult to prosecute successfully a false advertising claim is that puffing is a defense to false advertising. If a competitor gives a subjective statement about how much better his product is, then the law usually holds that this type of opinion is acceptable. Thus, claiming one's product is better than another will usually not be actionable. The Federal Trade Commission also regulates deceptive practices in commerce. This is very similar to the Lanham Act regarding false advertising. The Federal Trade Commission is particularly harsh against companies misrepresenting drugs and food. One of the challenges facing the Federal Trade Commission is regulating deceptive practices in commerce on the Internet.

Chapter Summary

A surety agrees to be primarily liable on a loan for the debtor, while a guaranty agrees to be liable secondary to the debtor on the loan.

If the creditor does not want to first resort to forcing a bankruptcy, it can employ a lien. Common liens include mechanic's liens and judicial liens. Mechanic's liens are for labor or materials that were not paid for and were used in improving real property. The mechanic's lien would then be against the real property that was improved. A judicial lien is one the creditor can request once the debtor has not paid. Then, the debtor can ask for a writ of attachment to seize personal property to pay off the debt. The creditor could also garnish the debtor's wages to get the loan repaid. If a mortgage is not paid, the mortgagor can foreclose on the loan.

If the debtor defaults, then the creditor or security party may take possession of the personal property. If the creditor can do so peacefully, he does not have to resort to the court system to do so. The creditor can keep the collateral and await further payment or he may sell the collateral.

For the creditor to have a security interest, he needs to maintain control of the personal property or have a written agreement regarding his rights to the property; have given something of value to the debtor; and the debtor must have some interest in the collateral. Then, after getting the security interest, the smart creditor will want to perfect his interest, as this gives him additional rights. He might do so by filing a statement that gives notice to the public of his interest.

Priority refers to who is paid first in bankruptcy court. Obviously, the closer to the front of the line, the more likely a creditor will be paid. A creditor with secured claims is paid first, priority claims second, and unsecured claims third.

One of the rights of debtors is that they can request an accounting of their debt to verify the accuracy of that debt. In addition, when the debt is paid, the debtor is entitled to a termination statement.

A petition begins the bankruptcy process. This process generally describes a Chapter 7 bankruptcy, which could be on behalf of a person or business entity. A bankruptcy judge is assigned to the case and the person filing for bankruptcy must go to credit counseling. The judge issues an order for relief. A trustee collects all the debtor's assets to distribute to the creditors. The debtor is put to a series of questions by the creditors. After the petition is filed, there is an automatic stay.

Key Terms

Accounting	Mortgagee
Attachment	Mortgagor
Automatic stay	Perfection
Collateral	Priority
Debtor	Right of reimbursement
False advertising	Secured party
Federal Trade Commission	Secured transaction
Garnishment	Security agreement
Guarantor	Security interest
Homestead exemption	Surety
Judicial lien	Trustee
Lanham Act	Unfair competition
Liquidation	Writ of attachment
Mechanic's lien	

Review Questions

1. How are a surety and a guarantor different?

2. In *JSV, Inc. v. Hene Meat Co., Inc.*, is Kennedy treated more like a surety or guaranty?

3. Does a creditor have to force a bankruptcy to get its money back?

4. Under *Indiana Surgical Specialists v. Griffin*, can a creditor garnish an independent contractor's wages? Why or why not?

5. What is a secured interest? What requirements must be met to have a secured interest?

6. In what order are disputes among creditors settled?

7. What laws are in place to protect the debtor?

8. What are the steps in a bankruptcy proceeding?

9. Why was the plaintiff in *Hebbring* not allowed to claim payments made to a retirement plan as exempt? What factors should be used in making this determination?

Web Links

The Federal Trade Commission, which helps regulate deceptive practices in commerce, has a website located at http://www.ftc.gov/.

Research, using the internet, the false advertising laws in your state.

Exercises

1. When would a creditor use a mechanic's lien?

2. Circuit City used to have a storefront and an online presence. Research whether the company went through reorganization and/or liquidation.

3. One diaper manufacturer claims its product is better than another diaper manufacturer's product. What can the maligned diaper company do about such a claim, if anything?

4. Give an example of how a manufacturer of a product could misrepresent the part of the world a product came from.

5. Choose one of the three cases in the chapter above and brief it.

Glossary

Acceptance: An acceptance, generally, is a voluntary act or words, which show agreement with the offer.

Accredited investor: To be an accredited investor, if it is a person, the person has to have a net worth of over a million dollars and an income greater than two hundred thousand dollars a year.

Accumulated earnings tax: The accumulated earnings tax states if the corporation has earnings beyond what is reasonable, and its purpose is to avoid having shareholders pay taxes on dividends, then the corporation will be subject to this tax.

Actual authority: Actual authority is when a principal purposefully gives the agent certain power.

Administrative dissolution: In an administrative dissolution, the secretary of state dissolves the corporation.

Age Discrimination in Employment Act: The ADEA stands for Age Discrimination in Employment Act. This act was instituted to prohibit age discrimination in hiring, promotions, pay, etc.

Agency by ratification: Agency can occur after the fact as well; a person may do something on behalf of another and if it is approved by the principal after the fact, then agency by ratification has occurred.

Agent: An agent is a person who has either an implied or express, verbal or written agreement to perform tasks on behalf of the principal, in regards to third parties.

Agent for service of process: An agent for service of process is a person or corporation designated to accept lawsuits and legal documents on behalf of a business organization.

Americans with Disabilities Act: Under the ADA, employers cannot discriminate against employees with a current disability, a past disability, or a perceived disability.

Apparent agency/authority: Note that apparent agency is caused by the principal making it look like there is an agency relationship even when there is not. The action is the principal's usually and not the agent's. There are three major factors to apparent authority. They include the conduct of the principal, which implies that a person is acting as his agent. Next, to have apparent authority, a third party must rely on that implication. Finally, the third party has to have acted to her detriment in relying on that implication.

Appraisal right: the shareholder might be bought out. This is known as an appraisal right.

Arbitrary mark: The fourth subcategory of mark is an arbitrary mark. This is a commonly known word, but it is arbitrarily applied to the particular product. A prime example of an arbitrary mark would be Apple for computers.

Articles of incorporation: public document for a corporation.

Articles of organization: A public document for a limited liability company.

Asexually: By asexually, the patent office means reproducing the plant through some other means other than just planting the seeds of the plant.

Assumption of the risk: Another defense to negligence is assumption of the risk. If the plaintiff understands the dangers and willingly goes ahead and partakes in a dangerous activity, then she has assumed the responsibility for the outcome of her actions.

Attorney in fact: An attorney in fact does not have to be an attorney at all. An attorney in fact can be someone who has authority, though a power of attorney, to act on behalf of another. In essence, an attorney in fact is an agent.

At-will LLC: If there is no specification in the articles of organization as to how long the limited liability company will last, then the LLC is known as an at-will LLC.

Authorized stock: Stock is authorized if it has been provided for in the articles of incorporation. Authorized stock is also known as the number of shares that could be issued.

Bilateral contract: With a bilateral contract, each party is exchanging a promise. In a bilateral contract, the offeree generally accepts by making a promise. Thus, there are mutual promises in a bilateral contract, otherwise referred to as a promise for a promise.

Blue sky laws: State regulations of securities laws are referred to as "blue sky laws." This references a desire in making laws to prevent investors from buying a valueless part of the blue-sky (kind of like selling someone swampland in Florida).

Bona fide occupational qualification (BFOQ): A bona fide occupational qualification is a necessary job qualification.

Business judgment rule: So long as the director made a decision in good faith, then he cannot be held personally liable for damages arising out of that decision.

But-for test: The but-for tests and substantial factor are used to determine actual causation. The but-for test is that the plaintiff would not have been injured but for the defendant's negligence.

Bylaws: The internal document of the corporation.

Certificate of limited partnership: the public document for the limited partnership.

Certification mark: A certification mark is a word, symbol, or logo used on either goods or services to certify the quality or locale of the product or services. A certification mark is the Good Housekeeping Seal of Approval.

Civil Rights Act of 1964: The goal of Title VII is to stop job discrimination due to race, religion, gender, or nationality.

Close corporation: A close corporation, family corporation, and a closely held corporation mean the same thing. A close corporation is one that is not publicly traded.

Collective mark: A collective mark is a mark used by an organization to show membership in the organization.

Commingling of assets: Commingling of assets is when the shareholders do not have their own separate bank accounts from the corporations. The shareholders might even use the corporation's bank accounts to pay bills!

Common stock: With common stock, the stockholder gets a percent interest in the corporation based upon the total number of shares he owns.

Compensatory damages: Compensatory damages are the damages that try to put the plaintiff back into the place he would have been had the injury not happened.

Complete performance: Complete performance occurs when a party to the contract has satisfied every duty that was required of them under the contract.

Consideration: Consideration is something of value that is exchanged between the parties.

Consolidation: Consolidations occur when Company A combines with Company B, and Company C is formed from those two corporations. Both Company A and B disappear. Company C starts its existence as a new corporation.

Contract: A contract is an agreement, which can be legally enforced. There must be at least two people involved in the contract, known as the parties. These parties must agree to do something or not to do something.

Contributory negligence: Contributory negligence holds that if the plaintiff contributed in some way to her own injury, then she is not allowed to recover damages from the defendant.

Copyright: Copyrights protect computer programs, movies, pictures (including film), music, some types of architecture, and literature. The copyright is for a certain tangible or fixed expression of a concept. The work must be original, though it does not have to be a new idea, and it must be made independently by the author of the work.

Continuity: Continuity is how long will the business last if it changes ownership.

Corporation by estoppel: An improperly formed corporation, also known as a de facto corporation.

Course and scope of employment: Course and scope of employment is the behavior expected of an employee as part of her job duties.

To court a white knight: To court a white knight is to seek out another company in which the target would prefer to merge itself with.

Crown jewels: When the corporation has a profitable asset, it can try to sell that asset to make itself less attractive to the aggressor. The profitable asset is known as a crown jewel.

Cumulative dividends: Cumulative dividends means that the preferred shareholders would get dividends for the prior year(s), in which dividends were not paid, as well as first year in which the corporation could again afford to issue dividends.

Cumulative voting: Cumulative voting is multiplying the shareholders' number of shares by the number of open positions on the board of directors.

Debenture: If a debt is long-term and unsecured, it might be called a debenture. A debenture may be for thirty or more years.

De facto corporation: An improperly formed corporation, also known as corporation by estoppel.

De jure corporation: A de jure corporation is a corporation that has been properly formed and is in good standing with the law.

Derivative action: A derivative action is one a shareholder can bring against a wrong-doer that has harmed the corporation, if the board of directors fails to bring suit themselves.

Design defect: A design defect occurs at the design of the product. Thus, all the products would be defective.

Design patent: A design patent is all about how the product looks. A design patent does not change the function of the product.

Direct action: A direct action is allowed when a shareholder has been directly injured.

Dissociation: Dissociation occurs when one partner leaves the partnership, and this can be done wrongfully or rightfully.

Dissolution: Dissolution is when the business ends, and it starts the winding up process.

Dividend: Dividends are how a corporation shares its profits with its shareholders. A dividend usually comes in the form of cash, shares, or property.

Domestic corporation: A corporation has existence in the state where it is domiciled. In the state wherein it is domiciled, it is known as a domestic corporation.

Double taxation: The Internal Revenue Service subjects corporate profits to double taxation. When a corporation makes a profit, it pays taxes on the profit. This is the first tax. When the corporation declares a dividend (thus giving the shareholders part of the profits), then the shareholders have to pay tax on those profits.

Downstream merger: When the parent company merges into the subsidiary, this is called a downstream merger.

Duress: Force.

Duty of care: The duty of care, also known as the duty of due care, requires the agent to use that amount of care a reasonably prudent business entity would use under similar circumstances.

Duty of loyalty: Duty of loyalty is also known as the duty not to compete with the principal or to help others compete against the principal. In addition, the duty of loyalty is the duty not to have a conflict of interest with the corporation.

Electronic Data Gather, Analysis, and Retrieval (EDGAR): To comply with securities regulations, certain companies must file a registration statement electronically on the EDGAR system.

Employee Retirement Income Security Act (ERISA): The Employee Retirement Income Security Act (ERISA) is supposed to protect employees covered by private pension plans.

Employer identification number: The Federal Employer Identification Number is used by the Internal Revenue Service. It identifies the business. It is similar to a social security number for a person.

Employment-at-will: Unless there is a contract for a certain amount of time, then an employer can fire an employee without cause, whenever the employer choses. There are exceptions to this general rule, such as the employer cannot fire employees for participating in union events.[1]

Estoppel: Estoppel is a public policy argument, which changes what the law would otherwise hold, based upon a "fairness" argument.

Exclusive remedy: The employee is normally only allowed to pursue a workers' compensation claim and not a civil lawsuit.

Exempt employees: When discussing the exempt and non-exempt status of employees, the reference is whether they are exempt or not from the Fair Labor Standards Act (FLSA). It applies more to private employees than to public ones. Typically, exempt employees do not have to be paid overtime, but non-exempt employees do.

Express agency: Principal-agency relationships made by oral or written words are known as express agency agreements.

Express contract: Express contracts occur when both sides to the contract state or write out all the terms of the contract.

Express warranties: An express warranty occurs when the seller makes representations to the consumer about the product.

Fair Labor Standards Act (FLSA): In general, the Fair Labor Standards Act regulates workers' wages as well as child labor.

Fair use doctrine: Prior to the expiration of the copyright, there is a limited right of the public to use copyrighted material under the fair use doctrine. Usually, this use is for critiquing the work or research. Another exception to copyright is that

---

1. This is upheld under the National Labor Relations Act and the Wagner Act.

work prepared by a United States government agency is typically not protected and can be used by the public.

False advertising: False advertising is using a description to describe goods or services in a misleading way.

Family and Medical Leave Act (FMLA): The Family Medical Leave Act was instituted in 1993. Eligible employees, working for covered employers, may receive up to twelve weeks of unpaid leave during a twelve-month period. In addition to the leave, the employer must continue the health care coverage and make sure that the employee will be able to come back to the same or a substantially similar position when they return.

Fanciful mark: The fifth and final subcategory of mark is a fanciful mark. These are provided trademark protection because they are distinctive. In fact, the word was entirely made up and not already in use in a dictionary. Kodak is an example of a fanciful mark.

Fictitious business name: When the client is not using their last name in a business name, then typically the client will need to file a fictitious business name statement so that plaintiffs suing the business can determine who owns the business. Basically, when the client does not use his last name in his business, then name of the company is a fictitious name.

Fiduciary relationship: The fiduciary relationship requires the agent to act responsibly or in good faith, in regards to the principal's money and interests.

First sale doctrine: Under the first sale doctrine, the buyer of a specific copy of copyrighted material is free to lend and/or resell the item without liability for infringement because they are now the owner of that copy.

Foreign corporation: If the corporation wants to "exist" outside of this state, it must seek permission from each other state wherein it wishes to exist. In these other states, it will be known as a foreign corporation.

Franchise: A franchise allows one party (here, the sole proprietor) to use the franchisor's name, trademarks, and other intellectual property to sell goods or services. The sole proprietor would be a separate business, apart from the franchisor.

Fraud: Fraud is when a party makes, intentionally, an incorrect statement of important information and the other side reasonably relies on that information to his detriment.

Frolic and detour: The second major exception to the course and scope of employment is the "frolic and detour" exception. With a frolic and detour, the employee's conduct is so far from a rational business purpose that the employer should not be liable for these actions of the employee. Basically, it boils down to the employee doing something to benefit himself rather than his employer during business hours.

Full shield: In the vast majority of states, full shield is the law. Full shield holds that a partner does not have personal liability for the contractual errors or negligence his partner commits.

General partnership: The Uniform Partnership Act of 1914 still provides a good definition of partnership: "an association of two or more persons to carry on as co-owners of a business for profit."

Generic: This type of mark is not offered trademark protection because it is not distinctive enough to warrant trademark protection. It is often the common name of a product or even a characteristic of the product. For example, calling your product the "best" typically would not be registerable under trademark law.

Genericide: Genericide is when a product's name is used so often as to become generic.

Going and coming rule: A major exception to the course and scope of employment rule is the "going and coming" rule. The going and coming rule holds that an employer is not vicariously liable for accidents that happen to an employee while the employee is either going to work or coming home from work.

Golden parachute: A golden parachute is the concept that if high-level managers are forced to leave the corporation, then the aggressor has to pay them an extreme amount of money.

Goods: Goods are anything that could be moved by the strongest mythical person in the universe, Hercules.

Goodwill: The goodwill of the business is that certain something that makes a consumer go to that business over another.

Guaranty: In a guaranty, the third party is secondarily liable after the person who incurred the debt.

Horizontal price fixing: When competitive companies make a contract to fix prices, this is dubbed horizontal price fixing.

Horizontal territorial agreement: When competitors agree to exclusive territories amongst themselves, this is known as horizontal territorial agreement.

Hostile takeover: A hostile takeover is a nonconsensual taking over of another company by going over the heads of that company's management.

House mark: There is still another type of mark, known as a house mark. Proctor & Gamble would be an example of a house mark, which is used to indicate a wide variety of products, all produced by the same quality of manufacturer.

Implied contract: Implied contracts are contracts formed by the conduct of both sides to the contract.

Inadequate capitalization: Not properly funding the corporation.

Incorporator: Usually, it will be the incorporator (often an attorney) or the directors named in the articles that hold the organizational meeting.

Indemnity clause: Hold harmless clause.

Infringement: Infringement occurs when an unauthorized individual makes, uses, and/or sells the patented item.

Initial public offering: The first offering of a corporation's stock to the public is known as the IPO, or initial public offering.

Intellectual property: Intellectual property is made up several types of law: patents, trademarks, copyrights, and trade secrets. Intellectual property is harder to quantify than real property, as it is sometimes intangible and the thoughts or creativity of someone.

Joint and several liability: Part of the reason liability is so terrible in a general partnership is because the concept of joint and several liability applies in a general partnership. The underlying reason for joint and several liability, is to make it easier for the plaintiff to sue someone when initially filling out the complaint. A plaintiff might not initially know all the partners' names in a partnership. The plaintiff could put down the name of the partnership, and then just the names of some of the partners. The partnership and the named partners would be held initially responsible for one hundred percent (100%) of any recovery the plaintiff obtained.

Judicial dissolution: Dissolution overseen by a court.

Judicial liquidation: Judicial liquidation occurs when dissolution is activated by the creditors, state, or shareholders. This would normally occur when the directors have acted improperly. The court does not feel that it can trust the directors to honestly or ethically conduct the liquidation. Therefore, the court appoints someone to handle the liquidation.

Lack of formalities: Lack of formalities is not holding meetings or taking minutes.

Last clear chance: This doctrine states that if the defendant could have avoiding harming the plaintiff at the last minute, then the defendant can be found liable.

The Learned Hand formula: There are two main tests for determining whether reasonableness has been breached. These are the Learned Hand formula and the risk-utility formula. With the Learned Hand formula, the test looks at whether the burden of taking precautions weighs more than the likelihood and possible severeness of the harm.

Letter of intent: In conducting a merger, both state and federal laws must be complied with. This generally requires some sort of negotiation at the start. If a deal is reached, then it is frequently written down as a letter of intent, which just indicates the parties' understanding.

Limited liability company: A limited liability company is often described a combination of a partnership and a corporation.

Liquidation: Taking all the assets that are not cash and turning them into cash.

Liquidation rights: Liquidation rights are the rights a shareholder has, after creditors are paid, to assets leftover, in an amount equal to their ownership percentage. The liquidation right is the right to a portion of any proceeds left after the corporation has dissolved and paid all its creditors first.

Living wage laws: While the federal government has a certain federal minimum wage, states are free to set a minimum wage that is higher than the federal minimum. These higher wages are called living wage laws.

Loss of consortium: Loss of consortium is the damage one spouse is entitled to by having his spouse injured and not receiving the benefits of marriage.

Marshaling of assets: There is also the concept of marshaling of assets in partnership as well. In that scenario, if a partnership is sued and does not have enough assets in its business accounts to pay the lawsuit, then the partners would be personally liable for the remaining amount of the settlement.

Material: Material means important. Material means the facts necessary to make a decision.

Mechanic's lien: Mechanic's liens are for labor or materials that were not paid for and where used in improving real property.

Merger: A merger is when company A combines with company B, and only company A survives. Company A would be dubbed the surviving corporation. Company B would be the merging corporation. Company A takes over all the assets, but also takes over all the liabilities of Company B.

Mirror image: The mirror image concept is that the acceptance must match the offer exactly. If it does not, then it is not an acceptance.

Misrepresentation: Misrepresentation is making a statement that is incorrect with the intent to mislead the other party.

Non-exempt employee: When discussing the exempt and non-exempt status of employees, the reference is whether they are exempt or not from the Fair Labor Standards Act (FLSA). It applies more to private employees than to public ones. Typically, exempt employees do not have to be paid overtime, but non-exempt employees do.

Nonjudicial liquidation: Nonjudicial liquidation can be brought about by a dissolution that is voluntary or even one that is sometimes administrative.

Nonobviousness: Nonobvious is just as it sounds; the invention cannot be obvious to a person with ordinary skills in that area.

Nonprofit corporation: Nonprofits are supposed to perform a public benefit, a mutual benefit, or a religious benefit.

Note: If a debt is short-term, either secured or unsecured, it might be called a note. Notes are usually for five years or less.

Novelty: Novel means that the invention not already be in use or known of in the United States and that it has not been discussed in a publication anywhere in the world.

Occupational Safety and Health Act: Federally, the major statute for protecting employees' health and safety is the Occupational Safety and Health Act[2] (also known as OSHA).

Operating agreement: The private document for a limited liability company.

---

2. 29 U.S.C. §§ 553, 651–678.

Organizational meeting: After the articles of incorporation are filed, then the first meeting of the corporation is held, called the organizational meeting.

Outstanding stock: Stock is outstanding if it has been sold.

Overtime pay: If an employee is eligible for overtime pay, the employee should be paid one-and-a-half time the regular pay rate for hours worked more than forty in a week.

Pac-Man: The Pac-Man is a reverse tender offer.

Partial shield: If a state is a partial shield state, then a partner does have personal liability for the contractual errors his partner makes, but not the tortuous errors his partner makes.

Par value: In the beginning, par value was close to the going rate for stock. The corporation could not cut a deal and sell stock to insiders at less than par. Nowadays, par value usually has nothing to do with the going rate. Some states have climinated the concept of par value; others put par value at a nominal amount, such as a dollar.

Pass-through tax status: Known as pass-through taxation because it passes through the entity to the members, this avoids the double taxation of a corporation.

Patent: A patent gives its holder a monopoly for a limited period. It allows only that person, the patent holder, to make, copy, use, and market the invention.

Patent infringement: Infringement occurs when an unauthorized individual uses and/or sells the patented item.

Patent prosecution: When the application process is actually started, it is called patent prosecution. Note that litigation has not started even though the process is called prosecution.

Per se illegality: Some contracts are so anticompetitive on their face that they are presumed illegal. This is known as per se illegality.

Personal property: Personal property is property that can be moved and is not attached to land.

Piercing the corporate veil: In general, shareholders do not have any liability for the corporation's debts other than what the shareholder invested in his stock. However, a major exception to this general rule is known as piercing the corporate veil. The limited liability the shareholder typically has is caused by a veil between the third parties and the shareholders that does not normally let the creditors of the corporation go after the shareholders. However, sometimes, this veil can be pierced.

Plan of merger: The plan will have a date, information about both companies' stock, and information about the surviving corporation (such as the name, location, and directors). There will be a discussion about whose shares will be converted.

Plant patent: A plant patent allows someone who invents a new type of plant, and who can reproduce the plant asexually, to obtain a patent on the plant.

Pleasure of doing business fee: A tax for using the state's highways and emergency system.

Power of attorney: A general power of attorney allows an attorney-in-fact to act for a principal on all issues, not just those of healthcare.

Poison pill: In a poison pill, the board may grant one additional right to each common share that is issued and outstanding. The poison pill would be triggered during the tender offer.

Predatory pricing: Predatory pricing occurs when the price is lower than the marginal cost. The company that sells below that price is willing to take the hit so as to drive out competition.

Preemptive rights: Preemptive rights give a current shareholder the choice to purchase enough newly issued shares to keep their ownership interest in the corporation.

Preferred stock: In general, preferred stock gets preferential treatment when it comes to dividend payments.

Preincorporation contracts: To start and organize a corporation, the promoter will often have to enter into contracts on behalf of the corporation, before the corporation is formed.

Presumption: Presumptions are principles generally held to be true until rebutted.

Price fixing: Price fixing is when competitors agree to charge the same amount of money for their similar products.

Principal-agent relationship: In agency, one person acts for another. The person acting is the agent and the person being acted for is the principal. The agent acts on behalf of the principal toward third parties. Both parties have to agree to the principal-agent relationship.

Principled negotiator: The type of negotiator who usually does the best in negotiations is a principled, otherwise known as a problem-solver, negotiator. A principled negotiator attempts to focus on the interests involved and not on the positions and wants each party to gain. The principled negotiator tries to look at all the options.

Products liability: Manufacturers and sellers of goods can be sued for injuries caused by those goods to a person.

Promise: A promise is a statement that this will or will not happen in the future.

Promissory estoppel: Sometimes, even when there is not a valid contract, the law will allow a plaintiff to recover. Promissory estoppel is one such way in which the plaintiff can recover. There are many different elements to promissory estoppel. A plaintiff must prove that she: has been injured; does not have a valid contract; had a promise, reasonably relied on that promise, and that there is an injustice as a result of that. A promise is a statement that this will or will not happen in the future. The person making the promise is known as the promisor and the person who has the promise made to them is known as the promisee.

Promoter: Promoters start the corporation. This can involve raising the money needed to capitalize the corporation, finding shareholders, finding directors, finding managers, finding employees (including attorneys and certified public accountants), drawing up a business plan, and determining where the corporation should be located.

Proprietary information: Proprietary information is nonpublic information that is considered the property of an employer. Employees are not supposed to misuse proprietary information.

Prospectus: A prospectus contains financial information so that the investor can make a well-informed decision.

Proximate cause: There has to be a connection between the work and the injury. Proximate cause is whether the plaintiff was a foreseeable plaintiff or not. Proximate cause looks at how closely connected the business entity defendant's actions were to the plaintiff's injuries.

Proxy: A proxy is basically an absentee ballot. A proxy gives another person authorization to exercise rights owned by the first person.

Proxy contest: A proxy contest occurs when the aggressor corporation attempts to have the target's shareholders vote for its management team.

Purchase of assets: Purchase of assets occurs when one company is going to purchase all or most of the assets of another.

Quantum meruit: Damages for quasi-contract are known as "quantum meruit." The plaintiff will receive as much as she is out.

Quorum: A quorum is the minimum number of people necessary to legitimately transact business. Depending upon the state, a quorum could be anywhere from one-third to fifty-one percent.

Reckless and willful: Reckless and willful behavior is behavior that is substantially likely to cause an injury.

Record date: Record date is used to determine which shareholders are entitled to notice of the meeting. Record date is a line drawn in the sand. The corporation arbitrarily picks a date, often one month before the meeting and states that whoever owns stock on that day shall get notice of the meeting.

Redemption rights: Redemption rights, if the shareholder has them, allow that shareholder to make the corporation buy back his shares.

Registration statement: The registration statement requires several things. This registration statement includes information about the security for sale, the operation of the corporation, and the managers of the corporation.

Reliance on others: To use the "reliance on others" argument, the director or officer will have to rely on an employee who is believed by the director or officer to be competent. Another way to use the reliance on others argument is for the director or officer to rely on attorneys, certified public accountants, etc., so long as that information is within their professional knowledge.

Respondeat superior: When an employee is responsible for torts he committed during the course and scope of his employment, then the employer is also responsible.

Revised Uniform Partnership Act (RUPA): The law that mainly governs general partnership law is now the Revised Uniform Partnership Act (RUPA).

Risk-utility test: If the enormity of the risk is greater than the utility of the action, then the defendant has breached his duty under this test.

Rule of reason: In the rule of reason, courts can only hold contracts in restraint of trade are illegal if the contract in restraint has *undue* or *unreasonable* restraints.

S Corporation: With an S Corporation, the corporation receives special tax benefits not available to a regular publicly held company.

Section 12 Company: Section 12 Companies have greater than ten million dollars in assets and greater than or equal to five hundred shareholders. As such, they have additional reporting requirements.

Secured debt: Secured debt is a promise to repay the debt that is secured by a piece of property, often the same property that the borrower took the loan out on.

Securities Act of 1933: The 1933 Act has to do with the original issuance of stocks in interstate commerce. It also makes it illegal to use interstate communication/ transportation to sell securities without providing certain basic financial information to potential buyers. This act requires a registration of securities. It also regulates prospectuses.

Securities and Exchange Commission (SEC): The goal of the SEC, in general, is to protect investors. The SEC is run by five commissioners. The president appoints these commissioners for five-year terms, which do not expire all at once.

Securities Exchange Act of 1934: The Securities Exchange Act of 1934 started the Securities and Exchange Commission.

Service mark: A service mark is something, whether it is a name, a phrase, or logo, used to identify and distinguish the services of one provider over another.

Share exchange: In a share exchange, the buying corporation will buy many or even all of the shares of the target corporation.

Sherman Act: The Sherman Act was enacted in 1890. In essence, the Sherman Act promotes competition in the marketplace.

Short-form merger: If the parent company owns ninety percent or more of the stocks, than it is not required to obtain shareholder approval for the merger. The reason that it does not have to be approved by either corporation is that the parent owns so much stock that a vote is unnecessary.

Short-swing profits: Directors, officers, and ten percent or more shareholders are not allowed to keep profits on buying and selling stocks within six months.

Sole proprietorship: A sole proprietorship is a business owned by an individual, which can be considered an extension of the individual.

Specific duty standard: For example, hospital personnel working around blood must be given gloves which are impermeable to blood. This is an example of a specific duty standard under the Occupational Health and Safety Act. These standards look at safety requirements for specific equipment, hazardous chemicals, machinery, procedures, etc.

Specific performance: Specific performance is when the plaintiff gets a court order stating that the defendant must go ahead and perform the contract as was agreed upon.

Specification: Specification goes over a description of the document, instructions on how to make the invention, and the subject matter of the invention.

Statement of denial: A statement of denial denies the authority of a partner to bind the partnership.

Statement of partnership authority: Many states allow general partnerships to file a public document, which gives general information about the partnership and puts the public on notice that the entity is in fact a partnership. Some states call this document a statement of partnership authority.

Statute of Frauds: Certain contracts are required, by the Statute of Frauds, to be in writing. This is to help make sure that these types of contracts have written evidence. These types of contracts are usually considered more important. These contracts include contracts for land, any contract that will not be completed within one year, debts, marital agreements, and goods worth over five hundred dollars.

Stock: Stocks are equity financing of the corporation.

Stock split: Stock splits are a way in which to increase the total number of shares. Do not confuse stock splits with stock dividends. Stock splits help encourage trading by reducing the price of shares.

Straight voting: Straight voting is one share equals one vote.

Substantial factor: With the substantial factor test, there were two or greater acts which caused the harm to the plaintiff. Was the defendant a substantial factor in causing the harm to the plaintiff? If yes, then the defendant was a substantial factor.

Substantial performance: Substantial performance occurs when one party to the contract has not made complete performance, but the party has tried to perform almost all of what that party is required to do. With substantial performance, the substantially complying party will still get paid, just less any damages to the other party.

Suggestive mark: The third subcategory of a trademark is a suggestive mark. This type of mark is distinctive because it requires some imagination to come to a conclusion about the nature of the goods.

Suicide pact: A suicide pact occurs when the manager(s) of the target corporation are fired. Even if only one of them is fired, the rest all agree to resign.

Surety: A surety is when the third person agrees to be liable for the debt.

Tender offer: To take over using a tender offer, the aggressor usually starts by buying stocks on the sly, but only up to 4.9%. The aggressor is normally going to offer prices which are currently above the market price. At 5%, the Securities and Exchange Commission makes the aggressor disclose the tender offer. Then, the aggressor tries to get a majority of shares.

Term LLC: If there is a specification in the articles of organization as to how long the limited liability company will last, then the LLC is known as a term LLC.

Tort: A tort is a wrong done by one person to another that results in jury to a person or her property. With a tort, money is often paid in order to try to compensate the injured party.

Trademark: Generally, a trademark is a word, phrase, or even a logo, which is utilized by a manufacturer to distinguish his product.

Trademark Electronic Search System: The USPTO's search engine, called the Trademark Electronic Search System (TESS) is available via the USPTO's website.

Uniform Electronic Transactions Act (UETA): This act was passed to try to even out the different laws the states have about e-signatures, in part.

Unilateral contract: In a unilateral contract, one party is promising for the other party's performance.

Unknown claims: Unknown claims can be brought against a dissolved corporation, so it is in the corporation's best interest to go ahead and pay all claims possible. In addition, the corporation should retain funds for any unknown claims. If it does not and there are unknown claimants, they may seek to get their money from the former shareholders.

Unsecured debt: Unsecured debt is a promise to repay the debt. While this promise can be enforced (much more easily if it is written down), it often has to be enforced by going to court.

Upstream merger: When the subsidiary merges back into the parent company, this is called an upstream merger.

Usefulness: Utility patents should be useful. The usefulness requirement just means it must be something that helps humans in some way.

Valid contract: Valid contracts are ones that are enforceable by law. A valid contract has met all the requirements needed for a contract, i.e. offer, acceptance, and consideration. In addition, for there to be a valid contract, the parties generally have to have the capacity to contract.

Vertical price fixing: Vertical price fixing occurs when the manufacturer tries to control the resale price of its manufactured goods.

Vertical territorial agreement: When a manufacturer and distributor agree to a distributor having an exclusive territory, it is known as a vertical territorial agreement.

Vicarious liability: Vicarious liability is when one person can be held liable for another person's negligence; this is often an employer.

Void contract: A void contract is illegal, and it does not matter if the parties to try ratify it. It is still illegal.

Voidable contract: A voidable contract is not necessarily illegal; it is just that one of the parties was in an unfair bargaining position, when the contract was entered into.

Voluntary dissolution: Voluntary dissolution is how most corporations dissolve. To be voluntary, the board of directors and the shareholders have to approve the dissolution.

Warranty of fitness for a particular purpose: This warranty states that if the seller tells the buyer that the product can be used for a specific purpose, then the product must be useable for that purpose.

Warranty of merchantability: This warranty holds that the product has to be safe for ordinary use.

Winding up: Winding up of a business is taking all the assets that are not cash and turning them into cash (also known as liquidation), paying off all the debts (including taxes), and then distributing anything left to the partners, members, or shareholders in accordance with their percent rights to the profits.

Williams Act: The Williams Act governs tender offers.

Workers' compensation: Workers' compensation allows the injured employee to receive money without having to prove that the employer was negligent in causing the injury. Therefore, workers' compensation is known as a no-fault system.

Index